JUSTICE FOR OURSELVES

The American South Series

Elizabeth R. Varon and Orville Vernon Burton, Editors

Justice for Ourselves

Black Virginians Claim Their Freedom after Slavery

John G. Deal, Marianne E. Julienne, and Brent Tarter

University of Virginia Press
in association with the Library of Virginia
Charlottesville and London

The University of Virginia Press is situated on the traditional lands of the Monacan Nation, and the Commonwealth of Virginia was and is home to many other Indigenous people. We pay our respect to all of them, past and present. We also honor the enslaved African and African American people who built the University of Virginia, and we recognize their descendants. We commit to fostering voices from these communities through our publications and to deepening our collective understanding of their histories and contributions.

University of Virginia Press

Printed in the United States of America on acid-free paper

First published 2024

1 3 5 7 9 8 6 4 2

Library of Congress Cataloging-in-Publication Data

Names: Deal, John G., author. | Julienne, Marianne E., author. | Tarter, Brent, author.
Title: Justice for ourselves : Black Virginians claim their freedom after slavery / John G. Deal, Marianne E. Julienne, and Brent Tarter.
Description: Charlottesville : University of Virginia Press in association with the Library of Virginia, 2024. | Series: The American South series | Includes bibliographical references and index.
Identifiers: LCCN 2023057973 (print) | LCCN 2023057974 (ebook) | ISBN 9780813951379 (hardcover) | ISBN 9780813951386 (ebook)
Subjects: LCSH: African Americans—Virginia—History—19th century. | Freed persons—Virginia—History—19th century. | Enslaved persons—Virginia—History—19th century. | BISAC: SOCIAL SCIENCE / Ethnic Studies / American / African American & Black Studies | HISTORY / United States / State & Local / South (AL, AR, FL, GA, KY, LA, MS, NC, SC, TN, VA, WV)
Classification: LCC F235.B53 D43 2024 (print) | LCC F235.B53 (ebook) | DDC 975.500496/07304—dc23/eng/20240108
LC record available at https://lccn.loc.gov/2023057973
LC ebook record available at https://lccn.loc.gov/2023057974

Cover art: The Freedman's Spelling-Book, Boston, MA: American Tract Society, 1866. (Monroe C. Gutman Library, Harvard University)
Cover design: Trudi Gershenov

CONTENTS

Foreword by Congresswoman Jennifer McClellan vii

Acknowledgments xi

Notes on Language xiii

Introduction 1

1. "I Ain't No Slave": Freedom in Virginia before the Civil War 11

2. "We Will All Be Free": Self-Emancipation during the Civil War 34

3. "To Own Oneself Is to Own One's Future": The Meaning of Freedom 60

4. "We Claim the Right of Suffrage": The Politics of Freedom 89

5. "Send a Colored Man": The Politics of Free Men 120

6. "Without Distinction of Color": Readjusters, Education, and Biracial Politics 150

7. "I Am Constantly Busy": Enduring Daily Life in Jim Crow Virginia 173

8. "To Take Our Place in the Business World": The Segregated Economy 194

Epilogue: "To Set Up Lofty Landmarks" 221

Afterword 231
Ajena Cason Rogers

Appendix: Virginia's Black Leaders, 1850–1900 235

Notes on Sources 243

Notes 247

Index 293

FOREWORD

My path to becoming the first Black woman elected to Congress from Virginia began in Petersburg, where I listened to the stories of my parents' childhoods and coming of age during the Depression in the Jim Crow South. I learned about poll taxes and literacy tests; sit-ins and boycotts; the *Green Book;* watching movies from the balcony and riding in the back of the bus; whispers of lynchings and race riots; redlining and racial covenants limiting where Black people could live; Black neighborhoods destroyed in the name of progress as colleges or highways were built; limited job opportunities for low wages and no worker protections; and hospitals that denied care to Black patients, stole their bodies for research, or conducted experiments on them without consent.

I did not learn these stories in school. These stories have rarely been part of our public history. But they should be. Without a complete and accurate—even when it's uncomfortable—history of our Commonwealth and nation, Americans cannot fully reckon with our collective past. *Justice for Ourselves: Black Virginians Claim Their Freedom after Slavery* seeks to fill this gap and tells the stories of African Americans facing those challenges.

When I was a newly elected member of the Virginia House of Delegates, I quickly realized that my colleagues' political philosophy and views on public policy were shaped by their life experiences and what they knew. I became keenly aware that my perspective as a thirty-two-year-old Black woman had been lacking in an assembly dominated by older white male legislators. Their families did not experience the worst of government in the way mine did. They did not learn these stories from their parents—or in school. As a result, they did not intuitively see the lingering impact slavery and Jim Crow has in our communities today.

A government by the people, of the people, and for the people reflects the perspectives—and therefore meets the needs—of the people who participate. Yet, for more than 175 years, "We the people" as described in our constitution did not include people like me, my parents, or my grandparents. Much of the story of our nation has been the struggle to make true the promises of our founding documents for all Americans. But many of the triumphs and tribulations of that struggle have been overlooked.

When I arrived at the Virginia General Assembly, I knew that I stood on the shoulders of Dr. William Ferguson "Fergie" Reid, elected in 1967 as the first Black man to serve in the House of Delegates since 1890, and Yvonne B. Miller, the first Black woman elected to the House, in 1981, and to the Senate of Virginia, in 1983. But until I became a member of the Virginia Dr. Martin Luther King Jr. Memorial Commission, I had no idea that twenty-four Black men served in the Constitutional Convention of 1867–68, which created a new state constitution after the Civil War, or that almost a hundred Black men served in the General Assembly in the nineteenth century before a backlash of racial discrimination, racial terror and lynching, and Jim Crow laws erased the political, social, and economic gains of Black communities in Virginia and across the South. As chair of the King Commission, I considered it a sacred duty to fill in gaps of Virginia's complicated history—the birthplace of American democracy and the birthplace of American slavery—in remembering its past. As a result of our work, plaques honoring the first Black legislators stand in the Capitol of Virginia and the Emancipation and Freedom Monument on Brown's Island commemorates the unsung heroes who participated in the struggle for equality.

Since learning their history, I've been inspired by these dauntless Black legislators of the nineteenth century who were ignored for so long, despite being a fundamental part of a critical period in the Commonwealth's history. As described in *Justice for Ourselves*, Black Virginians came together in the spring and summer of 1865 in public meetings across the state to declare their equality under the law and demand their right to vote as the most effective way to secure equality. They worked to advance issues for Black Virginians related to labor, civil rights, and especially the state's new public school system, as well as for local issues important to their constituents—both Black and white.

The story of Black Virginians claiming their freedom involves much more than politics, as *Justice for Ourselves* vividly illustrates through archival documents from the Library of Virginia. Because of de facto and de jure segregation, Black Virginians necessarily formed vibrant and successful parallel communities with their own businesses; newspapers; banks; churches; and a middle class of physicians, attorneys, and other professionals, as well as civic, fraternal, and social organizations. The establishment of historically Black colleges and universities helped develop leaders who would guide African Americans into the twentieth century and the fight for Black equality. The experiences of Black Virginians in the decades after the Civil War are much more dynamic and complex than we have previously understood and expand profoundly the story of Virginia.

But we can't appreciate our triumphs until we understand our trauma. *Justice for Ourselves* does not shy away from the losses Black Virginians suffered early in the twentieth century with the adoption of a new state constitution in 1902, one that removed most African Americans from the voting rolls for sixty years. And in that regard, this is a call to action for Virginians—and all Americans—to learn our complete, and often uncomfortable, history.

Congresswoman Jennifer McClellan

ACKNOWLEDGMENTS

We especially thank the scholars who accepted our invitations to research and write biographies of late nineteenth-century Black Virginians for the *Dictionary of Virginia Biography*. We also thank the present and former *Dictionary of Virginia Biography* staff members who contributed to the research, writing, editing, and fact checking of those biographies. At the Library of Virginia we thank Sandra G. Treadway, Gregg D. Kimball, and Catherine Fitzgerald Wyatt for their support of this project. Barbara C. Batson and Dale Neighbors assisted with illustrations. We are deeply grateful to our colleagues at the library who process the archival collections, many of which are also being digitized, that are at the heart of this work. We thank our partners at Virginia Humanities with whom we collaborated closely to commission, write, and post biographies on the period on its online *Encyclopedia Virginia*, including present and former editors Matthew Gibson, Brendan Wolfe, Peter Hedlund, Donna Lucey, Patricia Miller, and Caitlin Newman. We also thank the members of the General Assembly's Dr. Martin Luther King Jr. Memorial Commission, especially former Senator Jennifer L. McClellan, former Delegate Jean Cunningham, and chair Delegate Delores L. McQuinn, for encouragement and financial assistance. Through support from the Commission, Matthew Gottlieb provided invaluable assistance in preparation of the *Dictionary of Virginia Biography* entries at a crucial time in the project. Documentarians Lance Warren and Hannah Ayers helped secure the rights from VPM Media Corporation for the James A. Fields portrait, which they included in *How the Monuments Came Down* (2021). We thank the Menno Simons Historical Library at Eastern Mennonite University for permission to print the photograph of Jacob Yoder and his students from the Samuel Horst Collection. Leila Christenbury read the first draft and made valuable suggestions for revisions. Congresswoman Jennifer McClellan and National Park Service interpreter Ajena Rogers, a descendant of Black delegate James A. Fields, wrote the foreword and afterword, respectively. Acquisitions editor Nadine Zimmerli was enthusiastic about the project from the beginning and provided both encouragement and wise advice along the way.

NOTES ON LANGUAGE

In *Justice for Ourselves: Black Virginians Claim Their Freedom after Slavery*, the authors have endeavored to see more clearly how Virginians tried to create what Willis Augustus Hodges, a member of the state Constitutional Convention of 1867–68, called a "New Virginia" without becoming entrapped in old and out-of-date perceptions. These perceptions can be fueled by worn-out, imprecise, and incorrect language. For our purposes, the word Reconstruction invites a too-close focus on national politics and still conjures up misleading or erroneous ideas that white supremacists and apologists for the Confederacy created in the decades after the Civil War. Thus, we prefer to avoid that term and instead focus on how the competing aspirations of white and Black Virginians played out in their desires to construct that new Virginia.

We use the capitalized word Black with substantially the same definition that Judge Benjamin Watkins Lacy described when he defined the legal word colored in his 1892 opinion for the Virginia Supreme Court of Appeals in *Scott v. Raub*. The legal question in that case was whether the two parties to the case were legally "colored." In the nineteenth century, Virginia law defined every person with one-fourth or more of African ancestry as "colored." Reliable family history data often not being readily available, people sometimes had difficulty knowing whether a person with some observable or suspected African ancestry had more or less than one-fourth. In *Scott v. Raub*, Lacy and the court declared that the man and woman who were parties to the case "were both classed as colored persons, socially speaking, associated with colored persons, attended schools established for colored children, attended and joined a church established and attended by colored persons generally." The man in question "voted when other colored people voted, and not before." The woman "always passed as a colored person. It never has been questioned." Therefore, they "were socially of the class known as colored persons." The word Black here, in the same way that Lacy defined colored there, is not a physical description but a social and cultural identity. The lowercased word white, which does not have the same social and cultural anchor, refers to all other people except those who then self-identified as members of a Virginia Indian—Native American—First Nation—tribe.[1]

Some historical terms, phrases, and images presented here will be offensive to modern readers. These include manuscript collections with dehumanizing references to race, ethnicity, and enslaved or free status, such as registers of "free negroes" and county "free negro and slave records." Churches, organizations, and other institutions sometimes included "colored" as part of their names, including those established by Black Virginians. Books published in the nineteenth and twentieth centuries used terms that were accepted in scholarly literature at the time, such as Luther Porter Jackson's 1945 *Negro Office-Holders in Virginia, 1865–1890*. Quotations from Black people might be presented in demeaning dialects by white writers in such sources as contemporary newspapers and transcripts of interviews conducted by the Virginia Writers' Project of the federal Works Progress Administration program in the 1930s.

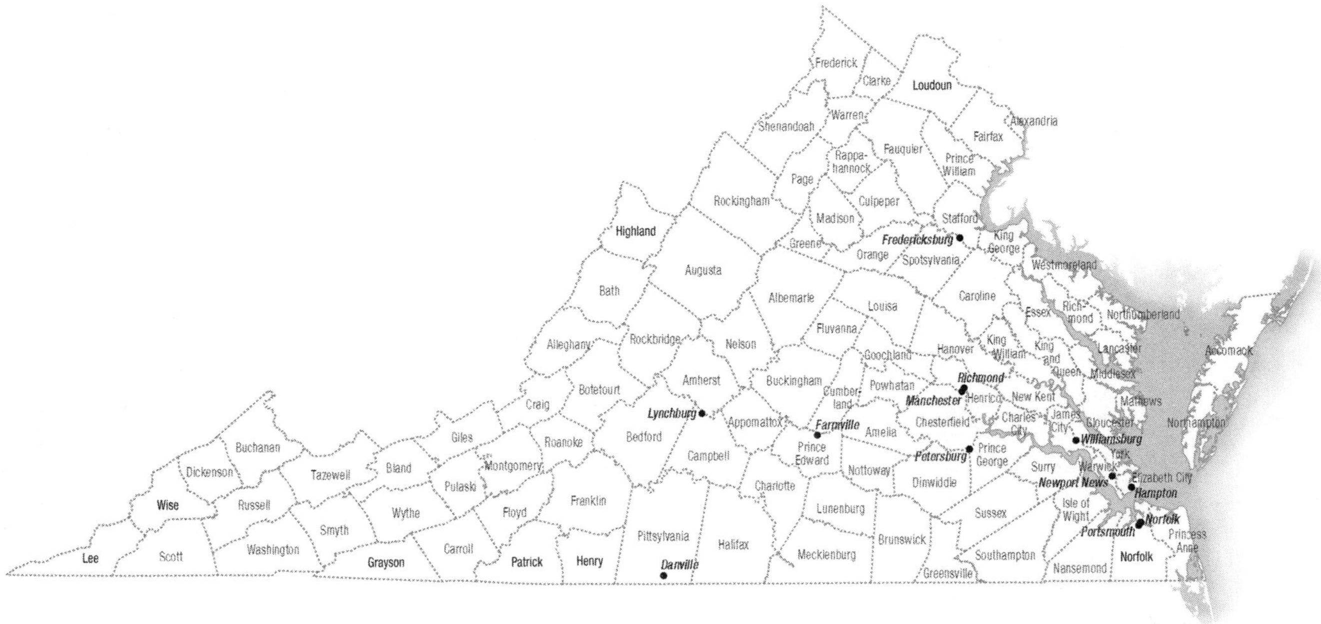

Virginia counties and selected cities and towns circa 1880. (Nat Case)

JUSTICE FOR OURSELVES

Introduction

In a June 1865 discourse published as *Equal Suffrage: Address from the Colored Citizens of Norfolk, Va., to the People of the United States*, its authors declared, "Give us the suffrage, and you may rely upon us to secure justice for ourselves."[1] Thomas Bayne, a dentist and political activist, led the committee that drew up the address. Born into slavery in North Carolina and known as Samuel Nixon, he escaped but was captured and sold to a dentist who relocated to Norfolk, Virginia. Nixon learned the trade, and his owner allowed him to make house calls at night. With this relative freedom of movement, he became an agent for the Underground Railroad before he escaped to New Bedford, Massachusetts, where he adopted the name Thomas Bayne and set up a dental practice. Returning to Norfolk near the end of the Civil War, he was elected to the Virginia Constitutional Convention of 1867–68 where he became one of the leaders of the Republican Party's radical faction.[2]

Like Bayne, Edward Whitehurst had his own story of self-emancipation. "I was free to all intents," he recalled in July 1877, "after the 27th day of May 1861, when my master went off" to enter the Virginia army "and left me." Like Bayne, Whitehurst was atypical of enslaved Virginians in that his master had illegally allowed him to live as if free and to earn money. Whitehurst had even leased a farm near Newport News, and he operated a small store and a bakery in the town. Although technically illegal, Whitehurst's actions illustrate that white authorities did not always enforce the laws restricting the behavior of enslaved people. He and his wife Emma had saved $500 toward purchasing their freedom. During part of the war he worked in a United States Army hospital. Soldiers of that army nevertheless raided his farm and bakery and carried away six hogs, fifty bushels of corn, forty bushels of potatoes, and two barrels of flour. They also seized two thousand pounds of fodder and cut down twenty acres of corn for forage. Edward and Emma Whitehurst gained their freedom during the war but lost everything else.[3]

Whitehurst had lived as if free before the war, but he recalled more than sixteen years later the exact date on which he actually became "free to all intents" and purposes. That date was of supreme importance to him, as was the date of freedom for Thomas Bayne and each of the almost half a million other Virginians who had lived in slavery. The end of their enslavement was a unique and momentous event in each of their lives. Decades later, when formerly enslaved Virginians debated what would be the best date to celebrate emancipation officially, Richmond grocer William Bell favored "April 3d when Richmond fell, because that was the day that I shook hands with the Yankees." William S. Selden, an undertaker, struck a more defiant tone and responded "I am in favor of April 9th, when Lee surrendered. For the day of the downfall of the Confederacy was the day of the uprising of the Negro."[4] It was undoubtedly the most revolutionary transformation they or their country ever experienced.

The end of slavery was of extraordinary importance everywhere, but it was not a single event in the history of Virginia or of the United States. For some people, it began prior to the war. For most it was a process that began with the war and continued for four or more years. The experiences of the freed people afterward were not all the same any more than the circumstances of their becoming free. Some of them were able to seize opportunities that freedom brought and achieve much more as freed people than many of them may have imagined possible when they were still enslaved. Other freed people, however, faced obstacles that they could not overcome and were unable to make the most of the precious boon of freedom.

Virginia's people are its history. This book is about Black Virginians and their families who strove to construct new lives in the aftermath of the abolition of slavery and during the remaining decades of the nineteenth century. Their hopes and fears as well as their successes and failures, individually and as members of families, communities, churches, and political factions, have been the subjects of numerous scholarly books and journal articles.

Black scholars produced the earliest studies of freed Virginians. Alrutheus Taylor's 1926 *The Negro in the Reconstruction of Virginia* is a detailed account of the politics of freedom in the second half of the 1860s. Luther Porter Jackson's 1945 *Negro Office-Holders in Virginia, 1865–1890* contains the first descriptions of the just over one hundred men who served in the Virginia Constitutional Convention of 1867–68 or in the two houses of the General Assembly between 1869 and the end of the nineteenth century. He also included an incomplete list of men who served in city and county government during those decades. Although he combed through local courthouse records and interviewed some of the men's descendants, a lack of access to subsequently available documentary evidence meant his biographical statements were less detailed than current research has uncovered. Still, Jackson's extraordinary work remains an essential starting point for investigating the lives of Black officeholders in the nineteenth century.

Community studies have laid the foundation for much of the modern scholarship on emancipation and its consequences in Virginia. Some focused on Richmond to explore the first critical years of freedom after the war as well as the long fight for the rights of Black labor in the capital city. Others examined the decades-long consequences of slavery on freed people in Hampton and race relations in the western railroad hub of Lynchburg. Important works have focused on rural areas such as Louisa County, contextualizing freedom and tobacco-growing economics, and in Montgomery County to explore formerly enslaved people navigating freedom in the decades after the Civil War. Several studies have looked back to the prewar years to delineate continuities and changes for freed people as a result of emancipation, while others have moved beyond Virginia to explore issues such as the confluence of race, gender, and public policy.[5]

This scholarship presents a wealth of evidence about changing conditions in Virginia following the abolition of slavery as well as detailed studies of several localities that enable us to make comparisons and see differences from region to region, especially between rural and urban communities. Those works and our own work and the research of other people who have written biographies for the *Dictionary of Virginia Biography* allows us to survey the whole period between the beginning of the Civil War and the disfranchisement of freed men in the Virginia Constitution of 1902 with an eye for revealing details and episodes that illuminate the obstacles and opportunities that freed people faced and to learn more about how they coped with the obstacles and took advantage, when they could, of the opportunities.

Much of what most people know—or think that they know—about the transition from slavery to freedom concerns the actions of radical Republicans in Congress to create new democratic economies and political systems in the states of the former Confederacy based on free labor and equal rights. Those national policies, white reactions against them in the Southern states, and the eventual abandonment of the campaign for reform contain competing interpretive narratives: one of an admirable attempt to create a new South based on free labor and equal rights; another that portrays that attempt as a failure doomed from the beginning; and a third that characterizes the end of the attempt as a white betrayal of freed people. Important as the actions of national politicians and their policies were, concentrating on them may slight what people of both races did in each of their separate states to create new economies and new political systems. Studying the people of a state adds valuable dimensions to the national narrative and illuminates local and regional variations and similarities.

Most of the life stories on which this work is based are found in the Library of Virginia's *Dictionary of Virginia Biography* (*DVB*), of which the authors are editors. All of the biographies, which the editors commissioned or wrote, are based on original research and contained new information. Beginning as a print publication and currently being published digitally, the *DVB* encompasses encyclopedia-length biographies of Virginians from across its history, especially highlighting women, Black and Indigenous Virginians, and men and women involved in fields of endeavor beyond politics, such as education, religion, business, fraternal orders, medicine, and arts and culture.[6]

In moving from a print to a digital format, the *DVB* partnered with Virginia Humanities' online resource *Encyclopedia Virginia* to develop "Freedom to Disfranchisement: The African American Experience in Virginia, 1861–1902," funded in part with grants from the National Endowment for the Humanities and the Virginia General Assembly's Dr. Martin Luther King Jr. Memorial Commission. The joint project published online at *Encyclopedia Virginia* comprises about two hundred *DVB* biographies, including all of the Black men who served in the General Assembly in the nineteenth century and in the Constitutional Convention of 1867–68, as well as entries on many influential Black Virginians in the decades immediately following the Civil War.[7]

By broadening the definition of who, and what, is important, these biographies have reshaped the narrative of Virginia's history. This is especially true when tracing the life histories of Black Virginians whose lives have been too-little studied. Most of the *DVB* entries are the first reliable biography ever written about these men and women. They have revealed so much new information that the authors of this work concluded that the entire history of the consequence of the abolition of slavery in Virginia required a full and fresh reassessment.

Diverse and fascinating life stories serve as the spine of *Justice for Ourselves: Black Virginians Claim Their Freedom after Slavery* as they drive the revised meta-narrative of post–Civil War Virginia. Weaving their way throughout the book will be themes central—though often misunderstood—to the nineteenth century Black experience, including self-determination, education, religion, entrepreneurship, the roles of women, and the condition of the family.

Meet James Apostle Fields, who, like Edward Whitehurst and Thomas Bayne was born into slavery. His life illuminates the changes that occurred during the final decades of the nineteenth century. Fields was born in August 1844, in Hanover County, the birthplace of Patrick Henry and Henry Clay. His parents, Washington Fields and Martha Ann Fields, lived on separate plantations. Virginia law did not recognize or protect their marriage or the integrity of their family. The separate residences of his parents and their status as enslaved people rendered their family and them individually vulnerable in many ways. Virginia law condemned Martha Fields's children to a lifetime of enslavement, but James Fields and his contemporaries lived through the abolition of slavery by the Civil War and attempted, with varying degrees of success, to take advantage of the new opportunities that freedom made available to them. Fields, in fact, lived a genuine American success story in the tradition of Horatio Alger's contemporary fictional white boys.[8]

Fields may have learned to read before the Civil War, which was not illegal, as many people have supposed. The General Assembly had made it illegal for people to operate schools for enslaved people early in 1831, a few months before Nat Turner's Rebellion, but not to teach individual people to read and write.[9] While Fields was tending horses for attorneys who conducted business at the Hanover County courthouse, he observed courtroom proceedings that later inspired his interest in the law. He could not have failed to notice the stark differences between the ways in which white lawyers sought to protect the rights and property of their clients and the ways in which the same laws and lawyers reenforced the harsh brutalities of slavery, which reduced enslaved people to the legal status of property, such as farm animals or plows.

During the Civil War, Fields fled after he suffered a particularly brutal beating from his master and eventually joined the rest of his family, who

James Apostle Fields was born into slavery and became a successful lawyer and civic leader in Hampton. (Luther Porter Jackson, *Negro Office-Holders in Virginia, 1865–1895*, Norfolk, Va.: Guide Quality Press, 1945. Enhanced image VPM Media Corporation)

had also escaped from enslavement. They reunited within the lines of the United States Army in the Hampton area. They were among many thousands of enslaved Virginians who freed themselves before the end of the war.

In Hampton, Fields attended a school that the American Missionary Association conducted at the army encampment, worked at Fort Monroe for the army's Quartermaster Department in 1864, and served as a watchman for the Bureau of Refugees, Freedmen, and Abandoned Lands in 1865 and 1866. Already literate, he was very fortunate to be able to take advantage of the new Hampton Normal and Agricultural Institute (later Hampton University) and was one of its first students in 1869. He then taught school for a year in nearby Williamsburg and graduated from Hampton in 1871. Early literacy and a chance for an education almost immediately after the war gave Fields many advantages. Men, women, and children who were not so fortunate did not always have an opportunity to enjoy the benefits of education, but they eagerly embraced it whenever they could.

Until 1886 Fields lived in Elizabeth City County, which included the town of Hampton. He was active in Republican Party politics and became known well-enough beyond his home that in January 1880 the House of Delegates elected him doorkeeper. He also attended Howard University, in Washington, DC, where he studied law with John Mercer Langston, another Virginia native and later the state's first Black congressman. Fields received a law degree in 1882 and began practicing law in the Hampton area. By 1887 he moved to Newport News, in Warwick County, where he served until 1891 as the county's commonwealth's attorney.

Fields easily won election in November 1889 to a two-year term in the House of Delegates to represent the counties of Elizabeth City, James City, Warwick, and York and the city of Williamsburg. As was the case with most legislators, including white men, much of Fields's work focused on issues of local importance to his constituents, such as authorizing construction of wharves on the Poquoson River. One of the last Black men who served in the General Assembly during the nineteenth century, Fields had a rare opportunity to help shape the laws that governed Virginia and its people. That he had little apparent influence was in many ways a consequence of the destruction early in the decade of the Readjuster Party, one of the most remarkable biracial political coalitions in Southern history that had given Black men substantial influence in state politics.

Befitting Fields's middle name, Apostle, he was active in Hampton's Third Baptist Church, instructing students at makeshift schools at Third Baptist and mentoring young men who aspired to enter the legal profession. Lawyers in and for the Black community were unusually influential citizens. They materially assisted freed people to obtain their own land, make wills, or charter fraternal organizations or corporations for conducting businesses, such as insurance companies and savings and loan associations. Dedication to the rule of law and to the importance of education ran in Fields's family. His brother, George Washington Fields, was an attorney in Hampton, and late in the 1920s his niece, Inez Catherine Fields (later Scott), became one of the first women to practice law in Virginia.

James A. Fields, the formerly enslaved boy, prospered. Estimates of his estate at his death in 1903 ranged from $25,000 to $50,000, amounts that most white families would have envied. The minority of the men and women who owned their own houses in the state's cities or their own farms in the country were more fortunate than the larger number who did not. To greater or lesser extents property owners were not as vulnerable as the majority to some of the financial and social limitations that the economics and politics of the time imposed on all of them. Property ownership, education, church membership, and family life were of the utmost importance and were measures of their successes as free Americans.

The professional and family life of James A. Fields paralleled the lives of a great many white Virginia men and their families. Among Virginians who remembered their lives in slavery or whose parents had been enslaved, he emerged as a prime example of how an educated, ambitious, professional family man could succeed in the radically altered environment after the abolition of slavery and give his own children a running start in life. Shortly before his death, however, white supremacists in the Constitutional Convention of 1901–2 stripped the right to vote away from men who had won the vote in the 1860s and then further imposed a rigid American apartheid that hardened into a racially segregated society and economy, crippling or destroying many of the opportunities that Fields and his contemporaries had taken full advantage of when they could.

Most of Fields's contemporaries did not fare as well as he did, either from the lack of as many good opportunities, because they could not obtain a good education, or because of the many high obstacles that unreconstructed white Virginians placed in their way during the generations after freedom. Fields's successful life and the less-successful lives of thousands of other Virginia men, women, and children illustrate the outer boundaries of what was possible for them and what was not during those transformative decades.

Fields's name and the names of thousands of other Virginians who shared the experiences of claiming freedom and living in a new Virginia without slavery have seldom appeared in a historical narrative or textbook. People do not know the stories of their struggles, their successes, and their sometimes-sad failures in pursuit of the American dream of liberty and prosperity. Children do not learn about them in school and of their achievements in the face of many obstacles even as they learn sanitized and inspiring versions of the lives of George Washington, Thomas Jefferson, and Robert E. Lee. Their stories are important and instructive, though, and just as inspiring in other and important ways. Part of the purpose of this book is to bring forward and understand how James A. Fields and his contemporaries lived, to enshrine their remarkable experiences into the master narrative of Virginia's multifaceted history, and to fill one of the many gaps in our knowledge and understanding of a past that all Virginians share(d).

Fields as a political leader and lawyer was unusual in several ways, but his life story intersects with most of the main themes of this history of the free and freed people of Virginia during the four decades that began with secession and Civil War. We carry their stories up to the dawn of the twentieth century, when the Jim Crow regime of white supremacy destroyed many of the opportunities that Fields was able to take advantage of with success.

THE STORIES OF James A. Fields and his contemporaries who experienced those changes and attempted to construct a new, egalitarian Virginia in a free labor economy are the subject of this book. The diverse tapestry of their prewar and wartime experiences shaped their postwar lives as they looked to define what freedom meant in terms of citizenship; political, economic, and civic equality; establishing marital status and reuniting families; forming separate church congregations; educating the old and the young; and engaging in land ownership or sharecropping.

As Black men voted and held elected office for the first time, we observe how they self-identified differently than white perceptions of their abilities. Studying their actions and votes in the Convention of 1867–68, the House of Delegates, and the Senate of Virginia related to universal manhood suffrage, establishing a statewide system of publicly supported schools, and democratizing the government enables us to discern what was most important to them immediately after they became free. Crucial to advancement in postwar Virginia, Black children—and adults—sought to take advantage of the new public school system. All the while, men, women, and children endeavored to navigate a minefield of societal behaviors in Jim Crow Virginia that shaped them at the time and for generations.

Essential to the story of Virginia is the brief experiment in biracial politics in the form of the Readjuster Party. With Black politicians playing a critical role, the Readjusters coalesced around the issue of the state's prewar public debt but also enacted such landmark legislation as repealing the poll tax, establishing Virginia Normal and Collegiate Institute (later Virginia State University), reforming the tax structure, increasing appropriations for public schools, and abolishing the whipping post as a punishment for crimes.

Community building and economic self-determination emerged by the turn of the century as Black Virginians carved out their own paths after white supremacists largely destroyed their ability to take a meaningful part in politics. Neighborhoods like Richmond's Jackson Ward developed in a segregated economy, which was cultivated by such institutions as the Grand Fountain of the United Order of True Reformers and the Independent Order of the Sons and Daughters of Saint Luke. These fraternal orders provided health and death safety nets and later established banks that spurred entrepreneurialism, while Black-owned newspapers provided an independent voice in the face of Jim Crow segregation. Local churches were the backbone of communities, while the Historically Black Colleges and Universities nurtured men and women to become educational, business, civic, and religious leaders in an emerging middle class that would continue the fight for Black equality into the twenty-first century.

1

"I Ain't No Slave"

Freedom in Virginia before the Civil War

When a woman who worked for the Virginia Writers' Project, part of the federal government's Works Projects Administration, asked Sarah Woodson Johnson in the 1930s for permission to interview her as part of an oral history project on slavery, Johnson agreed but insisted, "I ain't no slave—ain't never bin one."[1]

Johnson was about three years old when the Civil War began, one of approximately fifty-nine thousand Virginians whom the laws and social customs of the time identified as "free Negroes" or "free persons of color." She, her siblings, her parents, and her grandparents had all been free. Freedom and slavery had existed side by side in Virginia for almost two and a half centuries by then. About one in eight or nine Virginians with some African ancestry was free when Johnson was born and the Civil War began. In order fully to understand the context in which half a million enslaved Virginians became free during the war and their experiences in the aftermath of the abolition of slavery, we need to understand the lives of those free people before the end of slavery. They entered the new era of freedom with different personal and professional experiences than people who had been enslaved and as a result made the transition to a free labor economy differently than did formerly enslaved people. They enjoyed a greater degree of success and filled more leadership roles than their numbers alone would have predicted. As Johnson's emphatic, almost indignant, comment to the interviewer indicates, being free was of paramount importance.

The Lives of Free People in Virginia

At the time of the Civil War, Virginia had the largest population of free people of any slave state except Maryland; it also had the largest populations of enslaved people and of people who claimed ownership of them. A larger proportion of free people lived in the towns and cities of Virginia and the other slave states than lived in the countryside or on plantations. In the cities, more of them were women than men. The women for the most part earned livings doing laundry, working as seamstresses or cooks, and at other low-paying work; the men were to be found in many occupations, from unskilled laborers to barbers, riverboat hands, teamsters, and carpenters. In the countryside free people had to face the unpredictable terror of patrollers who often harassed them as well as enslaved people, but in the cities they faced equally unpredictable harassment and punishment from police officers and from mayor's courts that tried and punished free and enslaved people without the formalities of jury trials; and informal mobs of white people sometimes took it on themselves to punish free as well as enslaved people for behavior they deemed unsatisfactory.[2]

When Ira Berlin published his massive and deeply researched *Slaves without Masters: The Free Negro in the Antebellum South* in 1974, he neatly summarized in the title the scholarship of the time that he confirmed or supplemented with his own research into the primary source records of the slave states. Berlin concluded that most free men and women lived lives that laws and social customs constricted in so many ways that their condition resembled life in slavery more than the life that free white Southerners lived.[3]

In the decades after Berlin completed *Slaves without Masters,* other scholars published a large and important body of excellent scholarship on race and slavery in Virginia as well as an important body of excellent scholarship on free people in Virginia that contained many insights into the differences between the two populations. The most detailed and influential study on free people was Melvin Patrick Ely's *Israel on the Appomattox: A Southern Experiment in Black Freedom from the 1790s through the Civil War,* a fine-grained and richly insightful book that focused on a small community of people who lived for more than half a century near Farmville, in Prince Edward County.[4] Together with parallel investigations of free people elsewhere in Virginia[5] and in other slave states, the post-Berlin scholarship demonstrated that even within the many real legal, social, and economic limitations that free people faced, in many ways they were able to enjoy more freedom of action than the restrictive laws and earlier scholarship had indicated. Forty-five years after *Slaves without Masters,* Warren Eugene Milteer Jr. took into account all the new scholarship on the Southern states and, as had Berlin, did extensive original research into primary source records. In 2021 he published *Beyond Slavery's Shadow: Free People of Color in the South*. Its title indicates the extent to which it revised and to some extent superseded *Slaves without Masters*.[6]

Some free Virginians prospered. The lives of Richmond resident Joseph Abrams and of Petersburg resident Rebecca A. Gilliam Matthews may illustrate the outer boundaries of how successful a free person of color could be in the middle of the nineteenth century. Abrams was freed in 1844 at age fifty-three and worked diligently to earn money to purchase his wife, his daughters, and his six grandchildren, all of whom he freed in 1851. Abrams purchased two city lots and erected a comfortable house for his family. He prospered and at his death in 1854 had an estate worth nearly $1,500. For many years, he was a deacon at First African Baptist Church in the city and spoke to the congregation frequently. The white minister in nominal charge of the church reported that Abrams "was heard with far more interest than I was." Abrams was highly respected throughout the city and well known among Baptists elsewhere in the state. His funeral drew an estimated eight thousand people, including many of Richmond's white citizens.[7]

Matthews was the opposite of a slave without a master. If we could read the surviving records of her life without reference to the indications that she was free, we would scarcely be able to distinguish her life from the life of any of a number of upper-class, urban white women. In the 1820s, she, her sister, and their free mother each inherited several enslaved men, women, and children, as well as real estate in the city, from her father, a white Petersburg man who also owned plantations in Prince George and Goochland Counties. She married a free Petersburg man, James Z. Matthews, at the end of 1838 and had two girls and a boy. Her son, John Walter Boyd Matthews, whom she named for her father, won election to the House of Delegates in 1871.

At the time of her marriage, she executed a deed of trust that allowed her, through a white trustee, to manage her property. The common law doctrine of coverture routinely endowed a husband with all his wife's property at the time of the marriage unless she previously created what was called a separate estate. Such trusteeships were not uncommon among elite white families in the state. They preserved for a new wife ownership of family property that she brought into the marriage and prevented the husband from wasting it or endangering it by creating debts that her property could be seized to pay. With Matthews's resources thus protected from any interference her husband might wish to make and also (and this was even more important) against any actions of his creditors, she bought and sold real estate in Petersburg and probably became one of the most prosperous women in the city. She owned and lived in her own house that she insured in 1844 for $300. Her human property, by natural increase, included about thirty-five men, women, and children at the time of her death in 1849. The value of her estate then was nearly $7,000.[8]

Opportunities for Prosperity

Documenting the lives of Black Virginians such as Abrams and Matthews can be frustratingly difficult. In the absence of personal or family records, historians and sociologists use public records such as property transactions, tax records, local court papers, and census returns to learn about free people of color. Through local records, Ely's *Israel on the Appomattox,* about the people of the Israel Hill community of free people, contains detailed descriptions of people in a small free community that existed for more than half a century. Only a few of them owned real estate, and none of them owned very much. The men worked as day laborers or agricultural laborers on their own or some other person's property. Their incomes were small. Their chances for economic advancement were severely limited. The women, like farm women almost everywhere, cooked and cleaned, cared for children, and sewed and mended. Some of them may have taken in laundry or worked at menial tasks in a more prosperous person's house. Their freedom was in most instances their only valuable possession.

As in the case of Joseph Abrams, of central importance to the prosperity of free people was the ability to earn enough money to purchase the freedom of spouses, children, and other family members. Hercules Bland, a free Black cooper in Prince Edward County, purchased the freedom of his wife Mary Bland to ensure that their subsequent children would be born free. Their son James William D. Bland learned to read and write from an enslaved person in the household of his mother's former enslaver and later worked with his father as a cooper and carpenter. Beginning in 1864 he studied at an American Missionary Association school in Norfolk and later taught reading, geography, and mathematics.[9]

Enslaved people might be able to purchase their own freedom or that of their families, if allowed by their owners to hire out their own time and keep all or some amount of the earnings. Peter George Morgan was born into slavery in 1817, in Nottoway County, of mixed-race ancestry, possibly including Native American. Permitted to hire himself out as a shoemaker, he earned enough so that he could purchase his own freedom for about $1,500 in 1857. Later in the decade he purchased his wife and two daughters for $1,500. During the Civil War the family moved to Petersburg, where Morgan, in compliance with state law, registered as a free Black person in 1863. The following year he emancipated his wife, the two daughters he had purchased, and a third daughter who had been born in the meantime.[10]

Having a white parent could enhance opportunities for prosperity. Reuben Turner Coleman's white father owned property in Cumberland County, but his finances were precarious, and he was often in debt. While enslaved, Coleman sometimes acted as his father's agent in financial transactions, but was also permitted to enter into his own contracts, and his father emancipated him in 1860. After the Civil War Coleman used his keen financial sense and strong kinship connections with white family members to become a successful landowner and entrepreneur and operate a general store, a hotel, and a mineral springs company.[11]

Henry Turpin was born into slavery in 1836, in Goochland County and was one of the nine children of Mary James and the white man who enslaved her, Edwin Turpin. Their father freed all but one of them in a deed dated December 13, 1857. His elder sister Martha Catherine, who had been freed the previous year, was the wife of William P. Moseley, later a member of the Virginia Constitutional Convention of 1867–68 and the Senate of Virginia. In November 1863 Turpin paid his father $400 to purchase twenty-five acres of land adjacent to his father's place of residence in Goochland County.[12]

In some instances a white relative or family friend taught the rudiments of reading and writing. It was not illegal, as has often been said, to teach free and enslaved people to read and write; it was illegal only to open schools to teach them. In the case of Alexander Quincy Franklin, born in March 1852 in the city of Richmond, family tradition holds that he learned to read and write from a white Northern woman, who may have been his biological mother. Franklin's father had been enslaved before he purchased his freedom with money earned as a bricklayer.[13] While William Gilliam's parents were free people of color in Prince George County, he reportedly learned the rudiments of reading with the assistance of a white woman to whom he was related.[14]

Power of Kinship Networks

Some free people of color could trace their freedom back several generations or more on the eve of the Civil War. William Dennis Evans, born about 1831 in Prince Edward County, was part of an extended kin network of free Blacks who owned land in the county dating back to late in the eighteenth century. He apprenticed to learn the skilled trades of house painting and paper hanging. His freeborn wife Margaret, whom he married in 1855, worked as a clothes washer.[15] Likewise, Armistead S. Nickens was born in July 1836 to Armistead Nickens and Polly Weaver Nickens, both members of Black families in Lancaster County that had been free for several generations. Nickens was recorded as being literate in the 1850 census, and descendants believed that his father had taught him to read.[16] Goodman Brown's grandfather Scipio Brown received his freedom in 1804 in Surry County and later married Amy Johnson, a free woman. Both of their sons Herbert and Benjamin owned property in the county before the war. Goodman Brown's father Herbert married Parthena Bell Brown, also a free person of color. Goodman worked on his father's fifty-acre farm and attended a night school. In November 1862, near Cape Fear, North Carolina, Brown enlisted in the US Navy as a cabin boy aboard the United States *Maratanza*. He was discharged at Savannah, Georgia, on December 20, 1864.[17]

Kinship networks, especially those that crossed the racial divide, helped spur some free Blacks to live extraordinary lives, in spite of institutional racism in Virginia. John Robinson was born in the mid-1820s in Cumberland County. His father was likely a member of the Isbell family, white farmers in the county, while his mother Catharine "Kitty" Lipscomb was a free woman of mixed race who inherited land and two enslaved people. The extended Lipscomb family included at least a dozen free households in Cumberland and Powhatan Counties, several of whom owned land. White officials recorded Robinson's name in public documents as John Lipscomb until the 1850s or 1860s when he, his mother, and siblings adopted the surname Robinson, likely after Nathaniel Robinson, who had fathered his brother Jeter.

In April 1851 Robinson registered as a free man in Lynchburg, but it is unclear whether he remained long in the city. He registered again in Cumberland County in January 1857, two years after he purchased a small tract of land there and not long before he purchased another. He was likely the same free Black man named John Robinson who owned two parcels of land in the county containing twenty-four acres worth $705 and who owned one enslaved person. The census of 1860 listed him as Lipscomb and identified him as a wagon driver who owned real estate worth $700 and personal property worth $2,100.[18]

Martha Lipscomb, a free seamstress who owned her own land in Cumberland County, was also part of this kinship network. In 1850 her sons

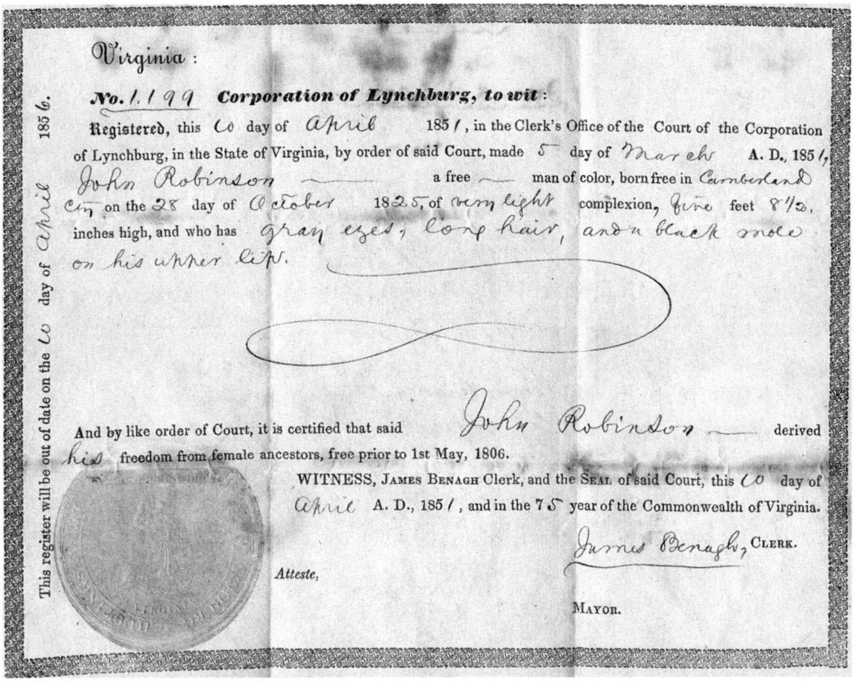
Virginia:

No. 1199 **Corporation of Lynchburg, to wit:**

Registered, this 6 day of April 1851, in the Clerk's Office of the Court of the Corporation of Lynchburg, in the State of Virginia, by order of said Court, made 5 day of March A. D., 1851, John Robinson a free man of color, born free in Cumberland Cty on the 28 day of October 1825, of very light complexion, five feet 8½ inches high, and who has gray eyes, long hair, and a black mole on his upper lip.

And by like order of Court, it is certified that said John Robinson derived his freedom from female ancestors, free prior to 1st May, 1806.

WITNESS, James Benagh Clerk, and the Seal of said Court, this 6 day of April A. D., 1851, and in the 75 year of the Commonwealth of Virginia.

James Benagh, Clerk.

Atteste,

Mayor.

This register will be out of date on the 6 day of April 1856.

Virginia law required that registers of free people include a physical description. John Robinson had a "very light" complexion, was 5 feet 8.5 inches tall, and had "gray eyes, long hair, and a black mole on his upper lip." (Lynchburg Free Negro Registration filed in Cumberland County, Free Negro and Slave Records, 1753–1865, Local Government Records Collection, Library of Virginia)

James F. and William Lipscomb and several other free laborers resided in Cumberland County. Late in the decade James F. Lipscomb left the county and by the summer of 1860 was living in Richmond, in the household of a prosperous white merchant for whom he was the carriage driver. The prosperity emerging from these kinship networks no doubt aided their postwar lives in which John Robinson sat as a member of the state Constitutional Convention of 1867–68 and of the Senate of Virginia, while James F. Lipscomb served eight years in the House of Delegates.[19]

Free People's Power and Free People's Restrictions

Free people were often important members of a community, which led some white people to treat them more politely or considerately than they might otherwise have. And in ways that a person who was merely familiar with the state's restrictive laws would not expect. For example, Virginia's laws had nearly always prohibited enslaved people from owning guns and regulated or prohibited free people's ownership of guns, but numerous references in many kinds of documents throughout the decades indicate that many free and enslaved people owned guns. Guns were important. For many families, including white families, they were essential to provide their tables with food and useful for any person with a chicken coop that foxes might raid. Guns were important; therefore, gunsmiths were, too. Early in the nineteenth century, John Wallace DeRosario was the foremost gunsmith in York and James City Counties. He enlisted the assistance of influential white men to endorse his application to the York County Court to allow him to own a firearm. In addition to the valuable services that he performed for the people of the counties as a gunsmith, he was also, according to the men who endorsed his application, a landowner and a respected man of honesty and integrity.[20] DeRosario was an unusual free man, not merely a slave without a master.

Nevertheless, the restrictions on free people were real and significant. Legislated restrictions on free people existed alongside, or made formal and legally enforceable, social and economic practices that were degrading and detrimental to their freedom. Most of them had origins in racism. Municipal ordinances in the state's cities made violations of white people's expectations of proper deference into petit crimes. The city of Richmond's comprehensive 1859 Ordinance Concerning Negroes prohibited free people to smoke tobacco in any public place, carry a cane in the night unless infirm, "use provoking language, or use or make insolent or menacing gestures to a white person," or fail to step aside, even into a muddy street if necessary, if "overtaking, or being overtaken by a white person on a side-walk."[21] And a Norfolk city ordinance earlier in the decade imposed a 10:00 p.m. curfew on the city's free people and authorized the mayor to fine "in a sum not exceeding one dollar" or punish "with stripes, not exceeding ten" any person taken up and thrown into the city's "cage," or lockup, for violating the ordinance.[22] There, as in other municipal and state laws, the word *stripes* referred to the wounds a person received for being tied to a whipping post and whipped, a punishment severe enough that it left bloody stripes on the back.

Such routine insults and humiliations reinforced the superior social status of all white people, even the poorest or least respectable. Free people also lived and worked under many other legal limitations that were more consequential. They could not vote (nor, before 1851, could white men who owned little or no real estate). They could not testify against a white man in any court. They could legally marry each other, but they could not legally marry an enslaved person or a white person; any children they had without a legal marriage were vulnerable to many forms of exploitation, and their parents had few legal means to protect them. Free people could be legally seized and hired out (as if enslaved) if they failed to pay the taxes levied on them or even be sold into slavery. They had to carry with them authenticated documentation that they were free, called free papers. After 1832, in the aftermath of Nat Turner's Rebellion, they lost the precious right to a jury trial if they were accused of a crime. They then faced what was called a court of oyer and terminer, a bench of county justices of the peace who conducted a trial without a jury and without all of the protections of the common law that white Virginians prized. If convicted of some non-capital offences, free people could be sold into slavery. And if convicted of a capital offence, they could be hanged or sold into slavery and deported from the country, just as enslaved people were.[23]

While free people had more options than enslaved people, they had not nearly so many as white people. Enslaved people convicted of felonies in a court of oyer and terminer ordinarily had no right of appeal to a higher court to reverse an alleged judicial error. They could only apply directly to the governor for a pardon or commutation of the sentence to some less drastic punishment.[24] If white judges made mistakes in reading or applying the law, free and enslaved people became victims with limited options. In 1843, though, after a court of oyer and terminer in Accomack County convicted a free woman, Elkaney Cropper, of stealing a shirt and a pair of socks and sentenced her to ten years of imprisonment, she appealed to the Virginia Supreme Court of Appeals. The judges overturned the conviction on the grounds that the court of oyer and terminer had no jurisdiction in cases of petit larceny, only in cases involving serious felonies. Instead of being tried without a jury in the court of oyer and terminer, Cropper should have been tried without a jury before a single justice of the peace and if found guilty would have been punished not with imprisonment but "by stripes, not exceeding thirty-nine."[25] A white person convicted of stealing a shirt and pair of socks would not have been imprisoned or tied to a whipping post and lashed up to thirty-nine times. That law and many others embodied the triple standard of justice in Virginia, one for white people, a brutal one for enslaved people, and an intermediate one for free people that was more severe than for white people.

The legal rights of free people appeared to be increasingly endangered by the 1850s as white Virginians contrived new ways to protect the institution of slavery. The state's 1848 law Of Offences Against Public Policy made it a felony for any "free person"—white or Black—to speak, write, or otherwise maintain "that owners have not right of property in their slaves" or for postmasters to distribute such publications through the mail.[26] The Virginia Constitution of 1851 contained several new provisions to protect slavery, including prohibiting the General Assembly from emancipating any person and endowing the assembly with authority to prohibit citizens from emancipating enslaved people. White Virginia politicians for decades had been trying to reduce the free population of the state, either by encouraging emigration to Liberia, promoting schemes of colonization to other places, or even enslaving the free population.[27] Chief Justice Roger B. Taney's 1857 opinion in *Dred Scott v. Sanford* proclaimed that people of African descent could never be citizens and that they did not therefore have standing to sue in a federal court.[28]

While some restrictions on the liberties of free people may have been routinely enforced, it is likely that white officials only sporadically enforced some others. Free people had to have certificates of freedom that proved that they were free, else they could be arrested and even, in the absence of proof of freedom, sold into slavery. Surviving records of registration, though, indicate that in many localities, few free people registered or clerks kept sloppy records, which could make it difficult to obtain a copy if somebody lost his or her free papers. Detailed studies of the enforcement of registration requirements in the central Virginia counties of Prince Edward and Goochland and in the Shenandoah Valley counties of Rockbridge and Augusta present ample evidence of the general laxness of registration enforcement with episodic bursts of registrations after events such as Gabriel's Conspiracy in 1800 and Nat Turner's Rebellion in 1831. The authors of all the studies concluded that even though many white officials disliked the presence of free people or believed in the abstract that free people posed a danger to public safety, they knew and seldom had reason to fear the free people who lived near them. Familiarity, then, bred trust, not contempt, and could lead to mutually beneficial or even friendly relations between white and free people or even enslaved people.[29]

While county and city registers were a means for local authorities to identify and exercise some level of control over free people of color and differentiate them from enslaved people, ironically they are crucial for our understanding of who they were. In the case of future state senator George Lewis Seaton, who was born free during the 1820s in Alexandria, then part of the District of Columbia, little is known about his early life. But the register of free negroes for Alexandria County (renamed Arlington County in 1920), described him in 1841 as about nineteen years old and "of dark mulatto complexion"[30] and in 1847 as about twenty-six and five feet ten and three-quarters inches tall. Most importantly, the 1841 register identifies six of his freeborn siblings by name as well as their parents, George Seaton and Lucinda Seaton. She had formerly been part of the enslaved community at Mount Vernon.[31]

Similar to the manner in which laws were unevenly enforced, enslaved peoples' chances for freedom were fundamentally determined by the level of autonomy that their masters allowed them, sometimes against the letter of the law. According to family tradition, William P. Moseley's Goochland County master allowed or perhaps enabled him to operate a boat on the James River prior to the Civil War. The absence of his name from census returns and local records suggests that he did not constantly reside in the county, but as a boatman probably would have resided on his boat. Moseley was free by 1857 when he married Martha Catherine Turpin, the recently freed daughter of a white planter, Edwin Turpin, and his enslaved woman Mary James.[32]

Distinction between White and Nonwhite

White Virginians often denigrated or insulted free people and enslaved people because of racial prejudice, which indicates that the distinction between white and nonwhite people was a more important distinction than the distinctions between free and enslaved people. For example, the white person who covered the mayor's court for the *Richmond Enquirer* on a day in April 1860 had nothing to report that he deemed newsworthy. "There was nothing of moment before 'His Honor' yesterday," the brief, two-sentence report began. "An average amount of niggerdom was ordered to be thrashed, and some half a dozen white people were fined in small sums, for violation of police regulations and city ordinances, of so slight a character that it is hardly worth while to publish them in a newspaper."[33] The report demonstrates that it was commonplace—scarcely worth reporting—that on one day in Richmond several people, perhaps including free people, received whippings—stripes—for infractions of order or decorum following a court proceeding in which the mayor alone, without a jury, decided guilt or innocence and ordered punishment. That at the same time the mayor fined a few white people indicates that the mayor punished free and enslaved people more severely than white people. Local and state laws often required harsher punishments for free people than for white people, as well as harsher punishments for enslaved people than for free people.

The newspaper report also exemplifies the callous way in which many racist white Virginians viewed the humiliating and often violent treatment that they routinely inflicted on both free and enslaved people. With the word *niggerdom,* the reporter lumped free and enslaved people together into a single degraded caste. For white racists, that leveled the status of free people downward toward slavery and acted like a corrosive acid in many other ways.

In some instances, however, derogatory reports contain valuable evidence of another kind. The white editor of a Petersburg newspaper reported at the beginning of December 1859 that a mixed-race crowd of children was reenacting John Brown's raid on Harpers Ferry outside his office. He characterized them as boys "who have nothing else but mischief and burlesque in their susceptible and humorous young minds." What his report demonstrated, though, was that the children of the city, most of whom were probably not literate, were well up to date on one of the most dramatic and politically important events of their time. "The insurgents are represented by the juvenile darkies," the editor reported, "with a large-headed white boy" taking the part of John Brown. Other white boys played the soldiers sent to capture them. "They arm themselves with tin shavings and wooden swords; and at this time, the 'armory' of one company is situated in the rear of our office, and glitters most formidably with the sheen of scrap tin picked up about the back doors of the tinneries. Their fights are highly amusing, the blacks and their white leader being always defeated, and treated to some hard slaps from the slender weapons of their patriotic adversaries. They run and fight everywhere, through the alleys and streets, climb trees and fences, throw egg shells, paper bullets, and in a word, carry on a most perfect counterfeit of guerilla war."[34]

Advantages of Urban Areas

Urban areas had many advantages over rural areas for free people and also some observable advantages for enslaved people. Cities were transportation and commercial hubs that provided enslaved people some opportunities to escape to freedom outside Virginia. Both free and enslaved people in the state's cities, which were all comparatively small, often lived under less strict supervision than on small farms and large plantations. And tobacco factories, ironworks, flour and textile mills, as well as railroads and steamboats and other commercial and industrial enterprises often had free, enslaved, and white people working side by side. In March

1829, the boiler of the steamboat *Potomac* exploded during a run between Richmond and Norfolk. Three firemen were at work together in the boiler room, John Dudley, who was white, Enoch Hay, "a free black, of Alexandria," and an enslaved man, George Wilson. According to a newspaper report, the steam from the boiler "shockingly scalded" all of them. Wilson died that night, and the other two died the following day.[35]

Free Blacks in urban environments could earn a living holding a variety of jobs not as readily available in rural areas. In Richmond, Joseph Cox worked for almost a decade in the rolling mills on Belle Isle and at the Tredegar ironworks. But he also worked in a tobacco factory and as a blacksmith, bartender, huckster, and day laborer. His wife Eliza, meanwhile, worked as a washer woman.[36]

There were also economic opportunities in urban life. The process of hiring out one's time enabled some enslaved people to accumulate funds to purchase their own freedom or that of their families. Joseph P. Evans, born into slavery in 1835 in Dinwiddie County, learned to read and write as a young child. By the age of twelve he had been moved to Petersburg, where he hired out his time as a whitewasher and plasterer. By 1859 he had earned enough money to purchase his freedom and enter Petersburg's substantial free community. During the Civil War he established a kiosk where he sold newspapers and magazines. He and his enslaved wife Josephine had at least four daughters and five sons, including William W. Evans, who during the 1880s served one term in the House of Delegates and edited the Virginia *Lancet*, a Republican newspaper.[37]

Enslaved persons in rural counties could be hired out by their masters to work in cities, allowing them to experience expanded freedoms from that of the farm. The Pendleton family in Caroline County owned Lewis Lindsey and his parents before he and his mother were sold in 1848 to another county resident. At the age of eleven he was sent to Richmond and hired out as a dining-room servant. Later employed at a female seminary, he learned to read and write, and also how to play the violin and bugle. During the Civil War Lindsey sold newspapers and served as a bugler in the fortifications around Richmond. He was whipped publicly for selling newspapers that he had allegedly skimmed from the publisher to soldiers in nearby camps. He reportedly played music at the governor's mansion during the Civil War and at the Hot Springs resort after the war, likely bringing him to the attention of politically influential Richmonders. In the spring of 1867 he was a member of the petit jury that was selected for the treason trial, which was never held, of former Confederate States president Jefferson Davis.[38]

Even for those enslaved people who lived somewhat independently in a city and managed to escape to freedom, the cruelty of slavery could be crushing. Born enslaved in 1818 in Norfolk, George Teamoh was orphaned when he was a young child. The Thomas family that owned him moved to Portsmouth about 1828. He developed a strong bond with the family matriarch, Jane Thomas, but when Teamoh was about twelve he was hired out to another family, where he was treated roughly. While working in a brickyard he taught himself to read by listening to white children singing the alphabet in school and identifying words on handbills and posters. His clandestine attempts at literacy were curtailed when the yard's brickmason discovered the used primer that Teamoh had found. For two decades beginning in 1833 he worked mostly around the city's shipyards as a caulker and carpenter.

In the summer of 1853 the family that owned Teamoh's wife and three children tried to sell them at Richmond's slave market. The ownership of the family being in doubt, the two older children were kidnapped and sold to parts unknown. Sallie Teamoh and their youngest daughter ended up in the hands of a liquor salesman who sexually abused both women. Jane Thomas arranged for Teamoh's escape from slavery by procuring him a job as a carpenter on the Bremen-bound ship *Currituck*, believing that he would not be subject to the Fugitive Slave Act while at sea. He ran away when the ship docked in New York City and eventually settled in Boston where he worked as a tailor. Teamoh returned to Portsmouth in 1865 and eventually found his wife in dire straits.[39]

Urban free people, unlike enslaved rural people, had some choice about where they lived, but in cities, many enslaved people also had some choice because industrialists or people who leased laborers may have exercised less close supervision than in the country. Some cities, such as the tobacco manufacturing centers in Petersburg, Richmond, Lynchburg, and Danville, passed municipal ordinances to prohibit enslaved people from living on their own or without proper supervision, but businesses often had no housing for the enslaved people they leased, so in the absence of any other options, the practice may have been fairly common.[40] Enslaved people enjoyed mobility and choices in urban areas that they did not have in rural areas, and they also probably interacted frequently with free people. The communities they formed were sometimes conspicuous and populous. And in the larger cities, such as Richmond and Norfolk, a small class of independent free men and women emerged almost in parallel to the new urban white middle class. Joseph Abrams, in Richmond, and Rebecca Matthews, in Petersburg, exemplified that small population of free

Virginians. For several years, free men and women in Norfolk staged an annual Ebony Festival complete with a ball at one of the city's hotels.[41]

Among the disadvantages for free and enslaved people in urban areas was the increased risk of epidemics, which struck commercial centers and shipping ports more frequently than elsewhere. Because people lived close together and associated more often in shops, churches, and places of work, epidemics of such pestilences as yellow fever and cholera were sometimes devastating. One enslaved woman, Jane Minor, was emancipated in 1825 because of her nursing skills during an epidemic the previous year in Petersburg, and she in turn emancipated more than a dozen women and children.[42] White people, of course, suffered, too, but at least some of them had resources that enabled them to escape the city and reduce the chance of becoming victims.[43]

In many respects, urban free families like Matthews's resembled urban white families, even though free families lived with restrictions and fears that white families never shared. Parents raised children, taught them essential skills, and tried to obtain some education for them. Norfolk had more than one school that free people attended.[44] In Richmond and Norfolk, and probably in other Virginia cities, free people formed associations of mutual benefit, such as burial societies or mutual aid organizations, to which they contributed small sums of money to be paid out to people or families in times of distress.

Importance of Urban Churches

The most important and conspicuous organizations urban people created were churches. In the countryside, free people, if they attended a church, probably sat in segregated balconies with enslaved people. All of the churches in the middle decades of the nineteenth century were entirely under the management of white men. In most of the cities, however, free and enslaved people formed their own congregations and for the most part managed the congregation's property much as white congregations did. In some, they also disciplined members for moral lapses or helped men and women reconcile family matters. After 1832, Virginia law prohibited free and enslaved people from preaching even in their own churches,[45] but some of the white clergymen appointed to oversee their churches allowed free and enslaved people to lead prayers during church services, and those prayers sometimes closely resembled sermons or even lectures on public events. Joseph Abrams was well known for his exhortation prayers in First African Baptist Church in Richmond.[46]

Williamsburg, Richmond, Petersburg, Manchester, Norfolk, Fredericksburg, and some of the smaller Virginia towns and cities had churches with *African* or *Colored* as part of the name.[47] Baptists appear to have outnumbered Methodists among the faithful church members, but free and enslaved people also attended churches of other denominations. The churches became influential centers of community life in the cities, sources of religious instruction and comfort, places to congregate relatively free of white oversight and regulation, and in effect community centers that could provide valuable assistance in times of need. First African Baptist Church of Richmond had the largest church building in the capital city and probably the largest congregation of any church in the state. Those churches, the free members of them, and their religious leaders became some of the most important institutions and leaders after the abolition of slavery.

Noah Davis became one of the most prominent church leaders. Born into slavery in 1804, he worked as a carpenter in Fredericksburg and eventually purchased his freedom and the freedom of his wife with money he raised in part by speaking in Philadelphia, New York, and Boston and by working as a missionary in Baltimore. He was a founder of Second Colored Baptist Church, in Baltimore, which was renamed Saratoga Street African Baptist Church when it opened in 1855. He purchased and freed a daughter and son with money that he raised on another Northern speaking tour, and with more money he earned by publishing his autobiography, *A Narrative of the Life of Rev. Noah Davis, a Colored Man* (1859), he purchased two other sons. Altogether he raised and spent more than $4,000 to free himself and his family. So prominent a religious leader had Davis become, that in 1863 he was one of twelve members of the American Baptist Missionary Convention who met with President Abraham Lincoln and persuaded him to allow Black ministers to preach to Black soldiers.[48]

Families of Free and Enslaved People

As with enslaved people, free people sometimes lived apart from their spouses or children. That was more likely if one person was still enslaved. If both were free, they were at least spared the horror and indignity of being sold away or having close family members sold away from the family or leased to work at a distant site;[49] and if a mother was free, she did not have to fear that her children would be sold. In that respect, free people were spared one of the most tragic consequences of slavery. Caroline Hunter recalled in the 1930s, "During slavery it seemed lak yo'

An enslaved family posed in front of a wooden house in 1862, on the plantation of Dr. William F. Gaines, Hanover County, Virginia. (Library of Congress)

chillun b'long to ev'ybody but you."[50] Matilda Carter remembered about the same time that after her sister was sold "down South," her mother "never did get over dis ack of sellin' her baby to dem slave drivers down New Orleans."[51]

The major studies of free people in antebellum Virginia suggest that free families probably resembled white families in some respects. As with white families, some had a woman as head of the household, but a majority had men, and unlike a large number of enslaved families, free parents and children (and sometimes grandparents, cousins, nieces and nephews, or other relatives) often all lived together.[52]

Those families and the community ties that they had with churches and other free families were often very strong. An 1806 law required that people freed from slavery had to leave the state within or year or be re-enslaved. For decades after passage of that law, men and women petitioned the General Assembly or a county or municipal court for permission to remain, usually in order to continue to live with family members. An even larger number remained without obtaining that permission. As with the lax enforcement of registration laws, local white clerks of court, law enforcement officers, and justices of the peace allowed them to remain because they knew the people and believed that they posed no threat to public safety and held jobs that kept them out of the poorhouse.[53] One of the best evidences of the importance of families is that some people who became free petitioned to be re-enslaved rather than have to leave the state and therefore leave their families. Precious though freedom was, the family could be more so.[54]

On the other hand, large numbers of free people left Virginia to escape the difficulties of life there and to seek better opportunities elsewhere. Some families left together, but others left one by one.[55] The lives of the three Hodges brothers, of Princess Anne County (later the city of Virginia Beach), exhibit both the difficulties that free people had in Virginia but also some of the opportunities that enslaved people did not enjoy. The brothers all left the state at different times and for different reasons. Sons of Charles A. Hodges and his second wife, Julia Nelson Willis Hodges, they grew up on their parents' small farm and had relatives among some of the other free families there, on the outskirts of Norfolk.

The eldest, William Johnson Hodges, usually known as Johnson, went to school in Norfolk and learned to read and write. Suspected of forging free papers for enslaved people, he was convicted in April 1829 of changing a figure (forgery) on a bill that somebody hired him to prepare or copy and sentenced to five years in prison. Hodges escaped from jail, left Virginia, and traveled to Canada and then to Brooklyn, New York, where he opened and ran a grocery store. He married, or entered into a common law marriage, with a woman who emigrated from England. They had a daughter and a son, John Quincy Hodges, named for former president John Quincy Adams who at the time of the son's birth was conducting a campaign against the House of Representatives' gag rule that prohibited receipt of anti-slavery petitions. Hodges built a house for his family, resumed preaching in Baptist churches, which he had begun doing before he left Princess Anne County, and by the 1850s was a leader in the community's emerging Republican Party.[56]

The second son, Willis Augustus Hodges, received only a little schooling and was the object of several episodes of harassment and abuse at the hands of local white men and boys. He visited his brother in Brooklyn to look for suitable land for his family to farm, but he was displeased with how local white men there treated free people like him and his brother, so he returned to Virginia. In 1836 Hodges went back to New York and worked for a time in his brother's grocery store and improved his reading and writing with antislavery tracts. He returned to Virginia again in 1838 and purchased one of his father's farms, but after he and his younger brother, Charles E. Hodges, were arrested for preaching antislavery sermons, he left Virginia again and in 1847 formed a short-lived partnership to publish an antislavery newspaper in New York, the *Ram's Horn*.

Through it he formed a friendship with and exchanged letters with John Brown, the white antislavery agitator who was hanged in 1859 after he led the assault on the federal arsenal at Harpers Ferry. Hodges joined the Union Temperance Benevolent Society and in the 1840s attended conventions of Black people in Albany, Troy, Utica, and Syracuse. He also lived for a time in upstate New York with other people who had escaped from the South and wrote an autobiography in which he described the many instances of violence and harassment free people were routinely subjected to in Princess Anne County. It was published in 1982.[57]

The youngest of the brothers, Charles E. Hodges, inherited his father's home farm and, like his brother Willis, was the frequent object of harassment. At the end of the 1840s, he paid taxes on two farms that together contained 143 acres of land and were worth more than $500. In February 1850, a white man swindled him out of one of the farms. The white lawyer he consulted told him that he would not be able to recover the land and would be better advised to leave the state. In 1851, fearing for his life and the safety of his family, Hodges moved his family and widowed mother to Brooklyn. There, he became a Baptist minister and joined his brothers in participating in antislavery meetings. In August 1864 he presided at a public meeting in New York that condemned a proposal to resettle freed women and children in New York in the menial capacity of servants. All three brothers and John Quincy Hodges would return to Virginia before the end of the Civil War.[58]

Racial Classifications in Virginia

Racial classifications in Virginia law and society governed many aspects of the lives of all Virginians, free as well as enslaved, white as well as not white. People's complexions reflected part of their personal and social history. Sexual procreation among members of the various populations that inhabited Virginia had begun soon after the first English settlers arrived in 1607 and continued unabated through the Civil War.[59]

Even people who appeared to be white could be classified as not white and therefore vulnerable to being enslaved or treated as members of what was defined as the socially and legally inferior class of free people of color. That happened to William Hayden when he passed through Virginia in the 1830s on a trip from Ohio, where he lived, to New York, where he had been born. During a pause in Prince William County, he associated for the most part with free men and women. A man who associated with free people but had a white complexion and no free papers, Hayden was arrested and jailed until he could prove his freedom. He could not, and the deputy sheriff, as the law required in that circumstance, tried to sell him into slavery, first at the courthouse, then at Brentsville, and then in Fredericksburg and Richmond. No traders would buy him, though, because his white complexion made it impossible for them to sell him for a profit. A man who looked white could so easily escape and pass for white that prospective buyers would fear to lose a large sum of money. Before the authorities in Prince William County could dispose of Hayden according to law, he escaped from jail and presumably made it safely out of Virginia. All this is known because the deputy sheriff who had tried to sell Hayden then petitioned the General Assembly to be compensated for his expenses in the futile effort to enforce the law.[60]

Free people's freedom became more precarious in the nineteenth century because the mere physical appearance of a person, as in Hayden's case, was not always sufficient to identify a person as white, free, or enslaved. The language of liberty from the American Revolution had inclined hundreds or thousands of white Virginians to question the morality or political propriety of slavery and to free some of the people they controlled. But the moral urgency of that language began to erode in the nineteenth century. In 1806, George Wythe had observed in the High Court of Chancery that in the case before him, *Hudgins v. Wright*, some of the plaintiffs who claimed illegal enslavement because they were Indians were "perfectly white, and that there were gradual shades of difference in colour" through three generations. Relying on the Virginia Declaration of Rights, Wythe declared that "on the ground that freedom is the birthright of every human being . . . he laid it down as a general position, that whenever one person claims to hold another in slavery, the *onus probandi* lies on the claimant." Freedom was the default condition of all people.[61]

But all of the judges of the Supreme Court of Appeals ruled that the Declaration of Rights did not entitle all people to a presumption of freedom and adduced what they regarded as important racial distinctions to shift the burden of proof. As Judge Spencer Roane, for many years the dominant intellectual of the court, explained, "In the case of a person visibly appearing to be a negro, the presumption is, in this country"—that is, in Virginia—"that he is a slave, and it is incumbent on him to make out his right to freedom: but in the case of a person visibly appearing to be a white man, or an Indian, the presumption is that he is free, and it is necessary for his adversary to shew that he is a slave."[62] Less than a decade later, the Supreme Court of Appeals ruled in *Hook v. Nanny Pagee and Her Children* that a jury could determine by visual inspection of physical appearance as well as by documentary evidence and witness testimony whether a person was entitled to a presumption of freedom.[63] In a Richmond city court in 1851, the judge summoned people who had known a female defendant in her former place of residence to attest to her racial status in that community. Whether the defendant was perceived as a white or a Black woman would determine if witnesses of the alleged crime who were identified as free people could testify against her.[64] That may have occurred more frequently throughout the state than current scholarship demonstrates.

An episode in the Richmond family of John E. Ferguson and Harriet F. Crump Ferguson provides a vivid example of the subtle and slippery complexities of race, slavery, and freedom in Virginia. Early in the 1850s Ferguson was engaged in the barbering trade, which placed him among the elite of free Blacks in the city. During this period barbers performed simple medical procedures, including cupping and leeching. He owned several enslaved persons, who likely worked in his barbershop or as domestics. Ferguson's barbershop, which included a three-story brick dwelling insured for $4,200, was located near the prominent Exchange Hotel. His clientele probably consisted of prosperous white businessmen, which placed him in a position to foster business relationships.

He used those connections to conduct more than twenty real estate transactions in Henrico County and Richmond. He purchased one property from John Dove, a white physician and leader of the Freemasons, and later joined the city sheriff in buying a lot on Main Street. These transactions, along with the necessary credit, indicate that white businessmen held him in esteem. By 1859 he owned a dozen properties valued at almost $6,300.

In 1853 Ferguson and his wife had obtained a certificate from the hustings court of the city that because they each had less than the one-fourth African ancestry, by law they and their children were therefore "not negros." But five years later, when their son, William Ferguson, appeared in the Richmond Mayor's Court charged with assault, the mayor ruled that even though members of the Ferguson family were legally "not negros," young Ferguson was not therefore legally white. That ruling enabled another free Black person to testify against him. The hustings court consequently convicted and fined him. Despite the mayor's decision, the 1860 census identified Ferguson's children as white.[65] No matter how prosperous, free persons of color lived in a shadow world between slavery and freedom, not enslaved, but not fully free. And therefore always vulnerable.

Maria Griffin and her children should have been freed and well-provided for before the Civil War. The will of Robert Anderson, a white wealthy investor and former mayor of Williamsburg, as well as the father of her children, provided that she and their children all be freed following his death and that his estate pay for the children's education. The will also bequeathed to her a stated portion of his estate. Anderson had allowed Griffin to live in a house that his late, white mother-in-law had owned in Yorktown, and he probably lived there with her and their five children in the 1850s. His white heirs contested the validity of the will in court after his death early in 1859 and prevented it from being executed, which deprived Griffin and her children of the freedom Anderson wanted them to have. Even after they all became free when they moved to Philadelphia, and some of them returned to Virginia after the war, she and her children never received any of Anderson's estate. His many investments, debts, and accounts receivable created a tangle of legal complications so complex that the estate was not settled for several decades. Their son eventually purchased one or two Yorktown lots that Anderson had owned, but Maria Griffin and her children never received any of the material benefits that Anderson had tried to provide for them when he wrote his will.

The complexions of Griffin and her children were almost white. Her son Robert's United States Colored Troops military service record would describe him as five feet, four inches tall with black or hazel eyes and light-colored hair. Some of her children later passed as white. Their father in that one respect had somewhat eased the lives of his children who had been born into slavery and were therefore perpetually vulnerable to racially discriminatory laws and social practices in Virginia and elsewhere. In fact, Anderson recorded (somewhat confusingly) that either Maria Griffin was, or their children were, seventh-eighths and three-quarters white. By that, he probably meant that seven of eight great-grandparents were white and that the eighth was three-quarters white.

Still, in spite of Virginia law that dated back to the seventeenth century that defined any person with one-fourth or more African ancestry as "negro,"[66] after Griffin and her son Robert, who later served a term in the House of Delegates, returned to Virginia late in the 1860s, they associated largely with other men and women with African ancestry and were recorded on most census documents as of mixed-race ancestry. Like Richmond real estate entrepreneur John Ferguson and his wife, who had obtained a certificate declaring them as "not negros" because they each had less than the one-fourth African ancestry,[67] the Griffins were socially Black, but just because they were not legally Black in Virginia did not make them legally white.[68]

Freedom for Black Virginians prior to the Civil War was a complicated existence navigating local and state laws, social customs, urban versus rural circumstances, and, of course, profound racial prejudice from whites. Still, free people of color could carve out a place for themselves in their local community and even achieve some measure of prosperity. In the not-too-distant future free Black Virginians, especially those who were literate and ran their own businesses, found themselves in a position to become leaders of all Black people. But first a war over freedom for all Black men, women, and children had to be fought; a period in which some enslaved Black Virginians took the opportunity to free themselves in the circumstance of war.

2

"We Will All Be Free"

Self-Emancipation during the Civil War

At the beginning of 1861, two months after Abraham Lincoln was elected president of the United States, a law enforcement officer in the town of Manchester, across the James River from Richmond, arrested several men who "had said amongst themselves, that they expected to be free about the 4th of March," the day of Lincoln's inauguration. Because the men had only talked about the possible end of their enslavement and had taken no action, a judge ordered them whipped thirty-nine times each and then released.[1]

Talk could get an enslaved person in serious trouble with the law. On a Sunday in April 1861, a man named Sam (whose surname was not recorded) in the county of Mecklenburg, on the North Carolina border, told some friends, "I suppose we will all be free pretty soon." For that and other things Sam said, he was arrested and tried on a charge of conspiring to "make insurrection." One witness testified at the trial in May that Sam had explained, "from what I can find out, Old Lincoln is coming down the Mississippi river and will free every thing as he goes, and I think if we be pretty keen we will get our freedom too." Another witness recalled Sam's words to the same effect but without the confused reference to the Mississippi River: "thank God we will all be free after a while, for old Lincoln is going to free us all." The witness reported that Sam hoped that Lincoln "would make haste and do it, for he meant to get his freedom as quick as he could." Without any evidence or testimony that Sam had taken any steps toward conspiring to free himself or anyone else, the court convicted him on May 21 and sentenced him to "be transported and sold beyond the limits of the United States."[2]

The court's sentence repeated the language of the state's law that such convicted men be sold to some place outside the United States;[3] but

"The Village Magnates, 1861" by William H. Strother ("Porte Crayon") depicts three gentlemen discussing the Ordinance of Secession that the Virginia Convention submitted to the voters in a May 23, 1861, referendum. A Black man, perhaps enslaved, listens to the discussion as he crouches inconspicuously behind a fence. (Pierre Morand Memorial, Special Collections, Library of Virginia)

fast-moving public events made that sentence almost comical in its irony. Two days after the court sentenced Sam, a majority of adult white male Virginians voted to ratify the Ordinance of Secession to take the whole state of Virginia out of the United States. The governor commuted Sam's sentence to "labor on public works," which may mean that the state paid his master or mistress $540, which is what the judges at the trial agreed was a fair market price, so that the enslaver did not lose money because of Sam's actions.

Sam and the men in Manchester understood early in 1861 what Edward Whitehurst understood when his owner left in May to fight in the war and he became free "to all intents"—that the election of Abraham Lincoln as president in November 1860 had generated a political crisis that created new opportunities for almost half a million men, women, and children in Virginia to become free. A majority of all Virginians were not literate at the time of the secession crisis—free as well as enslaved; white, Black, and American Indian—but they all had ears to hear and brains to think. They knew what was going on and understood what the changed circumstances could mean for them.

Self-Emancipation

Some people did more than hope or talk. They acted. In Greenbrier County, in the mountains of western Virginia, Reuben (whose surname was not recorded) was arrested about the same time as Sam because he had announced that after white militiamen left the county to fight for the Confederacy, enslaved men in the county would then begin the fight for their freedom. A man testified at the trial that Reuben had predicted that "there would be a row kicked up nearer than Harpers Ferry." He explained, according to a witness, "with what arms they had and with what fire they could throw out they could take Lewisburg," the county seat. Reuben had also defiantly announced, "I will be damned if any white man shall be master over me." County officials arrested Reuben and discovered that he had acquired and hidden "a good deal of shot, powder, Bullets," a box of percussion caps, and four loaded pistols. The court convicted him in May 1861 and sentenced him to death. The governor refused to pardon Reuben, and the state government paid $340 from the public treasury to purchase Reuben in order that the enslaver not lose the value of his property by Reuben's actions.[4] The executed Reuben may therefore be regarded in some senses as an early casualty of the Civil War.

Other men elsewhere in Virginia prepared to fight for the Union and their freedom. The same week that courts convicted Sam and Reuben, some men near Winchester began a small uprising. A few Confederate soldiers put it down but in the process shot four men, one of whom was white.[5]

More often, people quietly escaped from slavery as they had done since the very beginning of slavery in the seventeenth century.[6] Milt (also known as Mitt or Milton) left a white family in Barbour County, north of Greenbrier, later in the year. By then, at least some white people had begun to understand how much had changed as a result of the political and military crises and that some things might never be the same again. A white neighbor, reporting on the man's successful escape to Ohio, sighed presciently, "Milt is among the things that were." She perceived that slavery and enslavement might not survive the war.[7] In the neighboring county of Upshur, another man, named Frank or Frank Little, whose master or mistress had hired him out to work for a year for a local white lawyer, told the lawyer's wife at the end of 1861, as she reported the conversation, that "he refuses to be hired out . . . he is agoing to do for himself." He was "agoing" to live as if free.[8]

People fled from slavery in the vicinity of Winchester in May 1861, and the following month about one hundred more from the same area made it safely to Pennsylvania. Late in the year, more people from the same vicinity arrived in Philadelphia, including some who had been the property of United States senator James M. Mason, who had been the primary author of the Fugitive Slave Act of 1850 that required the return of people who escaped from slavery. None of Mason's enslaved people returned.[9]

Erosion of the Slave Regime

Throughout the war Virginians freed themselves in increasing numbers. The slavery regime began to erode almost from the beginning. Events of the war provided people with more and more-varied opportunities than people had had before the war began. People found or made a great many different ways to emancipate themselves. White Confederate Virginians and civilian supporters of the Confederacy actually created new opportunities for escaping slavery. Samuel Ballton, for example, escaped slavery while working in the Confederacy on a railroad that leased him from his enslaver. Ballton later joined the United States Army to fight for his own freedom and for the freedom of millions of other Americans. After the war he settled in Greenlawn, on Long Island, New York, hundreds of miles away from Westmoreland County, Virginia, where he had been born and where the laws of his native state had condemned him to a lifetime of slavery. He began farming, acquired land, and prospered. His specialty was cucumbers. Long before Ballton died in 1917, he was well-known as the Pickle King of Greenlawn.[10]

Beginning in April 1861, state officials leased enslaved laborers and draft animals to construct defensive works in areas of eastern Virginia that were vulnerable to easy incursions of the United States Army. Documents preserved in the state archives show that white people who leased workers and animals to the government received a daily compensation that was identical for mules and enslaved men; they were recorded together on the same form.[11]

Both the state and the Confederate governments leased enslaved laborers to support rebel armies. Because the defensive works where many of them labored were then, and throughout the next four years, close to units of the United States Army, many of those men made opportunities to slip across shifting battle lines in many areas of Virginia to seek refuge and, eventually, freedom. Indeed, during the war, so many men escaped toward freedom from entrenchments, hospitals, and other Confederate installations that by 1865 the number of enslaved men in some Virginia counties may have fallen by as much as a half. Men who returned from that work often brought back news of events far from home, much as enslaved people who had been leased to work away from home brought back information about other parts of the state and country.[12]

Thousands and thousands of men and women emancipated themselves, the number rising as the war continued and battle lines moved back and forth across much of the state. It is probable, but by no means proved, that as during most of slavery, men may have attempted to escape slavery more often than women and may have succeeded more often. Inasmuch as governments dragooned many men, but not so many women, into working on Confederate entrenchments and at other Confederate sites, men probably had more opportunities than women to make their escapes from the lines of one army to the lines of the other.

James W. Hunnicutt, a white Methodist minister who edited the *Christian Banner* in Fredericksburg, often commented in its pages in 1862 on the hundreds of formerly enslaved men and women constantly passing through town "seeking the land of freedom" by crossing the Rappahannock River and heading north. Many had come from the nearby counties of Spotsylvania, Culpeper, and Orange, but others had traveled from as far away as Madison and Albemarle to reach the lines of the United States Army. Describing their efforts as "practical *secession*" and "emancipation with a vengeance," Hunnicutt, who opposed secession but supported slavery, recognized that enslaved Virginians "are determined *to be free*, and will certainly be free" as a result of the Civil War.[13]

Members of some families sought freedom together. Early in the summer of 1861, William Roscoe Davis, Nancy Moore Davis, and their children entered the United States Army encampment at Fort Monroe, in Hampton. He had earned his freedom, but she remained illegally enslaved because the heirs of her former master refused to execute a provision of his will that would have freed her. Davis family members were among the first of thousands of Virginians and residents of other slave states who entered army camps because they believed or hoped that the army would protect them and ensure their freedom. William Roscoe Davis was literate and often preached to Baptists in and near Hampton. An agent for the American Missionary Association, which helped the army take care of refugees from slavery, reported that summer that Davis was a "man of genius and piety" and also an eloquent and compelling speaker. In September 1861, when Davis preached to soldiers and escapees from slavery, he "melted every heart." The following year, the association paid for Davis to travel north on an extended tour to raise money to support schools for people who had freed themselves from slavery and to purchase clothing for them.[14]

Enslaved people took whatever advantage of the presence of United States troops anywhere they could. On Christmas Day 1861 in Buckhannon, in the western county of Upshur, a white woman loyal to the United States reported that at the same time that "Secesh" women paraded through town in their finery, the "*colored ladies* are flitting around in the gayest apparel and giving themselves such exquisite airs." She did not record whether the "colored ladies" were free and/or enslaved, but they nevertheless proudly and without being molested paraded through the little city's streets just as the white ladies did.[15]

Near a United States Army encampment in Charles Town, in Jefferson County (later in West Virginia), an army officer wrote home early in 1862 about "a sight that I would gladly photograph for you. A large wagon full of negro men, women, and children, overrunning like the old woman's shoe. It had come in from the farm, near town, of some disloyal Rebel."[16] Later in the year when the army advanced as far south up the Shenandoah Valley as Harrisonburg, people celebrated as if its very presence brought them freedom. A correspondent of the *New York Times* reported that a woman there "clapped her hands and threw them up in an attitude of glory, hallelujah, while her face lighted up."[17]

This family with all its possessions and four oxen may have been seeking freedom in 1862 as Confederate Army units under command of Thomas "Stonewall" Jackson approached Fredericksburg. (Library of Congress)

Martha Ann Fields chose not to escape slavery in May 1862 after a United States victory at nearby Hanover Court House. Facing the threat of being sold at auction the following year, however, she took her chance when a cavalry unit passed through Hanover County. With her seven youngest children, she followed the regiment with Confederate troops not far behind. Forced to wade through swamps along the Pamunkey River, the family managed to cross the river safely and reached a United States Army camp. An officer agreed to take them to Fort Monroe, where her family was eventually reunited, including her husband who had been enslaved at a different plantation, her son James Apostle Fields who had previously escaped, and three other children who had been sold away.[18]

An Alabama soldier wrote to his wife in August 1862, "I have been scouting & picketing up in Caroline Co between the North & South Anna Rivers. . . . I hear of many negroes leaving & going over to join the Yankees. They go in Squads of 20 so some of the citizens say and one told me that 20 or 30 passed his house[.] They had carts & seemed to be moving bag and baggage & that one of the Negroes had an old fiddle & another an old Banjo & that they were singing & playing at a great rate."[19] On the other hand, when Confederate advances forced the army back, the retreat alarmed—endangered—people who had tried to free themselves.[20] A soldier in the United States Army later recalled one such episode. "At every rough point in the road," he remembered after the war, "we found the vehicles of these poor fugitives thrust aside, broken, and overturned, their goods scattered, and the family weeping in despair."[21]

Nobody at the time could count, or later accurately calculate, the exact number of Virginians who left their homes to secure their freedom. Hundreds or thousands of people escaped successfully to free states, but others remained in Virginia. As many as 900 sheltered in Hampton in the summer of 1861. Owing to the presence of the United States Army, the population of Black residents in Alexandria tripled to 8,000 during the war, and the population of Washington, DC, rose from 13,000 to 27,000. In 1864, 8,000 refugees were in camps in Norfolk.[22]

Men and women who lived near military lines or battle lines undoubtedly found it easier to reach freedom than men and women who lived in the interior. Maria Griffin, who lived with her children in Yorktown, moved with her three young daughters and one son to Philadelphia in the free state of Pennsylvania on an unrecorded date during the war. There, they lived in poverty as members of a small household with her eldest daughter and the daughter's new husband.

Life in Refugee Camps

The United States Army created about thirty camps in Virginia to care for some of the many thousands of Virginians who escaped slavery during the war. The camps were near the Potomac River as far upriver as Harpers Ferry and near the lower reaches of the Rappahannock and York Rivers, as well as in Norfolk and Suffolk. The army established seven camps in or near Hampton and nearby Newport News. At Fort Monroe, alone, three thousand people congregated by December 1861, and the number rose rapidly to five thousand the following February and to twenty-five thousand by the spring of 1865. Conditions in some of the camps were sometimes terrible. In the beginning, the army had logistical difficulties even feeding and taking care of the soldiers, but refugees compounded the problem. People arrived in tattered clothing with few or no possessions. Some suffered from malnutrition or disease. In the close quarters in some camps contagious diseases may have killed people who had risked their lives for freedom.[23]

The best-known of the refugee centers in Virginia was the first, at Fort Monroe, where the family of William and Nancy Davis took refuge and sought freedom early in the summer of 1861. The commanding general of the army at the fort was Benjamin F. Butler, who was the first United States official who had to make decisions about what to do with refugees. During the night of May 24, Shepard Mallory, Frank Baker, and James Townsend entered Fort Monroe, the first refugees from slavery to arrive. The following morning, a Confederate officer demanded their return to their owner. They were people to be fed, housed, and cared for; but they were also a valuable resource for Confederates if returned and a potentially valuable laboring resource for the United States if not. With no official instructions from the army about what to do, Butler refused to return the men, whom he declared were "contraband of war." The phrase meant captured property of a belligerent. Butler's declaration recognized that under the laws of Virginia and the United States, Mallory, Baker, and Townsend were property. That inaccurate term stuck and was in common use throughout the war for people who had escaped slavery.[24]

Because the camps near Fort Monroe were among the first and because of Butler's description of the inhabitants as contraband, that camp was probably the best-known in the country. Quakers, members of the American Missionary Association, and other philanthropic organizations in the free states sent clothing, foodstuffs, and teachers and other volunteers to Hampton to assist the refugees, many of whom, like Edward Whitehurst, labored for the army. The schools that they established were immediately popular because enslaved people had largely been unable to obtain schooling even though they very well knew the value of education. In the houses refugees built, in the schools that they helped found, and in the church congregations they joined or created, they lived in a new kind of Southern community, a community that included only a few white people and where the refugees lived almost as if free. Some got married, although the services their ministers performed were not legal under Virginia or United States law during the war.[25]

Refugees in the camps at Hampton and elsewhere had more freedom than with their enslavers, but life was not always easy for them. Army officers and soldiers sometimes abused them and even raped some of the women. Officers sometimes forced men to work on fortifications without pay, and even later when required to pay the men, the army usually paid them less than it paid white men for comparable work. Refugees had access to schools for the first time and in many instances more freedom of worship, but some of the teachers and other white people from free states who traveled to the camps to assist the refugees did not understand the culture of the people they tried to help, which led to difficulties. Because of the unprotected status of enslaved people's families, men and women who had lived in slavery had different notions of family life that often confused or even appalled people from the North who learned that men and women who considered themselves married often had living former spouses from whom the slave trade had separated them. The men and women regarded the former spouses as if they were dead. The people from the North, with their backgrounds in solemn religious services that stressed doctrinal sophistication and uniformity, also failed to understand the emotional, less-formal worship of people who had been part of evangelical Baptist congregations in Virginia. Such tensions and conflicts inhibited the abilities of refugees to be able to take maximum advantage of the opportunities that were available in the camps and to make their self-liberation from slavery a genuine freedom.[26]

The presence of refugees almost on the front lines of the war during the Peninsular Campaign in 1862, when the United States Army massed in Hampton Roads to march inland in a failed attempt to capture Richmond, contributed in important ways to Abraham Lincoln's and the army's decisions to make use of the refugees as laborers in the war effort and eventually, later in the year, for the president to draft the Emancipation Proclamation.[27]

The other most-famous refugee settlement in Virginia was on the Arlington estate, across the Potomac River from Washington, DC. The federal government confiscated Arlington in 1863 because the agent of its owner did not take a required oath of allegiance to the United States. The owner was Mary Custis Lee, a great-grand-daughter of Martha Dandridge Custis Washington and the wife of Confederate general Robert E. Lee.

Freedman's Village was unusual in many ways, perhaps most notably in its long life. The army and the residents constructed one hundred one-and-a-half story houses as well as schools and churches. As at other camps, education was a high priority of people who had freed themselves. They and their children learned to read and write at the schools. Men learned new farming techniques, and women learned housekeeping skills. Men and women tended gardens for themselves. Several hundred people resided at Freedman's Village for more than two decades and regarded it and the houses where they lived and the kitchen gardens that they tended as their real home and the land and houses as their own property. What they regarded as their home in freedom, however, they lost later when the federal government forced them out of Freedman's Village by 1900.[28]

In 1866 Congress deeded 17.53 acres of the Arlington estate and the house that stood on the property near Freedman's Village to formerly enslaved Maria Carter Syphax. She was the daughter of George Washington Parke Custis, who was a grandson of Martha Dandridge Custis Washington, and she was therefore a half-sister of Mary Custis Lee, who inherited the 1,100-acre estate from their father. Custis had given Syphax the seventeen acres and permission to live there without executing a proper deed which, because she was enslaved, he could not do. After the war, Congress made certain that Custis's promise to Syphax could be honored. She lived on her small plot of land for the remainder of her life and was so highly regarded that local white newspapers published brief accounts of her funeral early in 1886. Her son William Syphax helped establish the public school system for Black children in Washington, DC, and her son John Syphax had a long career in the Republican Party in Virginia and served one term in the House of Delegates.[29]

Freedom for the Enslaved in Virginia

The Emancipation Proclamation that President Abraham Lincoln issued on January 1, 1863, is only the most famous of the legal abolitions of slavery before ratification of the Thirteenth Amendment in December 1865. The proclamation freed men, women, and children who were enslaved in areas defined as "in rebellion against the United States," while exempting areas then under the control of the United States Army. In Virginia that included Hampton Roads near the naval installations at Norfolk and Portsmouth and on the Eastern Shore between the Chesapeake Bay and the Atlantic Ocean. Because battle lines continued to shift back and forth during the war, in some places like Winchester slavery was legal under Virginia law on some days but illegal under the Emancipation Proclamation on others. That could have aided people who wished to escape slavery while the United States Army was nearby, but it could also have put white people on guard or made them more vigilant or violent in their attempts to keep what Virginia law still defined as their personal property.

The proclamation also exempted counties in the western part of the state, which soon joined the Union as the new state of West Virginia. Approximately one-tenth of all enslaved Virginians lived there. White western Virginia men who remained loyal to the United States began working immediately after secession to separate the western part of the state from the eastern part to create a new loyal slave state. By the time the West Virginia statehood bill was before Congress in 1862, many loyal men in the free states had come to believe, as Lincoln also came to believe, that the best way to save the Union was to destroy slavery in the rebellious states. Congress required that the proposed constitution for the new state provide for the abolition of slavery. The constitutional convention that had met in the winter of 1861–62 reconvened and submitted to the voters a revised section that included a gradual emancipation provision that was similar to some laws or constitutional requirements in Northern states that had already abolished slavery. The new section stated that every person born in West Virginia on or after July 1, 1863, would be born free; that enslaved persons ten years of age or younger on that date be freed at age twenty-one; and that enslaved persons between the ages of ten and twenty-one on that date be freed at age twenty-five. It left all adult former Virginia men and women who lived in West Virginia as of July 1, 1863, enslaved for life, however, which could have prolonged slavery there into the first decades of the twentieth century.[30] Very little scholarship documents the experiences of those Virginia natives who gained their freedom in the new state.

For the remainder of Virginia, the legalities were more complex than anywhere else in any slave state. Two state governments functioned in Virginia during the Civil War. The one with its capital in Richmond was for the state that had joined the Confederate States of America, and that government continued to enforce the constitutional and statute law that created and protected slavery. The other government initially did, too. The Restored Government was the government of Virginia that loyal men restored to the Union in the summer of 1861. At first, it included most of the counties and cities that eventually became West Virginia; then after the admission of West Virginia as a new state, it included a smaller number of counties and cities in the eastern part of the state where significant parts of the white population remained loyal or where the United States Army was in charge. About one-tenth of enslaved Virginians lived in those loyal/liberated/occupied portions of eastern Virginia.

On December 7, 1863, Governor Francis H. Pierpont recommended that the General Assembly of the Restored Government summon a constitutional convention to abolish slavery in Virginia. He had been a strong western critic of the overbearing political power that defenders of slavery in eastern Virginia had exercised before the Civil War, but he had been no abolitionist, and he never became an egalitarian.[31] The Virginia Constitution of 1851, under which he and his government functioned, prohibited legislative abolition of slavery, and the Emancipation Proclamation had no effect in some of the jurisdictions of his government. Enslaved residents, escaping refugees, and conflicting laws created confusion. Those conditions and other events of the war convinced Pierpont, as he explained to the assembly, "There can never be any peace and unity among the people so long as this institution exists." Pierpont recommended that the convention abolish slavery in Virginia and ask the federal government to compensate owners for the value of their property that was to be thereby destroyed. He did not, however, ask that the formerly enslaved Virginians be compensated for their years of forced labor.[32]

Voters loyal to the United States elected a total of seventeen convention delegates from the counties of Loudoun and Fairfax and the city of Alexandria in northern Virginia, from the counties of Northampton and Accomack on the Eastern Shore, and from Williamsburg, Portsmouth, and Norfolk and the counties of Warwick, Princess Anne, Norfolk, New Kent, James City, Elizabeth City, and Charles City, all in southeastern Virginia.[33] Members of the convention, who met in the federal courthouse in Alexandria, omitted from the revised constitution all references to slavery and the three sections that protected it in the Constitution of 1851. On March 10, they voted 15 to 1 with one delegate absent or not voting to insert into the new constitution two sections: "Slavery and involuntary servitude (except for crime) is hereby abolished and prohibited in the State forever"; and "The general assembly shall make no law establishing slavery or recognizing property in human beings." White people rang the city's church bells in celebration and fired a hundred guns in honor of the event. The *New York Times* and other newspapers in the United States reported the vote and saluted the Virginia convention.[34] The new constitution for the Restored Government of Virginia became effective on April 11, 1864, and slavery was legally abolished in loyal/liberated/occupied Virginia.[35]

Neither the Restored Government nor the federal government compensated any Virginia men and women who had enslaved other Virginia men, women, and children. Unfortunately, little useful scholarship documents what, if anything, state and local officials of the Restored Government did to enforce the constitutional abolition of slavery; whether or how people within its jurisdiction freed enslaved men, women, and children; or how enslaved people took advantage of the new opportunity during the twelve months between the end of the convention and the end of the Civil War.

On February 3, 1865, when the West Virginia legislature ratified the Thirteenth Amendment to the Constitution of the United States to abolish slavery everywhere forever, it then also immediately abolished slavery in West Virginia by statute.[36] Five days later, the Senate of the Restored Government in Virginia ratified the Thirteenth Amendment, and the following day the House of Delegates ratified it.[37] But slavery remained legal in all parts of Confederate Virginia until the United States Army took control during the spring and summer of 1865.

Free People of Color in Wartime

Little hard evidence or scholarship documents the wartime experiences of the approximately fifty-nine thousand Virginians whom the laws of the time usually referred to as "free Negroes" or "free people of color." Unlike William and Nancy Davis and Maria Griffin, free people could legally marry, have legitimate children, buy and sell property if they were men, in some instances make valid wills, and enjoy some protections of the law. As in other states, though, they were vulnerable to exploitation and discrimination and legally incapable of exercising some rights that free white people enjoyed, including for men the right to vote—they were victims of taxation without representation. They could be sold into slavery if they failed to pay their taxes; they (and also American Indians) could not testify in court against a white person. In those and in other ways they were less than fully free.[38]

Free persons of color navigated this treacherous world and usually lived inconspicuously in the increasingly more dangerous conditions of the Civil War. Men faced the threat of being impressed to work on Confederate defenses or conscripted to work as orderlies (janitors) in Confederate hospitals or in other facilities, not unlike enslaved men were. Free men, however, might not be paid as were the masters or mistresses of enslaved men. A document filed with Cumberland County records labeled "List of slaves ordered to be sent to work on fortifications, made 22d of September 1863, in Cumberland County, in compliance with requisitions of the Governor for 80 slaves from said County" includes the name of John Robinson, a free man who later served in the Constitutional Convention of 1867–68 and the Senate of Virginia.[39]

Also difficult for free men were entreaties to assist enslaved people to escape. William Breedlove, who operated a ferry service across the Rappahannock River, was arrested in November 1863 with his employee William Chandler for assisting an enslaved man to escape. They believed that the man possessed a pass that allowed him to travel, but an Essex County court convicted them and sentenced them to be "sold into absolute slavery."[40]

Despite the conviction, the prosecuting attorney and other authorities recommended gubernatorial clemency because they believed that Breedlove and Chandler did not know that the man was enslaved. Letters of support attesting to Breedlove's character, honesty, and standing in the community came from such public figures as Lieutenant Governor Robert Latané Montague. The governor pardoned Breedlove on January 29, 1864. Less than three years after the pardon, Breedlove won election to the Constitutional Convention of 1867–68.[41]

William Henry Brisby, whose father was free and whose mother was of Pamunkey origins, owned land and operated a blacksmith shop in New Kent County. He served for several months as a blacksmith for a Confederate cavalry unit in the spring of 1862 to avoid impressment to labor on Confederate fortifications. His true feelings for the Confederacy became evident the following year when he smuggled escaped prisoners of war and people fleeing from slavery out of Richmond where he sold fish and agricultural produce. Twice imprisoned at Richmond's Castle Thunder on suspicion of aiding the enemy, Brisby ultimately benefited materially from his operation. In May 1864, he presented testimonials to United States Army major general Philip H. Sheridan from three army officers that he had smuggled through the military lines. Sheridan returned to him three cows that the army had commandeered. Brisby, too, won election to the Convention of 1867–68.[42]

Unless their names appear in the public records, like Breedlove and Brisby, the activities of free men and women during the war are difficult to discover. Some of the men who had been free before the war began or who gained their freedom before the war ended emerged after the war as social, religious, and political leaders; consequently we know more about them than most. They appear to have remained at their homes and for the most part continued with their personal and professional lives, as did civilian white people. Some of them, though, given the opportunity, joined the fight for freedom.

Fighting for Freedom

Approximately 5,700 men enlisted in the United States Colored Troops (USCT) in Virginia beginning in 1863 when the army for the first time recruited regiments of Black men. The men served under white officers in racially segregated units. Many recruits had lived in slavery until the war gave them opportunities to escape and eventually to fight to save the Union and to free all the other enslaved people in the country. The army recruited five regiments of infantry, two of cavalry, and one artillery battery in Virginia.[43] They and soldiers of about thirty other USCT regiments also fought in Virginia and on other Southern battlefields. The official number recorded in War Department records is 178,975, but the first historian of Black soldiers in the United States, Virginian Joseph T. Wilson, estimated that the total number might have been as high as 220,000. The USCT fought in nearly 450 engagements and sustained 35 percent greater casualties than white regiments in the United States Army. About 20 percent of all soldiers in the USCT died before the end of the war. The USCT may have provided the critical margin of manpower that enabled the United States to defeat the Confederacy.[44]

On September 29, 1864, at Fort Harrison on the outskirts of Richmond, four Virginians in the USCT received the Medal of Honor, the army's new and only award for gallantry. The fighting was fierce and concentrated. After the battle, an army officer counted 543 dead soldiers in a space three hundred yards long and only a few feet wide.[45]

Thirty-year-old Sergeant Edward Ratcliff, who had escaped from slavery in James City County, took command of Company C, 38th Regiment, after the white commanding officer was killed. Ratcliff bravely led his company throughout the remainder of the engagement and was one of the first men to enter the Confederate fort. He received the Medal of Honor and was promoted to sergeant major. Not far from where Ratcliff rallied his company, Private James Gardiner, a twenty-year-old oysterman from Gloucester County, charged ahead of his comrades of Company I,

36th Regiment, shot a Confederate soldier who was standing on the parapet, then used his bayonet on a Confederate officer. Gardiner's conspicuous bravery inspired the other men in his company, who rushed with him into the enemy's earthen fort. Promoted to sergeant, Gardiner received the Medal of Honor in 1865.[46]

Corporal Charles Veal, Company D, 4th Regiment, a Portsmouth native, was free when he entered the army in Baltimore in July 1863. When the company's color bearer, who carried the flag in the front of a charge, was killed, Veal seized the flag and carried it gallantly for the remainder of the attack. Like Gardiner, Veal was promoted to sergeant and received the Medal of Honor for inspiring the members of his company. Another corporal, Miles James, of Company B, 36th Regiment, a thirty-four-year-old man from Princess Anne County, took a bullet in the left arm, which shattered the humerus bone and according to a surgeon made immediate amputation necessary. Nevertheless, James continued to load and fire his gun with his right hand and urged his fellow soldiers forward, all within about thirty yards of Confederate earthworks. Later in the day, the surgeon cut off James's mangled left arm and sent him to the hospital in Yorktown. The surgeon expected the brave soldier to die, but James survived, recovered, and even refused to accept a medical discharge that the army offered him. He appealed directly to General Alonzo G. Draper to intervene and help him remain in the army. "He is one of the bravest men I ever saw," the general wrote to the surgeon, "and is in every respect a model soldier. He is worth more with his single arm, than half a dozen ordinary men." The army promoted James to sergeant and awarded him the Medal of Honor in April 1865. Ratcliff, Gardner, and James all served on the frontier in Texas for several months after the war and were some of the first of the legendary Buffalo Soldiers.[47]

Several regiments of USCT participated in the siege of Petersburg in 1864–65. At the end of June 1864, miners dug a tunnel into a hillside under a Confederate fort and filled a space beneath the fort with gunpowder. After they set off a massive explosion that destroyed the fort and left a huge crater, United States Army soldiers, including USCT, charged into the crater, where they were slaughtered in one of the most famous episodes of the war.[48]

An unknown number of other Virginians, perhaps several hundred more, served in the United States Navy, which unlike the army did not segregate men by race. Virginian Robert Blake earned the Medal of Honor during action near Charleston, South Carolina, on Christmas Day 1863. Described in the records as "Contraband, U.S. Navy," he was born into slavery in Virginia. Navy records do not indicate the exact place of his birth. Blake served on the steam gunboat *Marblehead* in the Stono River when it came under fire from a Confederate battery. Severely damaged, the *Marblehead* managed to escape the enemy fire as Blake assisted at one of the ship's large caliber rifled guns and "carried out his duties bravely," according to his citation, "throughout the engagement." The gunfire forced Confederates to abandon their works, which left the United States Navy in control of the river.[49]

Most men fought in the army. Peter Jacob Carter, who later served four terms in the House of Delegates, was born into slavery in 1845 in the town of Eastville, in Northampton County. By 1858 his master Calvin Read, a schoolteacher who may have taught Carter to read, had moved to Baltimore. To repay $1,000 Read had borrowed from his wife's separate estate, on December 5, 1860, he deeded to her Carter, two siblings, and their mother, all enumerated in the deed as residing in Northampton County. United States troops had liberated/occupied the Eastern Shore since November 1861. Carter escaped from slavery, and on October 30, 1863, in Eastville he enlisted in Company B of the 10th Regiment United States Colored Infantry. Arrested for mutiny early in February 1864 and imprisoned, he was released in May after the charges were withdrawn and then returned to duty with his regiment at Bermuda Hundred, near Petersburg. Carter served with the quartermaster department from September through December 1865 and then on detached duty with the Bureau of Refugees, Freedmen, and Abandoned Lands from January through April 1866. He mustered out on May 17, 1866, at Galveston, Texas.[50]

Maria Griffin's son, Robert Gilbert Griffin, also a future member of the House of Delegates, enlisted as a private in Company K, 24th Regiment United States Colored Troops on March 28, 1865, in Frankford, Pennsylvania. The infantry regiment guarded Confederate prisoners at Point Lookout, in Maryland, and eventually was stationed in Burkeville, in Nottoway County, where it distributed food and other supplies to freed people and helped preserve order. The regiment's motto on its battle flag was "Let Soldiers in War be Citizens in Peace," which Griffin embodied with his postwar political career.[51]

John Montgomery Dawson, born into slavery in 1829 in Alexandria (then part of the District of Columbia), escaped and made his way to Cato, Cayuga County, New York, where in 1860 he worked as a barber. In 1862 he enrolled in the preparatory school attached to Oberlin College, in Ohio, where he studied for the ministry but did not receive a degree. In September 1864 he enlisted in the 3d Regiment New York Artillery.

The flag of the 24th Regiment, United States Colored Troops, which was recruited in Pennsylvania, bears the regimental motto, "Let Soldiers in War, be Citizens in Peace." (Library of Congress)

Following his discharge ten months later, Dawson continued his religious studies under the tutelage of a minister in Alexandria, and after the war served for decades as pastor at First Baptist Church in Williamsburg.[52]

James Thomas Sammons Taylor had his own route to the United States Colored Troops. Born in Berryville in 1840, he was the son of Fairfax Taylor, a Black shoemaker who had purchased his freedom, and his first wife Ellen Sammons Taylor. His father became a leader in Charlottesville's Black community in the decade before the Civil War and reportedly employed a private tutor for his son. Taylor enlisted in the USCT's 2d Infantry Regiment on August 24, 1863, in Washington, DC. Assigned to Company E, he was named acting commissary sergeant and was promoted to the post on November 10, 1863, with the rank to date from September 1. In 1864 and 1865 he sent letters to the New York *Anglo-African* describing military engagements and protesting the lack of Black officers. Taylor was accused of stealing from the commissary stores in 1864, but there are no regimental records of a trial, and he was restored to duty in March 1865.[53] While stationed in Key West, Florida, he met, courted, and on April 18, 1865, married Eliza Ann Delancy, the freeborn daughter of Bahamian immigrants. He was mustered out of the army on January 5, 1866, and took his wife back to Virginia.[54]

Thousands of native Virginians fought, and many of them died as members of USCT regiments that had been recruited in other states. Some Virginia natives in the USCT also received Medals of Honor that were credited to the states where the men had lived before the war. Powhatan Beaty, born in Richmond in 1837, is the most famous of them. He enlisted in Ohio in Company G of the 5th Regiment USCT. During the same fighting at Fort Harrison in which four other native Virginians earned Medals of Honor in September 1864, Beaty retrieved the colors after the color bearer was killed during a retreat and then led the remnant of his company in a second, successful attack. In 1999, the city of Richmond honored Beaty by placing a memorial photograph of him on the city's floodwall alongside portraits of other notable citizens.[55]

A few Virginia women may have disguised themselves and fought as men did (and as a few white women did who fought for the Confederacy), and others undoubtedly followed the army, as women had done for centuries, to cook, wash, and do other necessary work. Some women, as well as men, spied on the Confederacy and provided valuable information to officers of the United States Army and Navy. The most famous of them was Mary Richards Bowser, also known as Mary Elizabeth Bowser, who worked for a time in the household of Confederate president Jefferson Davis and conveyed what she overheard or learned there to the white woman, Elizabeth Van Lew, who ran the largest and most effective espionage ring in Virginia during the war.[56]

People of Color in the Confederate Army

In addition to the hundreds or thousands of men (and some women) who were conscripted to work at Confederate installations during the Civil War, other men accompanied their masters or members of their masters' families who served in the Confederate Army. Most of the men probably acted as body servants, but they may also have been assigned to tend horses, cook, or do many other hard labor chores that army life required. Those men materially aided the Confederacy, usually involuntarily. The state government in 1924 amended the pension law of 1902 to offer pensions to the civilian laborers "who actually accompanied a soldier in the service and remained faithful and loyal as the body servant of such soldier, or who served as cook, hostler or teamster or who worked on breastworks under any command of the army and thereby rendered service to the Confederacy."[57] Sixty years after Isaac Edmundson, of Halifax County, accompanied a Confederate officer as a "Body servant" during the final months of the war and fifty-five years after Edmundson was elected to the House of Delegates, he applied for and received a small pension.[58]

Much later in the twentieth century, the recorded presence of those men at Confederate camps (including reports of some dressed in what appeared to be Confederate uniforms) served as the inspiration, as if it provided incontrovertible evidence, for a revisionist interpretation some neo-Confederates created that characterized those men as volunteer supporters of the Confederate Army, as if they had agreed, rather than been required, to accompany enslavers to war. A small number of isolated and unverified reports suggest that some men offered to fight for the Confederacy, but historians have discovered no substantial body of evidence that Black Virginians actively supported the Confederate Army or the Confederate cause.[59] Nevertheless, the reinterpretation allowed neo-Confederates to maintain that the war was not about slavery and fitted into an even larger set of beliefs that made the federal government then and thereafter a destructive agent of the interests of white people.[60]

Such stray hints that survive in newspapers and documentary records should be evaluated with care. A few days after the Convention of 1861 voted to secede from the United States, James Read Branch, member of an influential white family of bankers and financiers in Petersburg, informed his father that "one hundred (100) free Negroes the pick of the place good & true men will offer their Services to the State," meaning to the Confederate state of Virginia, "& ask me to command them. I will do so if the Governor will give me captains commission."[61] The governor did not issue a commission to Branch. Either because Branch's report about the hundred men was imaginary or because it was merely wishful thinking, nobody recruited a unit of "free Negroes" in Petersburg. Branch, in fact, received a commission in a company of Confederate artillery about two weeks later.[62]

Late in the war the Confederate government offered freedom to enslaved men who volunteered to serve in the Confederate Army. So many white soldiers had been wounded or died, were unfit for service, or had deserted and gone home that the army was virtually incapable of mounting an offensive campaign and barely able to defend Richmond and Petersburg. The decision generated a very contentious debate, which indicates that the proposal to recruit enslaved men would be an innovation, not a modified continuation of an existing policy of enlisting free men.[63]

In March 1865, Oliver and George (no surnames survive), two enslaved men who had been sentenced to death for stealing flour, bacon, and other supplies, received pardons from the governor "with a view to put them in the army." Their enslavers agreed to free them, and the Richmond *Daily Dispatch* reported that they were sent to "the colored camp for instruction, and were regularly mustered in for duty."[64]

Almost no records survive to indicate that very many enslaved men volunteered to serve in the Confederate Army with the permission of their enslavers. The March 21 and 23, 1865, issues of the Richmond *Sentinel* and the March 25, 1865, issue of the Richmond *Examiner* reported that some Black troops in a new Virginia regiment had been seen going through their exercises in the city. The *Daily Dispatch* stated that a "company of negro troops which have been raised in Virginia" would participate in a military drill at Capitol Square on March 22, and other newspapers in Richmond suggested that some of them or some other men may have taken part in a nearby engagement.[65] If a few enslaved men answered the call of the Confederate state, that does not necessarily demonstrate their commitment to the Confederacy or to its defense of slavery even late in the war, much less earlier. As with opportunities to escape from slavery by running away or passing through enemy lines, the offer of eventual freedom for military service could have enticed those men to volunteer and risk their lives, as escapees often did, to become free. Indeed, body servants on or near the front lines might have had even better opportunities to escape slavery than men and women farther away.

Staying in Place

A majority of enslaved Virginia men and women did not escape to freedom during the Civil War. Most of them probably did not try to escape. Like white noncombatant Virginians, they remained where they lived when the war began. When armies were not marching or raiding through their neighborhoods, the war did not fill their thoughts or dominate their days during every waking moment. People continued to live their lives. Enslaved men, women, and children continued to do the bidding and the work that white Virginians required—plowing, tending farm animals, drawing water, chopping wood, carrying crops to market, sewing, taking care of children, cooking, cleaning. Many white Virginia families later praised those men and women as loyal and faithful, adducing their wartime behavior as evidence that slavery was not a brutal or unjust system, that enslaved people did not resent being held in slavery, and that enslaved people loved their masters and mistresses—that slavery was, in fact, a good thing for them, and that they knew it.

Even with the new opportunities that the war provided to some people, most people did not try to escape. For each, a complex web of motives probably worked to dissuade them from trying. Free and enslaved people all lived within communities that also provided reasons for enslaved people not to leave. Extended families, kinship networks, lifelong friends, and fellow laborers undoubtedly formed mutually supportive communities that people may have been reluctant to abandon in the risky attempt to escape. Churches, too, formed their own communities, where people went about worshipping, marrying, and burying their dead during the war. In October 1863 in Prince Edward County, a religious revival enlivened the spiritual lives of people; and in nearby Cumberland County waves of increased numbers of baptisms at Cumberland Baptist Church in July 1862 and October 1863 suggest revivals there as well as elsewhere.[66]

Thousands of enslaved people lived too far from a place of refuge. Thousands of enslaved people were afraid of the consequences of trying to escape and getting caught and punished. Thousands of enslaved people, even though they eagerly desired freedom, were reluctant to leave their families and friends and the places where they had lived. The pull of family life should not be underestimated. Abundant evidence indicates that family ties among enslaved Virginians were often strong in spite of fragmentation of enslaved families when fathers and mothers lived with different masters or mistresses—in spite of separation of family members when one or another parent was hired out to work elsewhere—in spite of families broken up as a result of distribution of the assets of estates (sale of slave property) or sales to satisfy debts—in spite of the domestic slave trade that tore thousands of families apart and separated husbands and wives, parents and children forever. Perhaps the many separations made the family even more precious than it might otherwise have been. In spite of the intense desire for freedom that the actions of enslaved or freed people revealed during and after the war, most chose to remain with a family within slavery during the war rather than take the risky chance of escaping to freedom.

Indeed, the dangers for escaping Virginians in some places may have been even greater during wartime than before. For decades, slave patrols had regularly terrorized the countryside, inflicting summary punishment on enslaved people (and free people, too) who were abroad at night or did not have a pass as the law required.[67] But in the environment of war—a kind of semi-anarchy—patrollers or other white people who made opportunities to profit from the slave labor economy could more easily capture enslaved people and carry them to a slave trader to sell for a handsome price.

Even during the Civil War, the domestic slave trade continued to be one of the largest business enterprises in the state—perhaps second only to supplying the military—involving thousands of enslaved persons and hundreds of agents and slave drivers. Few things so graphically illustrate the importance of slavery to the economy of Virginia, to the lives of its white population, and for its enslaved people as the persistence of the thriving domestic slave trade during the Civil War. It continued right up to the end. On April 2, 1865, Richmond trader Robert Lumpkin, who operated one of the largest slave jails and trading companies in the state, drove a coffle of enslaved people he had recently purchased to the railroad depot to transport them for sale to the southwest on the very same train that Confederate President Jefferson Davis and members of his cabinet rode to escape Richmond. The train was already too crowded, though, and Lumpkin and his slave merchandise got left behind.[68]

Ironically, the men, women, and children in Lumpkin's coffle, rather than being transported for sale to work in some distant slave labor camp for the remainder of their lives, became free within a day. Following the Confederate and state governments' abandonment of Richmond that day, soldiers of the United States Army, including some USCT units, liberated/occupied Richmond. That put the Emancipation Proclamation in force in the city, and when USCT soldiers let them out of Lumpkin's jail, they ran into the streets singing

> Slavery chain done broke at last!
> Broke at last! Broke at last!
> Slavery chain done broke at last!
> Gonna praise God till I die![69]

The rejoicing among the freed people stood in stark contrast to the gloomy despair of Richmond's white citizens, who watched as the business district of the city burned and their way of life disintegrated. The freed people jubilantly welcomed Abraham Lincoln to Richmond the next day and escorted him through the streets in a scene that almost nobody—certainly no white residents—could probably have ever imagined.[70]

An enslaved woman named Hannah Reynolds was not so fortunate and was never able to enjoy freedom. On April 9, 1865, not far from where the Confederate armies surrendered at Appomattox Court House that

"Receiving the President" depicts freed people's joyous reception of Abraham Lincoln in Richmond on April 4, 1865. (Paul Fleury Mottelay, ed., *The Soldier in Our Civil War: A Pictorial History of the Conflict, 1861–1865, Illustrating the Valor of the Soldier as Displayed on the Battle-Field,* New York: G. W. Carleton & Company, 1886, Library of Virginia)

day, Reynolds was fatally wounded when a cannon ball smashed through her cabin and through her arm.[71] She was one of the last casualties of the war in Virginia, as Reuben, who had planned to fight for his freedom in 1861, had been one of the first.

Becoming Free

For each man, woman, and child who escaped from slavery during the war or became free at its conclusion, the event was a life-changing moment, a personal experience never to be forgotten. Almost half a million Virginians gained their freedom in different places, at different times, and under different circumstances. It is also probable that in some of those places and at some of those times, the legal end of slavery did not coincide perfectly with the end of enslavement. Enforcement of the slavery regime probably began to collapse in portions of West Virginia beginning in 1861, in Restored Virginia beginning in or perhaps even before 1864, as well as in some other places in Confederate Virginia before the United States Army arrived to enforce the Emancipation Proclamation. Some enslaved people may not have learned about their legal freedom or been enabled to live free until weeks or perhaps even months later.[72]

It is unfortunate that only a few written recollections survive of the precise circumstances of people learning of their emancipation and of their feelings at the time. No doubt, family traditions preserved many such recollections, but family traditions are ephemeral things, unlike the written word, and are hard to recover. Because such a small proportion of emancipated people could write, they left few documents that described their experiences. Even the interviews that employees of the Virginia Writers' Project conducted for the federal government's Works Progress Administration in the 1930s preserved only a few of those memories. The instructions that the interviewers received directed them to ask many questions about specific aspects of enslavement but did not specifically instruct them to ask people about when and how they became free.[73]

Occasionally, their thoughts on becoming free appeared in Black-owned newspapers decades later. At a "Colored Peoples' Celebration" in Richmond in October 1890, Jackson Acres, a forty-five-year-old undertaker who grew up in Lunenburg County, recalled for John Mitchell Jr.'s *Richmond Planet*, "Although the Proclamation had been issued, I think the work was done April 3, when Richmond fell." William S. Selden, a forty-year-old funeral director, remembered clearly April 9, when Robert E. Lee surrendered to Ulysses S. Grant at Appomattox, "For the day of the downfall of the Confederacy was the day of the uprising of the Negro." Dr. Robert E. Jones, a thirty-year-old Alabama-born physician, remarked, "it was conceded that when Lee surrendered to Grant the work was accomplished." Underscoring the personal nature of freedom, fifty-year-old grocer William Bell simply declared that he felt freedom on April 3, when United States troops entered Richmond, "because that was the day that I shook hands with the Yankees."[74]

More often, accounts of escaping slavery, or more properly snippets, come in official documents, as in the case of Robert Davis Ruffin. Born enslaved in King and Queen County in 1842, he probably worked as a body servant for his master, Alexander Fleet, a former member of the House of Delegates, until he ran away about the time of his twentieth birthday. Ruffin later testified before the Southern Claims Commission that despite being treated well in slavery, "I thought freedom was better than anything else." He also reported that he became a servant for an officer in the 123d Regiment Pennsylvania Infantry until early in 1863.

Ruffin moved to Yorktown, where he took over a store that his father had operated until his death in March 1863. The store was in the freed people's community outside the United States Army camp. That June, soldiers from the 99th New York Infantry ransacked it and stole goods worth more than $800. The Southern Claims Commission denied Ruffin compensation for his losses.[75]

Descriptions of people's reactions to the news of their freedom may best capture what they thought. For example, in the summer of 1864 when a reporter for the *New-York Tribune* accompanied the United States Army into Staunton, he informed a group of enslaved people that they were "now free, and at liberty either to go or stay, just as they pleased." The correspondent reported, "This announcement was received with great joy."[76] When the 8th Regiment, United States Colored Troops, arrived in Petersburg on April 3, 1865, among the first to enter the city after the Confederate army abandoned it, the commanding officer, brevet Brigadier General Samuel Chapman Armstrong, reported that the troops received "a most cheering and hearty welcome from the colored inhabitants of the city, whom their presence had made free."[77]

Seventy-five years later, Louise Bowes Rose vividly recalled her father's immediate reaction to his freedom. "Daddy was down to de creek," in Hanover County, near Ashland, the Virginia Writers' Project interviewer recorded Rose remembering. "He jumped right in de water up to his neck. He was so happy he jus' kep' on scoopin' up han'fulls of water an dumpin' it on his haid an' yell,' 'I'se free, I'se free! I'se free!"[78] For him, the moment was one of unrestrained jubilation, as it must have been for each of tens of thousands of other Virginians. He splashed about in the creek as if he were a joyous child about the age of his daughter. That is how the daughter recalled her father's actions. His actions spoke as loudly as any words. She might have gone further and drawn a symbolic parallel. As a Baptist minister might have baptized her father out of sin into salvation, he had baptized himself out of slavery into freedom. "I'se free, I'se free! I'se free!"

3

"To Own Oneself Is to Own One's Future"

The Meaning of Freedom

Louise Bowe Rose's father exemplified the immediate and visceral reaction to the news of slavery's demise. But perhaps the most important unanswered question that the abolition of slavery posed was this: What did the abolition of slavery actually mean? Was it to be more than the mere absence of slavery? Freedom meant that for the first time all people owned their own bodies and labor. As Gloucester County attorney and civic leader Thomas Calhoun Walker remarked in his memoirs, "To Own Oneself Is To Own One's Future."[1] That applied not only to "Oneself" but to one's families, too. Their actions in the weeks, months, and years after the end of slavery demonstrate clearly what freed people wanted the absence of slavery to mean.

"I desire to inquire for my kin people," Ann Brewers began an advertisement that she placed in the New Orleans journal, the *Southwestern Christian Advocate,* in July 1882. "I am the daughter of Summerset and Lucy Green. I had two brothers named John Richard and Summerset Green. I had two sisters, Mary and Lucy Green. We all belonged to George Mathews, a lawyer, and lived in Cumberland county, Va. I was sold in 1848 for $1,750, and taken to Louisiana." Seventeen years after the abolition of slavery and twice that long after the domestic slave trade separated Brewers from her Virginia family, she still longed to find her parents, brothers, and sisters.[2]

Brewers was one of the many people who bought advertisements in newspapers and magazines in search of their loved ones for decades after the war.[3] People also wrote or dictated letters to try to reunite with family members, such as the one Jennie Brown scratched out in the same month that Brewers published her advertisement. She directed it to the "Shairief" of "Masson Burge" (Mecklenburg) County, where she had been "Soled Before the War" and taken to Mississippi.[4] Some people managed after long searches across long distances to find or reunite with family members that the domestic slave trade had separated. In 1905, Ida Pryor, of Staunton, married Robert Anderson, then living in Hagerstown, Maryland. Back when they were enslaved, they had married, but he was sold away from her. Later, he heard that she was dead, and he married again, but after the death of his second wife, he learned that Ida Pryor was still alive. They reunited, and in 1905 they legally remarried.[5]

Anderson and Pryor were among the fortunate ones, as it is likely that more people failed to reunite with their families than succeeded. That Jennie Brown's letter remains on file with Mecklenburg County records suggests that the sheriff either did not find her family members or did not try. Something similar happened to John Brown, of Southampton County, who was about thirty-five years old when the war ended. Even though he was not literate, he had been able to maintain sporadic contact for nearly a decade—until the war began—with his wife, two daughters, and a brother who were all sold and carried away to Mississippi in about 1852. Brown was unsuccessful in reestablishing contact with them, however. In 1867 he dictated a letter to the local agent of the Bureau of Refugees, Freedmen, and Abandoned Lands (generally known as the Freedmen's Bureau) but never received a reply, perhaps because agents in Mississippi either could not find Brown's family members or did not even make the effort to find them. Brown was still wondering about the fate of his family in October 1867 when he won election to the constitutional convention that met later that year.[6]

Attempts to reunite separated family members began immediately after the conclusion of the fighting. On May 21, 1865, Stephen Flemming wrote from New Orleans to the governor of Virginia about "a very important affair, concerning my happiness." He began, "About 16 years ago, I was Sold as a Slave, from the State of Virginia, Bowling green, near Fredericksburg, in to the State of Louisiana I left behind Me a wife, and 5 living Children I never heard from her Since, and I wish her to Know (if she is alive) where I am, and for her to write to me, in order to determine for the future." Flemming provided the additional information that his wife's name was "Polly Roy before she was married to me" and that their children were named Mary Jane, Mary Ellen, Henry Paul, William Silas, and William Henderson, who was "a baby in Arms." That Flemming's letter remains on file with other letters that the governor received suggests that nobody in the governor's office was able to find his family.[7]

After escaping slavery George Teamoh returned after the war to Portsmouth, where he had lived enslaved before his wife and daughter were sold. He found his wife in Richmond living in a stable "emaciated, pale and almost speechless."[8] Grace Herbert Walker and her three-year-old son, Thomas Calhoun Walker, of Gloucester County, had been taken to the Blue Ridge Mountains late in the war. After the end of the war and the abolition of slavery, they headed home. Passing through Richmond, they paused at the notorious slave jail of Robert Lumpkin, where, providentially, her husband found them. Their son grew up to have a long and productive career as a lawyer.[9]

In May 1867, Hawkins Wilson wrote from Galveston, Texas, to the agent of the Freedmen's Bureau in Richmond in search of information about his sisters. "I have never heard from them since I left Virginia twenty four years ago." Wilson named his sisters, their closest family members, and the owner of the land where they had lived in Caroline County. He also sent a letter addressed to his sister, Jane. "Your little brother Hawkins is trying to find out where you are and where his poor old mother is," he began, with a long recitation of how after being freed in Texas, he had married, learned to read and write, and become a sexton in the Methodist Episcopal Church. From the pages of the long letter to his sister, Wilson's recollection of being sold away from his nearest relatives nearly a quarter of a century earlier leaps from the page, an indelible speck of poignant memory: "I shall never forget the bag of biscuits you made for me the last night I spent with you." That letter, too, seems not to have been delivered or deliverable.[10]

The separation of family members that the domestic slave trade had inflicted on thousands of Virginians and the dislocations that followed the abolition of slavery left many children homeless and forced to live on city streets without adult care or supervision. In Richmond, Lucy Goode Brooks, wife of and mother of the children of livery stable owner Albert Brooks, began a long career of civic engagement immediately after the war. They had been enslaved by different owners but were allowed to live together and raise their family. One of their daughters, however, was sold away to Tennessee despite a promise that she could remain in Richmond while her father raised the money to buy her out of slavery. Having lost a child to the slave trade, Lucy Brooks had a particular concern for the plight of parentless children, and she worked with the Cedar Creek

Society of Friends to establish the Friends' Asylum for Colored Orphans. The city government provided land, the orphanage constructed a building, and in 1872 the General Assembly incorporated it. The orphanage continued its work until the 1930s.[11]

Legal Protections

The first postwar session of the General Assembly enacted laws that altered fundamentally the status of freed people and assisted them in creating new lives. Others, as we shall see, inhibited formerly enslaved persons in the full expression of their new freedom. On February 27, 1866, the General Assembly repealed all "acts and parts of acts relating to slaves and slavery" and eliminated differences in punishments for white people, "colored persons," and Indians.[12]

On that same momentous day, the assembly legalized marriages between "colored people," one or both of whom had been enslaved and who had regarded themselves as married or had lived together as if married, which had not been legal under slavery. Commonly known as the Cohabitation Act, it also allowed fathers to identify their children and register them as legitimate, which was intended in part to prevent children from becoming wards of the state. The legalization of tens of thousands of Virginians' marriages and the legitimation of children was of extreme importance to the freed people and their families. For the first time, they had legal protection for their marriages and families. Widows and widowers for the first time could inherit property from their spouses, and children could inherit property from their parents in the absence of a will. In keeping with the patriarchal beliefs of the times, however, the law authorized men to identify their wives and legalize their marriages and to identify and legitimize their children, but it did not authorize women to identify their husbands and legalize their marriages or to identify and legitimize their children.[13]

Freed people took maximum advantage of the opportunity to legalize and protect their families. In Charles City County, Robert G. W. Jones and Frances (or Francis) J. A. Harris married on March 15, 1866, to legalize their union that dated to the 1840s, when one or both of them had been enslaved.[14] "You see, it's dis way," Minnie Logan, of Fishersville, in Augusta County, explained the old laws that had prevented marriages of enslaved people many years later to a Black interviewer of the Virginia Writers' Project, "God made marriage, but de white man made de law."[15]

Cohabitation Registers survive for about two dozen localities in Virginia in the collections of the Library of Virginia, in county courthouses, and as part of the Freedmen's Bureau records.[16] A detailed study of the movements of married freed people in some of those localities has produced maps documenting that they often traveled to many parts of the state and long distances in search of family members or work.[17] In Floyd County, Martha Sheler and Brock Wells had married in 1837, but were separated when Wells was taken to Missouri. After the war he made his way home to rejoin his wife.[18]

Regulating Freed Virginians' Freedom

Thousands of freed Virginians went in search of their "kin people,"[19] and others left the plantations, small farms, or town houses where they had lived to make new starts elsewhere. So many relocated, in fact, that the General Assembly in January 1866 revised the state's old vagrancy law and added another obstacle to the many that freed people faced. The 1866 law declared homeless or rootless people without income to be vagrants and classified them as public nuisances because they could become beggars or even threats to the public safety as thieves or robbers. The law defined people who were without work or "refuse to work for the usual and common wages given to other laborers in the like work in the place where they then are" as vagrants and imposed severe penalties on them.

The preamble to the Vagrancy Act began, "Whereas it is represented to the general assembly, That there hath lately been a great increase of idle and disorderly persons in some parts of this commonwealth, and unless some stringent laws are passed to restrain and prevent such vagrancy and idleness, the state will be overrun with dissolute and abandoned characters, to the great detriment of the public weal." With its unmistakable reference to the abolition of slavery that had "lately" taken place, the act implicitly applied to freed people. Nothing comparable happened to any appreciable number of white Virginians that sent them about the countryside searching for their kinfolk. The law authorized local authorities to arrest people they identified as vagrants and to hire them out for a term of three months or employ them on public works projects, such as roads. Vagrants who ran away before the expiration of the term could be forced to work for an extra month wearing a ball and chain and not be paid or even jailed and fed bread and water, only.[20]

None of the state's previous laws authorized any private person or public authority to require vagrants to be forced to work wearing a ball and chain. That was how penitentiary officials treated convicted felons who worked on public projects or were leased to private employers. The authorization to hire vagrants out to private employers almost certainly reminded freed people and others of the old practice from slavery days that allowed counties and cities to require free people who were in arrears in their taxes to be hired out to work for other people as if they were enslaved.[21]

Nine days after the assembly adopted the law, however, the commanding general of the United States Army in Virginia, Alfred H. Terry, issued an order to forbid civil and military officials in the state from enforcing it. "In many counties of this State," he explained why the law was intolerable, "meetings of employers have been held, and unjust and wrongful combinations have been entered into for the purpose of depressing the wages of the freedmen below the real value of their labor, far below the prices formerly paid to masters for labor performed by their slaves" they had leased to other people. As a consequence, "wages utterly inadequate to the support of themselves and their families have, in many places, become the *usual and common* wages of the freedmen." The statute would therefore "compel the freedmen, under penalty of punishment as criminals, to accept and labor for the wages established by these combinations of employers . . . and it is easy to foresee that, even where no such combinations now exist, the temptation to form them, offered by the statute, will be too strong to be resisted, and that such inadequate wages will become the *common and usual* wages throughout the State." Terry concluded, "The ultimate effect of the statute will be to reduce the freedmen to a condition of servitude worse than that from which they have been emancipated—a condition which will be slavery in all but its name." It is unclear how effective Terry's order to prohibit enforcement of the law was in the short term, but the law remained on the books and was enforced from time to time throughout the state until the beginning of the twentieth century.[22]

One of the most important new laws that freed people objected to during the subsequent decade and that legislators they elected beginning in 1869 tried to repeal or modify was the state's 1866 Act Relating to Fences, and for the Protection of Crops. The old law required landowners to erect a fence at least five feet tall to confine farm animals and prevent them from straying and damaging the crops or property of neighbors. People who had failed to erect such a fence and keep it in repair were liable for damages that their escaping livestock might inflict.[23] In the changed circumstances after the war, when many fences had disappeared into army campfires, the General Assembly declared that "the boundary lines of each lot or tract of land" were thereafter to be "a lawful fence." No need for a property owner to construct a fence, which could be time-consuming and expensive work. An unmarked, even invisible, property line became a lawful fence. That and similar laws elsewhere shifted the burden and cost away from landed families and onto landless families. Rural freed people often let their few hogs or cows run wild in the woods and fields. The new law made them, not the owners of land, liable for damages done to crops on private property and in effect required them to keep constant control over their animals and not allow them to cross what in many instances were unmarked boundaries.[24] The fence law allowed each county government to decide whether to enforce it, and when the law was new and all local officials were white, a large number of counties put it in force. During the 1870s, delegates and senators whom freed people elected introduced numerous bills to authorize local referenda on whether to cease enforcement of the law in their constituencies and relieve a burden on their constituents.

Freed people clearly believed that the end of slavery meant full and complete freedom, not merely the absence of slavery. But as the Vagrancy Act and Fence Law demonstrated, many influential white people did not agree. Instead, white Virginians often treated formerly enslaved people much as they had treated enslaved people or free people before the war, as second- or third-class citizens. For the most part, white legislators in the first years after the abolition of slavery did little to change the political economy of old Virginia, a political economy based almost entirely on slavery.[25] When freed people later entered the political arena, they made very clear their claims to full citizenship and all of its rights. In the near term, though, freed people, in effect, gambled on their futures in a game in which white legislators, judges, landlords, and employers dealt from their own decks of marked cards.

Assistance from the Freedmen's Bureau

Freed people could turn to the agents of the Freedmen's Bureau for assistance in combating the countless restrictions on their movement and behavior by white Virginians. Congress created the Bureau of Refugees, Freedmen, and Abandoned Lands in March 1865 to manage all matters related to formerly enslaved men, women, and children. Commissioners and agents opened offices across Virginia and among many other duties, they helped freed people find family members, provided clothing and food rations, and set up refugee camps, schools, and hospitals. Agents also performed the important task of supervising labor contracts between white landowners and men and women who were no longer enslaved.

Freed people nearly all entered their new freedom facing severe disadvantages. More than 90 percent were not literate as of 1870. Few had

Petersburg district headquarters of the Bureau of Refugees, Freedmen, and Abandoned Lands in 1866 shows free men, women, and children who relied on white bureau agents for rations immediately after the Civil War and for schooling, enforcement of labor contracts, and protection from white violence between 1865 and 1869. (Special Collections, Library of Virginia)

any experience functioning independently in a free labor economy. Only a minority had skills in trades or crafts that could earn them a living. The large majority of freed people who lived in rural areas had to make their ways without their own land, farming implements, or draft animals, all of which had belonged to landowners during slavery. Landowners had effective control over freed people's access to farmland and to paying work, as well as to implements, draft animals, and credit. Freed families therefore started out poor, with few or no resources by which to aid themselves, and often had to rely on other family members or close friends for mutual assistance. Faced with the effects of the intergenerational trauma of slavery, freed families faced almost insurmountable obstacles in climbing out of their poverty.[26]

In the beginning, it is possible that in many places, as a study of Montgomery County documented, freed people worked for families that had formerly enslaved them.[27] In Hanover County, nine men and women entered a contract in June 1865 with the man who had owned them in slavery. He promised to pay the men between $2.50 and $5.00 a month, or

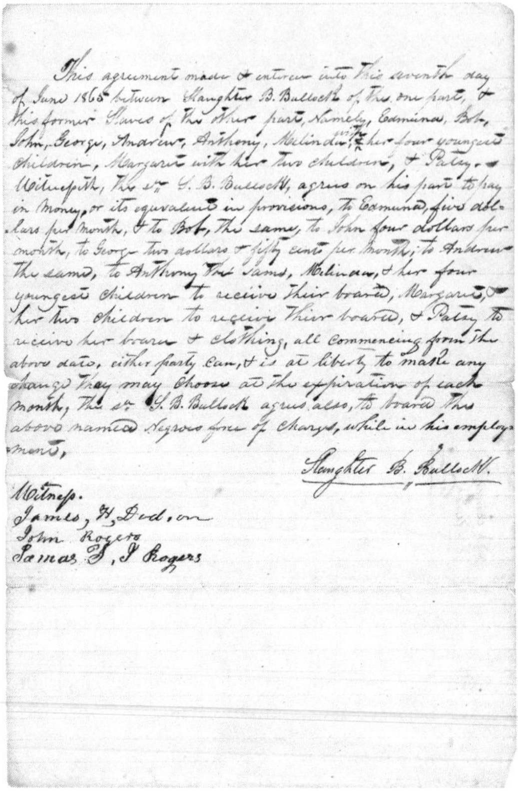

This agreement made & entered into this seventh day of June 1865 between Slaughter B. Bullock of the one part, & his former Slaves of the other part, Namely, Edmund, Bob, John, George, Andrew, Anthony, Melinda with her four youngest children, Margaret with her two children, & Patsy. — Witnesseth, the sd S. B. Bullock, agrees on his part to pay in Money, or its equivalent in provisions, to Edmund, five dollars per Month, & to Bob, the same, to John four dollars per month, to George two dollars & fifty cents per Month, to Andrew the same, to Anthony the same, Melinda, & her four youngest children to receive their board, Margaret, & her two children to receive their board, & Patsy to receive her board & clothing, all commencing from the above date, either party can, & is at liberty to make any change they may choose at the expiration of each month, the sd S. B. Bullock agrees also, to board the above named Negroes free of charge, while in his employment,

Slaughter B. Bullock.

Witness.
James, H, Dodson
John Rogers
James T, J Rogers

Labor contract dated June 7, 1865, between Slaughter B. Bullock and "his former Slaves" Edwina, Bob, John, George, Andrews, Anthony, "Melinda with her four youngest children," "Margaret with her two children," and Patsy, specified the wages they would receive, including room and board, and the terms of their employment. As was common before freedom, the white man, perhaps a Freedmen's bureau agent, who drafted the contract did not include the freed people's surnames. (Slaughter B. Bullock Papers, 1760–1910, Accession 23932, Personal Papers Collection, Library of Virginia)

an equivalent amount of provisions, and to provide the women and their children room and board as well as clothing for one of them.[28]

But in other places, freed people reported to a Freedmen's Bureau agent that they would rather starve before working for their former slaveholders who sold their children and fought to keep them enslaved.[29] At Hickory Hill plantation, also in Hanover County, men and women left in large numbers; women, in particular, almost disappeared from fieldwork once freedom allowed them to choose where, or whether, they wanted to work. Some women undoubtedly considered that caring for their families at home was more important than working for low wages that did not provide them with enough to support their families.[30]

The experiences of white planter family members indicate that many formerly enslaved household servants as well as field hands left and no longer worked for white families, even for wages, which dismayed many white people and left them with the humiliating choice of doing what they regarded as degrading manual work themselves.[31] Responding to language from former Confederates that the formerly enslaved had "forgotten what happened while they were slaves" and had been "so fond of their old masters," Charlottesville teacher Isabella Gibbons, who had been owned by a University of Virginia professor, wrote to the New England Freedmen's Aid Society in 1867 that, "This is a grand story for them to tell, but let us answer them. Can we forget the crack of the whip, cowhide, whipping-post, the auction-block, the hand-cuffs, the spaniels, the iron collar, the negro-trader tearing the young child from its mother's breast as a whelp from the lioness? Have we forgotten that by those horrible cruelties, hundreds of our race have been killed? No, we have not, nor ever will."[32]

Free People and the New Labor Economy

Freed families faced racial hostility and class prejudices that most white families could avoid. When a white landowner hired six men and women on the first of January 1866 to work on his Lunenburg County farm for the year, the labor contract specified the pay, lodging, and rations they would receive. But the contract also required that Bob, David, George, and Patrick (no surnames listed) rise by dawn and be at work by sunrise. It allowed them one hour for dinner each day and required them to be polite and obedient and to labor at the direction of the landowner or his agent. The agreement also imposed restrictions on when the workers could leave the plantation or receive visitors. If any of the workers violated any provisions of the contract, he or she forfeited all benefits for the year.[33]

The General Assembly passed a law in February 1866 that probably worked to the benefit of freed people in some respects and to their detriment in others. The law required that employment contracts "between a white person and a colored person, for the labor or service of the latter for a longer period than two months" be written, signed, and notarized. The law also required a "justice of the peace, notary, clerk or overseer of the poor, or the witnesses, to read and explain the contact to the colored person, before taking his acknowledgment thereof."[34] Such legal agreements appeared to protect the rights of working people. A related law of 1866 repealed a law from slavery that had prohibited "colored persons and Indians" from testifying against white people in court so that they would be able to enforce the terms of labor contracts and protect their rights.[35]

The white legislators who enacted these laws understood the importance of the judicial process in the new free labor economy. Written labor contracts should have protected the interests of both the employer and the employee. Freed people, however, most of whom were illiterate and had no prior experience with such contracts—or had been victims of contracts between white people who owned enslaved people and other white people who leased them—might not have always clearly understood the formal legal language of the contracts. They might not have understood that such contracts limited their abilities as free men and women to quit unsatisfactory employment before the expiration of the term of the contract or to move elsewhere without penalty. Nor may they all have understood that if the employer failed to comply with the terms of the contract, they had legal remedies in courts of law; or that in order to enforce those legal remedies, they had to have the assistance of a lawyer or a sympathetic person who could help them through the legal processes. The number of surviving labor contracts and complaints about them in county court records and in the files of the Freedmen's Bureau indicate that employers often failed in their responsibilities or even failed to pay their employees and that freed people in some instances attempted to enforce their contractual rights. We have no way to estimate how many working people failed to seek justice after being wronged.

Entering into a contract was, according to law, a voluntary act. Despite the law former enslavers often treated hired laborers as if they were still enslaved. A Prince Edward County landlord complained to the Freedmen's Bureau early in June 1866 that a woman (unnamed) who worked for him refused an order he issued to her, as if she were his slave property and obliged to obey all of his orders. He then informed her husband that he was going to deduct an amount of money from his wages. The husband objected, threw down his hoe, and stalked off. The other men who were working in the field also walked away, which left the employer without any hands to harvest his wheat.[36] During slavery the man and his wife would almost certainly have been punished for disobedience. After slavery, they had a few options and might hope to escape unfair treatment or being whipped; but by their refusal to obey the employer's demands, they may have lost their jobs and their ability to find work elsewhere in the neighborhood.

Untampered with, laws of supply and demand should have allowed wages to rise in a time of labor shortage, but what was essentially a rigged labor system kept wages low even as the supply of workers declined in rural areas.[37] Men and women who worked as farm laborers or at other jobs like washerwomen, seamstresses, cooks, or day laborers received very low pay, scarcely enough to provide them with essential food; and as time passed, an increasing number worked other people's land as sharecroppers. Contracts for sharecroppers, which usually ran for one year, obliged the cropper to plant, tend, and harvest the crop. Landlord and tenant shared the crop or divided the profits after the harvest. But before the harvest, tenant croppers still had to feed, house, and clothe their families. They sometimes had to borrow money and put up a portion of the anticipated crop earnings as collateral, called a crop lien. Such borrowing against the future was risky and made it difficult to prosper or to move to another place and work for another landlord because tenants had to remain and produce the crop with which to pay the debt.[38]

A tenant cropper who failed to meet some obligation of the labor contract could be sent packing before the harvest and receive nothing at all. In spite of all the work a person had devoted to plant and raise a crop, the cropper had no legal ownership interest in it until the division of the earnings after the harvest. The Virginia Supreme Court of Appeals affirmed as much in an 1884 case, *Parrish v. Commonwealth*. Without citing any Virginia laws but relying on contract law and a long list of legal treatises, a majority of the judges of the court overturned the conviction of a white landlord for killing a desperate sharecropper, A. J. Mitchell, who attempted to take some corn and tobacco before the distribution of the shares. The court ruled that the landlord was justified in using deadly force to protect what was still legally his property.[39]

Skilled Free People and the New Market Economy

Many freed people faced work environments not so different from slavery, but for some Black artisans the removal of slavery meant being able to employ their skills and abilities in a free market economy. Men who had been born free or secured their own freedom, were literate, possessed a skill such as carpentry or shoemaking, and were already familiar with an economy not bound to slavery had distinct advantages in post–Civil War Virginia, and some quickly became leaders in their communities. King William County resident Jesse Dungey belonged to a free family of mixed African, Pamunkey, and white ancestry. A shoemaker who had acquired land in the 1850s, he provided goods to Union authorities during the war. Afterwards he donated land and lumber for constructing a school, where he also taught, and raised funds for constructing a new church, both in West Point, in King William County. In October 1867 an agent reported that "when he gets his school & church in order he will start a Temperance Movement."[40] William P. Moseley had been allowed by his owner to operate a boat on the James River and achieved his freedom by 1857. He began buying property in Fluvanna and Henrico Counties before the war was over, and in March 1867 a Goochland County Freedmen's Bureau agent placed Moseley's name atop a list of six of the most influential Black men in the county. A writer for the *National Anti-Slavery Standard* later reported that Moseley was educated but "makes no display of his intelligence."[41]

Brothers Daniel Norton and Robert Norton escaped from the Gloucester County planter who was probably also their father and made their way to New York in the 1850s. Both had become prosperous barbers in Springfield, Massachusetts, before they returned to Virginia in the second half of 1865. Daniel Norton opened a store in York County, perhaps in partnership with his brother, and they founded Lone Star, a beneficial organization that enabled them to build a political power base. In 1866 York County freedmen elected Daniel Norton to the Freedmen's Bureau's local court. Such temporary courts had been authorized to address the unequal treatment of freed people and to adjudicate problems between them and white people. Federal authorities rejected Norton, but he was elected on two more occasions despite instructions to the freed people to do otherwise. After the third election an army officer ended the proceedings, which led to the assembled group chanting Norton's name and shooting off their guns.[42]

Limits of the Freedmen's Bureau

Freedmen's Bureau agents sometimes exercised their power to take labor disputes out of local or state courts and settle them in the bureau tribunals. That authority became increasingly important as the number of labor contracts increased and the number of disputes about enforcement of their terms increased. The degree of relief that agents were able to offer differed according to the agents' dedication as well as to local conditions, including the amount of resistance white people exhibited to the agents' work for the benefit of freed people. The very fact that freed people moved about the countryside and sought to enjoy their liberty made many white people fearful, and among the files of letters bureau agents received are numerous requests that the bureau disarm freed people whom white people regarded as dangerous.

White people often condemned or ridiculed the bureau and its agents, nearly all of whom were from states that had no slavery before the war and who were perceived as enforcers of the federal government's policy to construct new democratic governments, societies, and free labor economies with equal rights for all people. Some white people even exploited tragedies unrelated to the bureau for the purpose of condemning it. Early in October 1866 after a "negro woman" was found dead of starvation on a street in Richmond, a reporter for the Richmond *Daily Dispatch* could not resist the opportunity to blame the Freedmen's Bureau and contrast its care of freed people with the old slavery regime. He concluded "that no such cases were known while the American citizens of African descent were in a state of servitude."[43]

For the most part, it appears that most agents attempted to be helpful to freed people but in many instances were not successful.[44] Witness what happened to Benjamin F. Jones and his siblings who had been freed by and inherited land in King William County from their owner, who was also the father of some or all of them. In spite of their clear ownership of the property, white men cut down and sold some of the timber, causing the property's value to depreciate. Jones appealed for assistance to the local Freedmen's Bureau agent, who sympathized with Jones's plight but was unable to stop the timber cutting.[45]

In some cases freed people drew the ire of local bureau agents. After John Watson made a spring 1867 speech in a Mecklenburg County community where some freed people had acquired a small number of old muskets, the local agent caustically described him as an "ignorant and most violent fellow, who insists upon talking about what he does not understand & can't, or wont, be made to comprehend the amount of harm he is doing. . . . He is a bad man, but when charged with his petty offences against good order, denies all, & the freedmen fear to testify against him."[46]

The Freedmen's Bureau agents varied widely in their dedication to the work and also in their reactions to the freed people and to the extreme poverty in which many families lived. Marcus Sterling Hopkins, assigned to the bureau office in Gordonsville, exhibited some contradictory attitudes toward the people he was supposed to assist. He recorded privately in his diary on a cold day in January 1868 that he had been engaged "all day with all manner of cases involving questions of law and individual rights and morals generally. The freedmen are being outraged and swindled," he continued, but the remainder of that day's diary entry revealed some of his prejudices or perceptions. People were being "outraged and swindled to about the extent that such an ignorant, stupid and yielding subservient class would be anywhere else." Following those unflattering words, he went on, "There are many cases of desertion of wives and husbands and sometimes of young children on the part of the freedmen. They are very sharp to get children who are old enough to earn something and to hire them out. In such cases their parental and guardianship disciplines are very severe. The relatives of orphans apply to me often for such as are old enough to be profitable but I can seldom get them to take the slightest care or interest in infants. Blood don't seem to thicken as the phrase goes until children get to be about ten years of age."[47]

How much other agents shared Hopkins's analysis of the plight of freedmen's families remains unclear. It is also unclear whether his conclusions about parents' exploitive attitudes toward children accurately reflected reality in Gordonsville or elsewhere. The extraordinary efforts that thousands of freed families made to reunite or to hold their families together suggests that Hopkins's comments—however much they revealed about his perceptions—may have misrepresented the importance that most freed people attached to their families. Desperate freed people may have had few choices other than to hire out or apprentice working-age children.[48]

A law that the General Assembly enacted early in 1866 provided some protections to the children of freed people in keeping with Article IV Section 20 of the Constitution of 1864 that authorized "Courts of competent jurisdiction" to "apprentice minors of African descent on like conditions provided by law, for apprenticing white children." Before that time, only the children of poor white or poor free people could be apprenticed to learn a trade. The new law required that masters not only teach the trade specified in the apprenticeship agreement but also teach their apprentices "reading, writing and common arithmetic, including the rule of three."[49] More than a third of white Virginians were illiterate in the 1860s, though, and they may not have been able to fulfill the law's requirement to educate their apprentices. However beneficial to those children the terms of the act appeared to be, in practice courts composed entirely of white judges sometimes took children out of freed people's families and bound them out to learn a trade in the households of strangers, perhaps at a considerable distance from the children's families, which disrupted families much as hiring out or the slave trade had done.[50]

Schools and Education

With the end of slavery, children and their parents were quick to take advantage of the opportunity to go to school. One of the major accomplishments of the Freedmen's Bureau was supporting the establishment of schools for freed people throughout Virginia and the former

Confederate states. Long before the bureau's creation, however, Black Virginians started opening schools in areas where the United States Army took control. Norfolk native Mary Smith Kelsey Peake, the daughter of a white man and a free Black woman, who had attended school outside of Virginia during the 1830s, taught students of all ages secretly in her Hampton home before the Civil War. As enslaved people seeking freedom took refuge at Fort Monroe, Mary Peake started a school nearby in September 1861. Enrollment at her school, which was located within the present grounds of Hampton University, grew from six to more than fifty students within a few days. She was a dedicated instructor, teaching children and adults until her death from tuberculosis in February 1862.[51] In Alexandria, also under United States control, freeborn Sarah A. Gray, who had been sent to a Catholic academy for girls in Maryland, opened a school in October 1861 for people who had come to the city fleeing slavery. After the war, with assistance from the Freedmen's Bureau, she established the Excelsior School, where she taught reading, writing, math, and geography, and also trained her female pupils in needlework as a way for them to earn a living.[52]

The army had also encouraged volunteers who traveled to Virginia during the war to establish schools in refugee camps, and volunteers continued to arrive after the war to establish more schools or to teach in new schools that the American Missionary Association and other philanthropic organizations created. The freeborn brothers William Johnson Hodges and Willis A. Hodges returned from Brooklyn, New York, to their native Princess Anne County before the end of the war to assist freed people. In September 1865, Johnson Hodges applied to the Freedmen's Bureau for permission and funds to open a school in neighboring Norfolk County. Underscoring the negative attitudes that even prosperous Blacks encountered, the local bureau agent characterized Hodges as "a troublesome designing, unprincipled man" with a "worthless, mischievous, incendiary character." Perhaps the agent knew that Johnson Hodges and his son John Quincy Hodges assisted others in preparing claims against the federal government related to the army's actions during the war and dealings with the Freedmen's Bureau. Still, in October the agent supported a Norfolk County group led by Johnson Hodges seeking assistance from the American Missionary Association to open a school.[53] Willis Hodges successfully petitioned the Freedmen's Bureau in 1867 to open a school in Princess Anne County. By 1865, more than 450 teachers conducted classes for nearly twelve thousand students, including the first high school, Beulah Normal and Theological School, which Clement

Robinson, who was born into slavery in Petersburg and educated in the Ashmun Institute in Pennsylvania, opened in Alexandria in 1862.

While missionary and aid societies provided most of the funding to pay teachers, the Freedmen's Bureau provided funds to construct new buildings. Some of the contracts went to Black craftsmen. George Lewis Seaton, who had been born to a free family in Alexandria and trained as a carpenter, received contracts to construct two schools, along with tables and hundreds of desks, in the city. Seaton also was a trustee of the First Free School Society of Alexandria, which raised about $1,600 in the African American community to purchase the two lots where the new schools were constructed.[54]

Altogether, between 1866 and 1870, the Freedmen's Bureau spent between $190,000 and $225,000 on schools in Virginia and educated more than fifty thousand people.[55] Those children enjoyed a government benefit that few white children had been able to enjoy in Virginia, a system of schools created for their benefit. It may be the only instance to that time in Virginia's history that the needs of white people came second because Virginia had no statewide system of public schools for white children before 1870. The eagerness with which parents and children embraced their first opportunity for education clearly demonstrated that enslaved people had understood the value of education. Freed people took maximum advantage of the opportunity as soon as they could. Despite the extreme poverty many of them experienced in the aftermath of the war, freed families across the state contributed approximately $55,000 over four years to support teachers in the Bureau's schools.[56]

About one-third of the teachers who moved to Virginia to teach in bureau schools were white.[57] Many teachers of both races stayed for several years or even permanently. Jacob Yoder, a white Pennsylvanian, went to Lynchburg in 1866 under the auspices of the Pennsylvania Freedmen's Relief Association, returned to teach in a bureau school and remained to teach in the city's public schools for many years afterward. He was very sympathetic to the freed people and admired their ability to make new lives without exhibiting much animosity toward their former enslavers. In June 1866, he witnessed a parade of people, dressed in their finest apparel, who celebrated the founding of their new Sunday school. "So short time ago," Yoder recorded in his diary, "a people pressed down by a proud aristocracy now rejoices in their freedom for which, as an old man tremblingly said today, 'I have prayed sixty years.'"[58]

Yoder also witnessed their poverty. He had seen nothing comparable in Pennsylvania. One old blind woman he visited, perhaps the mother of

Jacob Yoder, back row, and a teacher and their pupils in the new public school in Lynchburg in 1871. A Pennsylvania native, Yoder had taught in the city beginning in 1866, first under the auspices of the Pennsylvania Freedmen's Relief Association and later in a Freedmen's Bureau school. (Menno Simons Historical Library, Eastern Mennonite University)

one of his students, paid "three dollars a month for a small room nearly in the ground and nothing inside only the roughest kind of wall. The house stands out of town almost inapproachable on a piece of ground valueless for anything except for poverty." Nevertheless, he concluded that although she was "poor in this world's goods; yet I do believe she is rich in heavenly treasurers."[59] The poverty that Yoder witnessed in Lynchburg was so severe that during the cold early months of 1868 some children stayed at home because their tattered clothing was insufficient to protect them from the cold.[60] The year before that, the Freedmen's Bureau agent in Hanover County requisitioned two hundred suits of children's clothing for the poorest freed families so that their children could attend school.[61]

Some teachers had political careers, too. William P. Lucas, who was born into slavery and forced to work in a Confederate hospital during the war, attended a school that a missionary society sponsored and later not only taught in the state's public schools until his death but also served a term in the House of Delegates.[62] One of Yoder's first pupils, Samuel Kelso, began to teach even before he completed his education and worked in the public schools for several years as well as represented Campbell County in the Constitutional Convention of 1867–68. He introduced a resolution that the new state constitution "guarantee for the future, a system of common school education, to be supported by the State, which shall give to all classes a free and equal participation in all its benefits."[63] The constitution required the General Assembly to establish a statewide system of free public schools for all children.

Two of the first historically Black colleges and universities in the South had their origins in Virginia in the 1860s. Shortly after the end of the war, Mary Lumpkin returned to Richmond from Philadelphia, where she and her children had lived since before the war began. She was the formerly enslaved mother of the children of notorious Richmond slave trader Robert Lumpkin and heir of the remnant of his estate, most of which the war and the abolition of slavery rendered worthless. His slave-trading headquarters, with its jail for holding his human merchandise, remained, though, and she permitted people to open a school in the building. It endured, and through a series of later mergers evolved into Virginia Union University, probably the only historically Black university a woman helped found.[64]

General Samuel Chapman Armstrong, who was a Freedmen's Bureau agent in southeastern Virginia from 1866 to 1868, founded Hampton Normal and Agricultural Institute, which opened its doors to students in April 1868. It evolved into Hampton University and was almost from the beginning one of the most famous college-level schools intended to prepare freed people to be teachers and for professional careers. Its early emphasis on craftsmanship and trades eventually overshadowed its role in preparing teachers, in part through the national influence of one of its earliest graduates, Franklin County native Booker T. Washington.[65]

Many white Virginians felt threatened by Northern and Black teachers who advocated social equality. Across the state teachers, students, and schools faced violence, including thrown rocks, gunfire, and arson. White and Black teachers were terrorized, including one man in Page County who was taken from his bed and carried to a boat in the Shenandoah River and held underwater.[66] In Norfolk, teachers reported broken school windows, vandalized classrooms, stolen books and supplies, and fires.[67] A resident of Isle of Wight County informed the American Missionary Association in 1867 that "the burners of colored schoolhouses are still unpunished in our vicinity."[68] Despite the numerous obstacles, freed people continued to construct school buildings, seek an education, and become teachers themselves.[69]

Violence as Enforcement

Violence or the threat of violence was the main engine for enforcement of the slavery regime. Violence continued after freedom, but its character changed. White men individually or in groups, and even United States Army officers and soldiers, used violence or the threat of violence to limit freed people's freedom or to enforce state and local laws left over from slavery that were not immediately repealed. To prevent overcrowding in Richmond, authorities revived the order that people must have a pass (as enslaved and free people had to have before the war) to enter or move about the city. Freed people strenuously objected, individually when confronted with officials who demanded to see their passes, and jointly at a large public gathering. Under slavery, enslaved and free Blacks in Virginia had been forbidden from assembling together for any purpose. Taking advantage of their new freedom, thousands crowded in to Richmond's African Baptist Church on June 10, 1865, to protest the abuses against them. They prepared an address that Fields Cook, a Baptist minister who had secured his freedom before the war, and a delegation of men presented to the president of the United States a few days later.[70]

The mass meeting that appointed the delegation complained that in the city of Richmond, "military and police authorities will not allow us to walk the streets by day or night, in the regular pursuit of our business or on our way to church, without a *pass*, and passes do not in all cases protect us from arrest, insult, abuse, violence and imprisonment, against which we have thus far had no protection or redress." Among the vulnerable were some of the many freed people from the countryside who traveled to the city to search for family members who had been hired or sold away, "thus preventing the reunion of long estranged and affectionate families."

Albert Brooks the livery stable owner, for instance, testified, "I am an old and well-known resident of Richmond, was a slave, but bought myself, my wife and six children, have kept a livery stable for 10 years, and have now a license for running three carriages, signed by the military authorities, and which I was told, was necessary to save my carriages from confiscation, and for which license I paid $37.50; I employ several colored men and pay them $35 per month; I was arrested by the police and put into the city jail, on the plea that my pass was not good." Brooks's testimony and a large number of other statements of similar purport filled a large part of the front page of the June 17, 1865, issue of the *New-York Tribune*.[71]

The speedy restoration of civilian municipal government in Richmond had unfortunate consequences, and the delegation also presented these to the president. Chief among them was that Mayor Joseph Mayo resumed holding sessions of his Mayor's Court, which with its police powers had terrorized both free and enslaved people before and during the Civil War. "For a long series of years," the delegation explained, "he has been the Mayor of Richmond, and his administration has always been marked by cruelty and injustice to us; and the old rebel police, now again in power, have been our greatest enemies. It was Mayor Mayo who, in former days, ordered us to be scourged for trifling offences against slave laws and usages, and his present police, who are now hunting us through the streets, are the men who relentlessly applied the lash to our quivering flesh, and now they appear to take special pleasure in persecuting and oppressing us."[72]

Freed people increasingly asserted their rights as citizens. They behaved and demanded to be treated like a free people rather than like a subjected people. In response, white people often resorted to force to reassert and to maintain what they regarded as proper subordination to white authority. In August 1866, in Lynchburg, for example, two young white men ordered three Black men to step aside and let the white men pass along the sidewalk, as would have been done during slavery. When the men refused, the two white men assaulted them. In the same city, a white working man objected to the behavior of a woman's child. He charged that she became verbally abusive, so he went to get his shotgun, loaded it, and shot and killed both the woman and her child.[73] White children in some instances emulated their elders and harassed freed people's children, who, not surprisingly, defended themselves, episodes that white newspaper reporters sometimes characterized as race riots.[74]

White peoples' fear of Black peoples' violence toward them sometimes spurred false accusations. Prince George County native Peter Randolph had been freed in the 1840s and went to Massachusetts and New York, where he was ordained a Baptist minister and published two editions of his autobiographical *Sketches of Slave Life: Or Illustrations of the "Peculiar Institution"* during the mid-1850s. He returned to Virginia as the war ended to aid and minister to the freed people. He carried a letter of introduction from the governor of Massachusetts and met Virginia governor Francis H. Pierpont, who consulted him when a rumor circulated among the white population that some Black men in Chesterfield County "were about to rise up and kill all the white people in that section." Informing the governor that he did not believe the report, he suggested that it was a ruse for white people to justify the murder of Black people. Randolph praised Pierpont, who "paid no attention to the rumor, by sending militia, and there was no riot. A few colored men were out hunting rabbits, and the whites cried, 'Negro uprising.'" In his memoirs, *From Slave Cabin to the Pulpit,* published in 1893, Randolph explained that such instances constituted "one of the sham tricks of the South, to get up a Negro riot, call out the militia or citizens in arms to butcher the blacks, for the purpose of keeping them in their places, as they say."[75]

On February 3, 1866, six men from southeastern Virginia who were in Washington, DC, trying to see the president took the opportunity to testify before the Congressional Joint Committee on Reconstruction. In response to questions about how white Virginians viewed and treated freed people and whether freed people were victims of violence, they all agreed that violence was endemic, although they did not all agree on how hostile former Confederates were. Daniel M. Norton, of Yorktown, who had escaped slavery and trained as a medical doctor in New York, informed the committee that "in some cases" white people treated freed people well, "but in more cases they have not. A number of persons living in the country have come into Yorktown and reported to the Freedmen's Bureau that they have not been treated well; that they worked all the year and had received no pay, and were driven off on the first of January. They say that the owners with whom they had been living rented out their places, sold their crops, and told them they had no further use for them." He also responded to a question whether freed people would feel safe if the army withdrew, "I do not think that the colored people would be safe. They would be in danger of being hunted and killed. The spirit of the whites against the blacks is much worse than it was before the war; a white gentleman with whom I was talking made this remark: he said he was well disposed toward the colored people, but that, finding that they took up arms against him" by joining the United States Army during the war, "he had come to the conclusion that he never wanted to have anything to do with them, or to show any spirit of kindness toward them."[76]

"The only hope the colored people have is in Uncle Sam's bayonets," Thomas Bayne, of Norfolk (spelled "Bain" in the published records), responded to the same question. Without the protection of the army, "they would not feel any security; and what is true of the colored people in that respect, is also true of the Union men; the secessionists do not seem to discriminate between them; they do not seem to care whether a northern man is with us or not with us; if he is a Yankee, that is enough; they hardly wait to examine what his views are; it is not uncommon to hear such threats as this: 'We will kill one negro, at least, for every rebel soldier killed by them.'"[77]

Madison Newby, who was born free in Surry County, testified about working conditions for the freed people there. "They work if they can get anything for it," he told the committee, "but the rebel people down there who have got lands will not let the colored people work unless they work for their prices, and they drive them away. They expect colored people down there to work for ten or eighteen cents a day. Six or eight dollars a month is the highest a colored man can get." He then described the coercion that he had witnessed. "In Surrey county," he reported "they are taking the colored people and tying them up by the thumbs if they do not agree to work for six dollars a month; they tie them up until they agree to work for that price, and then they make them put their mark to a contract. . . . A man cannot endure it long." Asked whether employers whipped freed people as they did before the war, Newby answered, "Just the same; I do not see any alteration in that." He continued, "There are no colored schools down in Surrey county; they would kill any one who would go down there and establish colored schools. . . . They patrol our houses just as formerly."[78]

Richard R. Hill, a freed man who lived in Hampton, responded to questions about interracial sex. The last was whether "blacks would have a strong inclination to unite with the whites in marriage." He declared, "I do not think that the blacks would have so strong an inclination to unite with the whites as the whites would have to unite with the blacks," which suggested that from his observations, at least some white men continued as during slavery to exploit women as sex objects.[79]

Freedmen's Bureau agents sometimes intervened or took control of prosecutions, but they were not able to stop the violence. Agents counted seventy-two "Outrages in Virginia" from March through July 1866 and ninety during the year 1868. How many went unreported or uncounted is not known. Among the reported "Outrages" were the burning of a school and church in Nansemond County in March 1866 and the "murder of a colored man by unknown parties" in nearby Isle of Wight County on the same day. In June an agent reported that "outrages are of Constant occurrence" and described how "a party of white ruffians perambulated the Streets of Suffolk assaulting every Negro the[y] met," but that white citizens "took no notice of them." Another agent reported that "the house of a Negro named Ballard living near Windsor Isle of Wight Co. was broken into—he was Shot, probably fatally—his child was also wounded and his wife whipped." In Richmond at the end of June, an agent reported on the

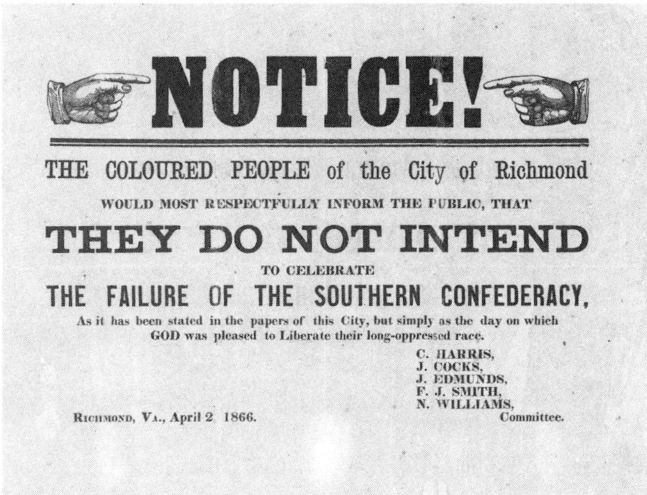

NOTICE!

THE COLOURED PEOPLE of the City of Richmond

WOULD MOST RESPECTFULLY INFORM THE PUBLIC, THAT

THEY DO NOT INTEND

TO CELEBRATE

THE FAILURE OF THE SOUTHERN CONFEDERACY,

As it has been stated in the papers of this City, but simply as the day on which GOD was pleased to Liberate their long-oppressed race.

C. HARRIS,
J. COCKS,
J. EDMUNDS,
F. J. SMITH,
N. WILLIAMS,
Committee.

RICHMOND, VA., April 2 1866.

This "Notice" dated April 2, 1866, informed the white majority in Richmond that freed people who celebrated the first anniversary of freedom that day did not intend to offend anybody by celebrating the failure of the Confederacy. (Virginia Museum of History and Culture)

"Assault of James B. Smith (white) on Peggy Rich (colored) with a stick. Smith was arrested and released on bail," after which he "again assaulted the woman—was again arrested and acquitted."[80]

King William County resident Benjamin F. Jones, who was not reticent about seeking the aid of Freedmen's Bureau agents, was shot by a white man on his property. A jury in King William County sentenced the shooter to thirty days in the local jail and a fine of $100, which Jones believed to be insufficient punishment for his injuries. He wrote to local agents and even the military commander of Virginia asking for a new military trial because of "the impossibility of obtaining justice at the hands of the civil authorities in consequence of the existing prejudice against persons of my race," but his request was not successful.[81]

The churches that free people had built in Petersburg before the war were burned at the beginning of May 1866, an event that attracted nationwide attention. The Richmond *Daily Dispatch* printed two long articles on the fires, other newspapers reprinted the articles, and an engraving of the "Ruins of the Colored Baptist Church of Harrison Street" appeared in the national magazine, *Harper's Weekly* on May 19.[82] And that was only a small portion of the documented instances of white on Black violence during a few months at the beginning of decades of white

"Fires at Petersburg, Virginia—Ruins of the Colored Baptist Church on Harrison Street" appeared in *Harper's Weekly* on May 19, 1866, and showed Americans nationwide part of the damage done earlier in the month when white men in Petersburg burned several Black churches and parsonages. (Library of Virginia)

attempts to reassert and maintain control in their own interests after the abolition of slavery.

Terrible as those actions were for the people involved, in Virginia, which had larger white and Black populations than most other states of the former Confederacy, Freedmen's Bureau agents reported fewer murders, episodes of arson, and other kinds of violence directed against Black people in 1867 and 1868 than did agents in other states. In April 1868, agents in Virginia reported that the Ku Klux Klan staged several nighttime attacks or demonstrations that may have been intended to terrorize Black people, but the Klan was evidently not so active in Virginia as it was in Tennessee and some other states.[83]

Black Churches

The first in the long list of complaints addressed by the attendees of the June 1865 mass meeting in Richmond concerned their churches and the old Virginia laws that vested in white trustees the actual ownership of church buildings and other congregational property, "which we have paid for," the men informed the president of the United States "out of the scanty earnings of years of toil." Those men spoke for the long-established churches in Richmond, which under the law had white ministers. "Now, in the reconstruction of our church matters," they continued, "we wish to employ clergymen of our choice and faith, and to hold our own property. The obnoxious clergy we may gradually get rid of, but how to get possession of our church property, passeth our understanding."[84]

Numerous congregations parted along racial lines in the years after the Civil War. Early in May 1866, a committee of "the Col^{d} members" of Cumberland Baptist Church, in Cumberland County, asked permission of the church's white board of directors "to withdraw from this church for the purpose of forming a Baptist church of Col^{d} members." The board agreed and ordered the church's clerk to "furnish them the necessary evidence of membership. Whereupon the new church was organized under the name of 'New Constitution,' and, on motion, it was ordered by the aforesaid committee, that the new church above-named do meet at Booker's Meeting house on the 3^{d} Sunday in this month to receive the report of their committee and to elect a pastor and church officers."[85] Likewise, freed members of a Baptist church in Montgomery County enlisted the assistance of the church's few remaining white members to affiliate with a church in neighboring Roanoke County and eventually to establish the new Elon Colored Baptist Church.[86] Similarly, white church members in Lynchburg assisted men and women who formed their own congregations.[87]

Before Peter Randolph returned to New England at decade's end, he served for four and a half years as pastor of Richmond's Ebenezer Baptist Church, where he helped establish the Shiloh Baptist Association for Black Baptist congregations in the central part of the state. While in Richmond, Randolph abolished the old practice of seating male and female members of the congregation on different sides of the aisle. "Before I left the church," he boasted, "the women not only had a voice, but voted in the business meetings."[88]

Throughout Virginia, freed people separated from their old congregations and formed new churches for themselves. Most separations were apparently amicable.[89] The long-term result was an almost complete racial segregation in religious worship. Unlike before the Civil War, when most enslaved people attended churches that white people controlled, freed people afterward attended and controlled their own churches. Within a short time, freedmen established several Baptist associations parallel to the older associations of churches that had included members of both races. An early example in southwestern Virginia was the formation of the Colored Valley Baptist Association that consisted of churches not affiliated with the old and by then all-white Valley Baptist Association.[90]

Those separations, amicable or not, did not settle the question of legal ownership of church property, but in 1867, the General Assembly of Virginia provided a means. It adopted a law to create a legal process for "communicants and pew holders and pew owners over twenty-one years of age" or members of divided congregations "entitled to vote by the ordinary practice or custom of such church or society" to decide by majority vote who should own the congregation's property.[91] Article XI of the Virginia Constitution of 1869 contained a new provision that could have made it more difficult for freed people to obtain ownership or control of church property. It declared that no events of "the late civil war" could alter ownership of church property and prohibited the General Assembly from passing any law that allowed or required any person or group other than original owner(s) "or the legal assignees of such original parties" to obtain ownership. How, if at all, that influenced the futures of congregations with their own buildings remains unclear.

Churches had always been important institutions and gathering places for free and enslaved people. After the end of slavery the importance of churches increased, especially in urban areas. The Colored Monitor Union Club of Norfolk held its meetings in the spring and summer of 1865 in the city's churches. Men such as Charles E. Hodges, in Princess Anne County, and John Montgomery Dawson, in Williamsburg, served for decades as ministers to their respective Baptist churches, while also serving in the General Assembly, and were important and essential community leaders.[92] The chair of the large Richmond meeting that composed the address to the president of the United States in June 1865 and who actually presented the address on their behalf was Fields Cook, who was then emerging as one of the state's ablest and most influential churchmen. He was then a leader of a Baptist church in the coalfields of Chesterfield County, near Richmond. He had been born into slavery and written a long autobiography in 1847, about the time that he gained his freedom. In 1865 he was one of the most important advocates of freed people in and around Richmond, and he went on to be a state leader in organizing freed people politically. Cook served as pastor of Third Baptist Church and then of Ebenezer Baptist Church in Alexandria from 1870 until his death in 1897.[93]

When Peter Randolph arrived in Richmond in April 1865, Fields Cook met him at the dock and escorted him to the comfortable home of John Adams, a prosperous building contractor whose son later won election to the city council. "The scene that opened before my eyes as I entered Richmond," Randolph wrote in *From Slave Cabin to the Pulpit*, "cannot be accurately described by word or pen. The city was in smoke and ashes," and "colored people from all parts of the state were crowding in at the capital, running, leaping, and praising God that freedom had come at last."[94]

Urban Opportunities

Increasing numbers of people migrated to the state's cities after the war in search of paying work or sought jobs on railroads or in other industrial settings. They were not always successful. The city of Richmond, for instance, had two racially segregated almshouses, and both were crowded during the 1860s.[95] As was the case in the countryside, wages were kept low for freed men and women, which some workers protested. In Lynchburg tobacco factory workers gathered one night and "adopted resolutions no longer to work at the price heretofore paid them." The manufacturers agreed the next day to increase their wages for three months, after which the workers went on strike again.[96] In Petersburg, striking men were less fortunate when the tobacco factory owner fired them instead.[97] George Teamoh, who had been hired out in the Portsmouth shipyards before escaping to Massachusetts in the 1850s, returned to the region in 1865. His experiences working on the docks focused him on workers' rights and he advocated equalizing the pay for white and Black laborers at the Norfolk Navy Yard.[98]

Despite the numerous obstacles, many Virginians were prepared to succeed. In Petersburg, Armistead Green gained his freedom by virtue of the Civil War and found work in a tobacco factory. He bought a town lot with a partner in 1869 and within a few years was identified in city directories as a grocer, likely benefitting from the large prewar community of free Blacks in Petersburg that helped the city's freed people fare better than in most Virginia cities.[99] Samuel P. Bolling entered the postwar free economy with distinct advantages, having gained skills in farm management by virtue of being able to hire himself out. In 1866 he was able to obtain two lots in the town of Farmville from the family that had owned him, and during the 1870s established a profitable brickyard there.[100] Just outside Manchester, across the James River from Richmond, James B. Carter purchased two lots in 1866 and worked as a cobbler, a skill he probably learned while enslaved in Chesterfield County. Two years later he bought another lot and opened a grocery store with a partner.[101] Countless other Black entrepreneurs could be found all over the state. In Lynchburg, for example, men and women acquired, owned, or operated more than sixty business establishments by 1880, including ten groceries, two livery stables, thirteen produce stalls at local markets, two bathhouses, a funeral parlor, and three saloons.[102]

Additionally, many freed men and women took advantage of their new opportunities to work together and provide mutual support by organizing benevolent associations that provided financial assistance at times of illness or death. The Freedman's Savings and Trust Company, known generally as the Freedman's Savings Bank, was chartered by Congress in March 1865, enabling freed people to save money, although it did not offer loans or credit. Before the bank's collapse in July 1874 as a result of speculative investments by some of the white trustees and the Panic of 1873, numerous Virginians and associations deposited their money there for safekeeping.[103] In some instances, the existence of those accounts is the only surviving evidence of those associations. The Freedman's Savings Bank in Richmond, for example, had accounts from more than one hundred such associations by 1869 and about four hundred by 1874.[104]

The January 1, 1874, issue of the Richmond *Daily Dispatch* included lists of white and Black fraternal and service organizations. At that time, the city's Black population had two militia companies; six Masonic lodges; six Odd Fellows lodges; twenty-eight temperance societies, including four with women officers; sixteen lodges of Good Samaritans for men and seven for women; twenty-five "Female Benevolent Orders"; and forty other organizations, including a Young Men's Christian Association, the Independent Sons and Daughters of Peace, the Rising Sons of the Vinyard, Rising Sons of America, Rising Daughters of America, a Shoemakers' Union, a Teamsters' Union, a Mechanics' Union, and eight separate councils of the Order of St. Luke with a combined membership of 360.[105]

In addition to caring for members at times of unemployment, illness, and death, such groups also served as social associations that organized public celebrations and parades despite the threat of harassment by white Virginians. In April 1867 John Watson and several men from a Mecklenburg County fraternal organization "mounted on fiery steeds, their white sashes flying, and batons in hand" led a thousand freed people through the streets of Boydton.[106] Lone Star, the association founded by Robert Norton and his brother Daniel Norton in Yorktown sponsored a July Fourth celebration in 1871 that included seven thousand members carrying banners and a hundred mounted officers who paraded through town.[107] These public demonstrations emphasized Thomas Calhoun Walker's remark that "to own oneself is to own one's future" and signaled to the white community that Black people were prepared to fight for their freedom.

4

"We Claim the Right of Suffrage"

The Politics of Freedom

Black Virginians organized in ways that undoubtedly took white leaders by surprise to fight for the rights they believed were theirs as a result of emancipation—especially the right to vote. Neither the Emancipation Proclamation nor the Thirteenth Amendment abolishing slavery (ratified in December 1865) delineated the rights of those who had been enslaved, but some men were determined to claim the same rights that white men possessed.

Sixty men who represented twenty-three cities and counties attended the "Colored State Convention," the first gathering of its kind in Virginia, in Lyceum Hall in Alexandria from August 2 through 5, 1865. They elected eight honorary delegates from Virginia as well as two from Baltimore, two from Washington, DC, and a white quartermaster in the United States Army who arranged for the flag of the United States that "graced the stand" during the proceedings. The delegates adopted resolutions drafted by Baptist minister Fields Cook, of Richmond, that appealed to the federal government and the citizens of Virginia for the protection "which is essential for the safety of our persons or our property, our wives or our children." This was necessary, they explained, because of "the assaults of the vile and vicious to do with us as they please, and we are left without redress." Indeed, during the convention, the delegates received a death threat: "Beware! beware! Fields Cook, you and other negroes will die." Undeterred, the delegates declared, "We claim, then, as citizens of this State, the laws of the Commonwealth shall give to all men equal protection; that each and every man may appeal to the law for his equal rights without regard to the color of his skin; and we believe this can only be done by extending to us the elective franchise, which we believe to be our inalienable right as freemen. . . . We claim the right of suffrage."[1]

Organizing for Political Action

Black men began to organize politically even before the Civil War ended. On February 27, 1865, men in Norfolk asked that the United States Army and the president guarantee that when regular civilian government resumed in the city it would be loyal to the United States and on an "equal basis." On April 4, the day after the army liberated/occupied the capital city of Richmond, "a public meeting of the colored people of Norfolk was held at the Mechanics Hall," with William Johnson Hodges presiding. They founded the Colored Monitor Union Club to protect and advance the interests of themselves and their families. Like the members of the later state convention in August, they insisted that as free American citizens they were entitled to, and for their own protection needed, the right to vote. They chose as president of the club Dr. Thomas Bayne, who had escaped from slavery in Norfolk and like Hodges had returned before the war ended.[2]

On May 25, at an election in Norfolk for members of the House of Delegates and state Senate, the club was able to assemble more than a thousand men in the Bute Street Methodist Church. How they got the word around the city is not clear, but that so many men attended the meeting and took part suggests that the club had an effective system of communication within the community. The men sent messengers to each of the four wards in the city to enquire whether election officials would receive their votes. Officials in the first, third, and fourth wards refused but those in the second ward agreed to record their votes on separate tally sheets. These tallies were identified as containing the votes of men whose qualifications were uncertain even though the state's constitution then limited the franchise to white male citizens. Then, 354 men who lived in the second ward went in small parties to the polling place and cast every one of their votes for white candidates who pledged to support suffrage for them. At the church, 712 other men who lived in the other three wards recorded their votes for the same candidates. The candidates for whom they voted failed to win election. If their votes had been counted, the candidates who supported suffrage for Black men would have won easily.[3]

At another meeting of the Colored Monitor Union Club in the Catherine Street Baptist Church on June 5, 1865, the members, who identified themselves as the "Colored Citizens of Norfolk," adopted a long and eloquent address to the people of the United States and listed "a few considerations touching the present position of the colored population of the southern States generally, and with reference to their claim for equal suffrage in particular." They explained, "We do not come before the people of the United States asking an impossibility; we simply ask that a Christian and enlightened people shall, at once, concede to us the full enjoyment of those privileges of full citizenship, which, not only, are our undoubted right, but are indispensable to that elevation and prosperity of our people, which must be the desire of every patriot."[4] They did not ask for "expensive aid from military forces, stationed throughout the South, overbearing State action, and rendering our government republican only in name," but instead they demanded, "give us the suffrage, and you may rely upon us to secure justice for ourselves, and all Union men, and to keep the State forever in the Union."[5]

Later in the year, the club had its history and public declarations, along with supplemental documents that supported full citizenship rights for freed people, published in a pamphlet, *Equal Suffrage: Address from the Colored Citizens of Norfolk, Va., to the People of the United States*. By identifying themselves boldly as American citizens, they claimed the full rights of citizenship—the right to vote being the most important and in effect the guarantor of them all—long before the federal or state governments recognized them as citizens or granted them the right to vote.

Black Virginians who were determined to claim their rights organized similar groups in other parts of the state. Men in Hampton founded the Union League in March 1865, and men in Williamsburg founded the Colored Union League in May.[6] Richmond residents formed the Colored Men's Equal Rights League of Richmond, Va., on May 9, in "the interests of colored men generally." The league declared that its purpose was "to encourage sound morality, education, temperance, frugality, industry, and promote everything that pertains to a well-ordered and dignified life, and to obtain by appeals to the minds and consciences of the American people, or by legal process when possible, a recognition of the rights of the colored people of the Nation as American citizens."[7] Men elsewhere did likewise. In the summer, Norfolk's Colored Monitor Union Club invited the "Secretaries of all Political, Labor, and Land Associations formed among the colored people of Virginia" to communicate with the club's officers.[8] Surviving records do not indicate how many men organized how many associations and where, but it is likely that the twenty-three cities and counties that sent delegates to the state convention in August all had political organizations by mid-summer.

Black men in Virginia expressed almost identical sentiments and goals with Black men in Northern states and other Black men, many of them recently freed from slavery, in states of the former Confederacy. They all understood suffrage to be an essential means of protecting their new freedom and making freedom more than an absence of slavery. Men in Virginia and elsewhere also argued that without the vote, ex-Confederates and former enslavers would soon retake control of state governments. Many radical white men in the Northern states fully appreciated the political benefits of extending the vote to freedmen.[9]

Some Freedmen's Bureau agents may have played a part in facilitating political organization in the countryside. In the spring of 1867, the commanding general of the bureau in Virginia instructed the agents to compile lists of the most respectable and influential men in their counties. Of the more than six hundred men the agents identified, almost all were native Virginians, the majority were literate, about a third had mixed-race heritage, and about a third had been born free or had achieved their freedom before the end of the war. They and their acquaintances could have enabled other men to organize Union Clubs or become involved in local Republican Party affairs.[10] The agents may have relied too heavily on the recommendations of white men and not enough on public opinion among Black men. This reliance was misplaced because in some counties Black men whom the agents did not identify apparently formed the bases of local Republican Party organizations.[11]

Surviving records of discussions about whether women should be enfranchised are too few and scattered to indicate whether many people seriously discussed the possibility. In August 1867, both white and Black men and women crowded into First African Baptist Church in Richmond to observe the Republican Party state convention there. Women seated in the gallery made their opinions known about some of the issues the male delegates discussed. Even without obtaining endorsement of proposals to enfranchise women as well as men, the women took an active part in the party's debates on important issues.[12]

White Reaction to Black Suffrage

Some native white Virginians supported suffrage for freed Virginians. Some of those men had remained loyal to the United States during the war or had quickly accommodated themselves to the new realities without slavery. Opponents of change called them by the insulting name scalawags. Other white men settled in Virginia during or after the war and also supported creation of a new inclusive democratic politics. Opponents of change called them by the insulting name carpetbaggers. Many of those white men understood that they would remain a permanent and politically impotent minority party if they did not make a political alliance with enfranchised freed men. As early as the end of June 1865, some of those white men formed the Virginia Union Association in order, among other things, to "secure the elective franchise to our colored population, as soon as it can be safely done" so that Virginia could have a government by people who had always been loyal to the United States and not by former Confederates.[13]

Even before any Black men obtained the right to vote and have their votes counted in Virginia, a very small number of men held the public office of juror in the federal district court of Judge John C. Underwood. He had moved to Virginia from his native New York early in the 1850s to establish a dairy and cheese-making enterprise that employed only free laborers in an attempt to demonstrate to Virginians the superiority of free labor over enslaved labor. So openly critical was Underwood of the Virginia slavery system that in 1856 his wife advised him that it was not safe for him to return home from the Republican national convention being held in Philadelphia. Underwood did not return until after the Civil War began. By the end of the war he was the only federal judge in the state and a widely known supporter of full citizenship rights for freed people. He was also openly eager to hold treason trials for Jefferson Davis, Robert E. Lee, and other Confederate leaders. Underwood may have admitted Black men to jury service in his courtrooms in Norfolk and Alexandria and he definitely did in Richmond, both for trial and grand jury service. In the spring of 1867, he empaneled a biracial jury to try Davis for treason, but the federal government declined to prosecute, and Underwood had to release Davis on bail.[14]

The prospect of freed people's service on juries and participation in politics alarmed many—probably a large majority of—white Virginians and led to more violence. As Congress began to take action for the first time to protect freed people's rights, the state's population became increasingly polarized on the many questions that the abolition of slavery and the grant of citizenship to freed people posed. Congress passed a Civil Rights Act in the spring of 1866 that declared that all people born or naturalized in the United States were citizens, including freed people, and it prohibited states from denying any people basic civil rights.[15] Congress submitted the Fourteenth Amendment to the states for ratification in June 1866 (but it wasn't adopted until July 1868). It included the basic provisions of the Civil Rights Act and prohibited states from paying any public debts incurred in support of the rebellion.[16]

The polarization between Black and white citizens was clearly demonstrated on April 16, 1866, when freed people in Norfolk commemorated the passage of the Civil Rights Act. Anxious white residents watched as the men paraded through the street carrying banners that read "The Ballot Box Free to All," "The Rising Sons of Freedom Society," and "The Monitor Union Club." A few marchers and a few of the white bystanders were armed. Somebody fired a gun, which alarmed an off-duty police officer who may have been drunk. He tried to arrest the person who he believed had fired the gun, but some men broke away from the parade and chased him through the streets. Robert Whitehurst, a young Confederate veteran, emerged from his house armed and fired several shots, probably at the men who were pursuing the policeman. Somebody, in turn, shot and killed Whitehurst. During the following night, armed bands of white people roamed the streets and injured several Black men and killed at least two. The so-called "riot" was widely reported in the press and led to a congressional investigation and publication of a sixty-eight-page report. The investigators were unable to ascertain who had fired the first shot that set the fatal sequence of events in motion or who had shot Whitehurst.[17]

Calling a Constitutional Convention

Radical Republican reformers in Congress became increasingly alarmed at the violence that freed people suffered, disappointed at the failure of state governments to protect them and their rights, and annoyed at efforts by former Confederates to shape public policies in their states with as little change from prewar conditions as possible.[18] Accordingly, Republicans enacted the first of several laws to reshape the economies, societies, and governments of the states of the former Confederacy on the bases of free labor and equal rights, including the right to vote. On March 2, 1867, Congress, over the president's veto, passed the Act to Provide for the More Efficient Government of the Rebel States, sometimes referred to as the First Reconstruction Act. It created military districts throughout the former Confederacy and designated Virginia as the First Military District. The law required the commanding general of each district to supervise the actions of state and local government officials, and it required Virginia and most of the other states of the former Confederacy to adopt new state constitutions.[19]

In preparation for the constitutional conventions, the law authorized the army to register voters in each state, including freed men, to allow Black men to vote and run for office, and to allow them to serve in the conventions if elected. It also prohibited former Confederates and active supporters of the Confederacy from registering to vote if they refused to disavow their Confederate pasts and take an oath of allegiance to the United States. Just three days after passage of the law, more than 1,300 Black men in Alexandria turned out during heavy rain and a hail storm to vote in a municipal election for city officers and councilmen. Black men and a few white radicals asserted that the new law allowed Black men to vote in any election, but white city officials did not allow their votes to count.[20]

During the registration of potential voters, so many disapproving white men throughout the state refused to register or could not register because they had not taken the required oaths that only 120,101 of them qualified to vote. Almost as many Black men registered, 105,832, a larger proportion of the eligible adult population than of white people.[21]

On October 22, 1867, Black men voted for the very first time in Virginia and had their votes counted and reported. Army officers at each of the polls required voters to deposit their ballots in separate boxes for Black and white voters and also recorded votes of Black men and white men on separate tally sheets. Ballots and tally sheets preserved in the archives at the Library of Virginia and the results published by the commanding general of the First Military District indicate that nearly all of the registered Black men voted.[22]

Voters of both races cast ballots rather than voted orally because the election took place under the authority of acts of Congress and not of the

"First Vote" appeared on the cover of *Harper's Weekly* on November 16, 1867. The magazine contained reports of Black men voting in several states of the former Confederacy for the first time. In Virginia, they voted on October 22, on the question of holding a constitutional convention and in the election of delegates to the convention. In reality, army officers, not white civilians as depicted here, supervised the election. (Library of Virginia)

constitution or laws of Virginia, which then required viva voce voting.[23] Voters cast two ballots that day, on the question whether to hold the convention and for candidates who wished to serve in the convention if the voters authorized it. Having voters approve the convention (as voters had approved proposals for state constitutional conventions in 1829 and 1850) gave the convention a legitimacy based on the votes of Virginians in addition to the authority of acts of Congress. The vote broke sharply along racial lines, with 92,507 Black men providing a large majority of the 107,342 votes for holding the convention and white men all but 638 of the 61,887 votes against. Almost all Black men voted for candidates who favored radical reforms, and most white voters opposed those candidates.[24]

Black Delegates at the Constitutional Convention

Black voters were more numerous and Black candidates for the convention were more successful east of the Blue Ridge Mountains and south of the Rappahannock River, the region which had the largest concentration of Black residents than elsewhere in the state. In Petersburg, Black men overwhelmingly elected saloon proprietor Peter G. Morgan, who advocated a tax increase on property of more than four hundred acres, a poll tax, and the removal of all race-related words from the state constitution. In Fluvanna County, political activist James D. Barrett had led efforts to educate and organize Blacks to seek their rights as citizens. He ran for a seat at the convention against a white candidate who was clerk of the county court. About one hundred more Blacks than whites voted in the election, and Barrett carried the county by fifty votes.[25]

During the campaign, a division of opinion among Black leaders became evident. Radical Republicans among them differed with more moderate men, probably a smaller number, who attempted to work together with moderate white men who were identified in the press as Conservatives (with a capital letter) even though they did not formally establish the Conservative Party until December.[26] For example, John Brown, a formerly enslaved candidate in Southampton County, had a ballot printed that may have signaled to white voters, and thereby reassured them, that he did not hold a grudge against the people who had enslaved him and thousands of other people in the county. On election day, however, militant white men in several communities tried to intimidate men who wished to vote for radical Republicans or later deprived those voters of their jobs.[27]

In Charlotte County, where about 64 percent of the population had lived in slavery in 1860, candidates Edward Nelson and Joseph P. Holmes

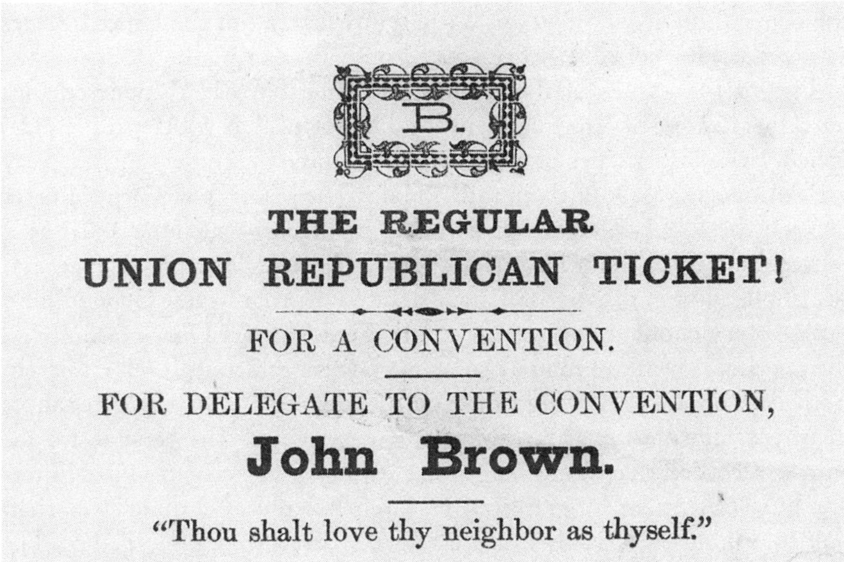

B.

THE REGULAR
UNION REPUBLICAN TICKET!

FOR A CONVENTION.

FOR DELEGATE TO THE CONVENTION,

John Brown.

"Thou shalt love thy neighbor as thyself."

One of the ballots cast for freedman John Brown, a successful candidate for the constitutional convention in Southampton County. The phrase, "Thou shalt love thy neighbor as thyself," may have been intended to reassure white men that the freedman held no grudges against white men who had enslaved Black men. Brown was one of twenty-four Black men who won election to and served in the Virginia Convention of 1867–1868. (Military Rule Election Records, Virginia Secretary of the Commonwealth, 1867, 1869, State Government Records Collection, Library of Virginia)

addressed a letter to the *Daily Richmond Whig* in June 1867 supporting the radical Republicans and criticizing the moderate proposals of white Republicans. Reflecting the county's racially polarized politics, in October registered Black men outnumbered white men 2,080 to 913, as some former Confederates were ineligible, and others, as elsewhere, seemingly refused to participate. Edward Nelson won election to the convention, with incomplete unofficial returns from two of the county's four or more voting districts indicating that all the men who voted for him were Black. Holmes also won election to the convention to represent the counties of Charlotte and Halifax.[28]

Of the 104 delegates who attended the convention, 24 had at least some African ancestry and a few also had some American Indian ancestry, the first such men to serve in public office in Virginia. Erroneous reports in some newspapers identified Frederick W. Poor, of Orange County, as one of the "negro" delegates, and his name appeared in the early scholarship on the convention. Poor, however, was a white veteran of the United States Army and a former clerk for the Freedmen's Bureau.[29]

Few of the names of the twenty-four men have ever appeared in a narrative history of Virginia or in local histories that white people published. Scholarly studies of the convention and its members include very little information about them individually. The research of Luther Porter Jackson disclosed enough that he could include one or more short sentences on each of them in his 1945 *Negro Office-Holders in Virginia;* and the publication in the 1990s of an annotated list that Major General John McAllister Schofield, commander of the First Military District, compiled during the convention made available a few more details. Unfortunately, both Jackson and Schofield obtained incomplete and in some instances incorrect information about some of the delegates. The general, for instance, recorded that about half of the twenty-four delegates were illiterate, but subsequent biographical research has revealed that fewer than half that number, possibly as few as two or three, were unable to read or write more than to sign their names. Among the men Schofield labeled as illiterate was Willis A. Hodges, who had edited an antislavery journal in New York in the 1840s, written an autobiography, and represented his native Princess Anne County.[30]

The membership was the most diverse by occupation, background, class, and race of any Virginia constitutional convention before or since. About half the twenty-four history-making delegates had been enslaved until the Civil War, but at least eight had been born free; two or three more had obtained their freedom before the war; and three—George Teamoh, Daniel Norton, and Thomas Bayne—had escaped from slavery and gone to the North before the war. Teamoh had worked in the navy yard at Portsmouth; Norton was a medical doctor; and Bayne was a dentist.

The delegates included four shoemakers or cobblers, one stonemason, one operator of a canalboat, two blacksmiths, two carpenters, three day laborers, and five men who after the war earned their meager livelihoods primarily as farmers or agricultural laborers. Hanover County delegate Burwell Toler, who was probably born into slavery, had since become a Baptist minister. William H. Andrews, from Surry County, had been a schoolteacher in New Jersey before he came to Virginia. Albemarle County delegate James Thomas Sammons Taylor, whose father had purchased his freedom and taught him the cobbler's trade, had served during the war as a commissary sergeant in a United States Colored Troops infantry regiment.

The twenty-four men were almost the only Black Virginians who ever took part in writing a state constitution. The exceptions were civil rights attorney Oliver Hill, who served on an advisory commission on constitutional revision in 1968 and 1969, and dentist William Ferguson Reid, the first Black person in the twentieth century to serve in the General Assembly, in 1969 and 1970 when it rewrote the state constitution that voters ratified.[31]

The white delegates were also much more diverse in origin and occupation than at any other constitutional convention in Virginia's history. They included a dozen natives of New York, four of Great Britain, one of Canada, and half a dozen or more natives of other states, an unprecedented number and percentage of delegates who had not been born in Virginia. Among them were nearly two dozen lawyers, six other physicians or dentists, several clergymen, and two newspaper editors. At least seven men had served in the United States Army or Navy during the Civil War, and three others had held federal government offices. Those white immigrants to Virginia were probably responsible for many of the democratic features that the constitution they wrote contained. On the whole, loyal and immigrant white Virginians embraced a more democratic and more inclusive view of politics than most of the Virginians who had supported the Confederacy.[32] White supremacists in Virginia nevertheless later blamed the twenty-four Black delegates for the democratic character of the constitution because for more than a decade after the constitution went into operation, voters that the constitution enfranchised played very important and influential roles in state politics and government; and for nearly two more decades they appeared to hold the balance of power on election day.[33]

Perceptions of the Constitutional Convention

The constitutional convention met in the chamber of the House of Delegates in the state Capitol from December 3, 1867, through April 17, 1868. The Capitol was easy to find, even for the many men who had never been to Richmond. It stood by itself in a park on a hill near the center of the city, surrounded by trees that had shed their leaves. The governor's house, city hall, and several churches and hotels were only a few paces away, as were the rented offices of the Freedmen's Bureau Bank. The redlight district and the notorious jails of the slave trade were also nearby, just a few blocks away through the city's busy streets. Perhaps busier than usual, because white and Black carpenters, brickmasons, and other workmen

Richmond following the evacuation fire of April 1865. When members of the Constitutional Convention of 1867–1868 arrived in the city in December 1867, they would have seen white and Black men busily reconstructing the city's business and industrial districts. (National Archives and Records Administration)

were rebuilding the burned business district between the Capitol and the James River.

For many of the convention members, it was probably their first time in Richmond, for some of them their first time in any city. Coming as some of them did from farms or small towns, they would have found the sounds and smells of the city as unfamiliar as the many large buildings and crowds of people. For decades, Richmond residents had heated their homes and cooked their meals using soft, high-sulfur coal dug from shallow pit mines just outside the city. Visitors sometimes complained that the city's buildings were grimy with coal smoke and the air sometimes suffocating. Steam locomotives pulled passenger and freight trains through the streets to within a short walk of the Capitol. Large brick industrial buildings or burned-out hulks lined the north bank of the James River.

How the men elected to the convention reached Richmond is not known for certain. Railroads sometimes offered free passage to legislators, a good-will gesture that they hoped would pay off when members of the General Assembly worked on the annual revision of the state's tax law. If some railroad companies offered free rides to convention members, that would account for how only some of them got to Richmond because many parts of the state had no convenient access to railroads.

Horses, mules, wagons, or stagecoaches probably carried a considerable number of men to Richmond or to railroad stations far from their homes for the final leg of the trip to the capital. Some delegates probably took steamships from Norfolk or Portsmouth or from landings on the shores of Chesapeake Bay or the navigable rivers that emptied into it.

Members of the convention were entitled to a travel allowance and a per diem payment for each day they attended the convention, but they did not have access to the money in advance, so the logistics of their traveling to Richmond are not known. Nor is it known how the twenty-four Black men found lodgings and places to eat at a time when boardinghouses, hotels, and eating establishments that served white people probably did not welcome Black customers.

When the men reached the Capitol, they climbed one of two exterior staircases on either side of the building to enter and reach the main floor. The ground floor had meeting rooms and other office spaces, but the legislative chambers were on the main floor, up the stairs. On the northwest side of the classical Roman design Capitol, the men would have passed by a very large bronze equestrian statue of George Washington and smaller bronzes of such Revolutionary War leaders as Patrick Henry, Thomas Jefferson, George Mason, and John Marshall.

The Capitol was shabby in 1867. Its peeling, faded brown paint, set off with white trim and columns on the south front, had not been refreshed since long before the war. The interior was in need of new paint and many repairs, too. Both the Confederate Congress and the General Assembly of Virginia had used the building. The upstairs library was in disarray, and remnants of the looted archival records were still scattered about on the floor of the attic. Aside from the addition of two small galleries on the short ends of the chamber of the House of Delegates, where the convention met, no significant structural changes or maintenance had been done for decades. Some of the floors sagged.[34]

To reach the high-ceilinged chamber, the men entered through a beautiful rotunda lit by a concealed skylight that was suspended beneath the roofline and not visible from outside. A full-length marble statue of George Washington stood in the center, just outside the entrance door to the chamber of the House of Delegates. The chamber was rectangular, with the entrance on one of the long sides and the ceremonial chair of the Speaker of the House of Burgesses, left over from colonial times, opposite it between two large windows. The president of the convention occupied that historic chair. The floor was crowded with about a hundred chairs and desks that members of the House of Delegates had used before the General Assembly adjourned at the end of the previous April. We do not know whether the Black members gravitated together when they selected their seats. Most of them were unacquainted with one another or with the white members, which might have led the Black men to join together in company.

The men were members of the third constitutional convention to assemble there. James Madison, James Monroe, John Marshall, and other famous Virginians had met there during the winter of 1829–30 to rewrite the state's Revolutionary-era constitution; and a second convention had met there from the autumn of 1850 through the summer of 1851 to write the state's third constitution. John Marshall had presided over the treason trial of Aaron Burr in that room, too. The chamber had also been the home of the Virginia Convention of 1861 that submitted an ordinance of secession to the voters for ratification. The walls of the chamber, if they could speak, would have told of many famous men who had done many important things there. Scarcely any of those things were as remarkable as what convention members began to do on Tuesday, December 3, 1867.

Radical Republicans, including men of both races, formed a majority in the convention, and almost all of the most important and/or controversial votes divided the members along the same lines.[35] Black men and women crowded into the galleries in the Capitol day after day to watch the first Black officeholders in the state's history participate in writing a state constitution. In keeping with ideas about gender roles at the time, only men occupied the west gallery, but "ladies and gentlemen accompanying them" sat in the east gallery until early in February 1868 when the convention ordered that "no distinction shall be made, in admitting persons in the galleries."[36]

Not only did the visitors witness the unprecedented participation of freed people in a constitutional convention, they also heard the convention's white president and some of the white delegates address them in proper parliamentary language as "Mr." or refer to them as "gentlemen." The official published journal and the published record of the debates preserve evidence of that practice that no free or enslaved men had enjoyed before the war. Unfortunately, the stenographer and the printer published nothing after the debates of January 29, 1868, which left more than half of the convention's debates unrecorded.

Hostile white journalists for the Richmond *Daily Enquirer and Examiner* and the Richmond *Daily Dispatch* reported on the debates selectively, often in a racist and partisan manner but did not reproduce speeches verbatim. Too few copies of the Richmond *New Nation*, a radical Republican paper that white convention delegate James W. Hunnicutt published,

This ugly line drawing from the *Southern Opinion*, December 7, 1867, depicts convention delegate Lewis Lindsey dancing barefoot on the Constitution of Military District 1. The illustrator used racist tropes to denigrate the work of Black and white convention members who worked together. (Library of Virginia)

survive to preserve much record of delegates' actions and words.[37] Curious white journalists focused their attention on the two dozen Black delegates. They lampooned some of the delegates with crude language and unflattering line drawings. Most of the twenty-four men engaged in the debates only rarely, leaving them vulnerable to charges that they were ignorant and did not know what they were doing—but that was also the case with a majority of white delegates. When Black delegates did speak their mind, they were often lampooned.

Writers for the Richmond newspaper *Southern Opinion* used overtly racist and demeaning, even nasty, language.[38] Sometimes, even when belittling those delegates, journalists inadvertently disclosed that the delegates did know what they were doing. About David Canada, of Halifax County, a writer for the *Southern Opinion* described him sitting silently like a sphinx as if oblivious to what was going on around him. Canada "never speaks," the reporter concluded, "though his nod is Radical," which indicated that Canada understood the nature and importance of the subjects being discussed and on which he voted.[39] So offensive were some of the reports in the *Southern Opinion* that George Teamoh proposed to expel one of its reporters because he had used the words *convict* and *pup* to describe "loyal and legally delegated members of this Convention," but a motion that the convention "indefinitely postpone the resolution" carried.[40]

Richmond's other white daily newspapers also treated the convention contemptuously. Ten days after the Constitutional Convention first met, the city hosted the founding meeting of the Conservative Party of Virginia to make certain that Virginia "is, and ever shall be, '*a white man's government*.'"[41] The editor of the Richmond *Daily Enquirer and Examiner* contrasted the two conventions. "A Convention will organize in this city to-day," he explained, "having for its object the preservation of that magnificent fabric of Caucasian civilization which for two centuries has kept Virginia in the front rank of modern States. . . . The Convention which meets in the theatre to-day, although imposing in numbers, will not contain a delegate who has been flogged for larceny, nor a single incendiary who is awaiting trial for inciting the negroes to murder and arson." On the next day the editor resumed, "The silent contempt with which eight hundred Virginia gentlemen treated the vile rabble called a 'Constitutional Convention,' which is performing in the Capitol, was especially worthy of commendation."[42]

Speaking for Liberty

Willis A. Hodges, of Princess Anne County, was one of the few of the twenty-four members of the convention who was known outside of his constituency. He had attended state and national Black conventions during the years he lived in New York. Journalists from New York and elsewhere who visited the convention recognized the large, thick eyeglasses that he wore. "Specs Hodges," some people called him. His notoriety may explain why in the only published image of the convention, Hodges stands at the center with his back to the other delegates and facing the illustrator. Thomas Bayne, who won election as one of two Republican delegates from Norfolk, was the most vocal advocate of the rights of freed people in the convention and thereby became the most famous of the twenty-four delegates.

Hodges initiated the first important discussion on December 12 (the second day of the founding meeting of the Conservative Party) when he proposed formation of a select committee to suggest measures "to put a stop" to the "intimidating of loyal Union laboring men by disloyal landholders in this State" that occurred during the election of delegates. Hodges improvised on the words of Jesus as recorded in Matthew 8:20 and Luke 9:58 and told the delegates, "The birds of Virginia have nests, and the foxes have holes, but the loyal, Union men of the State have scarcely a spot where they can rest, oppressed as they are by those who

"The State Convention at Richmond Va., in Session" in *Frank Leslie's Illustrated Newspaper* of February 15, 1868, depicted the Constitutional Convention of 1867–1868 at work in the chamber of the House of Delegates in the Capitol in Richmond. President John C. Underwood presided in the Speaker's chair. Delegate Willis Augustus "Specs" Hodges, the best-known Black member of the convention, appears in the center facing the illustrator. (Library of Virginia)

voted this State out of the Union, and who are now gathered together to oppose whatever action we may determine upon. I fully hope that the delegates elected here by the Republican Union votes of the State, will rise to protect their oppressed brethren."[43] When a white delegate proposed substitute language to the same purpose, Hodges agreed but objected to its inclusion of "the word colored" and explained, "We don't recognize the terms white or colored voters now."[44]

Bayne spoke at length in support of Hodges's proposal and emphasized that white radical voters had been intimidated, too. He concluded, "I ask the Convention seriously and earnestly, for the sake of saving life, and to protect the material interests of the State, to interpose their power in behalf of the Union white men and Union black men, who, without such protection, will be expelled from their homes this winter."[45]

James W. D. Bland agreed, even though he favored a more conciliatory attitude toward moderate white Conservatives than Hodges and Bayne. The freeborn cooper and carpenter who lived in Farmville responded to white objections that it was "discreditable" for the convention to set aside its regular business and act like a court. Bland declared, "I think it is discreditable to us, or for any body of men representing the people of a State, whether loyal or disloyal, to say to the people of such State, who are going down to ruin—who are being destroyed—that we have no power to put a stop to that course. . . . It is the duty of a representative body, whether a constitutional body or a General Assembly, to protect the people they represent."[46]

Hodges and Bayne spoke more often than the other delegates. They and the others focused more on the proposed Bill of Rights and the article on suffrage than on other subjects. The lack of stenographic records for the important February, March, and April discussions of the provisions of the new constitution leaves their remarks on most other topics unrecorded. On February 25, for example, when the report of the Committee on the Elective Franchise was under discussion, the journal records only that "Mr. Bland resumed his remarks," and that "Mr. Carter"—Chesterfield County delegate James B. Carter—"obtained the floor and spoke until the hour for recess, when the Convention adjourned until 4 o'clock P.M."[47] In fact, that brief entry included more information than most about who spoke on which subjects.

Bayne spoke often during debates on the Bill of Rights and made very long and eloquent speeches on the necessity of universal manhood suffrage[48] and on the plight of poor freed people.[49] Delegates of both races sometimes complained about the expense that the convention ran up by its extended debates, but Bayne wanted every clause of the proposed constitution fully debated and voted on separately. "If it takes ten days for them to discuss one resolution," he explained, "let them be fairly satisfied. Then, when you have made a constitution, when you have gotten through, the minority cannot complain that they did not have sufficient time to be heard."[50]

Hodges also made a very long speech that described the plight of poor freedmen and criticized some Freedmen's Bureau agents for doing too little.[51] He proposed a measure to relieve the "many poor laboring men in this State" by having the new constitution include a section, "that all woodland, swamps, marshes, creeks, rivers, lakes and bays in this State, shall be free for all persons to hunt, gun and fish on or in, as the case may be, provided, they do not destroy any private property in so doing."[52] He later added some condemnations of the harmful effects of hateful ideas and behavior.[53] "I am not ashamed of my color, and I am not ashamed of my principles," Hodges proclaimed one day. "There are but two classes of men in this Convention that I recognize as having any power, and these are loyal Union men and rebels. The rights of the loyal Union men are my rights."[54] On another occasion, Hodges looked forward to the future. "I hope we will soon be able to re-organize Old Virginia, or New Virginia, as it will then be. The old one has passed away with a great noise, and we are now coming to new things."[55]

More than two-thirds of the twenty-four delegates introduced important substantive or procedural motions during the convention, including David Canada, the supposedly illiterate sphinx. He proposed to extend the deadlines for "the payment of all debts as to give such farther indulgence, not exceeding four years, as may be deemed right and proper"[56] and to reform the county taxation system.[57] Canada offered two resolutions that appeared in the constitution in modified forms, to create an office of state geologist "to discover and develop, as far as he can, the mineral wealth of the State,"[58] and an office of "State Chemist, who shall give particular attention to agricultural chemistry; also to set apart a tract of land to be used as an experimental farm."[59]

Proposals that other delegates made suggest which subjects were most important to them. Joseph R. Holmes, who represented Halifax and Charlotte Counties, proposed an inquiry to determine whether "disloyal officials" were using their offices as collectors of taxes "as an engine of vexation and oppression to many of the loyal people of this Commonwealth."[60] To protect the civil rights of freed people, Peter K. Jones, a freeborn delegate from Petersburg, proposed "a clause prohibiting any distinction whatever in public conveyances" and that "all public institutions, such as railroads, steamboats, &c., chartered for public purposes, shall make no such distinction."[61] Lewis Lindsey, a sharp-tongued Richmond delegate, wanted "to protect all persons in the full enjoyment of all their political rights"; to require that "all public institutions and incorporated companies, or public places, where licenses or charters are granted under the laws of Virginia, shall be accessible to all persons alike"; and to prohibit differences in treatment in the penitentiary "on account of family standing, or anything else."[62] And William P. Moseley, who had earned his freedom running a barge on the James River, made a motion "That no licensed minister of the Gospel shall be required to perform militia duty, work on roads or serve on juries in this State."[63]

James T. S. Taylor insisted that because "the disloyal men of Virginia are seeking by every means in their power to prevent the free exercise of the elective franchise," all voting be by ballot, "the palladium of American liberty."[64] He undoubtedly hoped that ballots would make it more difficult for opponents of reform to intimidate radical voters on election day than if voting was by voice vote. James W. D. Bland proposed several measures relating to suffrage. One of his proposals was less harsh on former Confederates than the language that made it into the constitution. His stated, "'That the right to vote, to hold office, and the privilege to act as a juror, shall never be denied to any of the male inhabitants of this State having all the prescribed constitutional or statutory requirements; nor shall any public privilege or civil right ever enjoyed by citizens prior to the year 1861, be denied or refused to any person now, or heretofore, citizens of this State."[65] The final clause should have appealed to white men. Perhaps as an inducement to white voters to accept the radical reforms that the constitution embodied, Bland unsuccessfully proposed late in the convention that "All persons who advocate the adoption of this Constitution, or vote for a candidate or candidates for office favoring the same, shall be relieved from all disabilities imposed by the above section, so far as it relates to county, city or town officers."[66]

Bland introduced two resolutions to allow people who moved since they registered to vote in their new places of residence,[67] which would benefit freed people in search of work or lost family members. Samuel Kelso, of Lynchburg, introduced a similar measure.[68] Joseph Cox, of Richmond, introduced several proposals to deny the vote and the right to hold office to men who, "during the late rebellion, inflicted, or caused to be inflicted, any cruel or unusual punishment upon any soldier, sailor, marine, employee or citizen of the United States, or who, in other ways, violated the rules of civilized warfare"; who refused to "accept the political equality of all men before the law"; had been "convicted of treason, embezzlement of public funds, malfeasance in office, crime punishable by law with imprisonment in the penitentiary, or bribery"; as well as men who were "idiots or insane," or who refused to swear an oath disavowing secession and accepting "the political and civil equality of all men."[69] All but the first of those requirements was included in the new constitution. Cox also proposed that cities be laid off in wards and that only residents of the wards be allowed to vote in them, which he may have suggested in order that Black men have a better chance to elect local officials of their own color;[70] and to insert in the constitution "a clause requiring of all foreigners a residence of ten years in the State of Virginia, and one year's residence in the community where they offer to vote, before they can exercise the right of suffrage." The new constitution created a Bureau of Agriculture and Immigration, and it is possible that Cox wanted to make it difficult for Conservatives to pack voting booths with recent white immigrants.[71]

Public Schools

Samuel Kelso, a school teacher from Lynchburg, introduced one of several proposals on public schools. He recommended that the constitution "guarantee, for the future, a system of common school education, to be supported by the State, which shall give to all classes a free and equal participation in all its benefits."[72] Thomas Bayne moved to amend Kelso's resolution to prohibit racial discrimination in the schools, but because the resolution had already been sent to committee the president ruled the amendment out of order.[73] Later, Bayne proposed a similar amendment to the draft article on education to require that schools be "free to all classes, and no child, pupil or scholar shall be ejected from said schools on account of race, color, or any invidious distinction." The white majority defeated Bayne's motion 56 to 15.[74] Rejection of the amendment left the question of racial segregation legally unanswered, but in practical terms it meant that unless the General Assembly directed otherwise the schools were certain to be segregated.

Several white delegates introduced their own proposals for public education, but Eustace Gibson, a white delegate from western Virginia, proposed, "There shall be separate schools for white children and for colored children; and the capitation tax derived from white polls shall be devoted exclusively to education in the white schools, and that from colored polls to education in the colored schools." Lewis Lindsey was immediately on his feet to offer an amendment, "And there shall also be a separate Legislature, for the convenience of all classes." James B. Carter moved to "lay the proposition and amendment upon the table," which killed Gibson's proposal by a vote of 41 to 15.[75] In the nineteenth century and early into the twentieth, influential white political leaders often objected that it was unfair or unjust for their taxes to be spent on the education of Black children. Those men clearly understood that Black families were often poor and that as a consequence if revenue for schools were collected and spent based on race, schools for Black students would almost always receive less money than schools for white students.[76]

Samuel Kelso also introduced a second resolution relating to public schools, but it did not make it into the constitution. He proposed that the General Assembly not be permitted to appropriate any money for "the support of colleges or high schools until the common school system . . . shall be in operation throughout the State," with the exception that in the meantime, normal schools to train new teachers "shall be considered a portion of the common school system."[77] That would have given preference to the common schools for all children instead of the then-existing high schools and universities for white students. William Breedlove, a freeborn farmer and former ferryboat operator in Essex County, proposed that two-thirds of the money collected by poll taxes "be applied exclusively in aid of the public school fund" and the remainder for the use of county and municipal governments.[78]

Financial Issues

A majority of the twenty-four delegates who made substantive motions introduced measures to relieve poor people. John Robinson, for instance, a freeborn delegate from Cumberland County, introduced a measure to limit payment of poll taxes to "twenty-five cents per annum."[79] The colonial and state governments had taxed adult white men and enslaved men, women, and children old enough to work since the seventeenth century—a poll tax, or tax on each head, or person—but had not linked it to the right to vote; however, in 1866 opponents of change amended the state constitution to restrict the vote to men who paid state taxes, and Robinson evidently believed that many poor men would be unable to pay a higher poll tax and would therefore lose the right to vote. He also proposed "That where property was voluntarily sold during the late war by consent of all the parties concerned, the sales are hereby ratified and confirmed," which could have reassured both white and Black property owners, but that "the values on purchases remaining unpaid at the close of the war, shall now be paid in United States currency at the rates of the value of the 'so-called Confederate money' in gold at the time of said purchase."[80]

Samuel Kelso proposed a constitutional cap for the maximum allowable interest rate in the state at 8 percent,[81] but the convention ultimately settled on a cap of 12 percent on a negotiated debt but a flat 6 percent if the instrument of debt did not specify a rate. Lewis Lindsey moved to require due notice before any person garnished wages or salaries for payment of back taxes.[82] George Teamoh proposed to extinguish all debts that arose for the purchase of enslaved people, which would punish former enslavers, and to tax uncultivated land at a higher rate than tilled land, which would hit large landowners (mostly white people) harder than (most) Black people.[83] Other proposals relating to taxes revealed other concerns. James T. S. Taylor wanted to allow formerly enslaved people to sue their former enslavers to recover wages not paid between April 9, 1865, and January 1, 1866.[84]

John Watson, a formerly enslaved delegate from Mecklenburg County, proposed that the convention ask Congress to repeal a tax on tobacco, which was "injurious and oppressive to the agricultural and laboring interests of this Commonwealth." He also made a motion that the constitution create a $1,000 homestead exemption to prevent indebted people from having all their resources seized for nonpayment of a debt.[85] The convention also received a petition from tax-paying residents of the First Congressional District, in eastern Virginia, in favor of a homestead exemption,[86] and the constitution included the first homestead provision in Virginia. Lewis Lindsey introduced motions that the General Assembly purchase a parcel of land in each county, town, and city "for the purpose of establishing a public burying ground for the benefit of the poor persons and strangers who are unable to obtain means through their labor";[87] to grant a homestead exemption until age twenty-one for orphans of soldiers;[88] and to exempt from paying the poll tax "all loyal soldiers, disabled from wounds received during the late war, in suppressing the late rebellion."[89]

Joseph Holmes introduced a resolution to consider the consolidation of Richmond and York River Railroad with the Richmond and Danville Railroad.[90] And Burwell Toler inquired about how properly to transfer management of Eastern Lunatic Asylum from military to civilian authority,[91] and asked for an inquiry into appropriations made before the war for constructing a railroad between Fredericksburg and Gordonsville, work on which was suspended during the war.[92]

Buckingham County's Frank Moss conceived of himself as "a working man" and a representative of "the whole class of colored people in this State." He advocated land ownership as a boon to freed people. "When we get the land," he announced, "notwithstanding the burthens of taxation may be upon it, we would—or at least I would—rather pay a high tax upon land and work it myself than to work for other people for nothing."[93] A letter writer to the Richmond *Daily Enquirer and Examiner* identified as Rebellus—*rebel us?* an unreconstructed Confederate?—not long thereafter dubbed him "Francis-Forty-Acres-and-a-Mule Moss."[94] The nickname derived from the common hope among freed people and fear among white people that the army would confiscate the property of Confederates and distribute forty acres of land and a mule to each freed person.

Proposals that Black members of the constitutional convention introduced reflected their expectations of what freedom meant. They worked on behalf of Black Virginians to facilitate education through public schools, to expand their access to the ballot, to integrate public spaces and conveyances, to assist the needy, and to protect property ownership. By majority votes, the convention defeated most of their proposals.

White Allies in the Constitutional Convention

Some white delegates spoke frequently and eloquently on behalf of the freed people. Some believed rights were universal regardless of race, while others believed Black voters and politicians could aid their own causes.[95] Among them were radical newspaper publisher James Hunnicutt; John Hawxhurst, who represented Alexandria City and had served in the General Assembly of the Restored Government and been a member of the Convention of 1864;[96] and Edgar Allan, a former officer in the United States Army who settled in Prince Edward County and served in the convention from the same district that James W. D. Bland represented. Allan was so firm a Union man and Republican that in spite of his birth in Ireland, he was known until his death early in the twentieth century as Yankee Allan.[97] Nottoway County delegate William H. Robertson suggested that the convention send a committee to Washington "and respectfully ask the Congress of the United States to take some legislative action looking to the amelioration of the deplorable condition" of the freed people, but it was defeated.[98] Samuel D. Williamson, a white delegate who with teacher Samuel Kelso represented Campbell County and Lynchburg, proposed "That the right of suffrage should be as universal as liberty itself."[99]

President John C. Underwood relinquished the chair during discussions on the franchise on January 16, 1868, to deliver a long speech that praised abolitionists (including John Brown, who was hanged for his attack on Harpers Ferry in 1859), condemned the exploitive and wickedly luxurious lifestyles of Virginia enslavers, and openly supported the rights of freed people in ways that offended the old Virginia elites. Underwood not only favored full civil rights and suffrage for freed men, he also proposed to enfranchise "female citizens,"[100] but nobody made a formal motion to that effect.

Not all white delegates were so sympathetic to Black aspirations, and many were clearly hostile. On January 21, 1868, Underwood appointed a five-member committee, including Samuel Kelso, to invite General Ulysses S. Grant, who was then in Richmond, to visit the convention. Hugh H. Lee, a white delegate from western Virginia, declined "to go on a committee with a colored man." Bayne immediately moved "that the gentleman be relieved of that burden." (Pity that nobody recorded what tone of voice Bayne employed or how the other delegates reacted.) Underwood appointed a replacement for Lee.[101] The following day when the committee issued the invitation to Grant, the four white delegates reportedly left Kelso alone in the parlor of Grant's hotel when they met with the general. The reporter who covered the event for the Richmond *Daily Enquirer and Examiner*, a newspaper that was not always respectful or even fair toward freed people, nevertheless wrote that Kelso "dresses well, and is certainly as well worthy of respect as any negro that could have been appointed."[102]

The New Constitution

The new constitution resembled mid-nineteenth-century state constitutions elsewhere in the country more than it resembled any former Virginia constitutions.[103] Changes that the members made to the state's Bill of Rights in Article I signaled how different from the state's first four constitutions their new constitution was. They added a new section that condemned secession and the Confederacy, and another section disavowed the doctrine of state's rights that had underpinned white, proslavery Southern politics since the American Revolution. Those sections were definitely and perhaps intentionally insulting to supporters of the former Confederacy. Delegates rewrote and transferred the prohibitions on slavery from the body of the loyal Restored Government's Constitution of 1864 to a new section in the Bill of Rights, "That neither slavery nor involuntary servitude, except as lawful imprisonment may constitute such, shall exist within this State." The delegates added a very important new section, "That all citizens of the State are hereby declared to possess equal civil and political rights and public privileges."

Most or all of the delegates regarded the word *citizens* as encompassing adult males, only, as was the case with the white male members of Congress who proposed the Fifteenth Amendment to grant the vote to adult Black men.[104] The new constitution almost completely ignored the state's women, as had the state's first four constitutions and its sixth, the Constitution of 1902.

Early in the convention, however, Henry Moseley Bowden, a loyal white man who won election along with Thomas Bayne in Norfolk, proposed that the new constitution include protection for married women's right to own and control their own property,[105] and the Committee on Limitations and Guarantees recommended something similar.[106] Convention delegates declined to make or even seriously consider such an important modification in legal practices, gender relations, or family law that had been in place in Virginia from the beginning of English settlement.[107] Not until 1877 did the General Assembly adopt a married women's property act. Virginia was the last of the then-existing states to allow women equal rights with men in the ownership of real property.[108]

With one hand, the new constitution granted the vote to "Every male citizen of the United States, twenty-one years old, who shall have been a resident of this State twelve months, and of the county, city or town in which he shall offer to vote three months next preceding any election"; but with the other hand, it disfranchised all former federal, state, and local officeholders who "shall have engaged in insurrection or rebellion" against the United States "or given aid or comfort to the enemies thereof." The General Assembly, with a three-fifths vote, could reinstate these voting rights on a case-by-case basis. The constitution required that all men elected or appointed to public office had to swear allegiance to the Constitutions of the United States and of Virginia and to "recognize and accept the civil and political equality of all men before the laws"—to accept the fact and finality of the abolition of slavery and the citizenship of Black Virginians.[109]

Those proscriptions on voting and holding office by men who had in any way supported the Confederacy were capital victories for the most radical men in the convention. Delegates also required that voting be by ballot and for the first time in a Virginia constitution established a qualification for jury service linked to the suffrage and thereby made unrepentant Confederates ineligible to serve on a jury. Article III banned all active and most passive supporters of the Confederacy from the ballot box and public office unless they renounced their past allegiance to the Confederacy. As a result, Article III was the source of considerable controversy from the very beginning, which delayed ratification of the new constitution for more than a year.

The new constitution contained several provisions beneficial to freed people. The convention inserted a section to allow men to claim a homestead exemption of up to $2,000 in real property or implements required for their employment. Virginia was one of the last states to enact a homestead exemption by statute or place a homestead clause in its constitution.[110] The constitution defined the militia as consisting "of all able bodied male persons between the ages of eighteen and forty-five years" without reference to race, which for the first time allowed and required Black participation. The article also required the assembly to encourage the establishment of active and reserve militia units, though they were always racially segregated during the remainder of the nineteenth century.[111]

Among the important reforms that almost certainly came from Northern-born white members, the new constitution for the first time granted the governor authority to veto bills that the General Assembly passed, subject to a two-thirds vote to override in each house. Also, probably at the suggestion of Northern-born members, the constitution created new administrative and judicial structures for counties. The new constitution abolished the old county courts on which, since the seventeenth century, white, unelected justices of the peace had served, largely without legal training, to exercise executive and legislative powers in their counties and also sit en banc as the local court of first resort.[112] The article on local government created the form of county government that persisted in modified form to this present writing. It greatly extended local democracy in Virginia by creating numerous township and county officials, such as tax collector, road commissioner, and school supervisor, and allowing voters to elect them. Both white and Black men won election to those offices during the subsequent years. It is almost certain that the extension of local democracy allowed a large number of middle- and lower-class men of both races to serve in public office for the first time.[113]

The new constitution provided for payment of the very large public debt that the state had incurred before the Civil War to stimulate construction of toll roads, bridges, canals, and railroads, and made it almost impossible for the state to create a large new public debt for that or any other purpose. One of the most important articles in the new constitution, inspired in part by Samuel Kelso's proposal, required the General Assembly to establish a "uniform system of public free schools, and for its gradual, equal and full introduction into all the counties of the State." Funding the new public schools and paying the public debt created problems that in the 1870s led to the creation of a new biracial political party.

Road to Ratification

The convention adopted the new constitution by a vote of 51 to 26 on April 17, 1868.[114] President John C. Underwood was extremely pleased that the convention concluded its work and enabled him to sign the official document seven years to the day after the Convention of 1861 had voted in the very same room to secede from the United States.[115] Few things gave the high-tempered, openly partisan judge more pleasure than belittling or insulting secessionists and former Confederates. Underwood even displayed on the wall of his Alexandria law office one of the original signed copies of the Virginia Ordinance of Secession by way of keeping everyone's mind focused on the wickedness of slave owners and traitors.[116] Later, it became commonplace for people in Virginia (of both races) to refer to the proceedings as the Underwood Convention, and the document that it wrote as the Underwood Constitution. White men initially did so as a means of condemning the constitution. Underwood came to personify the radical Republicans who gave Virginia all that white supremacists despised about full citizenship and voting rights for Black men.

Members of the convention scheduled a ratification referendum for June 2, 1868, but military district commander General Schofield indefinitely postponed it. He had supervised the state government with a rather mild hand since March 1867 and believed in leniency toward former Confederates who took the required oaths and peaceably accepted the new realities of life in postwar, post-slavery Virginia.[117] Schofield believed that the disfranchisement provisions defeated that purpose and predicted that with so many educated white men disqualified and so few experienced Virginians available to serve in public office, government under the new constitution could not properly function. Under the pretense that the convention had spent all the money appropriated for it, he never directed the army to conduct the ratification referendum.[118]

The unintended consequences were numerous and significant: no ratified new state constitution as Congress required; no election of state or local government officers; no elected senators and delegates to meet in the General Assembly to elect judges and revise the laws to comport with the new constitution; no meetings of the assembly at all between April 1867 and October 1869; no assembly ratification of the Fourteenth and Fifteenth Amendments as Congress required; no quick end to military oversight of the state's government; and no state or congressional authority for Virginians to vote in the presidential election of 1868.

Those serious consequences eventually convinced some Conservative Party leaders to try to salvage what they could and reach a compromise. In January 1869, a nine-member committee of Conservatives traveled to Washington and negotiated an agreement with President-Elect Ulysses S. Grant and Republican leaders of Congress. They agreed to hold the required ratification referendum in the summer and at that time allow voters to vote separately on the sections that disfranchised and barred from public office supporters of the former Confederacy. The price Conservatives had to pay was to accept suffrage for Black men and full and equal political rights for all male Virginians.[119]

On July 6, 1869, eligible voters ratified the new constitution by an overwhelming vote of 210,585 to 9,136. On the same day, they rejected the clauses that disfranchised former officeholders and Confederates by a vote of 124,360 to 84,410, and that barred them from holding office by 124,715 to 83,458. Despite this victory for Conservatives, the number of negative votes indicated that a very large number of Virginians were still unwilling to allow supporters of the former Confederacy to be fully enfranchised citizens and have a role in the state's government.[120] On October 8, 1869, members of the Senate and House of Delegates, who had been elected on the same day as the ratification referendum, overwhelmingly ratified the Fourteenth (birthright citizenship and equal protection for all under the law) and Fifteenth (the right to vote shall not be denied on basis of race) Amendments as Congress required before it seated the state's senators and representatives in Congress.[121]

Among the few who voted against the amendments was Isaiah Lyons, a New Jersey native and former member of the USCT, who represented the district comprising Elizabeth City, Surry, Warwick, and York Counties in the Senate of Virginia. The lone Black legislator to vote against the amendments, he objected that since many white legislators could not take an oath required by Congress stating that they had been loyal to the United States before and after the Civil War, he consequently regarded the assembly as illegitimate and its actions as illegal. That action drew criticism from Northern and Republican newspapers but rare praise from the hostile *Richmond Whig and Advertiser*.[122]

On January 26, 1870, President Grant signed An Act to Admit the State of Virginia to Representation in the Congress of the United States. Because of the delayed ratification referendum on the new constitution, Virginia was the last of the states of the former Confederacy to have its senators and representatives take their seats in Congress. Moreover, the law prohibited any changes to the new constitution "to deprive any citizen or class of citizens of the United States of the right to vote who are entitled to vote by the Constitution"; to deny any person the right to hold office "on account of his race, color, or previous condition of servitude"; or "to deprive any citizen or class of citizens of the United States of the school rights and privileges secured by the constitution of said State."[123]

After ratification of the Constitution of 1869, Virginians lived in a completely transformed political system. Half a million Black Virginians were now citizens. Although women did not obtain all the rights of citizenship, all adult men—not merely white men—gained a constitutionally protected right to vote and hold public office. Legislators represented their constituents, not the vested interests of enslavers.[124] Popularly elected local governments replaced the old undemocratic county court system that tobacco planters and slave drivers had created in the seventeenth century.

Moreover, with ratification of the Thirteenth, Fourteenth, and Fifteenth Amendments, the federal government became empowered to guarantee equal citizenship rights and voting rights, anything in state constitutions and laws to the contrary notwithstanding. In short, the elite, white, male oligarchic government of Virginia formed in the early decades of the seventeenth century had been entirely swept away by 1870. In its place men of all races and classes (for the first time) had equal opportunities to participate in government, and the creation of a statewide system of free public schools promised (also for the first time) that in the future a broadly educated electorate would determine who served in that government.

In the years immediately following the end of the Civil War and the beginning of freedom for those who had been enslaved, Black Virginians quickly and aggressively sought to exercise their new right of suffrage. In the constitutional convention—the first election in which Black males could vote for candidates and to which they overwhelmingly elected Black representatives—Black delegates worked with white radicals to transform the state's governmental structures and responsibilities, and in the process transform the state's political culture profoundly.[125] The state constitution adopted in 1869 gave Virginians the chance to construct the "New Virginia" that Willis Hodges envisioned during the convention.[126]

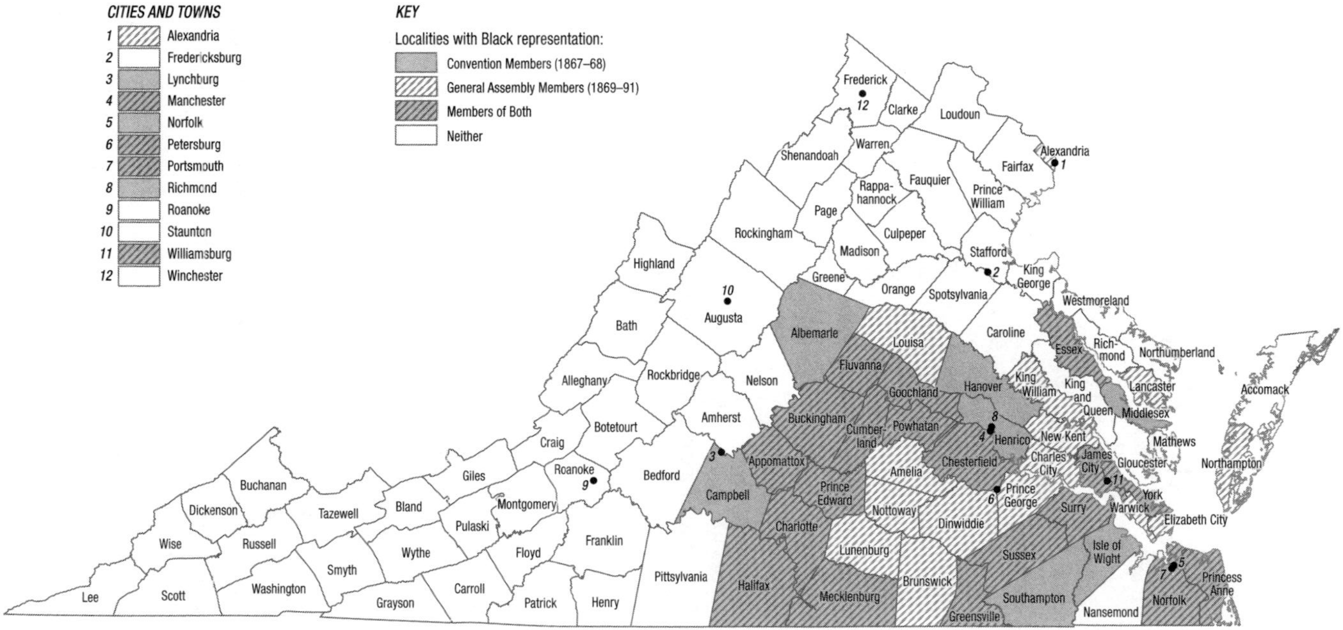

Localities represented by Black members of the Convention of 1867–1868, and in the House of Delegates and Senate of Virginia, between 1869 and 1891. (Nat Case)

5

"Send a Colored Man"

The Politics of Free Men

Mark R. DeMortie, a Nottoway County businessman and twice an unsuccessful candidate for the House of Representatives, told the editor of the weekly Black newspaper, the Petersburg *Lancet*, in 1884 that for a decade he had argued "that the Fourth district should send a colored man to Congress, and thereby break the color line."[1] Before that time, no Black Virginian had ever won election to a statewide office or to Congress, even in the majority-Black Fourth District, which comprised counties south of Richmond to the North Carolina border where the enslaved population had approached 70 percent.[2] DeMortie was of mixed-race Haitian ancestry and had been born into slavery in Norfolk. He was emancipated at age twenty-one and assisted enslaved people to escape to freedom in New England and eventually moved to Massachusetts himself. There, he participated in Republican Party politics and was briefly sutler of the famed 54th Massachusetts Infantry. Late in the 1860s, DeMortie returned to Virginia and operated a large plant in Burkeville to extract oil from sassafras roots for sale to manufacturers of medicines, soap, and a popular new beverage, sarsaparilla, or root beer. Prosperous and married to the daughter of a wealthy and famous Black caterer, he often spent summers with her family in Newport, Rhode Island. DeMortie never won election to public office, but for more than a decade he, just like many other men, attended county, district, and state political conventions, always in the interests of Black men.[3]

The years during which DeMortie was active in Virginia politics were unprecedented. Between December 1867 when two dozen Black men took their seats in the constitutional convention and December 1891 when the terms of the last state senator and delegates expired, 106 Black men

"Electioneering at the South," a drawing by Virginia illustrator William Ludwell Sheppard, appeared in *Harper's Weekly* on July 25, 1868, and depicts a Black candidate addressing a small audience that includes not only men who were eligible to vote but also women and children. For all of them, voting was key to securing their rights as American citizens. (Library of Virginia)

won election to the convention or one of the two houses of the General Assembly; more, including DeMortie, made unsuccessful campaigns for the convention, the assembly, or Congress; and scores, perhaps hundreds, of others served on city councils and in county offices. Unlike in some of the states of the former Confederacy, they never won a majority in the state assembly or in any city or county legislative body; but until the 1890s they voted in sufficient numbers to threaten the dominance of the Conservative Party and later of the Democratic Party. Indeed, Republican president Ulysses S. Grant received 50.5 percent of the vote in Virginia when he ran for reelection in 1872, and Republican presidential candidates very nearly carried the state in 1884 and 1888. Republican candidates for governor nearly always received more than 40 percent of the vote. The votes of Black Virginians formed a large proportion of the impressive totals and enabled Black voters to influence public policy. White Virginians, however, feared that Black voters would shift the balance of political power in the state.[4]

Shifting Political Landscape

On July 6, 1869, when voters ratified the new state constitution, they also elected members of both houses of the General Assembly and a new governor, lieutenant governor, and attorney general. Radical Republicans nominated Henry Horatio Wells for governor, Joseph D. Harris for lieutenant governor, and Thomas R. Bowdon for attorney general. Wells had been provisional governor by military appointment since the spring of 1868, and Bowden was the Republican incumbent who had remained loyal to the United States during the Civil War. The nomination of Harris was an extraordinary event, the first nomination of a Black man for statewide office in Virginia. Harris had been born free in North Carolina, grew up in Ohio, traveled to the Caribbean, and become a medical doctor. Late in the Civil War he was stationed at the United States Army hospital in Portsmouth. Shortly before the state Republican Party convention nominated him for lieutenant governor, Harris had married a Northern white woman.

Harris's nomination contributed to the Republicans' defeat. The backlash against his candidacy, together with the radical platform of the Republican Party, produced an alliance of white Conservatives and moderate Republicans who supported an alternative ticket that included a native of New York, Gilbert Carlton Walker, as candidate for governor and loyal white Virginians for the other two offices. Not surprisingly, the Conservative-Republican coalition won the election. Harris received the lowest number of votes among the six statewide candidates, but even then he garnered about 45 percent of the vote and probably received the votes of some radical white Republicans. The significant number of votes for Harris provided opponents of change with a frightening example of the potential strength of allied white and Black voters; had all the white Republican voters supported the radical Republican ticket, all three candidates, including Harris, might have won election.[5]

The political landscape of Virginia had changed after the Constitutional Convention of 1867–68. The white radical Republicans who had cooperated with Black members of the convention had largely retired from the field after the ratification referendum (which removed the disfranchisement of former Confederates from the new constitution) and the defeat of the radical Republican candidates for statewide office at the same time. Many of the radical white Republicans most likely believed that with the new democratic state constitution, they had achieved their principal objectives and did not choose to pursue additional reform measures that Black voters desired.[6]

The Republican Party of Virginia had initially attracted most Black voters, most or all native Virginians who had remained loyal to the United States during the Civil War, and a substantial portion of immigrants and of Virginians who adapted themselves to the new realities of postwar, post-slavery Virginia. Without the white radicals, Black voters had fewer allies and faced a well-organized new opposition. The Conservative Party, which was founded in December 1867, was almost exclusively the party of native white men. Most Conservatives probably voted for Democratic candidates for president, but Virginia had no formally organized Democratic Party. Within the context of state politics, they identified themselves as Conservatives until 1883, when the leadership of the Conservative Party reorganized it as the Democratic Party, led by white supremacists who subsequently controlled politics in Virginia for decades.

Black Mobilization

While the political sands were shifting in postwar Virginia, more than 1,200 working men gathered in April 1870 to form a laboring men's union to serve their interests in the new free market economy. They organized a Richmond chapter of the new but short-lived Colored National Labor Union. Most of the men who attended the gathering were apparently affiliated with one of the numerous labor organizations that men who worked in tobacco warehouses or factories, as stevedores, carpenters, shoemakers, bakers, coopers, teamsters, and the like had formed after the end of slavery. Some of the men who attended were fairly successful in their fields, such as building contractor John Adams, who had been free before the war and by 1870 owned his own house and lot and about twenty other pieces of property and was worth perhaps as much as $4,000. His son, John Henry Adams, won election to the Richmond City Council not long afterward.[7]

The 1,200 men elected John Oliver president of the meeting. He had been born free in Boston and moved to Virginia after the war. According to the report of the event in the *New Era*, a weekly Black newspaper published in Washington, DC, Oliver accepted the office with "a graceful bow" and a speech that captured the political moment almost perfectly. "He felt honored" to be elected president of the meeting of laborers, the report of his address began, because "he was himself a laborer, being a carpenter. If there was anything he could do, it was to build a house." Observing that the meeting purposely excluded talk of politics, he continued that "the colored people have had political meetings since the war and nothing good had been achieved. Let us now, said he, learn how to make home comfortable by associating ourselves upon a firmer basis than politics." Instead, such meetings should focus on "devising the best means practicable for the protection of labor."[8] That is to say, Black working men—he did not say men and women, but he probably could have—were on their own.

Black Virginians, having won the precious right to vote with the ratification of the constitution in 1869 and in the following year with ratification of the Fifteenth Amendment, continued to vote and remained active in politics, though without as many influential allies. Almost all of the successful candidates for the convention and assembly during the nineteenth century won election in districts with a white minority or a very small white majority. Some delegates and senators represented districts that included more than one county, but in each at least one county had a Black majority. The few exceptions included Willis A. Hodges, who represented Princess Anne County in the convention, his brother, Charles E. Hodges, who was elected to the House of Delegates from the district of Norfolk County and Portsmouth in 1869, and their nephew, John Quincy Hodges, who was elected to the House from Princess Anne County on the same day. The city and two counties, together with the city of Norfolk, in the southeastern corner of Virginia, had white majorities, but among those majorities were numerous white men who had remained loyal to the United States during the Civil War, some of whom joined the radical Republicans.[9]

Election of 1869

The 1869 election campaign, as had the 1867 election of convention delegates, disclosed differences among the state's Black political leaders, who sometimes opposed one another on election day because of differences of opinion, as members of rival groups within their party, or because of competing personal ambitions. The most radical reformers, eager to replace the state's old elite, white, male political culture with a more inclusive and representative politics, differed with one another about how much reform was possible, how hard to push for it, or how much change was a necessary minimum. Others believed that cooperation with white men, who formed a majority, might yield better results without so much strife or creation of so much stiff opposition from unsympathetic white men. In some communities those political differences produced long-term divisions within the ranks of Black voters.

On the same day as the state constitution ratification referendum and the election of a new governor, voters elected 24 Black men to the 138-member House of Delegates and 6 to the 43-member Senate of Virginia.[10] Of these 30 elected men, 9 had served in the convention a year and a half earlier. While 30 was the largest number of Black members ever to serve in the General Assembly at any one time, white members of the Conservative Party won majorities in both houses in 1869 and in every assembly until 1879. Even at their most numerous, Black men were always in the minority, nearly always received low-ranking seats on comparatively inconsequential committees, and always needed white allies to pass legislation.

A British observer described the scenes in both houses of the General Assembly during a short special session at the end of October 1870 when some of the thirty Black men were present. When he visited the Senate, he caught sight of "two coloured Senators among the number, quite black, but senatorial enough, and like men who in Africa would probably have been chiefs. In the Lower House the coloured delegates mingled freely with the other members, but in the Senate these two sat in a corner by themselves. Yet they seemed to take a cordial interest in the proceedings, and manifested all sympathy with the Senators who addressed the House." The observer favorably compared the decorum in the Senate with that in the British House of Lords. Unfortunately, he did not name the two senators or any of the delegates who were present.[11]

One of the two senators could have been James W. D. Bland, the former member of the constitutional convention. He won election in 1869 from the district of Prince Edward and Charlotte Counties, and he was one of the few members appointed to a genuinely important committee, the Committee for Courts of Justice. Bland introduced the bill to incorporate Hampton Normal and Agricultural Institute to enable it to receive federal land-grant money. Described as "thoughtful and sagacious," as well as "being active yet unobstrusive, ambitious yet modest, an ardent champion of the oppressed and persecuted," he was popular with his colleagues and the press.[12]

His cooperative attitude toward Conservative Party members may have led him in the spring of 1870 to switch or to contemplate switching from the Republican to the Conservative Party. On April 27, Bland was in attendance when a very large crowd assembled in the courtroom in the Capitol to hear the judges of the Supreme Court of Appeals issue their opinions in a case concerning who was legally mayor of Richmond. Under the weight of the crowd, the floor of the courtroom crashed into the chamber of the House of Delegates below, which killed Bland and about sixty other people and wounded even more. The Senate passed a memorial resolution in his favor, and the assembly appropriated money to pay for his funeral. More than two hundred people, including white legislators, attended his funeral and burial in Farmville.[13]

During legislative sessions, Black assembly members often shared lodgings, as did Delegates Henry Cox, George Fayerman, Benjamin F. Jones, and George Seaton, who boarded together during the 1870 session. The Union Hotel and the Maison Dorée, a three-story brick hotel with ten rooms, were among half a dozen hotels and rooming houses operated by Black managers that served Black visitors to the city.[14] Republicans often held political meetings in them. Laws did not then require racial segregation in public accommodations, but hotels and rooming

"Legislature of Virginia, Session 1871 and '72," contains formal portraits of many of the members of the House of Delegates who were elected in November 1871. Thirteen African American portraits are segregated together on the bottom row. In most instances, these are the only known photographs of Black legislators in nineteenth-century Virginia. Soon thereafter, white General Assembly officials ceased including photographs of Black men on these collections of legislators. (Special Collections, Library of Virginia)

houses probably practiced segregation, and their customers probably expected it. When legislators boarded together, they had ample opportunities when they were not at work in the Capitol to confer, plan strategy, or reinforce one another's courage. Late in 1876, Guy Powell and several other members of the House of Delegates moved out of the Eagle Hotel, the most substantial available to Black customers at that time, and sought lodgings in private residences. The Black proprietor protested, boasting in a newspaper advertisement that his accommodations were as fine as any available to white customers at other city hotels. Believing that their integrity had been impugned, the delegates responded with their own public letter describing the crowded conditions, lack of gas and water amenities, and being forced to eat in a separate temporary structure with no heat.[15]

In 1871, officials of the House of Delegates commissioned formal photographs of the members and framed them together. The composite of portraits of members of the House of Delegates has photographs of thirteen Black delegates segregated from the white delegates on a separate but otherwise equal bottom row. Within a few years, though, photographs of Black delegates had been excluded entirely, leaving the impression that the General Assembly was again, as it had been since 1619, all white.

Who Were These Black Legislators?

Ninety-two Black men served in either the House of Delegates or the Senate of Virginia in the three decades following the end of the Civil War and slavery. Fifteen sat in both legislative bodies, and Frank Moss, of Buckingham County, served in both houses of the General Assembly and in the state constitutional convention. Nineteen members of the House of Delegates won reelection to a second term, and one state senator, Daniel Norton, served two consecutive terms. Caesar Perkins served two nonconsecutive terms in the House, with a remarkable sixteen years separating his service representing Buckingham County (1869–71) and Buckingham and Cumberland Counties (1887–88). Ross Hamilton, of Mecklenburg County, impressively won election to seven consecutive terms (1870–83), while several other delegates also served in multiple consecutive terms in the House.

Almost two-thirds of these assemblymen were born into slavery, while one-third identified as mixed-race, including several with Pamunkey Indian ancestry. At least five legislators escaped from slavery and returned to Virginia after the war. Several were freed or purchased their freedom

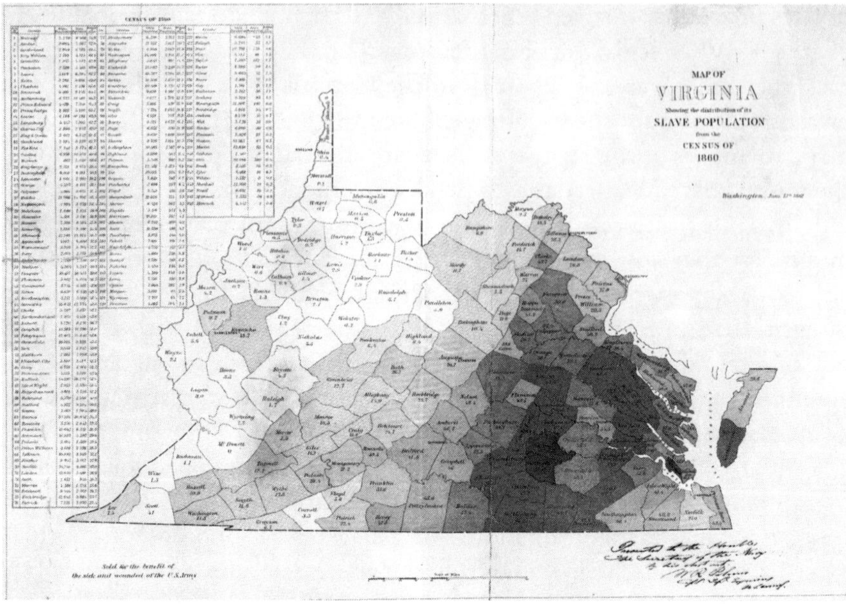

"Map of Virginia Showing the Distribution of Slavery Population from the Census of 1860," was published in 1861. This map includes the northwestern region of Virginia that became the separate state of West Virginia in 1863. The darkest areas shown on the map had the largest percentage of enslaved people. From the election of 1867 through that of 1889, voters in those counties, which had the largest percentages of Black residents, elected nearly all of the state's nineteenth-century Black legislators and convention delegates. (Special Collections, Library of Virginia)

prior to the Civil War. Among those who achieved their freedom or were born free, seven served in the United States Colored Troops. At least eight legislators were born outside Virginia, including several from Northern states and George Fayerman, who may have been from Jamaica or Haiti. Three of these non-native Virginians joined the USCT. At least ten Black assemblymen are known to have had white fathers, with some having a white father who was also identified as their owner. The value of literacy is highlighted by the fact that 94 percent of the Black legislators were literate at a time when more than a third of Virginians older than age ten were unable to read.[16]

Geographically, all the legislators came from areas of Virginia east of the Blue Ridge Mountains to the Eastern Shore at the Atlantic Ocean. Southside Virginia, the region south of the James and Appomattox Rivers to the North Carolina border, was especially well-represented. This is perhaps not surprising, considering that Petersburg had the largest free

Black population before the war, and Amelia, Brunswick, Dinwiddie, Halifax, Mecklenburg, and Nottoway Counties had substantial populations of enslaved people. During the period, voters in each of those counties elected two or three Black legislators.

Some Black members of the General Assembly could boast about family political connections. One prominent family is the Nortons—brothers Frederick, Daniel, and Robert—who represented the city of Williamsburg and surrounding counties. Another prominent family was the Hodgeses. Charles E. Hodges and his nephew John Quincy Hodges represented Norfolk County and Princess Anne County, respectively, in the House of Delegates during the same term. Phillip S. Bolling represented Buckingham and Cumberland Counties in the House of Delegates from 1883 to 1885 and was succeeded by his father Samuel P. Bolling for the 1885–87 term. (Because their names were similar and some documents confused P. S. Bolling with his father S. P. Bolling, the younger Bolling's election as a delegate has not been included in works on nineteenth century Black political life.) Joseph P. Evans represented Petersburg in the House of Delegates (1871–73) and the district of Petersburg, and Prince George and Surry Counties in the Senate of Virginia (1874–75). His son William W. Evans represented Petersburg in the House of Delegates during the 1887–88 term.

These members of the General Assembly were quite diverse in their occupations, from farmers and laborers to grocers and merchants. The majority came from the skilled trades such as barbers, carpenters, and blacksmiths, and the professional class, including ministers, attorneys, and teachers. Almost three-quarters could be confirmed as working at more than one occupation, with the occupational combinations being as varied as the men themselves.

Frank Moss obtained a license to sell alcohol in Buckingham County in 1873 and a license to perform marriages in 1878. Armistead Green worked in a tobacco factory about 1870, and by the middle of the decade, Petersburg city directories listed him as a grocer. In the 1880s, after his time in the House of Delegates, he ventured with partners into the mortuary business and a brick manufacturing company. He may have even been a member of the Petersburg police corps. William Faulcon, who represented Surry and Prince George Counties for one term in the House of Delegates, operated a blacksmith shop near Surry Court House. In 1879 he set about farming and began acquiring land in Surry County in increments: fifty acres of land one mile south of the town in May, then another ten acres in 1881, and a nearby thirty acres in 1884. His personal property by 1890 included a clock, a sewing machine, and $20 worth of musical instruments.[17]

Some legislators were entrepreneurs. Greensville and Sussex Counties delegate Henry D. Smith identified himself as a carpenter and farmer in the 1870 census. Two years later he received a license to sell alcohol at his Greensville storehouse. In the mid-1870s he purchased four tracts of land totaling almost a thousand acres, on which he raised corn and cotton, and later operated a sawmill and a cotton gin. By the 1890s he produced brandy and whiskey at his distillery, operated a large sawmill, and was described as the wealthiest Black person in the county. Robert M. Smith worked as a wheelwright and blacksmith for many years in Hampton, where he owned property, and he formed a partnership in 1880 with a brother-in-law to operate a grocery store. In nearby Yorktown, Robert Gilbert Griffin owned or co-owned several lots beginning in the 1870s and with a partner operated a gristmill.[18]

Griffin's work with Daniel and Robert Norton in helping the Republican cause in Yorktown earned him appointment as the town's postmaster effective May 1880. Other legislators also obtained federal patronage jobs that included working for the post office, as keepers of lighthouses, or in the customhouses. Those jobs were often welcome rewards for loyal party work, and the salaries enabled them to purchase property. Elizabeth City County's Alexander Lee could boast of a job at the customhouse in Old Point Comfort by 1871. After his service in the House of Delegates at decade's end, he obtained a federal patronage appointment as a keeper of the lighthouse at Thimble Shoal, though he lost the position with a new Democratic administration in 1885. James Richard Jones served as postmaster in the town of Boydton, in Mecklenburg County, from August 1880 to January 1885.[19]

Jones and Robert Griffin were among the 90 percent of legislators who owned real estate property and the 90 percent who owned some kind of taxable personal property. Cumberland County tax rolls for 1861 indicated that John Robinson, a future member of the constitutional convention and state senate, owned two parcels of land totaling twenty-four acres worth $705, and that he also owned one enslaved person. New Kent County delegate William Henry Brisby may have inherited land from his father in the county in the 1850s. Brisby, whose mother was of Pamunkey Indian origins, established himself in the free Black community. Working on the construction of the Richmond and York River Railroad, he purchased a set of blacksmith's tools and with a partner established a blacksmith shop at Talleysville in 1859. The following year Brisby bought his partner's tools, and in January 1860 purchased the lot where his shop was located.[20]

Most landholding was modest, but some Black legislators owned substantial amounts of property. Norfolk County delegate Richard Gault Leslie Paige was born into slavery but escaped to Boston. During his ten years there he worked in a metalworking shop and accumulated land and personal property worth more than $4,000. After returning to Virginia he acquired land, some on his own and some in partnership with others, including in 1880 the local burial ground for Black residents (later Mount Olive Cemetery). Paige also began reading law in Boston, and in 1880 qualified to practice, making him perhaps the first Black attorney in Norfolk and among the earliest in the state. At the time of his death in 1904, he owned at least ten properties and five buildings in the town of Berkley and Norfolk County valued at more than $6,500. Such was Paige's wealth that his widow Lillie Paige erected a twelve-foot-tall, engraved obelisk over his grave.[21]

New opportunities after the end of slavery enabled Black men and women to buy, sell, and mortgage their property to pay debts, go into business, or to buy land or expand their holdings. In 1870 formerly enslaved Ellis Wilson, who may have constructed coffins for the Freedmen's Bureau, purchased more than eighty acres of land for $200 in Dinwiddie County. Representing the county in the House of Delegates at this time, he became a successful farmer and did not engage in state politics after his term concluded the following year. In 1904 he paid taxes on five tracts of Dinwiddie land that numbered more than 550 acres and was worth more than $1,400. Among his other sources of income from the property was the occasional sale of timber.[22]

Shortly after the Civil War ended, Robert G. W. Jones and another man borrowed $900 to purchase five hundred acres in Charles City County, although the property was sold later to pay off their debt. While Jones was a member of the General Assembly in the summer of 1870, he paid $179 to purchase a seventy-acre tract of land and as a trustee of the Union Baptist Church, which had been formed in Charles City during the Civil War, he contributed funds to help purchase land for a burying ground. Financial challenges were not uncommon, however. Jones and his wife pledged their farm as security for the purchase of shares in the Lincoln National Building and Loan Association in 1893, but within the decade they had failed to keep up their monthly payments.[23]

Jones was among the 34 percent of General Assembly members who were known to have joined civic groups, religious organizations, political associations, or fraternal orders, often in leadership roles. Many others for whom no documentation exists probably did, too. Black Virginians established their own associations to encourage home ownership. In Norfolk, R. G. L. Paige cofounded the Virginia Building and Savings Association, while master carpenter and Alexandria delegate George Lewis Seaton advocated organizing the Colored Co-Operative Building Association. In Prince Edward County, the formerly enslaved Tazewell Branch used his literacy and skill as a shoemaker to prosper soon after emancipation. He owned property in Farmville and served on its town council and was among the trustees to purchase land by 1869 for what became Beulah African Methodist Episcopal Church.[24]

Seeking to promote further economic prospects for Blacks, in 1886 Dinwiddie County's A. W. Harris and Petersburg's William H. Jordan organized the Colored Agricultural and Industrial Association of Virginia to establish an annual fair to exhibit farm and industrial products from Black Virginians. Harris was its first president, and Jordan served on the first board of directors and as general manager, while other legislators, including William Faulcon, of Surry County, and Amos Andre Dodson, of Mecklenburg County, helped obtain its incorporation from the General Assembly and were among the first trustees.[25]

Some legislators—who were also ministers—sought to provide assistance for Black Virginians through religious and relief organizations. Shed Dungee, a delegate representing Buckingham and Cumberland Counties, served as a trustee of the Baptist Aid Society in Buckingham County during the 1870s. A licensed preacher, he helped establish the Slate River Colored Baptist Association in 1877. Charles E. Hodges served as an elder in the Roanoke Missionary Baptist Association, which included churches in northeastern North Carolina and in southeastern Virginia, and was a founder of a relief society for the widows and orphans of the association's ministers. Louisa County's Fountain Perkins sat on special committees of the Colored Shiloh Baptist Association, while Buckingham County's Caesar Perkins served as treasurer of the Slate River Baptist Association. John Montgomery Dawson established himself as a leader in the Norfolk Virginia Union Baptist Association. During his tenure on the executive board and serving as moderator during the 1870s, the association established educational and foreign mission boards to organize the collection of funds.[26]

The experience of Peter George Morgan, who had purchased his freedom and that of his family with money he made as an enslaved shoemaker, may have led him to join men of both races in establishing a dual board for the Petersburg Relief Association in 1868. Assistance to Black residents continued to lag behind that for white people, causing Morgan and other Black leaders to form a separate Impartial Relief Association, of which Morgan was elected president in 1869.[27]

Legislative Priorities for Black Delegates

Bills that members of the General Assembly introduced beginning in 1869 reveal some of the obstacles that freed people encountered after the abolition of slavery as well as some of their common aspirations. This is especially true with respect to establishing fraternal orders, to which many legislators belonged because they provided important services to the community. James P. Goodwyn, of Petersburg, introduced a bill that passed both houses and became a law in 1875 to incorporate the Masonic Temple Association of the City of Petersburg so that the city's Freemasons could raise money to erect a "suitable building" for their use.[28] During the 1876–77 session, Robert Marcus Smith, of Hampton, introduced the bill that passed to incorporate the Jonathan Lodge, No. 1434, of the Grand United Order of Odd Fellows, a fraternal mutual service organization that provided relief and burial benefits for poor people. He later served as grand treasurer of the Grand United Order of Odd Fellows in America during the mid-1890s and early 1900s.[29] In the 1883–84 session, Robert Gilbert Griffin, of Yorktown, introduced a bill that chartered the Band of Brethren Lodge, Number One Thousand Nine Hundred and Fifty, Grand United Order of Odd Fellows, and was a member of the first board of directors.[30]

John H. Robinson, of Elizabeth City County, introduced bills that passed to incorporate the Newport News Cemetery Company (later Greenlawn Memorial Park)[31] and to hold a referendum in Warwick County about moving the county courthouse to Newport News.[32] He introduced bills that did not pass to prohibit certain oystering tongs for use in the James River, to authorize construction of a bridge over the northwest branch of the Hampton River, and for the financial relief of three former public school teachers in Elizabeth City County.[33]

Like Robinson's three unsuccessful bills, most of the legislators' proposals failed to win enough votes from white majorities in either house of the General Assembly to pass. In fact, most died in committee and never even came to a vote on the floor. Some proposals were of small genuine consequence but of large symbolic importance, such as the resolution that John B. Miller Jr., of Goochland County, introduced early in the

1869–70 session to have the House of Delegates invite Black ministers to open sessions with prayers;[34] James P. Goodwyn and William Gilliam, of Prince George County, introduced similar resolutions in subsequent sessions.[35] Other proposals had large consequences for individual people but were otherwise of limited importance, like the proposal that Alexander Owen, of Halifax County, made in 1870, "That Alice Lucado and Josephine Johnson, who have been keeping apple-stands for some time past in the vestibule of the capitol for Mr. Hagerty, be permitted to keep an apple-stand of their own at said place."[36] Interestingly, Charlotte County delegate William H. Ragsdale inquired about the propriety of giving to Fourth Colored Baptist Church in Richmond several benches removed from Sycamore Church, where the House of Delegates had temporarily met following the April collapse of the upstairs courtroom into the hall of the House, which killed more than sixty people.[37]

Other bills were related to specific needs of constituents, especially in areas of labor and transportation. William Gilliam proposed to allow Prince George residents to trap small animals to supplement their diets, as well as a successful motion to authorize construction of a pier for a local company.[38] William D. Evans introduced several bills to improve roads in Prince Edward County during his two terms late in the 1870s.[39] William H. Patterson, who represented New Kent and Charles City Counties, introduced a bill to prohibit cutting trees or other actions that would "obstruct the free passage of boats, canoes or other floating vessels, or fish" in the lower reaches of Sycamore Creek in New Kent.[40] In separate legislative sessions, Halifax County delegates John Freeman and Matt Clark each proposed a bill to authorize county residents to vote on establishing a free bridge at South Boston either by purchasing the existing toll bridge there or erecting a new bridge.[41]

Black legislators opposed efforts by white men to impose racial segregation in all areas of public life. John B. Miller Jr., of Goochland County, introduced an unsuccessful proposal to prohibit conductors on railroads from discriminating against passengers on the basis of color.[42] Armistead Green, of Petersburg, introduced a bill to ensure that no racial discrimination would exist when the state furnished convict labor for extending the Danville and New River railroad.[43] In February 1870 the Committee on Asylums and Prisons introduced a bill to establish a mental hospital near Richmond, after which a white delegate insisted that it be designated for Black patients. Some of the radical delegates, including Peter G. Morgan, of Petersburg, protested what he called "class legislation" to keep the races separated. Nevertheless, the bill designating Central Lunatic

Asylum for the "treatment of colored persons of unsound mind" passed in June, making Virginia the first state to establish a public mental hospital for Black patients. The white editor of the *Norfolk Virginian* reflected the fears of many white Virginians when he complained about the "aggressive temper" of Black and Radical politicians who insisted on "equality, not the 'equality before the law' . . . but that social equality which demands association in schools, and asylums, in hotels, cars and places of public amusement."[44]

Reflecting the precarious existence Black Virginians faced in a post-slavery world, Rufus Sibb Jones, who represented Elizabeth City and Warwick Counties, presented a resolution that called for the Committee for Courts of Justice "to inquire into the expediency of reporting a bill defining the authority of sheriffs and constables in making arrests, and preventing said officers from striking, shooting or abusing persons whom they arrest, except in self-defence."[45] A native of Gettysburg, Pennsylvania, and formerly a member of the USCT, Jones proposed another bill to amend sections of the code adopted in 1860 that related to "offences against morality and decency" that prohibited interracial marriage, provided different penalties for free and enslaved persons who committed adultery, and targeted issues of prostitution, lewd conduct, grave robbing, and desecration of churches. Neither of Jones's bills, the second of which he probably intended to curb white male exploitation of Black women, passed.[46]

Many of the bills sought to relieve freed people of some of the systemic obstacles that delegates and their constituents faced, such as that of Alexander G. Lee in 1878 to require the judge of Elizabeth City County to select jurors "without regard to race or color."[47] Similarly, Petersburg's Joseph P. Evans and Nottoway County's Archer Scott introduced measures to require that juries consist of equal numbers of white and Black members.[48] Early in 1880, R. G. L. Paige made a passionate speech that the *New York Herald* printed in support of a resolution he introduced in the House of Delegates to request the governor to offer a reward for the capture and punishment of men who lynched Black men in Amherst and Fauquier Counties. The white majority killed Paige's resolution.[49]

Black legislators also introduced measures to remove economic obstacles. John B. Miller Jr. introduced a proposal to establish a maximum ten-hour day for farm laborers with a minimum wage of $1.00 a day and $0.25 per hour for every extra hour. It did not pass.[50] Neverson Lewis, of Powhatan County, tried but failed to repeal an 1875 law that taxed owners of all dogs in that county to create a fund to compensate owners of sheep that roaming dogs killed, almost certainly a law designed to protect the sheep of white people from the dogs of Black people.[51] Reflecting emerging issues of property ownership, Henry C. Hill supported an unsuccessful bill to compensate owners of land for damages done by residents of adjacent property.[52] In successive legislative terms in the mid-1870s, Robert H. Whittaker proposed a bill to permit a referendum in some Brunswick County districts on whether to enforce the state's fence law, and another bill to repeal the fence law in several county districts. Neither bill passed.[53]

William P. Lucas, a teacher in Louisa County, introduced a bill in 1875 that did not pass to reduce the mandatory five- to ten-year prison sentences for people convicted of stealing property worth more than $5 and that also imposed a prison sentence of three to eighteen years for any person convicted of stealing a horse, mule, or jackass.[54] During the next session of assembly, Lucas made a motion to establish "a normal school, for the instruction of colored teachers, to be under state control,"[55] but the assembly did not do so until 1882.

Senator Cephas Davis, who represented Mecklenburg and Charlotte Counties, proposed to establish a college in Chase City.[56] Both William Gilliam early in the 1870s and Robert Marcus Smith, of Hampton, in 1876 unsuccessfully tried to persuade the General Assembly to appropriate money for Hampton Normal and Agricultural Institute.[57] And Henry Clay Harris, who may have attended Oberlin College in Ohio during the war, introduced a bill that did not pass to construct new buildings at Hampton. Perhaps not surprisingly, a bill that he introduced to pay for repairs to the greenhouse at the governor's mansion in Richmond did pass.[58]

Before 1882 when the General Assembly finally took positive action, McDowell Delaney, of Amelia County, called on the Committee for Courts of Justice to submit a bill repealing the use of the whipping post for punishment of crimes, a painful and humiliating relic of slavery.[59] Halifax's Asa Coleman was one of many Black legislators to support abolishing the whipping post, and he supported an unsuccessful attempt to end the practice of prison chain gangs being hired out to private employers or work on public projects.[60] John Walter Boyd Matthews, of Petersburg, proposed a similar bill in 1872 to abolish chain gangs, to which Black prisoners were most often sentenced. He also introduced a resolution to inquire what legislation was needed to enforce the new provision of Article I Section 20 of the Constitution of 1869, "That all citizens of the State are hereby declared to possess equal civil and political rights and public privileges."[61] George Fayerman, also of Petersburg, made a proposal about the same time to protect the equal rights of all citizens,[62] and Gilliam introduced a bill to protect the rights of voters.[63] Charlotte County's

Dabney N. Smith unsuccessfully introduced a motion to abolish petty larceny conviction as a disqualification from voting.[64]

Ballard Trent Edwards, a freeborn man and property owner who lived in the town of Manchester across the James River from Richmond, introduced many bills indicating his concern about the vulnerabilities of and difficulties that freed people encountered in the first years after emancipation. The bills he introduced represented a catalog of obstacles that they faced. In the 1869–70 session of the assembly, Edwards proposed to regulate the practice of paying wages in company scrip rather than in cash, so that working people did not have to spend their incomes where their employers required; to limit the length of the workday for laborers on public projects so that they would have time to attend school; to require that farmers enclose their lands with good fences; to forbid railroads, steamboat companies, and other common carriers from adopting rules "which shall have a tendency to make a difference in travel on account of race or color"; to reduce the toll on the existing bridge between Manchester and Richmond or to construct a free pedestrian bridge to enable residents of Manchester to go to work in Richmond without having to pay any toll at all; to pay salaries to magistrates; and to repeal the Vagrancy Act, which forced into employment any person who appeared to be unemployed or homeless. During the session that met in the winter of 1870–71, Edwards suggested that a bill be drafted to require that railroads fence their lines because railroad companies did not compensate people when trains killed their livestock. None of Edwards's numerous proposals passed.[65]

In contrast to Edwards, Henry Turpin introduced few bills during his single term representing Goochland County. In 1872 he offered one of several amendments to revise a law that provided artificial legs to men who lost limbs during the Civil War. His amendment stated, "Colored men who lost legs as soldiers or employees in the late war shall be entitled to the benefits of this act." The General Assembly enacted the bill with Turpin's amendment, which permitted wounded veterans of the United States Colored Troops and also free and enslaved men who had been wounded after being impressed to work on Confederate defenses to receive the state benefit originally intended for white Confederate veterans.[66]

Black Legislators Silenced by History

Peter Jacob Carter had one of the most successful political careers of any member of the General Assembly but has largely been forgotten to history. He grew up enslaved in Northampton County, on the Eastern Shore, served in the United States Colored Troops during the Civil War, attended the new Hampton Normal and Agricultural Institute for two years, and in 1871 won election to the first of four consecutive two-year terms in the House of Delegates. For a time, Carter gained statewide fame. He was a vice president of the Republican Party state convention in July 1873 and presided as temporary chair at the opening session of the state convention in April 1876. Carter remained involved in politics after he lost a race for the Senate of Virginia in 1879 and was no longer a member of the assembly. An excellent public speaker, he campaigned both before and after he left office for other Republican candidates throughout the large First Congressional District that included counties on both shores of Chesapeake Bay. When the board of the new Virginia Normal and Collegiate Institute met in 1883, the members elected him the first rector. Carter also owned a farm and after his service in the assembly was keeper of the lighthouse at Cherrystone Inlet, a federal patronage appointment.[67]

Ross Hamilton, who had been born into slavery in Mecklenburg County on the North Carolina border, had the longest career as a legislator. Well-known in his time, his achievements have since nearly been forgotten. He won election to the House of Delegates to complete the two-year term of former convention member John Watson, who died in December 1869, and won full terms in every election from 1871 through 1881. Hamilton lost his seat to Republican Amos Andre Dodson in 1883, failed to regain it in 1885 when a rival and former friend, James Richard "Dick" Jones, won the nomination, but won again in 1889, although he was unseated in an election challenge. Throughout the two decades, Mecklenburg County always had at least one Black delegate. When Hamilton was not in the assembly, he held minor posts in the federal bureaucracy in the county or in Washington, DC. A major player in the turbulent politics of the county, he made friends and enemies throughout his career. Hamilton's political life was unusually long, but his personal experiences and difficulty making a living were more nearly typical of the other men who sought or won election to public office. Hamilton owned a few small pieces of property, but he struggled financially all his life. He also had political rivals within the Republican Party, both white and Black, as did some other legislators.[68]

Most men who served in the General Assembly held office for one or two terms and had less influence on public affairs than did Carter and Hamilton. Miles Connor, for example, worked as a house servant during slavery but was literate and was an elected member of the Norfolk County board of supervisors in 1875 when, on the fourth ballot, radical members of the Republican Party county convention nominated him for the House of Delegates. He won election and was appointed to a low-ranking seat on the Committee on Militia and Police. Connor rarely spoke during his two-year term and did not introduce any bills. He did not seek reelection in 1877, when Republicans did not even nominate a candidate for the General Assembly from his district. In October 1882, Connor paid $900 for fifty acres of land and four years later helped establish the Churchland Grove Baptist Church. He was a trustee of the church, helped acquire the land on which to build a sanctuary, and served as a minister to the congregation. In the spring of 1887 he was elected to the first of two two-year terms as a justice of the peace. After Connor died in 1893, his name seldom ever appeared in the local history literature that white men wrote.[69]

Johnson Collins was another legislator whose name was almost lost to history. He was probably born into slavery and in the 1870s lived with his wife and sons and did farm labor in Brunswick County. He was elected to the House of Delegates in 1879 and served one term. While a member of the assembly, he proudly identified himself to the census enumerator in 1880 as a legislator, as did several other members that year. Collins never owned any land and did not run for reelection in 1881. A few years later he moved his family to Washington, DC, where the former state legislator worked for two decades as a watchman.[70]

Nathaniel M. Griggs was listed in Philadelphia city directories as a porter prior to his death in 1919. Formerly enslaved, he had lived in Farmville, taken part in politics for several years during the 1870s and 1880s, and after serving one two-year term in the House of Delegates and one four-year term in the Senate of Virginia took a patronage job in the printing office in Washington, DC. There, according to family tradition, he caught the eye of the politically influential owner of Wanamaker's Department Store and moved to Philadelphia where he worked as a jeweler. Griggs's identification as a porter, a term that at the time embraced a variety of largely menial or custodial tasks, suggests that he did janitorial or some similar work, instead. From time to time, he returned to his wife and family in Farmville and was there at the time of his death.[71]

For some legislators, much of what is known is confined to their legislative service. That can be challenging for understanding delegates such as George William Cole, who represented Essex County in the House for one undistinguished term (1879–80), and for whom we know little else, except that he came from Georgia to attend Hampton Normal and Agricultural Institute and became a farmer and a teacher.[72]

On occasion a legislator's personal behavior interfered with his service in the assembly and caused him to disappear from the public record.

William H. Andrews, a former member of the convention who won election to the House of Delegates from Surry County in 1869, was an alcoholic. He was arrested in Richmond on a charge of being drunk and disorderly in March 1870. Less than two weeks later, William Henry Brisby charged that Andrews had struck a House page with a whip and called for him to be expelled. Andrews apologized to the House, paid a fine, and immediately departed for the city's saloons. After several more drunken incidents, a justice of the peace jailed Andrews in the summer. In the next session of the assembly early in 1871, he came under suspicion for accepting a bribe from a railroad lobbyist. Escaping expulsion, he stopped attending legislative sessions and disappeared shortly thereafter.[73] His conduct reflected badly on other and abler Black legislators. Andrews was one of several former members of the General Assembly who so far disappeared from the public records that the times and places of their deaths are still not known.

Legislative Milestones

Late in the session of the General Assembly that met from December 1870 through March 1871, nearly all of the thirty delegates and senators voted on two measures that were or became extremely controversial and had long-term consequences for state government and politics.

On March 31, 1871, the assembly passed a law that was customarily referred to as the Funding Act of 1871. Before the Civil War, Virginia had sold bonds to raise money with which to buy 40 percent of the stock in new railroads in order to allow for rapid capital accumulation and construction. The Funding Act provided for refinancing the debt with new bonds that matured in thirty-four years and paid 6 percent annual interest in two semiannual installments. It seemed like good business sense at the time for the state to honor its old financial obligations, and nearly all of the thirty Black legislators joined the majority of white legislators in voting for the bill.[74]

The governor and the assembly, however, overestimated how much revenue the state would collect. They also did not anticipate the losses from bond holders being allowed under a provision in the Funding Act to pay taxes with the interest-bearing coupons attached to some of the bonds. That significantly reduced the amount of money that the treasury received. Taxes paid with coupons yielded no money with which to pay for ordinary government operations or to support the new public school system.[75] In addition, the abolition of slavery had destroyed one of the state's most-valuable kinds of taxable property, second only to the value of the land, itself; and without enslaved laborers, much of the state's farmland was valued for tax purposes at a lower rate than before the war. As a result, the state ran a deficit nearly every year for the next decade.[76]

At almost the same time that the General Assembly passed the Funding Act, it voted to sell the stock in almost all of the railroad companies that the state owned. The sale of the stock beginning in 1871 was part of a larger movement within the state to consolidate some of the shorter lines into long, trunk lines and to remove the state from involvement in ownership and allow private capital to control railroad construction and operation. The prices that the state accepted for sale of the railroad stock were surprisingly low, which further exacerbated the problems created by the original underestimation of available revenue by the governor and legislators. At the time and for a long time thereafter, critics charged that railroad lobbyists had purchased the votes of some members of the General Assembly, including the notorious William H. Andrews, with money, alcohol, or prostitutes.[77]

Senator George Teamoh recalled later that a railroad lobbyist came to his room one cold winter night and laid out a map to explain how consolidation of railroad companies would benefit Virginia. Then he told Teamoh, "that if I would consult my individual interest as well as that of the people's I would—after all that has been said and written—vote for the measure." Then, Teamoh went on, "Softly adjusting the folds of his map and placing it in his heavy portfolio, he drew from the latter a package of green back money consisting of Ten Thousand Dollars, ($10,000) made up of Five hundreds, One thousands, Twenties Tens and hundreds." Teamoh refused to accept the money and stated his objections. The lobbyist remarked "that if it required argument to over come my objections, there was no use in talking the matter over any longer. He left and I went to bed."[78]

Alexander Owen was not as forthright as Teamoh and came under some suspicion at that time because of the role he had played in railroad politics. A one-term delegate from Halifax County, he was elected to the House of Delegates as a moderate Conservative Republican, and it was widely known that he regularly returned home during the first sessions of the assembly to consult with his former enslaver, William L. Owen, who was possibly a close relative. In the summer of 1870, Alexander Owen told a newspaper reporter that when a bill to consolidate several of the state's major railroads was before the House of Delegates, his white Conservative colleague from Halifax County told him, "Alek, if you don't vote for this Bill, I will cut your darned ears off and send them back to H—x; you son of a gun"—or stronger words to that same effect. Owen responded, "I 'spect you, Colonel, will make about $25,000 by this bill, and I like you and will go for it certain."[79]

During the next session of the assembly, an investigator asked Owen whether he knew if any member received money for his vote on the consolidation bill. "I know one," he answered, "and that is myself, sir. Before this bill came to the test, sir, I went to my county. My constituents asked me to vote for it [the Pennsylvania Central]. They told me it would be the life of the country, and I told them that I would vote for it. I have received nothing from any other party save those who elected me, and from them only their good will. I know of no other party who has received anything."[80] Alexander Owen's practice of consulting William L. Owen suggests that the white man was his principal constituent. Owen appears to have been under the influence of the leading white men in his county. In that, he may have been very nearly unique among the Black men who served in the General Assembly. Conservatives then, and white supremacists later, regularly charged (for the most part falsely) that Black men who engaged in politics were often under the dictation of white Northern radicals. That was definitely not the case with Owen.[81]

The most important law that the General Assembly of 1869–71 passed was the act to create the state's first public school system.[82] When the bill came out of committee and was considered on the floor of the Senate in June 1870, it contained a clause that required racial segregation in the schools. Senator William P. Moseley, of Goochland County, who in the constitutional convention had voted for Thomas Bayne's motion to prohibit discrimination,[83] introduced an amendment to delete the requirement for segregation, but the white majority defeated it. Perhaps as a silent form of protest, three of the six Black senators absented themselves and did not vote when the bill passed.[84] A few days later in the House of Delegates, John B. Miller Jr., also from Goochland County, made a motion similar to Moseley's. That motion also failed, as did a motion that William Nash Stevens, of Petersburg, introduced, "that no distinction shall be made in the appointment of the school trustees" in the counties and cities "on account of race or color." Then, most of the twenty-four Black delegates voted against passage of the bill as their only means of objecting to what they believed was a denial of the full rights of equal citizenship that they gained with the abolition of slavery and ratification of the Fourteenth Amendment to the Constitution of the United States.[85]

Obstacles to Black Political Participation

Thirty Black men won election to the General Assembly in 1869, and between eighteen and twenty won in each of the elections of 1871, 1873, and 1875. The assemblies in those years had little positive impact on the prospects of freed people and their families. Partisan and personal disagreements and rivalries divided members of both parties as well as divided the voting population.

Because many white voters objected to the participation of Black voters, election day was often a tense or sometimes even violent time. In Petersburg in October 1873, a few days before the election of members of the General Assembly, partisan crowds of Black and white men encountered one another during street demonstrations and began shouting at each other and throwing rocks. The following night brought more rock-throwing, and some white men fired guns at the Black men. Apparently, nobody was seriously wounded or killed. On election day, James P. Goodwyn and a white Republican, Godfrey May, both won.[86]

The campaign for the Republican nomination for Congress in the district three years later revealed deep fractures within Republican ranks that had at least some of their roots in race. Mark DeMortie ran to represent Black voters, and a white Republican, Joseph Jorgensen, the postmaster of Petersburg, ran with the blessings of the party's white leaders. On the same day in mid-August, Black and white Republicans held separate conventions in Farmville that nominated DeMortie and Jorgensen. Late in September the district and state party committees endorsed Jorgensen, but DeMortie campaigned until election day, challenging the white leaders and arguing that the district's Black majority should send a Black man to Congress. Jorgensen persuaded President Ulysses S. Grant to dispatch a company of soldiers to Petersburg on election day to keep the threatened peace. Jorgensen received far more votes than DeMortie and narrowly defeated the Conservative Party candidate.[87]

Black voters faced serious difficulties in electing the candidates they preferred. The abolition of voice voting in the 1860s and the introduction of the ballot did not insulate voters from intimidation. Before 1894, the government did not provide a standard ballot to voters. Each candidate printed a ballot for the voter to take to the polling place, or each party printed a ballot with all of its candidates' names on it. The ballots were

First published by *Harper's Weekly* on October 19, 1872, "One Vote Less" illustrates violence used to intimidate or eliminate Black voters in Virginia. On the wall behind the corpse of a Black man is scrawled "Negro Killed" and "Greeley Ratification," which refers to the 1872 presidential candidacy of Horace Greeley and the 1870 ratification of the Fifteenth Amendment. Immediately to the left of the dead man's left hand are the letters "KKK." (Library of Virginia)

oftentimes on paper of a different size or color than the opponents' ballots. Thus, everybody could see how everybody voted or intended to vote. That left voters vulnerable to threats on election day or retaliation afterward, the same as with voice voting. Moreover, at some polling places, officers of election required voters to hand their ballots to the official who placed it in the ballot box, which allowed dexterous men to replace a Republican ballot with a Conservative ballot or fold several together to stuff the ballot box. Conservatives and Democrats often made white and Black voters wait in separate lines and allowed the white men to vote first or forced the line of Black men to move slower than the line of white men so that all Black men might not get a chance to vote before the poll closed. Or election officials might allow known Conservatives or Democrats to vote first and Black men, together with known or suspected Republicans, to vote later. Republicans, when they had the opportunity, often retaliated with similar unfair or illegal tactics. Challenges to election results based on charges of various kinds of fraud and intimidation, including violence, increased substantially after the introduction of the ballot.[88]

Conservative Party majorities in both houses of the General Assembly imposed other obstacles to the political success of Black candidates. In 1874, voters, a majority of whom were white, ratified an amendment to the state constitution to change the names of townships in the counties to magisterial districts—the word *township* evidently reminded old-line white Virginians too much of New England democracy. The amendment also eliminated several elected township officers (clerk, tax assessor, tax collector, and commissioner of roads). The amendment authorized the election of one county surveyor and one county tax commissioner rather than several separate tax commissioners in each township, streamlining the structure of county government and reducing the expense to taxpayers by decreasing the number of elected officials in each county. By limiting the number of public offices that men of both races might hope to hold, the amendment may be understood as restricting local democracy for everybody, as well as being a means of limiting the political influence of Black men.[89]

Two years later in 1876, the assembly submitted and voters ratified an amendment to require that men pay an annual poll tax in order to qualify to vote, and it also disfranchised every person convicted of "petit larceny." The poll tax placed a new financial burden on the franchise with the deliberate intention of making it too expensive for Black men to vote. What was called the "chicken-thief" clause was based on a racist assumption that Black people were inherently more dishonest than white people and that they often stole things like chickens in the same way that enslavers had believed that enslaved people had often taken foodstuffs from them during slavery. The 1876 amendment also made important changes to the article on the General Assembly, some ostensibly to save money. It allowed the assembly to create districts for the election of not fewer than 90 nor more than 100 delegates (reduced from 138) and from 33 to 40 senators (reduced from 43).[90]

The combined consequences of the poll tax, the disfranchisement of people convicted of petit larceny, and the reduction in the number of legislative seats made it more difficult for Black men to vote and for Black men to win election to the General Assembly. Only eight were able to win seats in the General Assembly in 1877, the smallest number since Black men won the vote, and the number remained low through the election of 1889, when voters elected the last four delegates for seventy-eight years and the last senator for eighty years.

Holding Local Offices

A decline in the number of Black men elected to local offices was almost certainly another consequence of the 1874 and 1876 amendments.[91] Sound scholarship on local office holding and data about the numbers of local officeholders in the state's cities and counties is too scarce to permit thorough analysis. Luther Porter Jackson identified a large number of men whose political success at the local level he discovered while researching his pioneering *Negro Office-Holders in Virginia*,[92] but later scholarship on the subject contains much more evidence of how white legislators and other politicians made it difficult for Black men to become officeholders than about how many men won election when and where.[93]

Almost half the ninety-two Black members of the General Assembly in the nineteenth century held local offices, such as on city councils or county boards of supervisors, overseers of the poor, road commissioners, and county justices of the peace (though that office was no longer so influential as it had been before the Civil War). Henry Johnson served for fourteen consecutive years on the Amelia County Board of Supervisors before he was elected to the House of Delegates in 1889. Maclin Wheeler served three consecutive terms on the Brunswick County Board of Supervisors following his tenure in the House of Delegates. And Daniel Norton was a justice of the peace in York County for many years after the end of his long political career. Petersburg delegate Peter George Morgan held a seat on Petersburg's city council, while also receiving a patronage appointment as a revenue collector at the customhouse. Black men never won a majority on any county board of supervisors or city council, but a coalition of Republicans of both races, including Morgan, held a majority of the city council in Petersburg from 1870 to 1874, and a similar coalition was victorious in Norfolk in 1884 and 1888.[94]

The capital city of Richmond is the subject of the best study of local officeholders. In 1871, the all-white council gerrymandered the city and created a new Jackson Ward, which had a Black majority.[95] That enabled some Black men to win election to municipal offices in the ward, but white majorities in the city's other five wards guaranteed white majorities on the city council and the board of aldermen. Thirty-one Black men won election to the city council or the board of aldermen (which was created in 1874) between July 1871 and June 1898. About three-quarters of the victorious councilmen and aldermen were of mixed-race backgrounds, and they were better educated and more prosperous than most citizens. Despite electing more than two dozen Black officeholders in the city of

Richmond, voters there were never able to elect a delegate or senator to represent the city during the nineteenth century.

Local Black officeholders succeeded in persuading the city to erect a new school in Jackson Ward and to create a night school for children who worked during the day. They were able to provide improved street lighting in the ward and fuel for cooking and heating during the winter. They campaigned successfully for abolition of the chain gang for convicted men who worked on the public works. They were able to defeat a plan to locate a smallpox hospital in the ward and put a stop to the illegal practice of grave robbing to provide the (white) medical schools in the city with (Black) cadavers for dissection; but they were not able to prevent the construction and operation there of a foul-smelling incinerator to burn garbage and dead animals or to have the city create a public park in the ward. A second gerrymander, in the 1890s, combined with a sharp reduction in the number of men who voted, resulted in the election of no Black councilmen in Richmond for half a century after 1898.[96]

Confronting White Intransigence

The Black members of the General Assembly during the 1870s were for the most part unable to achieve their most important objectives, such as preventing mandatory racial segregation in the new public schools and passing new laws to guarantee equal civil and political rights, because they were always outnumbered. White opposition to their proposals usually prevailed, and they were unable to prevent white legislators from enacting measures that they deemed harmful to Black men and women.

Some Black legislators' proposals were more symbolic than substantive. In 1871, for example, the General Assembly appropriated $600 to purchase a portrait of Robert E. Lee to place in the Capitol. Senator Frank Moss objected because "Gen. Lee had fought to keep him in slavery, and he couldn't vote to put his picture on these walls."[97] Four years later, Moss again, this time as a member of the House of Delegates, led the opposition to appropriation of money to erect in Capitol Square a statue of General Thomas J. "Stonewall" Jackson that some admiring British men had commissioned and given to the state. Ten other Black delegates and three white Republicans voted with Moss against the appropriation.[98] The legislators lost the first rounds in a decades-long campaign of white Virginians to commemorate and glorify the Confederacy with public art that had the effect of reinterpreting the Civil War as a struggle of noble white men against a tyrannical federal government, that minimized slavery as the cause of the war, and that ignored the war's most important consequence, the abolition of slavery.

By the mid-1870s, many Black political leaders had grown impatient with the ineffective white leaders of the state's Republican Party, who appeared to ignore their interests. They organized to take charge of their own political destinies and promote the interests of Black men. Almost thirty sitting, former, or future legislators and constitutional convention delegates were among the approximately one hundred men who met in Richmond for a three-day state convention that began on August 20, 1875. Senator John M. Dawson, who was also pastor of First Baptist Church in Williamsburg, called the meeting to order. The members elected Delegate Peter J. Carter temporary chair, then they chose as president Robert D. Ruffin, a former Alexandria County (later Arlington County) sheriff and recently elected member of the House of Delegates from Dinwiddie County.

Members of the convention condemned the inadequate support for the public schools; the proposed constitutional amendment to impose a poll tax and to disfranchise men convicted of petty crimes; exclusion of Black men from juries; the painful consequences of the recent failure of the Freedman's Bank that cost thousands of men and women their savings; and the denial of the full rights of citizenship for Black Virginians. The men were also aware that the severe and prolonged economic recession that began with the national financial Panic of 1873 limited commercial and economic development in the state and contributed to the continuing difficulty their constituents experienced in trying to work their ways out of poverty. The convention resolved to establish the Laboring Men's Mechanics' Union Association to unite Black workers to enable men and women to "receive a fair compensation for a day's labor," purchase land for themselves, and join together to protect their rights as "American citizens."[99]

The public address that the convention's members adopted on the third day included an exhortation that avoided specifics and failed to set a clear political agenda. They advised Black people to take care "that no measure be incorporated in your laws which does not meet the necessities and circumstances of the whole people of Virginia. Pass no evasive acts which contemplate ruin and disaster to any man, whatever his complexion. Diligently strive to inculcate knowledge and intelligence, and let it be known and remembered that the safety of our institutions and the preservation of liberties depend upon the liberal support of a broad system of public instruction." The address concluded, "The colored people of the State confront their white fellow-citizens to-day upon high and honorable grounds. Eager to adjust all differences for the good of all, they speak wholly for themselves and put forth these sentiments to intelligent minds and a just God."[100]

That they chose the verb *confront* rather than some more-friendly verb may be an indication of the measure of their frustration or of their determination in the face of the opposition that they faced, had faced, and anticipated that they would face during the remainder of the 1870s. It is nevertheless a tribute to the strong belief among Black voters that voting offered them their best chance for full citizenship in spite of the many obstacles and frustrations. This would be demonstrated over the next two decades as "sending a colored man" to the General Assembly resulted in Black legislators working tirelessly—often with white political allies—to improve the political, material, economic, and educational fortunes of their fellow Black Virginians.

6

"Without Distinction of Color"

Readjusters, Education, and Biracial Politics

On February 25 and 26, 1879, at Mozart Hall in Richmond, men of both races met to create a new political party with the immediate objective of refinancing—of adjusting or, as they put it, readjusting—the public debt that Virginia had incurred before the Civil War. "Wm. T. Jefferson (colored)," of New Kent County, as a newspaper report identified one of the men, announced that he was delighted to attend "in response to the call which convened the people of Virginia without distinction of color." The newspaper reported that he went on to state that "All the colored people in his district are Re-Adjusters and ready to shake hands with all other Re-Adjusters. . . . As to the debt, we don't want to pay a cent of it. We think we paid our share of it, if it ever was justly chargeable upon us, by long years of servitude. And then, as Virginia has been reconstructed in her territory"—by the formation of West Virginia during the Civil War—"and in her government"—by the Constitution of 1869—"we think that her debt should be reconstructed too." After the applause for his remarks died down, Jefferson concluded, "We are humble citizens—the humblest in the Commonwealth—and we treat white people invariably with a great deal more courtesy than we receive, because we are anxious not to offend you, and to win your good will. We are for peace, and we accept the overture made to us as heartily as it is tendered for we feel that your interests and our interests are identical," which brought another round of applause.[1]

A public debt created in the 1840s and 1850s to stimulate railroad construction hardly seems a suitable rallying point in 1879 for Virginians "without distinction of color," especially for Black people such as Jefferson and his neighbors, who had been struggling since the abolition of slavery to create new lives and communities for themselves and their families. But it was not the debt that was the problem; it was the injurious consequences that the high cost of paying interest on the debt had for the new statewide system of public schools that was very popular with Virginians "without distinction of color."

The Early Years of Public Schools in Virginia

Realizing the necessity of education, people of both races were seemingly eager to send their children to school. According to the 1870 federal census, about 44 percent of all people in the state older than ten could not read. One of four white Virginians older than ten and nine of ten Black Virginians older than ten could not write.[2]

The public school system, which initially provided "elementary education for children and youth," went into operation speedily after passage of the July 1870 law that created it. The State Board of Education, consisting of the governor, attorney general, and a white superintendent of public instruction, whom the General Assembly named, appointed a white superintendent for each county and city and about 1,400 white school trustees. As was common in the nineteenth century, the first schools were open to Virginians between ages five and twenty-one, and they opened in November. In referenda in May 1871, voters in seventy-three of the state's ninety-nine counties imposed additional taxes on themselves to supplement the $345,517 that the state distributed to the local schools in that first year.[3]

According to the superintendent of public instruction, "the difficulty, and often impossibility, of procuring qualified teachers for the colored schools" delayed the opening of schools for Black children. Nevertheless, by the end of 1870, between 8,000 and 10,000 Black children attended school, and in the following spring and summer almost 39,000 were enrolled in 706 schools that employed 335 Black male teachers and 158 Black female teachers.[4] William Henry Ruffner, the superintendent of public instruction, published in his first annual report a twenty-five-page argument that good public schools for Black children were essential for the future prosperity of all the people of the state.[5]

Hampton Normal and Agricultural Institute furnished some of the teachers for the new public schools. The word *Normal* in the institution's title meant that one of its primary responsibilities was to prepare people to teach. With a focus also on agriculture, Hampton prepared its students

"Primary Class" was published in *Frank Leslie's Illustrated Newspaper* on July 21, 1883, and shows a woman teaching Black boys and girls. Schools like this were extremely popular among freed people in Virginia. (Library of Virginia)

to operate farms, manage greenhouses, practice animal husbandry, and prepared students for careers in various professions, from carpentry and masonry to home economics. Students at Hampton learned trades by constructing the buildings, producing the food, operating the laundry, as well as learning to sew and cook and manage households.

One of the trades Hampton taught was printing. In January 1872 the institute published the first issue of the *Southern Workman*, printed by the students under faculty supervision. The monthly magazine, which was edited by white staff members, served purposes beyond teaching men and women how to publish a newspaper and was intended during its first decades to inform white philanthropists and supporters of Hampton about the activities and needs of the students.[6] Each month for more than sixty-five years, the *Southern Workman* printed editorials about morals, religion, and the value of education; advice on teaching; articles on people in Asia and Africa; literature and poetry; news of the Indigenous peoples who attended the institute; and reports of events interesting to Black people anywhere and everywhere. A regularly recurring feature of the *Southern Workman* during the first years were reports from graduates, many of whom taught in the public schools of Virginia and other states. As Black freed people left little in the way of personal recollections, these reports from Hampton graduates provide eyewitness accounts of the obstacles that Black children and adults encountered in undoing more than two centuries of being denied an education.

The Experience of Teachers

Teachers in the new public schools of Virginia had very different experiences depending on the attitudes of Black and white people where they taught.[7] Mary C. Robinson wrote from Thaxton's Switch in Bedford County on January 10, 1873, "The people are all very anxious to have the children learn, now that their minds are aroused." At first, some farmers were reluctant to spare their children from work on the farm, but the number of her students increased in the first month from sixteen to thirty-five and continued to grow. "The children's parents were so pleased with the progress of their children that they sent them from their work," Robinson reported; but "The school house has no boards, no maps, or anything that should be in a school house. It is a very small house, and can only hold ninety or a hundred people, though it is used as a church for the people to worship in as they have no church. . . . Some of the people have a little land and a plank house, but the most of them are living on the white people's land in little log houses, some with no windows or anything to give light. The people have treated me very well, both white and colored. Some of the whites are very much opposed to free schools and colored teachers but they have always treated me with respect, I am happy to say."[8]

Nancy Ellison Wallace wrote in 1874 from Clarksville, where she and her husband, both 1870 graduates of Hampton, taught in a school "with eighty scholars." She reported, "Mr. Wallace's health is declining from constant teaching. He has lost twenty pounds within eighteen months. Two physicians have advised him to resort to some other business, though the county superintendent and trustees are unwilling to give him up." She also commented on the condition of the people there. "The colored people, in general, are advancing. There are five or six prosperous colored merchants in the town. The finest church in town is owned by the colored people. It is built on a hill and its spire can be seen and bell heard for miles around. Good ministers and teachers are what they need most. A great many are buying land in small quantities and building on it."[9]

About the spring of 1875, William C. Boyd, who taught at Hale's Ford in Franklin County, reported on the stark illiteracy he found near his school in the Blue Ridge. "I am sure you don't have any *idea* what a bad condition it is in regards of an education," he wrote to Hampton's superintendent:

> It is almost past all hopes; ignorance and poverty are walking hand in hand. No longer than to-day I have had a white lady to come and

> ask me to back [write] a letter for her. Since that is the case with these whites you may imagine [how] it is with the poor colored man who has never had an opportunity of being cultivated. It is true they are all free, but it reminds me more of the time when I was a slave than anything else. It is master and mistress just as it was twenty years ago. Now it may seem strange to you, but it is true; for all of them are ignorant, white as well as the *black man*.[10]

In Halifax County early in 1878, a teacher wrote, "Both white and colored are wide awake here about the schools. We have pupils coming five and six miles (daily), and you would be astonished to see them in the school-room after such a walk. They seem as fresh and bright as they can be, and as a general thing are first in their places."[11] Another teacher wrote in April 1878, "Before Christmas the people were so slow in sending their children to school that I was about to be sent to another neighborhood. . . . I have told them, and will try and prove to them next Friday, that the scholars of whom I can boast, are not those that were kept away from school because of dress, but those who came regularly though with the poorest of clothes on their bodies. I have even stood and gazed on some of my pupils' dress, wondering which was the original piece of their garment, girls as well as boys. Many of their heels were well protected from the weather, but their toes were just the opposite."[12]

An educator identified in the *Southern Workman* as "M" wrote about a new school in one county ten years after the founding of the public school system: "There was never a school here until I opened one last March," she recalled, and she believed that "the children and their parents are worse off than when they were slaves, freedom only excepted. Why I say this is, they tell me when they were slaves their masters kept them in clothes and kept their cabins in quite good order. Now I come and find some of them without one decent garment, and living in log huts I can't stand up in." The teacher allowed "all ages and sizes" of people to attend her school, "as they had all helped to raise the money. So among my students I have from grandma to an infant 8 months old. The mother brings her baby and a quilt that it may lie down when she recites. Occasionally it gets its spells and a passerby might think from the noise, I kept a nursery instead of a school."[13]

A former Hampton student began to teach school in 1874 in King and Queen County. He later recalled that the school building "was very frail and rough; the floor made of logs split and fastened to the sleepers with wooden pins. There were no windows but one, very small one, and

A twentieth-century photograph of the school building in which Thomas Calhoun Walker received his first education in Gloucester County in the 1870s. Small frame buildings like this were common during the early decades of public education in Virginia, especially for Black schools. Thomas Calhoun Walker, "Lawyer Walker of Gloucester—As Told to Two Northern Friends," ca. 1950. (Special Collections Research Center, Earl Gregg Swem Library, College of William and Mary)

no blackboards or desks. Some of the people told me it was a very poor neighborhood, and if they were in my place, they wouldn't go." When he asked the school trustees for money to purchase proper windows, blackboards, and the like, "They said there was no money in the treasury, and I must see the patrons of the school. I went to them. Some were willing to do what they could;—others said they had paid their taxes, and thought the trustees ought to put the house in good order." He described the harsh conditions of his "place of boarding," in which "The room upstairs in which I slept had no windows save the cracks in the slab cover, which were large enough, some of them, for me to put my hand through." Nevertheless, his work teaching was its own reward. "I felt amply repaid," he concluded, "for all of the very hard work I had done, and the disadvantages and suffering."[14]

"D.," a young woman teacher who also had poor lodgings, reported that she "got a hammer and nails and some pine slabs last Saturday, and made my room tighter" and also "stopped the cracks, and then pasted up all the paper I could get. . . . I mean to get in some glass windows next." Not only did she do carpentry work that under ordinary circumstances only men did, she also preached at a local church because the congregation had no minister.[15]

Northern philanthropic organizations continued to send teachers to Virginia, but the supply of teachers educated at Hampton and other institutions could not keep up with the demand. Black parents repeatedly, but not always with success, demanded that the schools their children attended have Black teachers, who they believed would treat the students better than white teachers and better understand their needs.[16] On July 7, 1880, what a Richmond newspaper called "One of the largest and most enthusiastic public meetings ever held in this city took place at the Second Baptist church (colored)." The "colored citizens and tax-payers of Richmond" formally addressed the local school board and asked it "to appoint colored teachers in all colored public schools of this city, and to raise the grade of the same to a level with that of the white schools."[17] Four years later, a man in Stony Creek, in Sussex County, addressed the editor of the Petersburg *Lancet*. "Do you know of any teacher we can get to teach school in this county," he asked; "if you do tell them to write to me at once. There is a school vacant here because the people here will not have a white teacher."[18]

Some Black boys and girls born late during slavery or afterward who attended the schools later taught in them. Samuel Kelso, who had introduced one of the resolutions in the constitutional convention to require creation of the public school system, taught in Lynchburg's public schools until he took a job transferring mail between the post office and the railroad depot.[19] Beverly Allen, son of one of the first elected town councilmen in West Point, graduated from Hampton Institute in 1881, taught in West Point's public schools, and was principal of the Black school there until his death in 1918.[20]

Education was one of the few professions available to Black women. In 1870, the first year of the public school system, 158 women held teaching jobs. A decade later, after budget cuts closed about half the schools, 254 women were public school teachers. Black women outnumbered Black men by 1890, when 1,043 women taught in the public schools.[21]

Amanda Virginia Thomas Clark probably attended the public schools in her native Isle of Wight County in the 1870s and 1880s before she received a teaching certificate from Virginia Normal and Collegiate Institute. She taught in the public schools of Newport News and was also a civic and religious leader in the community into the 1940s.[22] Josephine B. Mathews Norcom was born in 1873 in or near Wytheville and attended public schools and graduated from Virginia Normal and Collegiate

Institute before she taught in schools in Salem, Pulaski County, and Lynchburg. She settled in Portsmouth with her husband, I. C. Norcom, where he was a high school principal, and she joined the local Colored Woman's Club and rose to be an officer in the Virginia State Federation of Colored Women's Clubs. Widowed, she returned to teaching in Portsmouth and Newport News before she went to work for the Young Women's Christian Association in Ohio and Michigan.[23]

Maggie Lena Mitchell attended the public schools in Richmond and graduated in 1883 from the Richmond Colored Normal School. She taught in the city's public schools for three years before she married Armstead Walker, also a graduate of the normal school. Under her married name of Maggie Walker, she became one of the most famous Black Virginians. She was a very successful business leader, advocate for education and for the rights of women and children, and not only the publisher of a newspaper but the first Black woman bank president in the United States.[24]

Another Richmond woman, Rosa Dixon Bowser, also graduated from the Colored Normal School and married an alumnus. She taught in Richmond for many years and in the 1880s helped organize the Virginia Teachers' Reading Circle, the first professional organization for Black teachers in the state. Before the end of the century and well into the twentieth, Bowser was a state and national leader in movements beneficial to Black women and in the Colored Women's Clubs. The first public library open to Black citizens of Richmond, founded in 1925, was named for her.[25]

Private academies and schools that some religious and philanthropic organizations supported also provided educational opportunities. Prior to his service in the House of Delegates, John W. Poindexter taught school at Louisa Court House, one of many teachers whom the New England Freedmen's Aid Society supported.[26] William Horace Ash attended a private school in Leesburg after the Civil War, graduated from Hampton in 1882, and taught for several years at the Ingleside Seminary, an academy for Black girls that the Presbyterian Church supported in Burkeville. In the summer of 1884, shortly before Ash won election to the House of Delegates, he took part along with Bowser in founding the Virginia Teachers' Reading Circle.[27] James Solomon Russell worked to pay his tuition to attend a private school in his native Mecklenburg County before he entered Hampton Institute and later became an Episcopal minister. His belief in the importance of education animated much of his life. Russell was a founder of and the first president of the Saint Paul Normal and Industrial School in Lawrenceville from 1888 until his death almost fifty years later.[28]

School Funding and the Rise of the Readjusters

Throughout the 1870s and into the 1880s, many influential white Virginians remained opposed to spending tax money to educate freed people and their children. They also feared that Northerners who taught in the state's public schools and others who wrote the textbooks would infect the students with democratic ideas that were unsuitable for the life that those white Virginians expected Black Virginians to live. Wendell Phillips Dabney remembered an encounter with one such person. The son of the famous caterer and barkeeper John Dabney, he was born late in 1865 and attended the public schools in Richmond. With the education he received, he became a nationally known musician, civil rights advocate, and publisher of a newspaper in Cincinnati, Ohio. Dabney recalled in an incomplete, unpublished autobiography that one day when he was walking home from school with his history book tucked under his arm, a "tall, thin, cadaverous looking 'rebel'" accosted him and demanded, "'Here boy, let me see that book.'" The man began to read the chapter on the Civil War. "Then," Dabney remembered, "the floodgates of profanity opened to their fullest extent. He cussed every Yankee S—of a B—in this world, and hoped every damned rascally dog of them would die in torture and particularly the 'low-life scoundrel' who wrote that damned lie about the South." The old rebel hurled the book into the street. Dabney retrieved it, recalling that "Fleetness of foot saved me from the heavy cane he always carried."[29]

In 1877, when Dabney was in school, Virginia had 3,442 public schools that enrolled almost 140,000 white students and 1,230 schools that enrolled about 65,000 Black students. Total expenditures on the schools that year (as for each of the three preceding years) exceeded $1,000,000. Based on the amount of taxes the state collected, the school fund should have been much larger and the number of schools, teachers, and students correspondingly larger, too. In some years, nearly half of the state's revenue came into the treasury in the form of tax-receivable coupons from the bonds issued when the General Assembly refinanced the debt in 1871, and the state could not spend a penny of that revenue on the schools or on anything else.[30] Throughout the 1870s the school system should have received from $300,000 to $450,000 more each year than it did. Superintendent William H. Ruffner complained from the very beginning that teachers' and superintendents' salaries were too low to attract and keep the highest quality educators, and he advocated increased funding for public education throughout his tenure. The General Assembly, however, routinely diverted large sums of the (inadequate) budgeted funds allocated to the schools and other programs to pay interest on the public debt. Between 1877 and 1879, the legislature drastically slashed the school budget from more than $1,000,000 to $570,000. The result was disastrous. About half the schools in the state closed, their teachers lost their jobs, and half the students in the state received no education.[31]

Largely to rescue the public schools from those reductions, people who favored refinancing the debt emerged as a readily identifiable and influential political faction by the middle of the 1870s. Readjusters, as they became known, desired to reduce the interest rate, the amount of the principal to be paid, or both. Some white members of the Conservative Party became what people called Funders; they insisted on paying the full principal and interest on the debt regardless of consequences. They argued that defaulting on the debt or reducing the interest rate would be a dishonor to Virginia and would permanently damage the state's ability to build a strong economy. William Mahone, of Petersburg, became the leader of the Readjusters. A former Confederate brigadier general and railroad executive, he had been at the center of the political controversies concerning the consolidation of railroads in the state after the war. He had made powerful enemies among his competitors at that time as well as among some of the nation's leading bankers and agents of bond speculators.[32]

Adamant Funders inadvertently made the Readjusters' advocacy of refinancing easier. In February 1878, the General Assembly passed a bill to require that the portion of the state tax revenue that the law dedicated to support the schools be paid with money that the state could spend and not with useless coupons clipped from the public bonds. During debate in the Senate, the white senator from Lynchburg, John Warwick Daniel, denounced the bill as a subterfuge to cheat the bondholders. "He said," according to a newspaper report, which he later confirmed was accurate, that "he would rather see a bonfire made of every free school in the State, and a bonfire then made of his own home, than that this bill and those that are to follow it should pass."[33]

Governor Frederick William Mackey Holliday vetoed the bill with a blunt and insulting message that drew a sharp class line and placed the interests of Black Virginians and poor white Virginians together. "Our fathers did not need free schools to make them what they were," he lectured the assembly, implicitly referring to the white founding fathers who were all comparatively wealthy planters who had been educated privately. "They would not have tolerated them on the soil of Virginia had they to be established by the denial of their honest debts. . . . Public free schools are not a necessity." People who wanted to educate their children should pay to do so, Holliday went on, as if poor white and Black parents could afford to educate their children the same way as prosperous white parents such as his had always been able to do. Holliday clearly believed that the state should not unfairly burden those prosperous people with a responsibility to pay for the education of the children of poor people, white or Black.[34]

Those episodes and others like them were why advocates of readjustment "without distinction of color" attended a convention in Richmond in February 1879. The perils that the public school system faced demonstrated what "Wm. T. Jefferson (colored)" referred to then when he informed white attendees that "your interests and our interests are identical."[35] Readjusters stressed issues like public education and taxation that affected families of both races and muted references to other issues that could have divided Black and white voters. That made it easier for advocates of refinancing to appeal to Black and white voters with one inclusive, democratic campaign message. Readjusters framed the critical public debate about the debt as a question of whether voters wanted their tax money to be paid to bond speculators or to be spent for the education of their children. Formation of the Readjuster Party guaranteed that Funders would face well-organized opposition in the 1879 legislative elections and the 1881 election of statewide officers.[36]

Black Political Identity and the Readjusters

In spite of the difficulties that white Conservative legislators had imposed on Black voters in the middle of the decade with the constitutional amendment that required payment of a poll tax as a prerequisite to register, Black men made the necessary sacrifices and took the necessary risks in order to vote.[37] In the general election in November 1879, Readjusters won majorities in both houses of the General Assembly. Twelve Black men won election to the House of Delegates and two to the Senate, more than had won since ratification of the poll tax amendment. The campaign and the Readjuster victory likely gave added energy to Black people who followed politics. The December 1879 issue of the *Southern Workman* was the first that had extensive reports on a state election. It printed excerpts from several letters from Hampton graduates. One reported that a longtime Democratic incumbent in a Black majority county lost his bid for reelection because he was a Funder; one of the correspondents believed that the Democrat's reelection would "injure our free schools, which are poor enough. The colored people in this county are repudiators, and, as they have a majority, usually carry elections, if they only 'get rights' as they term it." The correspondent reported that Black voters "did not contract the debt, and cannot see why they should help pay it." With no outright repudiators to vote for, they voted for Readjusters. In another county, "The majority of colored voters here are in favor of not paying the debt. . . . The reason they give for their vote is that when this debt was made, they were held as property as security for it, and they had no hand in making it. Therefore, they hold that they should not be taxed to pay it, nor the money taken from their free schools and their children left destitute of education."[38]

Because of the governor's veto power, the Readjuster majorities elected in 1879 were not able to enact a law to refinance the debt or pass any other of the Readjusters' proposals.[39] They did, though, elect William Mahone to the United States Senate and took the first step in the protracted process to amend the state constitution and remove payment of the poll tax as a prerequisite for voting. The amendment process required that both houses of the General Assembly pass the amendment and that after the next legislative election both houses pass the same amendment again. The assembly could then submit the proposed amendment to a referendum at which voters by majority vote could ratify or reject it. It is instructive to notice that all of the senators and delegates who participated in drafting the amendment to abolish the poll tax and guided it through the General Assembly in 1880 were white, not Black.[40] It was to the advantage of Readjusters to preserve the ability of Black men and also of poor white men to vote because together they formed the basis of the Readjuster electoral success. Readjusters of both races were apparently committed to preserving the democratic franchise for all men, which white Conservatives by and large were not.

Shortly after the General Assembly adjourned in March 1880, fourteen Black legislators issued a public statement and explained that they had charted their own course and not followed the leadership of white Republican or Readjuster leaders. They recognized that they had wielded the balance of power and boasted that "by our action the whole machinery of the State has been changed." They appealed to the white people of Virginia to "Consider well the popular idea of giving to the colored people their full and every political right" and not "be afraid and so prejudiced but what you will be willing to give us a fair and equal chance in the race of life; you cannot lose and must gain." The legislators concluded by directly addressing the "colored people" of the state "to ever keep before us those bright principles of liberty which the laws of our country guarantee us, but which we can only enjoy by the common consent of the people with whom we live."[41]

A major partisan realignment had taken place in Virginia. Electoral politics ceased for a few years to be contests between Republicans and Conservatives or Democrats and became contests between Readjusters (including both Conservatives and Republicans, as well as Black political leaders) and Funders (including Republicans, Conservatives, and Democrats). The July 1880 Readjuster Party state convention included more than forty Black delegates. The white and Black members of the convention adopted resolutions that promised to refinance the debt, revise the state's tax laws to make them more fair, and—what was almost certainly aimed at holding and attracting more Black voters—"the Readjusters reiterate their purpose to vindicate and maintain the constitutional rights of the citizen to the exercise of a free and priceless suffrage."[42]

The pivotal event in the Readjusters' eventual success may have been a meeting of almost three hundred Black Republican men in Petersburg on March 14, 1881, with state Senator Daniel Norton in the president's chair. White Mayor William E. Cameron in a cordial speech welcomed the men to Petersburg; and early in the day a telegram arrived with news that when Mahone took his seat in the United States Senate that day, he joined the Republicans. The delegates applauded and cheered the fact that the most prominent Readjuster in the state had joined their ranks.

Because of Mahone's choice, the delegates acted as if the Readjusters had already joined the Republicans rather than debate whether the three hundred Republicans should join the Readjusters, which was the principal item on the agenda. Many of the men were reluctant to risk alienating old white Republican allies, or to lose their own political identities as Republicans, but disillusionment with the state's white Republican leaders was strong. Members of the convention resolved to chart their own independent course of action. "We believe that the time has come," one of the resolutions they adopted asserted, "when the colored man cannot better vindicate his manhood and his title to citizenship than by boldly shouldering political responsibilities that have been too long assumed for him by others. If he would not always be a ward, he must now, at least, act for himself and determine his own course with that spirit of self-reliance which at once secures respect and achieves success."

The resolutions continued, "To the jury, the free schools and the ballot we look as the highest earnests and the best safeguards of all that is valuable in our citizenship, and it is with the most fervent aspiration that we seek the final obliteration in politics of that color-line which, disastrous to the Nation, the State, and all the people, has been especially hurtful to ourselves as a race." They concluded that even though the "National Republican party, from its advent to the present moment, has given too many evidences of its friendship for the rights of man for us to renounce our allegiance to it in any time of need," yet for the immediate future in Virginia, "*Resolved,* That the colored people of Virginia, in convention assembled in the city of Petersburg, regard the Re-Adjuster party with favor, and confidently believe that their interests will be better secured and preserved by aiding that party in its efforts to achieve and permanently settle the antagonism of races, which has unfortunately affected the prosperity of our State."[43]

On June 2 and 3, 1881, Readjusters of both races met together in the party's state convention to nominate candidates for statewide office. Published reports do not indicate how many of the 759 delegates were white and how many were Black. White men held all of the convention's offices, but James T. S. Taylor, who had served in the Constitutional Convention of 1867–68, and former members of the House of Delegates Henry Clay Harris and Caesar Perkins were members of the Committee on Credentials. Several Black members spoke, according to one report of the proceedings, among them both Daniel and Robert Norton, and former Senator William Nash Stevens.

The convention adopted a platform that pledged the party's members to refinance the debt and reduce both the rate of interest and the amount of the principal to be paid. The platform also declared, "The Readjusters hold the right to a free ballot to be the right preservative of all rights, and that it should be maintained in every State in the Union," and that the poll tax "restriction upon the suffrage in Virginia to be in conflict with the fourteenth amendment to the Constitution of the United States."

Black delegates supported different candidates for the nomination for governor, as did white delegates. After several ballots, the convention nominated Mayor Cameron of Petersburg, a former Conservative, for governor; John Francis Lewis, a loyalist during the Civil War and a former Republican lieutenant governor and United States senator from Rockingham County in the Shenandoah Valley, for lieutenant governor; and a former Confederate soldier Francis Simpson Blair, of Wythe County in southwestern Virginia, for attorney general.[44] The coalition won the election in November 1881. Cameron defeated Senator John Warwick Daniel (the man who would have burned the schools) to become governor.[45] At the same time, twelve Black men won election to the House of Delegates, and one more won election to the Senate of Virginia, which brought the total there to three. Readjusters would need Black and white voters to succeed in enacting a reform agenda.

Readjuster Coalition Triumphant

With the Readjuster Party's legislative majorities and a friendly governor, the General Assembly that met from December 7, 1881, through April 22, 1882, passed the largest collection of transformative legislation of any assembly to that time or for several generations thereafter. Indeed, the agenda was so packed that when the assembly reached the constitutional limit for the length of the session, the governor summoned a special session to meet immediately and complete the work.

The 1881–82 session of the General Assembly was the only one in which the Speaker of the House of Delegates (who was white) appointed several Black members to some of the most important committees.[46] Black delegates, perhaps emboldened at being part of the majority, introduced more substantive bills and resolutions than in any other session. They introduced multiple bills to limit operations of the 1866 fence law, and more than a dozen bills respecting the operations of the government of the county or city they represented,[47] including one that Richard G. L. Paige, of Norfolk County, proposed to create a county board of public health.[48] Delegates introduced several bills relating to catching and selling fish or harvesting wild game. More than half a dozen presented petitions that asked for, or introduced bills to authorize, local referenda on the sale of alcohol; Edward David Bland, who represented Prince George and Surry Counties, introduced three bills to incorporate temperance societies;[49] and Ross Hamilton, of Mecklenburg County, persuaded the House of Delegates to allow use of its chamber in the Capitol for "a lecture on the question of temperance in intoxicating drinks."[50]

Hamilton also proposed a bill to prevent people who did not live in Virginia from attending the tax-payer-supported public schools in Mecklenburg County, on the North Carolina border, and another to authorize election of local school trustees who under the school law of 1870 the state Board of Education had appointed.[51] Three delegates introduced bills to incorporate new railroad companies, and Paige introduced separate bills to incorporate two ferry companies.[52] He also introduced a bill "to authorize the trustees of Little Zion Baptist Church, Norfolk County, to borrow money and issue bonds for the same."[53] Alfred W. Harris proposed the bill "to incorporate the board of foreign missions of the Baptist foreign mission convention of the United States of America,"[54] which was the first large Black society to sponsor missionaries to foreign countries, initially to Africa. Armistead Green, of Petersburg, proposed to repeal the law that prohibited white people from marrying Black people and imposed prison sentences on any clergyman who performed such a marriage.[55] Littleton Owens, who represented Princess Anne County, presented a bill early in the 1881–82 session to amend an existing act "to prevent the seduction of females" and another a few days later "to suppress miscegenation in the state of Virginia."[56] Green and Owens almost certainly intended their bills to protect Black women from predatory white men.

The Readjusters elected new judges for the state's circuit courts and the Supreme Court of Appeals. They named Readjusters to all the important state offices such as treasurer, auditor, and second auditor. They appointed Richard Ratcliffe Farr superintendent of public instruction in the place of William Henry Ruffner whose term expired in 1882. Farr and the State Board of Education replaced nearly every county and city school superintendent in the state, all of whom the Conservative board had appointed. The new superintendents were viewed as more favorably disposed to allocate resources fairly to the Black schools than some of the Conservative superintendents had been.

Significantly, the Readjusters elected their legislative leader, Harrison Holt Riddleberger, to the United States Senate (where, with Mahone, he caucused with the Republican Party majority) and submitted the proposed constitutional amendment to abolish the poll tax to a November 1882 ratification referendum.[57] Voters ratified the amendment by vote of 107,303 to 66,131.[58]

Together, the Black and white legislators passed a bill that Riddleberger introduced (known as Riddleberger Act) to refinance the debt at a significantly lowered rate of interest and in effect repudiated part of the principal so that the cost of debt service would not in the future severely reduce the amount of money available for the public schools.[59] They reduced taxes on farmers, raised taxes on some businesses, and increased revenue by adjusting the calculation of property taxes railroads paid. As a result of refinancing the debt and changing the tax laws, Readjusters eliminated the chronic budget deficits that the state had faced every year since adoption of the Funding Act of 1871 and at the same time significantly increased spending on the public schools.

Of particular interest to the Black men who had helped elect the Readjuster majorities, the General Assembly created the Virginia Normal and Collegiate Institute (later Virginia State University). After Harris introduced the bill in February 1882, he explained to the white delegates that "while we have provided here for a Normal department" to train teachers, "we do not desire to simply become a race of teachers; we have ambition for the different learned professions for business, and some of us want the classical and scientific instruction" that the collegiate department would provide.[60] Armistead Green introduced a bill to authorize Petersburg's common council to donate a site for the school, which was built in nearby Ettrick, in Chesterfield County.[61] Twenty years later, white supremacists in the assembly restricted the school's academic offerings and renamed it the Virginia Normal and Industrial Institute.[62] White and Black Readjusters also voted to select a new site and erect new buildings near Petersburg for Central Lunatic Asylum, the first state hospital "for the reception and treatment of colored persons of unsound mind," which then operated just outside Richmond.[63] Seventeen years after the end of slavery and several failed attempts, they finally abolished the whipping post for punishing Black people. As with the poll tax amendment in the 1880 session, a white delegate introduced the bill that, with several changes, passed to prohibit punishment by whipping.[64]

A new political calculus operated in the General Assembly. Without the votes of white legislators, the most important bills that Black members favored could not have passed. As members of the biracial coalition, legislators of both races cooperated as part of the revolutionary new coalition party. Race, for once, took a backseat to other political issues in which white and Black voters shared interests. Education took the front seat.

A New Virginia?

The 1881–82 session of the General Assembly embodied a profound attempt to construct a new Virginia.[65] Governor Cameron's message to the next session of the General Assembly in 1884, which no longer had a Readjuster majority, gave him an opportunity to boast about what the coalition had achieved, reforms that he believed should become permanent parts of the state's public life. In particular, he bragged about the significant increases in spending on the public schools. "The executive of the commonwealth," he explained, setting himself as far apart as possible from his predecessor, "knows no higher duty than to contribute all in his power to furnish the means for teaching all the people to understand their rights, to know the limits of their privileges, and to feel and perform the full measure of their duties."[66]

The Readjusters took maximum advantage of the statewide political organization that William Mahone had put together and succeeded in large part because they emphasized the shared interests of white and Black voters and used egalitarian, democratic language to promote their agenda for all citizens, language that was very much like that of the March 1881 Petersburg convention. During the 1882 legislative session, Senator Mahone published a long letter that he sent to the men in Boston who invited him to give the major address on the occasion of George Washington's birthday. "Our people have just declared popular education to be among the most sacred duties and trusts of representative government," he wrote, "and are bravely executing that honorable decree. With valuable and beneficent results we are rapidly guaranteeing a priceless ballot to all entitled to it under the American theory. . . . Virginia has closed the long strife, which Mr. Jefferson foresaw and dreaded as he would dread 'the fire-bell at night,' over the status of the colored man. . . . In Virginia he is at last in the full panoply of acknowledged citizenship."[67]

About ten days before the November 1883 legislative elections, several hundred Black Virginians, including every member of the General Assembly, several candidates for the assembly, and scores of local officeholders and political leaders, published "AN ADDRESS *TO THE COLORED VOTERS OF THE STATE OF VIRGINIA*." They boasted about the laws that the Readjuster majority had passed in 1882, including abolition of "the whipping post—a relic of the barbarous ages," and the amendment that repealed the poll tax and "wiped away that requirement which, in former years, by Democratic manipulations, had disfranchised thousands of colored voters, and they made us free once again." The address also reminded voters that Readjusters had given Virginia "fifteen colored men as guards at the State penitentiary," an assistant postmaster in Norfolk, numerous local school trustees, and "a colored man as clerk in the First Auditor's office, and another bright-eyed, smart colored youngster as clerk in the Second Auditor's office." Black Republicans rejoiced in their achievements.[68]

During the 1883 campaign, an unknown Readjuster printed a broadside entitled "PUBLIC FREE SCHOOLS!" for distribution to Black women in the state. It included figures for the number of white and Black schools, white and Black teachers, and white and Black students in Virginia for each year from 1877 through 1882 with an exhortation, "*Let every Mother read, and by the facts which these figures below establish, determine for herself who are the friends to the Children.*" The clever designer used typefaces of different sizes to emphasize the differences between the numbers of schools, teachers, and students under Funder and Readjuster administrations.[69] The campaign document is important evidence that Black women

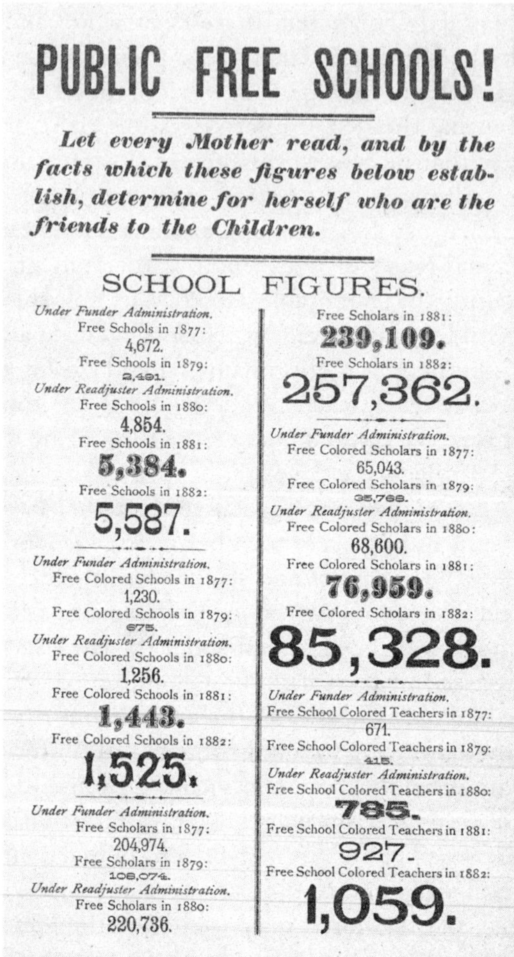

PUBLIC FREE SCHOOLS!

Let every Mother read, and by the facts which these figures below establish, determine for herself who are the friends to the Children.

SCHOOL FIGURES.

Under Funder Administration.
Free Schools in 1877:
4,672.
Free Schools in 1879:
2,491.
Under Readjuster Administration.
Free Schools in 1880:
4,854.
Free Schools in 1881:
5,384.
Free Schools in 1882:
5,587.

Under Funder Administration.
Free Colored Schools in 1877:
1,230.
Free Colored Schools in 1879:
675.
Under Readjuster Administration.
Free Colored Schools in 1880:
1,256.
Free Colored Schools in 1881:
1,443.
Free Colored Schools in 1882:
1,525.

Under Funder Administration.
Free Scholars in 1877:
204,974.
Free Scholars in 1879:
108,074.
Under Readjuster Administration.
Free Scholars in 1880:
220,736.
Free Scholars in 1881:
239,109.
Free Scholars in 1882:
257,362.

Under Funder Administration.
Free Colored Scholars in 1877:
65,043.
Free Colored Scholars in 1879:
35,768.
Under Readjuster Administration.
Free Colored Scholars in 1880:
68,600.
Free Colored Scholars in 1881:
76,959.
Free Colored Scholars in 1882:
85,328.

Under Funder Administration.
Free School Colored Teachers in 1877:
671.
Free School Colored Teachers in 1879:
415.
Under Readjuster Administration.
Free School Colored Teachers in 1880:
785.
Free School Colored Teachers in 1881:
927.
Free School Colored Teachers in 1882:
1,059.

"Public Free Schools!" was a campaign broadside likely printed ca. 1883. It included figures showing that during the years when the biracial Readjuster Party was in power, the number of Black teachers, students, the number of schools, and appropriations for the schools had been greater than when Funders dominated the General Assembly. The exhortation to mothers was a clear appeal to Black women to use their influence on their Black male relatives who could vote. (Special Collections, Library of Virginia)

were well-known to be interested in the political implications of the debt for their children and likely to let the men in their families know how they should vote.

The Death of Biracial Politics

The biracial Readjuster coalition was the most radical and successful reforming party in nineteenth-century Virginia—perhaps in all of Virginia's history. It was also the most brittle. As soon as the problems with the public debt dissolved with the 1882 Riddleberger Act that refinanced it, white Readjusters began to forsake the coalition. The inclusive, democratic language and the leaders' apparent treatment of their Black allies as equals alarmed many white Readjusters as well as white Funders, just as it attracted thousands of Black Virginians, who came to regard Mahone as their best white ally, their genuine friend and protector.

Black men and women wrote hundreds of letters to him to ask for advice or for financial assistance and to offer their help on election day. In November 1882 Isaac Dabbs, who represented Charlotte County in the House of Delegates, sent a letter to Senator Mahone affirming his loyalty and service to the Readjusters, while requesting for a young constituent an appointment as a railway postal clerk.[70] Willis William Robinson, pastor of Shiloh Baptist Church in Fredericksburg, appealed to Mahone for a federal appropriation to repair the church that had been damaged during the Civil War.[71] George Washington, of Richmond, sought Mahone's help in securing a job at the Smithsonian Institution in Washington, DC, because he had "Spent the Last Dollar I Had out of my pocket going Home to vote."[72]

Neither Mahone nor any other prominent white Readjuster conceived of Virginia society becoming fully egalitarian. Although Mahone courted Black voters and treated Black people respectfully, he never allowed any Black leaders to rise into the party's leadership. His language, however, could easily be interpreted as promising to raise Black Virginians to full social and political equality with white people—a stance that went entirely too far for a majority (probably a large majority) of white Virginians.

Mahone's implication provided opponents with an opportunity that they eagerly seized. To counter his influence and in anticipation of the November 1883 legislative elections, the leaders of the Conservative Party, who had ceased to be very effective, reorganized themselves as the Democratic Party. At the July 1883 state convention, they rather cynically jettisoned their Funder past and pledged themselves to maintain and defend the Readjusters' refinancing of the debt and to support the public schools properly.[73] That allowed Democrats to campaign on a platform of white supremacy as well as public education, and to woo white Readjusters away from what they claimed was Mahone's radical Black party. Democrats condemned Readjusters as a party of Black supremacy that threatened white men, women, and children. John W. Daniel bluntly explained in a campaign speech that year, "I am a Democrat because I am a white man and a Virginian."[74]

Tensions ran high as the election approached. Former Essex County delegate and local Republican chair Aaron Commodore denied allegations by Democrats that Black residents showed up to a polling place in

Tappahannock armed with swords.[75] A street brawl between a few Black men and a few white men in Danville a few days before the election swiftly became portrayed, through energetic and skillful work of Democratic Party propagandists, as an alarming race riot and part of a Readjuster plot to install Black supremacy in Virginia. White newspapers throughout the state reprinted an inflammatory appeal to white men that Danville business and political leaders circulated. The *Conservative Democrat* in the southwestern town of Marion, for example, reprinted the appeal and played on fears of race riots and William Mahone. "If you are a white man and a freeman," it warned its readers, "go early to the polls next Tuesday, and vote and work to redeem your state from the clutches of a tyrannical and unscrupulous Boss!"[76]

The ploy worked. In the November election Democrats narrowly won safe majorities in both houses of the General Assembly. The number of Black men elected to the House of Delegates dropped from twelve to nine, and only Daniel Norton retained his seat in the Senate.[77] That was the beginning of the end. Two years later in 1885, Democrat Fitzhugh Lee, a former Confederate general, won the governorship. Virginians both white and Black interpreted the event as the death knell for biracial politics in Virginia.

Political Realignment and the End of Black Political Influence

The long debt controversy and the rise and fall of the Readjuster Party had several important and lasting impacts on Virginia. The only one that was undoubtedly positive was that it generated additional political support for the public schools. Voters had repeatedly defeated candidates who failed to promise to support the public school system adequately. Former Conservatives who had opposed the public school system learned their lessons and became Democrats who supported it—or at least gave lip service to the value of public education in an age of universal manhood suffrage.[78]

Voters and members of the General Assembly who had supported the Readjusters fragmented into several groups. Political alignments after the Readjusters were not the same as before. White Readjusters, regardless of whether they had entered politics before the Civil War as Democrats or Whigs or after the war had been Conservatives or Republicans, divided into different political camps. Most former Conservatives and some white Republicans became Democrats. Nearly all Black Readjusters remained in the Republican Party. Some other white Republicans—the so-called "Straightouts"—who had not supported the Readjusters sought to reassert their leadership within the Republican Party.[79]

Senator Mahone was one of many white former Conservatives who traveled politically from the Conservative Party, through the Readjuster Party, and into the Republican Party. He ran for governor as the Republican candidate in 1887 and lost. Mahone had become by then a divisive figure both in state politics as well as in the party. That became painfully apparent to Black Republicans in 1888 when John Mercer Langston, the first president of Virginia Normal and Collegiate Institute, ran for the Republican nomination for the House of Representatives in the Fourth Congressional District. Mahone objected to the Black man's candidacy and recruited a white former Readjuster to run against Langston and the Democratic Party nominee. The Republican Party vote being split in the district, which had a Black majority, the Democrat won. Langston mounted a successful challenge to the Democrat's victory based on evidence of widespread electoral fraud and intimidation and was eventually seated for the final few months of the two-year term. Under the circumstances, he did not run for reelection.[80]

Mahone's unwillingness to allow Black men to rise to influential positions in either the Readjuster Party or the Republican Party frustrated and angered many of his political supporters. Daniel and Robert Norton turned against their old leader for that reason, and their brother Frederick Norton broke so sharply with his brothers and Mahone that he became a Democrat. In the cases of Daniel and Robert Norton, thwarted personal ambitions as well as an unwillingness to follow the lead of white political leaders intensified their disillusionment with Mahone.[81] That may also have been the case with John B. Syphax, who was a great-great-grandson of Martha Washington and a former one-term Republican member of the House of Delegates from Fairfax County. Readjusters singled him out in 1883 for being one of the hated "Straightouts" who assisted the Democrats. Syphax concluded his erratic political career in Virginia as a Democrat.[82]

For decades after the dissolution of the biracial Readjuster Party, nearly all Democrats in Virginia routinely condemned the Readjusters as corrupt and incompetent and as promoting Black domination in the state. That incorrect characterization allowed white supremacists to lump the Readjusters in with the Northern radical Republicans who immediately after the Civil War attempted to impose a new egalitarian politics in Virginia that included Black men with equal rights with white men. In both instances, many of the reforms failed, not because of lack of political support but because white politicians sabotaged them.

The worst consequence of the dramatic rise and fall of the Readjusters was the twenty-year campaign that white supremacists in the Democratic Party launched to make certain that Black voters could never again make an alliance with white voters and pose a serious obstacle to Democratic Party domination of the General Assembly, seats in Congress, and local government offices in Virginia. The number of Black men who managed to win election to the General Assembly gradually fell off by the 1890s to zero, and the number who won election to local offices fell almost to zero by the end of the decade. Hope for a world without "distinction of color" was dashed, if not entirely destroyed.

7

"I Am Constantly Busy"

Enduring Daily Life in Jim Crow Virginia

For Black men, women, and children, daily life in Jim Crow Virginia—in rural as well as urban environs—meant hard work almost every day and living under constant oppression and peril from white men, women, and children who implicitly and explicitly enforced white supremacy. Oppression came from de jure and de facto laws at the local and state level imposing racial discrimination and economic segregation. Peril for Black Virginians often arose from perceived slights and crimes against whites, with penalties from assaults to jail terms to summary lynchings.

A majority of Virginians lived on farms or in or near small towns. Farm life was a hard life for everybody but especially for Black men and women. Lucy Smith McKenzie, of Chesterfield County, the wife of a rural teacher, described her day in a letter that was excerpted in the Hampton Normal and Agricultural Institute's journal, *Southern Workman,* in 1893. She was the mother of a son aged five, a daughter aged two, and a baby girl aged two months. "I rise in the morning at half-past five," she wrote, to get her husband off to his school, "and from that time until night I am constantly busy. . . . Every morning by the time I get the dishes washed, the house put in order and give the baby her bath, it is near twelve o'clock. Then, as my husband is away, I feed the cow, pigs and chickens, have dinner, and after clearing up, nursing the baby, &c., sew until time to get supper ready. I have a great deal to keep me busy, yet I enjoy living out here in the country; my work is a pleasure to me."[1]

A man identified only as "H" in the *Southern Workman* who taught school, preached in two churches, and farmed a small plot of land to feed his family was also constantly busy. He reported that in 1887 he had raised

"25 bbls. of corn, 6 bushels of potatoes, 3 of peas and beans, a nice supply of vegetables, and I have 384 lbs. of pork, and fowls enough for our use." He believed himself very fortunate. "Most of the colored people would have homes," he lamented, "but for the following reasons: 1st. Wages for men are very low: from $60 to $80 per year, and from 25 to 40 cents per day. 2d. The lands are in large tracts and the owners will not cut them to suit purchasers. 3d. Most of them receive their wages in orders on the stores," much as miners who received their pay in company scrip that could be redeemed, or spent, only in the company store.[2] "H" may have been the same man who reported three years later that after "the great failure in crops this year" in his locality, "Most of the whites have turned off their hired help, saying that they are not able to pay, and most of the colored have gone to the railroads and other public works so as to make a living. We have never realized such times since slavery. Some few have homes and are doing well, but the rest are seeing hard times." He added, reflecting the deteriorating political conditions in the state, "The political feeling is not as strong between the races as it has been. The colored are not particular as to which party is successful."[3]

Life in the countryside was very different in many ways from life in a city or large town. Accidents or illnesses were more dangerous in the countryside than in a town. It could be a long walk and perhaps take several hours to reach the closest town, and even if a poor person owned a horse, nobody could summon assistance quickly. And white people, suspicious about Black people they did not know, could be anywhere and might be threatening.

Rural neighborhoods consisted of small farms and woodlots where some people worked their own land and a larger number of people worked for other people on the landlord's land. Farm labor, whether in the field or in the household, was hard work that required people to be up early in the morning and remain at work until as late in the day as possible. Within two or three miles of a person's place of residence, he or she would have known the residents of other farms, but social gatherings of more than a few people were likely uncommon except perhaps at churches and during holidays. Close family members and their nearest neighbors were probably the centers of their lives. Information about events at the county courthouse, in Richmond, or in Washington could take many days or a week or more to reach all of the rural areas in Virginia. As one person identified only as "M." noted late in 1877, it could be "a hard country and a lonely place."[4]

Colored Farmers' Alliance and Cooperative Union

Slavery had its own legal and social code to define and regulate people's behavior, but in the decades after its abolition a new regime of race relations evolved in the United States. The nineteenth-century tune "Jump Jim Crow" gave its name to the phenomenon. The negative stereotypes of the lyrics depicted Black people as impulsive, ignorant, comically credulous, irresponsible, unreliable, and dishonest. The Jim Crow regime was one of inequality and double standards, always to the disadvantage of Black people generally and of poor Black people especially. The economic, social, and legal barriers to any kind of success for freed people and their descendants were often high ones. That made it difficult or impossible for members of families like the farmers just quoted to escape the constant hard work and lonely life in or near poverty.[5]

The history of the rise and fall of the Colored Farmers' Alliance and Cooperative Union of Virginia in the 1890s illustrates how the lack of political power and the economic difficulties farmers faced combined to put them at a severe disadvantage. It was one of the largest organizations of Black Virginians in the nineteenth century. It was also one of the shortest-lived.

Founded in 1886 by Black farmers in Texas, the Colored Farmers' Alliance was one of many such associations founded throughout the Southern and Great Plains states by farmers of both races.[6] Those in the Southern states were racially segregated, including the Virginia Farmers' Alliance, which was for white farmers only. The Colored Farmers' Alliance, which included white officers, grew rapidly in the cotton-raising regions of the South. In Virginia most of its members were recruited from the tobacco-growing region, where Black farmers, like white farmers, saw the growth of large tobacco manufacturing firms as a serious threat to their economic survival. The large firms like the American Tobacco Company could control and reduce the prices they paid farmers for leaf tobacco and left farmers who refused to accept the low prices without any market. Farmers also had few or no options about where to purchase supplies or obtain credit. The farmers' alliances established exchanges where farmers could purchase seed, fertilizer, and equipment at wholesale prices and try to form joint marketing agreements to negotiate for higher prices with cotton buyers and tobacco manufacturers. The Colored Farmers' Alliance opened its first exchange in Virginia in Norfolk, where a white alliance official managed it. Membership was $2.00 a year.[7]

The white national leaders of the Colored Farmers' Alliance saw Black farmers as potential allies and tried to encourage farmers of both races to develop a class consciousness for united action. They hired men or persuaded volunteers to act as organizers and lecturers to inform farm owners and agricultural laborers about the alliance and to recruit members.[8] The alliance lecturer in Virginia beginning in the spring of 1890 was William H. Warwick, a Black man who was about twenty-seven years old and lived in Boydton, in Mecklenburg County.[9]

Representatives from alliances in Nelson, Madison, Louisa, Isle of Wight, Fluvanna, Dinwiddie, Cumberland, Charlotte, Appomattox, Amherst, and Albemarle Counties formally founded the Colored Farmers' Alliance and Cooperative Union of Virginia at a meeting in August 1890 at the Henrico County courthouse. "The object of the organization," according to one newspaper's account, "is to create a market for what the farmers produce and to obtain at cheaper rates what they purchase. They expect to accomplish this by uniting together and establishing exchanges throughout the State at which they can buy and sell at wholesale prices."[10] By that October reportedly about ten thousand Virginia farmers in twenty-five counties had joined the alliance.[11]

The convention delegates appointed a state board of directors, elected the white director of the Norfolk exchange as president, and named Warwick organizer and lecturer for the states of Virginia, Maryland, and West Virginia. Alliances allowed women as well as men to join, and on the second day of its organizational meeting, the Virginia alliance proposed that the national constitution of the Colored Farmers' Alliance be amended to require that women pay a twenty-five cent initiation fee and ten cents quarterly rather than $2.00 annual dues. The Virginia meeting also named Warwick one of the alliance's representatives to the national Colored Farmers' Alliance annual meeting that December in Ocala, Florida, where the all-white Southern Farmers' Alliance was also scheduled to meet.[12]

The Southern Farmers' Alliance had recently scored significant victories in several state elections in which Democrats endorsed its proposals. Some of those Democrats also promoted racial segregation and discrimination and endorsed plans to disfranchise Black voters.[13] Some very influential white Virginia Democrats also embraced some alliance proposals, but in the aftermath of the Readjuster movement they were openly hostile toward Black participation in politics. White leaders of the Virginia Farmers' Alliance were for the most part Democrats engaged in large-scale commercial agriculture, and they had little interest in poor farmers who owned or worked on small farms.[14] Members of the Colored

Farmers' Alliance, especially the men from Virginia, were disillusioned with an indifferent Republican Party and opposed to cooperation with hostile Democrats. They endorsed a radical proposal to create a third national political party to unite all advocates of agrarian reform.[15]

The Colored Farmers' Alliance appears to have flourished in Virginia during 1891, but few records survive to document the work of its leaders or the number of its members. By one unverified account it had enrolled twenty thousand members in forty-two counties.[16] The alliance held its second state convention in Richmond in August of that year.[17] White officials did not attend, and the Black delegates unanimously elected Warwick state superintendent, which gave the Virginia alliance exclusively Black management. The convention named two delegates and two alternates to the next national convention of the Colored Alliance, and Warwick announced that the weekly Boydton *Midland Express* would be the alliance's official newspaper. Unfortunately, no known copies of the newspaper survive from the time to document the alliance's work.

The convention also invited the president of the Virginia Industrial, Mercantile, and Building Association, a Black financial services company, to address the members. The alliance and the association agreed to cooperate for the mutual benefit of their two memberships. Before the convention adjourned, the delegates adopted a resolution that in effect declared independence from both the racially exclusive Virginia Farmers' Alliance and the Democratic Party. Members of the Colored Alliance, it stated, "are beginning to realize that our salvation rests in neither of the old political parties and are no longer slaves to either, but are organizing to protect ourselves, and thus free the toiling masses of our race from the deadly fangs of monopoly, and rings, and trust companies."[18]

This was tantamount to war. White leaders of the national alliance then withdrew support from the Virginia alliance. They denied Warwick access to the alliance's membership list, which made it impossible for him to collect dues. The exchange in Norfolk ceased functioning, and without support from the national organization the demise of the Virginia Colored Farmers' Alliance began. The white Virginia Farmers' Alliance offered no help other than printing an occasional news item about the Colored Alliance in its newspaper, the Richmond *Virginia Sun*. Warwick published a long letter in the *Virginia Sun* in June 1892 announcing that if necessary the Colored Alliance would pursue its own agenda. Black and white farmers shared the same economic problems, he explained, and "we are willing to act together with our white brethren and the people all over this country to bring about these reforms. We are one common people with a common interest in the same country, and we are here to stay. And no people better realize the need of unity of purpose and action to suppress the outrages perpetrated upon white and colored alike by class legislation, ballot-box stuffing, lynch law mobs, than the colored people. And we feel safe to say we voice the honest sentiment of every good and thinking colored man in this country when we say they stand ready to act with any party that will go to work to remedy these evils."[19]

In February 1892 Warwick had attended and was elected assistant secretary of the conference in St. Louis that founded the People's, or Populist, Party. Organized by agrarian reformers campaigning against monopolies, high railroad transportation costs, and political corruption, the Populists offered a third-party alternative. Warwick attended the national convention in Omaha that July when it nominated candidates for president and vice president. At that time he criticized the Republican Party for taking the votes of Black men for granted and indicated his willingness to cooperate with any party that worked for the benefit of Black farmers.[20]

Ultimately Black Virginians did not participate meaningfully in the very limited campaign that the People's Party waged in Virginia in 1892,[21] not even Warwick. The party's white Virginia leaders did not welcome Black men. So strong had been the backlash among opponents of the biracial Readjuster Party that political cooperation between the races, as occurred in neighboring North Carolina in the 1890s, was no longer possible in Virginia. By the end of 1892, the Colored Farmers' Alliance had completely collapsed nationwide following violence in southern cotton fields.[22] The Virginia alliance ceased to function, and Warwick moved across the state line to teach at Reedy Creek Institute in Littleton, North Carolina. He made an unsuccessful run for the Republican nomination for a seat in the North Carolina Senate later in the 1890s but then, like many other Black Americans, gave up on politics.[23]

Urban Life

Inhabitants of towns and cities lived in different conditions than did farmers and other rural residents, but in many instances economic conditions in urban areas were also deplorable. They also had to remain constantly busy to feed, clothe, and house themselves and their families. In a study entitled "The Negroes of Farmville, Virginia," that W. E. B. Du Bois conducted for the federal Department of Labor in July and August of 1897, he found that the town's 2,190 Black residents (almost twice the number of its white residents) included many people who moved there from the surrounding countryside. "At the same time," he noted, "Farmville boys and girls are attracted by the large city life of Richmond, Norfolk, Baltimore, and New York," and "the Negro population appears to have fallen off" since 1890. Women formed a slight majority of the adult population, but "The proportion of children under 15 is also increased by the habit which married couples and widowed persons have of going to cities to work and leaving their children with grandparents. This also accounts for the small proportion of colored children in a city like Philadelphia."[24]

Du Bois reported that "business enterprises in which Farmville Negroes are engaged on their own account" included "brickmaking, the grocery trade, barbering, restaurant keeping, furniture repairing, silversmithing and clock repairing, shoemaking, wood selling and whip making, steam laundering, contracting and building, painting, blacksmithing, wheelwrighting, hotel keeping, and farming." He explained that "While the range of employment open to colored men is not large, that open to women is peculiarly restricted, so that most girls have only the choice between domestic service and housewifery." Moreover, "There are no colored physicians or lawyers in the town, preachers and teachers being the only representatives of the learned professions. The position of preacher is the most influential of all positions among the Negroes, and brings the largest degree of personal respect and social prestige."[25]

"There are 92 common laborers" in Farmville, Du Bois continued, "including 17 porters and 3 janitors." About 162 other men and women, "some of whom are residents of the town and some not, are wholly engaged in domestic service. The men receive from $8 to $10 a month. The women receive from $1 to $5, according to age and work." Du Bois also recorded, "There is considerable dissatisfaction over the state of domestic service. The Negroes are coming to regard the work as a relic of slavery and as degrading, and only enter it from sheer necessity, and then as a temporary makeshift. Parents hate to expose their sons to the early lessons of servility, which are thus learned, and their daughters to the ever-possible fate of concubinage."[26]

Their residences varied in quality, perhaps more than in poor rural areas, but they were all, or nearly all, crowded. "The houses which the 262 Negro families of Farmville occupy," Du Bois discovered, "vary from 1 to 9 rooms each in size, but have generally 2 or 3 rooms. . . . Of the 262 families, 6.5 per cent occupied one-room homes; 51.1 per cent, two-room homes; 17.2 per cent, three-room homes; 11.8 per cent, four-room homes, and 13.4 per cent, homes of five or more rooms. . . . There are about 240 separate houses occupied by Negroes."[27]

"Of the 262 families of Farmville," Du Bois went on, "only 1 is Episcopalian and 3 are Presbyterian; of the rest, 26 are Methodist and 218 Baptist. In the town of Farmville there are 3 colored church edifices, and in the surrounding country there are 3 or 4 others." First Baptist Church had the largest congregation and largest building in the town, and he described it as the social center of the Black community. "The Methodist church, with a small membership, is the second social center of Farmville, and there is also a second Baptist church, of a little lower grade, with more habitual noise and shouting."[28] About forty or fifty women belonged to the Loving Sisters of Worship, a benevolent society that "has been in existence in Farmville for over twenty years," and the town boasted lodges of Odd Fellows, Masons, Good Samaritans, True Reformers, and other fraternal and social service organizations.[29]

Whether Farmville was typical of other small towns in Virginia is not certain because of the lack of reliable contemporary studies, but it seems likely that it was. The population of the state's cities, although containing more professional men and women such as teachers, physicians, clergymen, and lawyers, probably did not differ very significantly from what Du Bois documented for Farmville. Working conditions for Black men and women in Richmond are better documented than for elsewhere. Throughout the years beginning in the 1870s, Black men in Richmond, as in other cities, formed associations of workers in various industries, such as tobacco workers, confectioners, bakers, and the like. During the 1880s, the first large national labor union, the Knights of Labor, formed an active chapter in Richmond and promoted cooperation between Black and white men who did the same or similar work. It even held its national convention in the city in 1886 and in a move that generated controversy allowed men of both races to attend.[30] Coalitions of Black and white working men won a surprise victory in the municipal election in Richmond, and members of the Knights of Labor won control of Lynchburg's city council in 1887.[31] About that same time, though, when Black stone cutters in Richmond insisted on an opportunity to take part on equal terms with white workmen in the construction of a new city hall, the city government refused, which delayed construction of the building for several years.[32]

Racial Segregation

Charles E. Wynes, the most thorough student of late-nineteenth-century race relations in Virginia, concluded that Black residents of the state, with declining political influence, lack of material improvement, and rising overt racial discrimination, often had to resign themselves to a dimmer future than they had anticipated.[33] Local, state, and national officials seldom enforced constitutional and legal protections of civil and political rights of Black Americans. For instance, the Virginia Constitution of 1869 specified that qualified voters could serve on juries, but in Pittsylvania and several other counties, judges empaneled juries from lists of jurors that contained only names of white men who had qualified to vote. Congress passed An Act to Protect All Citizens in Their Civil and Legal Rights, known as the Civil Rights Act of 1875, that, among other things, prohibited states from excluding men from jury service on account of race. The Supreme Court of the United States ruled in *Strauder v. West Virginia* in 1880 that the law was an appropriate piece of legislation that the Fourteenth Amendment authorized Congress to enact to enforce the guarantees of freedom and citizenship that the amendment enumerated. In two companion cases on the same day, the Supreme Court ruled in *Virginia v. Rives* and *Ex Parte Virginia* that state judges could not legally exclude Black men from jury service by the subterfuge that the judges in Pittsylvania and other counties had employed. Nevertheless, neither the federal government nor the state government took effective steps to prevent local judges from excluding Black men from juries. In 1883, the Supreme Court of the United States in *The Civil Rights Cases* declared most of the provisions of the 1875 law unconstitutional.[34]

The General Assembly required that the public schools be racially segregated when the school system was created in 1870, and thereafter racial segregation crept in gradually throughout the society, which limited the opportunities and liberties of Black Virginians. Early in that year, the Orange and Alexandria Railroad introduced separate passenger cars for the races. The president of the railroad was John Strode Barbour, who responded to the success of the biracial Readjuster movement early in the 1880s by organizing the white supremacist Democratic Party. He was the first state chair of the party, and the General Assembly later elected him to succeed William Mahone in the United States Senate.[35] In January 1871, Kate Cummings, en route from New York to Lynchburg, sued the Orange and Alexandria after she was arrested for refusing to leave the first-class car and move into the smoking car. The federal court in Richmond awarded her $1,000 in damages. About the same time, Jonathan Jasper Wright, a judge of the South Carolina Supreme Court, rode in a first-class car through South Carolina and North Carolina on his way to Washington, DC, but when his train entered Virginia, the president of the Richmond and Danville Railroad personally ordered him to leave the car. Wright sued for $5,000 but settled out of court for $1,250. The state's other railroads did not attempt to institute mandatory separate seating until later in the century.[36] The Supreme Court of the United States allowed such mandatory racial segregation in public spaces in its *Plessy v. Ferguson* decision in 1896 so long as the separate facilities ostensibly provided equal quality.[37]

Residential racial segregation became conspicuous in Virginia's cities late in the nineteenth century, as Du Bois discovered in Farmville. Cities did not require segregation by law until the second and third decades of the twentieth century, but it was a fact long before that. During slavery, household servants and many other enslaved people had lived with or very near their enslavers, but after freedom, working Black people in many cities and towns lived in neighborhoods distinct from white ones. New street railways or bus services facilitated that residential segregation by making it easy for white people to move to new neighborhoods on the fringes of a city and commute to their work downtown as well as for the men and women who worked in their households as cooks, nurses, cleaners, washerwomen, gardeners, carriage drivers, and handymen to travel in the opposite direction each day to work in the white neighborhoods. *Richmond Planet* publisher John Mitchell Jr. counted on white people's reliance on their household servants' use of the city's street cars in 1904 when he organized a boycott after the street car company imposed mandatory racially segregated seating in the cars. Men and women also organized boycotts of city transit systems in Portsmouth, Petersburg, Norfolk, Newport News, and Lynchburg. Without adequate political influence, though, the boycotts all failed to achieve their objective.[38]

Interracial Marriage

Relations between white and Black Virginians deteriorated across the board late in the nineteenth century. Issues of race were a constant preoccupation of white people as racial classifications and regulations of Jim Crow replaced the laws and practices of slavery. The most intimate aspect of race relations, interracial sex, attracted the attention of white people. Virginia law had prohibited marriages between white people and Indigenous people and also between white people and free Black people since 1691.[39] Virginia law had also defined people with one-fourth or more of African ancestry—the laws sometimes used the word *blood*—to be "negro" or "colored." The legal definitions reflected the attitudes about racial differences in the society, specifically the beliefs of the white men who adopted and interpreted the laws. All of the Virginia laws about interracial marriage were laws about how racial identification controlled marriage options. They were not incorporated into the state's law of marriage, but into the state's law of race. The law of race replaced the law of slavery in the regulation and limitation of the lives of Black Virginians.

Newspapers in the years after the Civil War took notice of interracial marriages or liaisons and reported dozens of such occurrences across the state, including in the counties of Wythe, Smyth, Roanoke, Prince Edward, Henrico, Cumberland, Charles City, Buckingham, Augusta, and Amelia.[40] In 1873, the General Assembly added a new provision to the Code of Virginia. It declared, "All marriages between a white person and a negro . . . shall be absolutely void, without any decree of divorce, or other legal process."[41] That immediately annulled all interracial marriages that had been performed outside Virginia; and it violated the important legal doctrine of comity, which could be found in the "full faith and credit" clause of the Constitution of the United States. Comity required governments to acknowledge the legality of and to respect contracts and other legal agreements, such as marriages, legally entered into in other states or countries. But, as a judge of the Virginia Supreme Court of Appeals explained in *Kinney v. Commonwealth* in 1878, all of the former slave states, including Virginia, routinely ignored the comity doctrine in the one, single instance of interracial marriage; and nobody made them change.[42]

In the same year that the state's highest court handed down that opinion, the General Assembly amended and strengthened the state's law and explicitly made it illegal for "any white person and negro" to "go out of this state for the purpose of being married, and with the intention of returning" and then "cohabiting as man and wife. . . . The fact of their cohabitation here as man and wife shall be evidence of their marriage." The amendment also abolished the fine for interracial marriage but increased the prison sentence from one year to between two and five years for white people convicted of marrying "a negro" and for the first time imposed the same sentence on the "negro."[43]

During the years immediately following the 1878 amendments to the state code, the Virginia Supreme Court of Appeals handed down rulings on several appeals from convictions of people for violating the laws against interracial marriage. The judges insisted on strict interpretation of the code and overturned several convictions of people who were identified as Black in the court records but who had not been proved to have the required minimum of one-fourth African ancestry. That is not to say that the judges of the state's highest court ever approved of mixed-race marriage or even tolerated it. In 1884, they ruled on an appeal from the conviction in the Montgomery County Court of "Isaac Jones, a negro," for marrying "Martha A. Gray, a white person." Justice Thomas Turner Fauntleroy made that clear when he wrote that Jones "stands thus convicted of a crime, not only against the law of Virginia, but against the just sensibilities of her civilization."[44] When the case came back to the appellate court on a second appeal the following year, the judges overturned the conviction because the trial had not proved that Jones was "a negro." Judge Benjamin Watkins Lacy nevertheless explained the state's laws bluntly. "The charge against Isaac Jones," he wrote, "is, that he is a negro, and that being a negro he was married to a white woman. To be a negro is not a crime; to marry a white woman is not a crime; but to be a negro, and being a negro, to marry a white woman is a felony."[45] Interracial marriage, including interracial marriages performed outside of Virginia, remained illegal in the state until the Supreme Court of the United States decision in *Loving v. Virginia* (1967) that struck down Virginia's law prohibiting interracial marriages as a violation of the Fourteenth Amendment.[46]

As with laws during slavery that required free people to register or freed people to leave the state within a year or be re-enslaved, white officials sometimes neglected or refused to enforce laws against interracial marriage.[47] Local and personal considerations continued to influence white officials after slavery. A prime example is Reuben T. Coleman, a Cumberland County entrepreneur who had been born into slavery. During the course of his life, he married three white women and lived successively with them in Virginia. At least twice he married in Washington, DC. Closely allied with one of the leading white families in the county and himself a very successful businessman, Coleman evaded the law and prospered in spite of some of his white neighbors, who suspected him of poisoning his second wife as a ruse to escape prosecution. After a three-day investigation a jury determined she died of natural causes and found "nothing whatever to cause the slightest suspicion to rest upon R. T. Coleman."[48] Coleman's ability to live his life as he pleased did not shield his third wife from censure, though. She worked in his household, perhaps as a nurse or in some service capacity, before they married, but after he died in 1909, some of her white and Black relatives and neighbors shunned her for violating the law and what by then were widely accepted social conventions.[49]

Lynching

Thomas Calhoun Walker, a Black attorney in Gloucester County, dedicated himself to defending the interests of his Black clients in court, especially against charges related to what he described as "Jim Crow skirmishes." In the mid-1880s, one of these skirmishes inspired him to take up the law. As he recalled later, he stopped at the Gloucester courthouse where he witnessed the trial of a fourteen-year-old Black girl who "was being tried for housebreaking and larceny of a few dollars by a white family where she worked as cook and housemaid. You know how that is." Having no one to defend her at trial, she was swiftly convicted and sentenced to two years in jail. Believing the charges false and that a lawyer would have changed the outcome, Walker resolved then to become an attorney who could represent Blacks in legal proceedings.[50]

Throughout the final decades of the nineteenth century, Black men and women were vulnerable to violations of their rights and bodies. Lynching was the ultimate violation of human rights and the most atrocious. Most accounts define lynching imprecisely as a mob action that results in the death of one or more people without a judicial conviction. Those definitions exclude fatal or injurious attacks one or two people made on victims who were suspected of some wrong-doing. Similar nonfatal violence has seldom been tabulated, even though it was included in the original understanding of the Revolutionary-era verb *lynch* and phrase *lynch law* as any extralegal punishment of a supposed miscreant, not necessarily resulting in death.[51] The ubiquity of lynching spurred attorney Thomas C. Walker to remark that when he was defending a Black man accused of trying to rape a white woman, often a spurious charge, he went to great lengths to protect his client from what he called a "lynching bee," a clear reference to the common sewing bees of the time, in which small social gatherings of women made or mended clothes.[52]

An online compilation of lynchings reported in Virginia and Washington, DC, newspapers has identified more than one hundred victims of lynching in Virginia between the end of the Civil War and the end of the nineteenth century. The definition that the compilers have employed is an "extra-legal killing of a person by a group of at least three people acting under the pretext of service to justice or tradition." This excludes killings that one or two people perpetrated or that might have been regarded as personal conflicts not involving "service to justice or tradition." Files of small-town newspapers are very incomplete, too, which suggests that some episodes may never be identified, and that other murders or lynchings may never have been publicized. Some murders or assaults may have been prosecuted in the state's courts, but many of them went unpunished, unprosecuted, or even uninvestigated, especially in instances involving a Black victim.[53]

At least eighty-four lynchings of Black Virginians (including one woman) have been documented, and at least twenty white Virginians (including one woman) were lynched. Contemporary defenders of the practice used lynchings of whites in their attempts to show that the mob violence was not racially motivated. Of the reported events, more than forty arose from accusations of rape or attempted sexual assault. More than thirty-five involved charges of murder (including one murder of a Black man) or attempted murder, five of theft, and two (including one of the women) of arson. Only a few members of the many lynch mobs were ever prosecuted, and no member of a mob was ever hanged for the crime of murder.[54]

White newspapers routinely refused to accord a presumption of innocence to Black men who were arrested or even suspected of committing crimes, especially if a white woman was identified as a victim. For example, several newspapers printed accounts of the November 1889 lynching of Owen (or Orion) Anderson, a Black youth who had been arrested and accused of assaulting a white girl in Loudoun County. Under the headline, "THEY HANGED HIM. HOW A LYNCHING WAS CONDUCTED IN LOUDOUN COUNTY," one of the papers, the *Richmond Dispatch,* referred to Anderson as "the fiend," "the brute," and the "negro scoundrel," even though the girl could not make a positive identification. He reportedly confessed to that and two other attempted assaults on white women, but the newspaper did not indicate what pressure the sheriff or jailer put on him to confess. About 1:00 a.m. during the night after Anderson's arrest, twenty-five or thirty white men entered the jail equipped with "axes, crowbars, and sledges" to break Anderson out if necessary, but they forced the jailer to hand him over. The mob conveyed Anderson "down Church street to the depôt, where one of the *posse* on horseback put the rope through the hook on the derrick, and Anderson was raised up and was dead in a few minutes. Several pistol-shots were fired into his body. One ball struck in the head, one in the body, and one in the leg." As was customary, the newspaper reported laconically that the members of the lynch mob were "all unknown."[55]

In the rapidly growing city of Roanoke on September 21, 1893, a large mob estimated at four to five thousand people demanded that the jailer hand over Thomas Smith, who had been arrested and accused of assaulting and robbing the wife of a prominent local white farmer. The jailor, commonwealth's attorney, and mayor intervened and persuaded the crowd to disperse, but the mob returned later in the day. In spite of the presence of militiamen, the mob attacked the jail. The militia fired into the mob and killed nine white people, but the remainder of the mob overwhelmed the militia and removed Smith from the jail. They lynched him in downtown Roanoke, fired shots into his body, and later burned it. Authorities tried five men for lynching Smith, but only four of them were convicted and on the lesser count of burning his body. They received sentences of twelve months in jail.[56]

Two of the worst episodes took place in southwestern Virginia. Charles Miller, John Scott, and Robert Burton, miners who were visiting Clifton Forge, in Alleghany County, on a Saturday in September 1891, had their portraits taken as they posed in wild west garb and displaying pistols. A white man tried to arrest them, on what charge is not clear, so the three

A broadside exhorting "You Shudder at the Picture!" depicts a mass lynching near Clifton Forge, Virginia, on October 18, 1891. John Mitchell Jr. reprinted the image from his *Richmond Planet* of October 31 on a broadside as part of his courageous campaign against lynching. (David M. Rubenstein Rare Book & Manuscript Library, Duke University)

men quickly left town. A white posse pursued and attacked them, and during a gunfight two men were killed and two injured. The mob hanged Miller, Scott, and Burton and shot their bodies full of bullets. The white photographer who had taken their portraits earlier in the day exploited the situation for his personal advantage and printed cabinet cards with the three portraits and a photograph of their bodies hanging in a tree. He distributed them to advertise his studio.[57]

In southwestern Virginia's Tazewell County, early in 1893, five or six Black men were lynched on consecutive days.[58] A large mob lynched Jerry Brown, one of several men whom they suspected of killing two white men, on January 31, 1893. The next day, the mob reassembled and found and lynched John Johnson, Spencer Branch, Sam Blow, Sam Ellerson (or McDonald), and perhaps another man whose name is not known. The *Clinch Valley News*, published in the nearby town of Tazewell, reported that "none of the lynchers were in any way disguised," but in spite of a grand jury investigation they all escaped prosecution and punishment.[59]

John Mitchell Jr., editor and publisher of the *Richmond Planet* for many years, was the boldest and most tireless Virginia warrior against lynching. Mitchell had a remarkable eye and ear for the telling anecdotes that he used to remind his readers that all people involved in lynchings were individual human beings and not merely names and numbers in a violent event. Lynching was a concerted act of white on Black violence that law enforcement officers and the perpetrators' families and neighbors often did nothing to prevent and often even approved. Victims and their families and neighbors suffered, sometimes for years. Mitchell was peculiarly well talented at bringing those human dramas to his readers and making them angry at injustice or moving them to tears.[60]

Mitchell's damning coverage of lynchings was extensive, constant, and unflinching. He published a long editorial in the *Richmond Planet* on December 13, 1890, to condemn the lynching of Thaddeus Fowlkes, who had been arrested and charged with killing a white man in Charlotte County. "No one doubts," Mitchell acknowledged, that "he would have been legally hanged dead by the neck had he have been convicted." As armed deputies were transferring him to a jail in Danville, though, "a body of irresponsible white men, armed with shot-guns intercept the sworn officers of the law, defy the orders of a judge, sitting in a judicial capacity, and hang their trembling, cowering victim, helpless as he was to a tree, and stand and see him slowly strangled to death." The armed deputies on the scene did not intervene and by what

Born enslaved in Richmond, John Mitchell Jr. (1863–1929) became a prominent newspaper editor, politician, banker, and civil rights activist who fought against segregation, racial discrimination, lynching, and other violence against Blacks in America through the pages of his *Richmond Planet*. (W. N. Hartshorn and George W. Penniman, eds., *An Era of Progress and Promise, 1863–1910: The Religious, Moral, and Educational Development of the American Negro Since His Emancipation*, Boston: Priscilla Publishing Co., 1910. Library of Virginia)

Mitchell characterized as their "passive submission become accessories to the crime and are virtually as guilty as the scoundrels who pulled the rope, and sent into eternity a human being wholly unprepared to meet his GOD." The lynchers and the inactive witnesses, he explained in the plainest possible language, "are guilty of murder. They should be arraigned before a jury of their country-men to answer for their crime." Mitchell appealed to the governor to take action to bring the guilty men to justice. "*Lynch-law must go!*" Immediately below the blistering editorial, Mitchell printed a report on a South Carolina lynching with the headline, "A COLORED MAN ROASTED ALIVE."[61]

Before technological innovations that enabled Mitchell in the twentieth century to publish actual photographs of victims of lynching in his newspaper, he did his own sketches. One of the earliest signed engravings of Mitchell's art appeared on the front page of the edition for February 23, 1895. Entitled, "White Men to the Rescue," it depicts a mob of white men preparing to hang a Black man and another group, of "liberal-minded white men," approaching to stop them. Three and a half years later, though, Mitchell's lynching art suggests that he had abandoned much hope that "liberal-minded white men" would often come to the rescue. To illustrate one of the many lists he published of people lynched in the United States—not only in the Southern states—during the ensuing years, he reprinted the image of the Clifton Forge lynching victims hanging from a single tree with the headline "The Reign of Lawlessness" and one of the sub-headlines that declared "The Law Sleeps." Mitchell's bold persistence earned him the title the Fighting Editor.[62]

Local authorities often had to go to great lengths to prevent a lynching and follow the rule of law. In one instance in the summer of 1895, Lucy Jane Pollard, a white woman, was found dead in the yard outside her Lunenburg County farmhouse. Although some circumstantial evidence implicated her white husband, local suspicion quickly settled on four Black people, Pokey Barnes, Mary Barnes, Mary Abernathy, and William Henry (also known as Solomon) Marable. When the white sheriff first arrested some of them, he assembled a guard in the nighttime and secretly conveyed the prisoners to the jail of another county in order to prevent a possible lynching. Marable, Abernathy, and Pokey Barnes were all convicted. Marable was eventually hanged but not before three trials and a remarkable campaign that John Mitchell led to provide him with defense counsel and to publicize evidence that might have exonerated him and to cast doubt on the reliability of other evidence that appeared to condemn him.[63]

A charge of sexual assault was just one of several excuses that perpetrators of lynching and supporters of lynch law adduced to justify and explain the practice, but it became the most notorious and roused the most fear among white people. Historian Diane Sommerville documented the widespread fear that rapidly arose in the states of the former Confederacy, that after the end of slavery white women were under a new threat of sexual assault from Black men. Many white Southerners and Virginians believed that without the control over Black males' bodies and behavior that slavery had provided, Black men had become much more dangerous than enslaved men had ever been, while refusing to acknowledge that white men had a long history of exerting sexual control of and exploiting Black women.[64]

Fears and the memories of the fears endured into the twentieth century in popular literature, folklore, family stories, and the new medium of cinema. Edmonia Barksdale, a white Virginian who grew up during and after the Civil War, relied on and tried to take advantage of those memories and fears in a February 1914 public lecture in favor of suffrage for women. According to two newspaper accounts, she told her audience that "after the war she had recommended the carrying of firearms by girls as a measure of self-protection in lawless times. The women of this day needed the ballot as the women of that day needed the bullet, she claimed, for their own protection."[65]

White Southerners, including Virginians, had a highly inflated fear of violence directed at themselves. They were much less concerned about Black-on-Black violence. When the Jim Crow system was in its infancy, a Black man was tried in a rural county for killing another Black man. According to the recollection of the accused man's white lawyer—Joseph Bryan, then a young attorney who would later become one of the South's most important industrialists—a jury member told him afterward that the jury acquitted the accused man to give the lawyer a courtroom victory early in his career. Members of Bryan's family chuckled at the juryman's recollection: "'What's one Nigger more or less to us?' Says I: 'Let the d—d black rascal off,' says I, 'and help the young man along.'"[66]

Black Migration

As W. E. B. Du Bois noted in his analysis of Farmville's people at the end of the 1890s, a decade and a half after the destruction of the Readjuster Party, Black Virginians left the state in great numbers to seek better opportunities and to escape discrimination, poverty, violence, and the many humiliations that the Jim Crow regime imposed on people. In 1888, "B.," from an unidentified place, reported, "The times have been particularly hard this year; the men had to leave their wives and children and go off to other States to find work to do to support their families."[67] In 1890, a teacher in a rural area noted, "The people are all farmers. There is nothing to induce young people to stay here, so as soon as they are old enough to work for themselves, they are gone."[68]

Several former legislators, unable to support themselves and their families adequately in Virginia, emigrated, but there were many other reasons for emigration. Willis A. Hodges, who had served in the Convention of 1867–68 and had a long and tempestuous career in the politics of his native Princess Anne County, left for New York in 1878 after agreeing to leave the state following an arrest for a disturbance on election day. He lived in Brooklyn for several years, becoming active in Republican politics, before returning to Virginia early in the 1880s. His nephew John Quincy Hodges, who was a member of the House of Delegates in the 1869–71 sessions, also returned to his native New York in the 1880s after the death of his wife and several occasions in which he was arrested for drunk and disorderly conduct, for which he served short sentences in the city jail when he lacked the money for his fines. In New York he worked as a clerk in an insurance company. In 1900 the census enumerator recorded him as residing with his sister in Brooklyn and identified both of them and her husband as white.[69]

Three decades before what historians call the Great Migration, which began in the 1910s, tens of thousands of Black people began to flee Virginia and the other states of the former Confederacy. During the 1870s, the populations of Black and white Virginians increased at about the same rate, but between 1880 and 1930 the number of Black Virginians remained almost the same (between 631,616 and 690,017), while the number of white Virginians doubled (from 880,858 to 1,770,441). So many Black people left Virginia that the percentage of Virginians who were Black dropped during the fifty-year period from 41.9 percent in 1880 to 26.8 percent in 1930 and dropped below one-fourth during the next decade.

There were many reasons for the exodus. The loss of political power and of the ability to protect their rights was certainly a powerful one. The lure of good jobs elsewhere was undoubtedly another. During the serious and prolonged recession that began early in the 1890s, Virginians of both races had difficulty finding paying work. But many Black Virginians did not leave the state, either by choice or by circumstance. Despite the constant discrimination, they remained on the farm and in towns or cities where they and their families had built communities.

A large majority of Black men worked hard in low-paying jobs in the building trades, as hack or wagon drivers, in factories, on railroads, and in other occupations. Black women continued for the most part to work as they had done during slavery and afterward, as seamstresses, take in laundry, serve as domestic servants, cooks, or nursemaids in white households, as well as raise their own children, take care of their own houses, and do the cooking and cleaning. They were "constantly busy" with the work of everyday life while facing the constant effects of Jim Crow segregation.

When asked about these effects, Gloucester attorney T. C. Walker responded, "It is just the same as a quarantine sign for contagious diseases. . . . It generates a strange fear as of something 'catching.' The distance widens between the races; they become more suspicious and more ignorant of each other."[70] Anna Harris lived through, witnessed, and experienced all of that. As a girl in the 1860s, she became a free person. As a young woman later, she must have had the same hopes for an easier life as other freed people, but she was evidently frustrated at being unable to attain the dream. As a middle-aged woman she saw the imposition of Jim Crow with all of its limitations, humiliations, and ill treatment of Black men and women. These experiences produced very strong opinions that would endure throughout her life. As a very old woman in the 1930s, Harris exclaimed to an interviewer from the Works Progress Administration's Federal Writers' Project, "No white man ever been in my house. Don't 'low it. Dey sole my sister Kate. I saw it wid dese here eyes. Sole her in 1860, and I ain't seed nor heard of her since." Harris admitted that some Black people believed that "white folks is all right dese days. Maybe dey is, maybe dey isn't. But I can't stand to see 'em. Not on my place."[71]

8

"To Take Our Place in the Business World"

The Segregated Economy

At the August 1917 annual meeting of the Right Worthy Grand Council of the Independent Order of Saint Luke, L. Clarence Miller, business manager of the order's print shop, urged Richmond members to use his shop rather than pay white printers for producing necessary work for their fraternal orders, churches, and schools. He advised Black people to patronize Black-owned businesses. "We cannot build up our plant to compete with that of the white man's in a day, a week or a year," Miller explained, "but, thanks to the opposition, the oppression and the discrimination of the other races against us, we are being gradually cemented together in thought and action, and what may seem to be persecution may be a blessing in disguise, and may be the way Providence has willed it that we are to be a united race and to take our place in the business world now occupied by other races."[1]

Miller's comment regarding his print shop's capacity was prescient. Even though his printing press published the order's weekly newspaper, the *Saint Luke Herald*, and forms and necessary documents for the order's bank and the other businesses it conducted, his print shop was not big enough to produce the book that contained his recommendation and the fiftieth anniversary edition of the order's proceedings. A white printing office published the annual report.

Education

Education, as men and women of both races well understood, was one of the keys to success in business and other endeavors. That had been one of the lessons of the brief Readjuster Party experiment in biracial politics in which parents of both races united in pursuit of a common goal for their children and grandchildren. The state government, however, persisted in underfunding schools for Black children and relied on continued Northern philanthropic assistance. The Anna T. Jeanes Fund, among others, provided money and helped pay salaries for teachers at both public and private schools in Virginia. The Peabody Education Fund also supplemented tax revenue to support many schools. Petersburg's Colored High School, founded in 1870, was later renamed Peabody High School.[2]

In addition to the public schools, private philanthropy supported multiple private academies across Virginia. The Boydton Academic and Bible Institute, founded soon after the Civil War in the southside town of Boydton, in Mecklenburg County, offered elementary and secondary education in the large three-story building that Randolph-Macon College had constructed there before the war and abandoned when it moved to Ashland. Included among Boydton Institute's graduates was Britton

Ingleside Seminary in Nottoway County early in the 1890s, one of several academies that offered high-quality academic education to daughters of prosperous mid-Atlantic Black families. (*Catalogue of Ingleside Seminary, Burkeville, Virginia, 1892–94*, Library of Virginia)

Baskervill, who represented the county in the House of Delegates during the 1887–88 term.[3] The Presbyterian Church sponsored Ingleside Seminary in Amelia County and later moved it to Burkeville. A counterpart to the finishing schools for white women, it attracted students from as far away as New Jersey and New York.

Christiansburg Institute, in southwestern Virginia, was also established shortly after the Civil War with substantial Northern financial support and a white faculty and administration. It focused on teacher education and initially offered a rigorous academic curriculum. Early in the 1890s, Jennie S. Dean, who had been born enslaved in Loudoun County, began a fundraising campaign in Northern states to raise money for her proposed school near Manassas. The Manassas Industrial School for Colored Youth opened in 1894 and offered liberal arts classes as well as training for future employment for boys and girls.[4]

Higher education assumed increased importance during the final decades of the nineteenth century for both Black and white Virginians. In addition to institutions like Hampton Normal and Agricultural Institute and the Richmond Theological School for Freedmen that had been established in the 1860s, other private colleges opened during the 1880s and 1890s, sometimes with financial support from white Northerners. The white American Baptist Home Missionary Society, based in New York, sponsored the creation in Richmond of Hartshorn Memorial College for women. Chartered by the General Assembly in 1884, it emphasized moral instruction and offered normal, industrial, college preparatory, and college courses to achieve its goal of "lifting up and ennobling the women of the race." Hartshorn later became part of Virginia Union University, which had its roots in the Richmond Theological School.[5] The Virginia Baptist State Convention, composed of Black congregations, opened the Lynchburg Baptist Seminary in 1890. Renamed the Virginia Theological Seminary and College, it provided college classes and teacher training and later offered theological degrees. It continues to operate as Virginia University of Lynchburg.[6] Some ambitious individuals also established their own institutions of higher education. In 1892, John J. Smallwood, who had been born enslaved in North Carolina, established the Temperance, Industrial, and Collegiate Institute in Surry County to educate young men and women and build "race pride." For more than thirty years it provided collegiate preparatory classes in addition to college coursework, a teacher training department, and industrial education in dressmaking, carpentry, and scientific agriculture. Smallwood's call to "become intelligent men and intelligent women" and to "build colleges" was taken up by many Virginians.[7]

The faculty of Virginia Normal and Collegiate Institute a few years after the General Assembly had renamed it Virginia Normal and Industrial Institute. One of its main goals was the preparation of teachers for the state's public schools. (*Virginia Normal and Industrial Institute, Petersburg, Virginia. Twenty-Fourth School Year, 1906–1907,* Library of Virginia)

The Virginia Normal and Collegiate Institute that the Readjusters incorporated in 1882 in the town of Ettrick, near Petersburg, was the first state-supported institution of higher education for Black people in Virginia. It was coeducational, the only public college in the state that admitted both men and women. It was also unique in having a Black board of visitors, and its first president, John Mercer Langston, was a Black man. It focused on the education of teachers and evolved into Virginia State University. From the beginning, the institute had a high-quality faculty. Among them was James Major Colson, a freeborn son of a Black Petersburg merchant. Colson attended public schools in Petersburg and Middleborough, Massachusetts, graduated from Dartmouth College in 1883, and then joined the faculty of Virginia Normal and Collegiate Institute, where he taught Latin and other subjects. He was active in state and national educational organizations until his death in 1909. The science building on the campus that was erected in 1940 was named for him.[8] His daughter, Edna Meade Colson, joined the faculty in the year of his death and also participated in national educational organizations as well as being an early Black feminist and one of the first Black women in Petersburg to register to vote in 1920.[9]

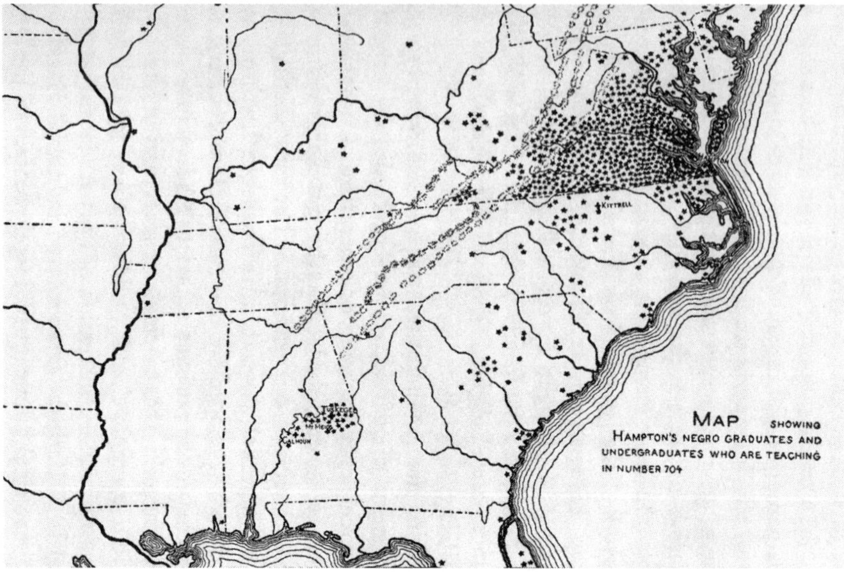

"Distribution of Negro Graduate Teachers (1894)," showing where 704 graduates of Hampton Normal and Agricultural Institute were then teaching or had taught. The regional and national importance of these early Black colleges and universities is almost impossible to overestimate. (Francis Greenwood Peabody, *Education for Life: The Story of Hampton Institute, Told in Connection with the Fiftieth Anniversary of the Foundation of the School,* Garden City, N.Y.: Doubleday, 1918, Library of Virginia)

The best known of all the educational institutions in Virginia at the end of the nineteenth century was Hampton Normal and Agricultural Institute, which became Hampton University in 1984. It had opened in 1868 under white direction and with considerable financial support from white Northerners. Hampton educated hundreds of teachers as well as provided training in agriculture, homemaking, and a variety of occupational fields, including building trades, sewing, and printing. Its combination of occupational education and teacher education earned widespread support among white Virginians who viewed the school as beneficial and non-threatening. For several decades the Hampton Singers entertained audiences throughout the country and in Europe with hymns and what at the time were regarded as plantation songs that blended Christian piety with rhythms and tunes that were in part influenced by African musical styles. The Hampton Singers spread the fame of the institute far beyond the United States.[10]

Booker T. Washington was one of the best-known natives of Virginia at the turn of the twentieth century, although by then he had resided for more than a decade in Alabama, where he was superintendent of Tuskegee

This photograph by Frances Benjamin Johnston shows students at Hampton Normal and Agricultural Institute learning the craft of fine carpentry. In addition to preparing students to teach, Hampton and the other Black colleges and universities also prepared young men and women to enter careers as skilled artisans. (Library of Congress)

Institute. Washington had been born into slavery in Franklin County and spent his childhood near Charleston (later part of West Virginia), where his parents worked in the salt industry through a lease agreement between their enslaver and the managers of a salt-producing company. After Washington graduated from Hampton Institute, he made a national name for himself at Tuskegee. He was very respected and influential among white people because he advocated what at the time was called industrial education to prepare Black students for productive careers of work in ways that did not threaten white supremacy or offer competition to white working people. As an advisor to Christiansburg Institute, his influence led to the transformation of its rather demanding academic curriculum into an industrial education more like Tuskegee's. Washington's emphasis on practical and achievable objectives put him at odds with Black leaders who advocated cultivation of the talents of the best young men and women—the race's so-called talented tenth—to serve as leaders and models for other people who could compete on equal terms with white men and women.[11]

The Emerging Business World

The decades of the 1880s and 1890s produced much hardship for Virginia's Black families, accelerated emigration from the state, and cemented racial segregation into place. It is a paradox that at the same time and for more reasons than Clarence Miller (of the Order of Saint Luke's print shop) adduced, racial segregation created business opportunities that enabled some Black Virginians to evade some of the worst features of Jim Crow and in a few instances even thrive.

The Black-owned businesses that grew large and established regional or national markets often were extensions of the small post–Civil War burial societies and cooperative organizations that provided rudimentary life- and burial-insurance services for members. The first one of those to succeed on a large scale began as a temperance society that William Washington Browne, who had been born into slavery in Georgia, established in Alabama in the 1870s as the Grand United Order of True Reformers. Browne moved to Richmond in 1876 at the invitation of the Grand Lodge of Good Templars. The Templars faltered, and he left the city for a time, but he returned in 1880 and took control of the Grand Fountain of Virginia.

From that relatively small beginning, he created what was then the largest Black fraternal order in the country. True Reformers' Hall was one of the largest commercial/fraternal buildings in the city. The True Reformers acquired a hotel, published a weekly newspaper, the *Reformer* (which boasted a circulation of 5,800 in 1898), owned a general store, operated a home for aged members, and in 1889 opened the Savings Bank of the Grand Fountain United Order of True Reformers. As president of one of the first Black-owned banks in the country, Browne was recognized nationwide and earned a coveted place among the eight Black men who, with Booker T. Washington, represented Black Americans at the 1895 Cotton States and International Exposition in Atlanta. Two years later when Browne died of cancer, his funeral in Richmond reportedly attracted the largest crowd of any Black citizen to that date.[12]

Even more successful was the Independent Order of Saint Luke, which had been founded in Baltimore, Maryland, in 1867 as a mutual self-help organization that spread to Virginia and other locations. It was unique among large-scale Virginia institutions in that a woman, Maggie Lena Mitchell Walker, was its guiding leader for nearly four decades. She joined the order while still in school and worked her way up through the ranks and in 1890 became the order's Right Worthy Grand Chief and nine years

A group portrait of delegates to the 1889 annual meeting at the Old Folks Home of the True Reformers, one of the many social service organizations, some of national importance, that men and women organized to serve their communities. (Special Collections, Library of Virginia)

later its Right Worthy Grand Secretary. Walker was responsible for the order's particular care of women and cultivation of their talents.

Even as a child, she had witnessed how women and their families suffered from the 1874 failure of the Freedman's Bank and Trust Company as a result of bad management by its white directors. About 20 percent of all the assets of the Richmond branch of the Freedman's Bank were in women's accounts. Kate Barber, of Winchester, struggled as late as 1884 to recover some of the $8.27—a small and yet important amount—that her sister, who had since died, had deposited in the bank in that city. The Independent Order of Saint Luke stepped in to help Richmond women in several ways and later, in 1903, created the Saint Luke's Penny Savings Bank with Walker as president. She was the first Black woman in the United States to be president of a bank, and one of the first women of any race. Even before the Independent Order of Saint Luke created the bank, Walker hired young women to work for the order, and when it founded the

This photograph of women sorting tobacco at the T. C. Williams factory in Richmond was displayed at the "American Negro Exhibit" at the Paris Exposition of 1900. The Saint Luke Penny Savings Bank was intended to help working women and men as well as more affluent customers save money and build community wealth. (Library of Congress)

bank, women formed a majority of its first account holders. At Walker's insistence, the bank treated women depositors and borrowers the same as it treated men, which was definitely not the case in white-owned banks.[13]

When in 1917 Clarence Miller urged Richmond men to patronize the order's printing office, he was repeating what Walker had advocated for years. In addressing an audience of Black Richmond men in 1906, she pointedly asked, "Is there one single colored man in here that will now deliberately go and carry his dollars to the white merchant so that he can fight us? Are you really going to feed the lion of prejudice and make him stronger and stronger so that he can all the more easily devour us?"[14] Long before her death in 1934, Walker was a nationally recognized business leader and advocate for women and the welfare and education of children.[15] She succeeded by all of the standards that white Virginia men prized. She quietly counted it as a major success when one day in a meeting in the governor's office a secretary addressed her respectfully as Mrs. Walker rather than with the customary and demeaning Maggie.[16]

The "Uprising" Segregated Economy

Black businesses generally succeeded in towns and cities where men and women were able to prosper in the segregated urban economy by providing necessary goods and services to their neighbors. "In 1882 I bought me a lot in this city," Patrick W. Oliver, who had graduated from Hampton Normal and Agricultural Institute and lived in Roanoke, later recalled, "and commenced building me a house which I now live in and use as a store. When I commenced my building I had $1050, in cash. With the small remainder left after building, I commenced a small grocery business, running for a few months." Then, in need of a loan, he obtained a letter of recommendation from a well-established businessman, "as I was not known as a merchant," and borrowed $1,000. Oliver boasted in 1890, "I am worth in real estate $15,500 besides my stock of goods and some R. R. stock. I own nine lots, some with buildings on them, and most of them are in the good part of town: my houses bring me $57 per month rent. The colored people are doing tolerably well here in town. Many of them are getting homes and earning from $25 to $60 per month."[17]

Each city and many of the smaller towns had a professional class of educators, clergy, physicians, insurance agents, grocers, bankers, and other men and women parallel to the middle-class and elite social, cultural, and business institutions that leaders in the white community formed. Black Virginians created and published more than forty weekly newspapers during the final two decades of the nineteenth century. Most failed within a few months or years, which was not uncommon for all newspapers at the time. Unfortunately, few or no copies of most of them survive, and the files of none of them are complete.[18] Religious institutions sometimes adapted to the changing economy of the professional class. Unlike in white churches, First Baptist Church in Petersburg held two services every Sunday, an early one for professional members and their families, and a later one for domestic workers such as cooks, nursery maids, and coach drivers.[19] Black women, like white women, formed the majority of most church congregations, but as in white churches, Black men always officiated as ministers, and committees or boards of Black men usually controlled management and finances for the congregation.[20]

W. E. B. Du Bois described the Farmville business community in 1898 when he published his study of that town. "The wealthiest Negro in the town," Du Bois then believed, "is the leading barber, who is reported worth not far from $10,000."[21] One of the other prosperous businessmen of the town was former legislator Samuel P. Bolling, who operated a large brickyard. An article on Southern businessmen in the October 23, 1886, issue of the *Cleveland Gazette* estimated that his business was worth $40,000.[22] His daughter, Eliza W. Bolling, not only taught in a nearby Cumberland County school, but according to an article in the *Southern Workman* she had "entire charge of all his books and accounts." Every Saturday morning she went into Farmville to audit his business accounts, make out the payroll, pay the employees ("sometimes thirty and forty in all"), and deposit the week's earnings in the bank. Then she returned home in the afternoon to pay the farmhand and the three day-laborers she hired to work on her father's six-hundred-acre farm. Samuel P. Bolling had "nothing whatever to do" with running the farm, the article concluded, because Eliza Bolling "has proved herself a successful farmer."[23]

Shortly after Du Bois completed his study of Farmville, Frank D. Banks, of Hampton, reported that his small city had three insurance agencies, three resident representatives of other insurance companies (that had their headquarters elsewhere); a building and loan association; a real estate firm; a large grocery store; and a mercantile company dealing in flour, coal, and wood. He concluded, "Business activity among a people is the best evidence of an upward tendency. . . . The observant man can detect evidences of almost a business *uprising* among our people. The growth in recent years of the business idea among Hampton students is, to my mind, significant. Many of our school-boys, aye and a considerable number of girls too, are preparing themselves for positions in stores, banks, insurance offices, and the like."[24]

Even though few historians have studied Black businesses in Virginia's cities and towns, city directories and tax records suggest that the business districts of Farmville and Hampton were not unusual. By 1910, fourteen Black-owned banks operated in nine Virginia cities.[25] In Newport News, not far from Hampton, Edward C. Brown, a Philadelphia native, was one of the insurance agents Frank Banks counted. Brown opened Crown Savings Bank in 1908. The following year he founded Brown Savings Bank in Norfolk and established a real estate office there. The business empire he started in Virginia and enlarged after he returned to Pennsylvania later collapsed in financial scandal, but his enterprises served residents of their communities well for a time.[26]

In Martinsville, the Black business district came to be called Baldwin's Block, for the town's Black physician, Dana O. Baldwin. A native of Chatham County, North Carolina, Baldwin graduated from Leonard Medical College of Shaw University in 1910, passed the examination of the

Virginia State Board of Medicine, and opened his practice in Martinsville. He began to acquire property and after service in a segregated army unit during World War I returned to the small city and prospered. Baldwin's Block eventually included not only his medical office and a dentist's office but also a brickyard, a textile manufacturing firm, a candy store, a poolroom, a barbershop, a beauty parlor, a theater, two restaurants, a drugstore, and a twenty-seven-bed hospital that he established.[27]

Businesses could prosper in rural areas as well. Reuben T. Coleman succeeded in the countryside by operating a resort where successful men and women who lived in cities could vacation and socialize very much as elite white men and women had for decades. Born into slavery but the son of a prominent white man, Coleman bought and sold property in Cumberland County beginning soon after the Civil War and became a prosperous farmer. In 1891 he incorporated the Colemanville Mineral Springs Company for bottling and selling mineral water from a spring. He opened Colemanville Hotel, which became a popular place for vacations and recreation of the elite of Virginia's cities as well as from Washington, DC, and elsewhere.[28]

Many farm families took advantage of new opportunities to improve their lives. Beginning in the 1880s, thousands of Black men, women, and children left the farms where they worked and moved to towns and cities elsewhere in Virginia or left the state entirely. Some fortunate families managed instead to purchase their own farmland. In Louisa County, for example, about 60 percent of day laborers left, but Black landownership increased. In 1870 Black men and women owned only about 2 percent of the land in the county, but by 1900 they owned 39 percent. Their farms were generally small and averaged only twenty-four acres, which meant that some of the landowners had to continue to work as day laborers to support their families. The 1900 census reported that "colored" farmers in Virginia owned 22,809 farms, while white Virginians owned 79,640 farms, nearly 78 percent of the state total.[29] In 1900, Black Virginians operated 44,795 farms, comprising more than 2.2 million acres, while white farmers tended 123,052 farms comprising more than 17.6 million acres. Black Virginia farmers worked an average number of 49.7 acres, compared to 143.7 acres for white Virginians.[30] Despite the disparities between Black and white farmers, at that time a larger percentage of Black men and women owned their own farms in Virginia than in any of the former Confederate states and escaped from the debt peonage of sharecropping.[31]

Jackson Ward

The largest and most prosperous and successful Black business district in Virginia was Jackson Ward in Richmond. The city government created it in 1871 by a gerrymander that placed most of the city's Black voters within one ward that allowed white voters from the other wards to elect a majority of white city councilmen. The True Reformers and the Independent Order of Saint Luke established their national offices and business enterprises in the ward. Early in the twentieth century, the True Reformers, which numbered more than two hundred thousand members nationwide, owned $700,000 worth of real estate in the ward; True Reformers' Hall was valued at more than $75,000; and its bank, valued at $50,000, did more than $1,000,000 in business annually. The order's insurance agency employed more than three hundred clerks, agents, and messengers. The headquarters of the Southern Aid Insurance Company was valued at $25,000, owned real estate worth ten times that, and did an immense amount of business. The American Beneficial Insurance Company also had its headquarters in Jackson Ward and employed several hundred agents and clerks. Other large companies in Jackson Ward included the Richmond Beneficial Insurance Company and the United Aid Insurance Company.[32]

By the first decade of the twentieth century, Black Richmonders, mostly in Jackson Ward, had developed the necessary institutions, businesses, and professions not only to function in an economy separate from whites, but to prosper. Several hospitals, asylums, and drugstores, along with dozens of physicians, nurses, and dentists, fulfilled the medical needs of the community. Eleven attorneys and eight notaries public represented Black Richmonders in legal matters. The skilled trades included dozens of blacksmiths, wheelwrights, carpenters, contractors, cabinet makers, watchmakers, jewelers, butchers, and plastering firms. Serving customers of both races throughout the city were eighty-three barber shops, one of the oldest businesses open to Black men dating back to the pre–Civil War days.[33]

The Independent Order of Saint Luke operated a dry goods and millinery business with $10,000 in stock; one furniture store owner could boast of $10,000 in merchandise. Scores of smaller merchants throughout the city flourished, including poultry, meat, fish, and confectionery shopkeepers; coal and wood dealers; booksellers, florists, photographers, and music teachers; and an impressive fifty dressmakers. At least one woman's exchange operated in Richmond, which provided a storefront where women could sell their homemade goods and foodstuffs on consignment.

This photograph of people posing at the *Richmond Planet* building located in the Jackson Ward neighborhood was displayed at the "American Negro Exhibit" at the Paris Exposition of 1900. (Library of Congress)

Several dozen restaurants, saloons, and caterers served the city's Black population, and more than a dozen Black-operated public halls throughout the city could accommodate groups ranging from 200 to 1,200 people.

Black entrepreneurs established banks, a cigar factory, steam laundries, and other concerns ranging from livery stables to boardinghouses to at least one music store. Four weekly newspapers could boast of a combined circulation of thirty-two thousand. Two schools for higher education thrived—Richmond Theological Institute, founded right after the Civil War, and Hartshorn Memorial College, which had been founded to provide higher education for young Black women in 1883. Several burial associations owned nine burial grounds, with at least ten funeral directors and embalmers serving the community.[34] The city's Black residents owned real estate and personal property worth a total of $2,574,071, and tax-exempt church property, orphan asylums, and other eleemosynary institutions were worth $3,264,646.[35]

Celebrating Black Accomplishments

In 1907, the state government sponsored a large, months-long exposition to commemorate the three-hundredth anniversary of the 1607 English settlement at Jamestown. The white directors planned it to be almost

"The Negro Building" was the largest structure at the 1907 Jamestown Exposition that commemorated the three-hundredth anniversary of the founding of the colony of Virginia. Black architects and construction workers designed and built the museum, which attracted some of the largest crowds at the exhibition. (Giles B. Jackson and D. Webster Davis, *The Industrial History of the Negro Race of the United States*, Richmond: The Virginia Press, 1908, Library of Virginia)

exclusively a celebration of white American success and virtually ignored Black and Indigenous Americans.[36] Undeterred, an enterprising committee of Black Virginians nevertheless raised private money and with the aid of a separate grant from the United States government—but no support at all from the state government—hired an architect and contracted with masons, carpenters, electricians, plumbers, and other necessary workers to construct and furnish what became the largest building on the exposition grounds. Every man and woman involved in the design and construction of the "Negro Building" and who contributed to the exhibits that it housed was a Black American.

The exhibits featured a series of tableaux designed by famed artist Meta Warrick depicting the history of Black Americans from freedom and its loss in Africa, through enslavement, and to freedom and prosperity in the United States at the beginning of the twentieth century.[37] The hundreds of items on exhibit demonstrated their success within the constraints of the segregated economy in meeting some of their lofty goals. The exhibits included photographs and displays from all over the country that showed well-dressed children in schoolrooms and churches; women and men working as bank clerks and teachers; examples of published novels, poetry, and history that Black men and women wrote; paintings and

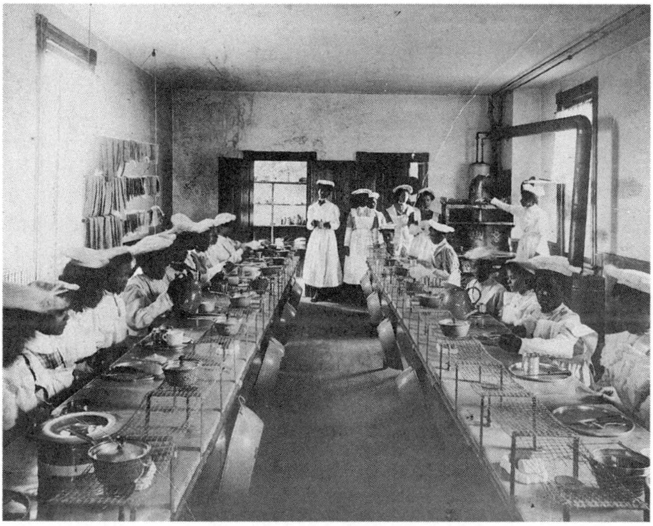

This photograph of a culinary class, titled "Laboratory for Colored Girls Designed by Mrs. Mary E. Dillard," may have been among the hundreds of exhibits in the Negro Building at the Jamestown Exhibition that documented the successes of Black Americans in the decades after the end of slavery. (Special Collections, Library of Virginia)

sculpture that they created; clothing and other textiles that they designed and manufactured; music that they composed and performed; innovative and useful practical devices that they invented; and other products of creative, skilled craftsmanship. Every item and image in the building and the building itself presented Black men, women, and children favorably and respectfully. The "Negro Building" was one of the most popular features at the exposition.

"The results were simply marvelous," the men who raised the money, coordinated the work, and collected the artifacts and images congratulated themselves afterward, "and we think it not too much to say that the Negro Exhibit was the central figure of the Exposition." Thousands of people "visited it each day and went away astounded at the marvelous display of every possible department of Negro thrift and industry." The exhibits "silenced the croakers, gratified the friends beyond expression, made friends of the enemies, and indeed it may be said that 'they who came to scoff, remained to pray.'"[38]

Giles B. Jackson, a Richmond businessman and attorney who coordinated the immense project from beginning to end, and Daniel Webster

Davis, a writer and accomplished poet, compiled and published a book to accompany the exhibition, *The Industrial History of the Negro Race of the United States*. The title is significant. In the small world of Black higher education, the word *industrial* suggested manual training for farming, manufacturing, and productive work, not an emphasis on intellectual achievements. Nearly everything focused on material success through work. Davis's especially subtle book-length history that accompanied photographs of Warrick's tableaux and photographs of hundreds of the items on display portrayed Black American achievements in a non-threatening way that met the high standards white Americans valued and that conformed to their expectations of what Black education should be.

Davis succeeded splendidly with his careful prose and boasted repeatedly of the accomplishments of Black Americans. His text used the singular, masculine pronoun throughout, as was common at the time to refer to people in general, as he deployed the evidence of Jackson's research to make their points. Since the abolition of slavery, Davis wrote of the state's Black citizens, "he has accumulated and owns one-twenty-eighth of all the land in Virginia. He owns one-sixteenth of all the land in Virginia, East of the Blue Ridge. He owns one-twelfth of all the land in twenty-eight counties out of one hundred counties in the State." Black men and women were "acquiring land at the rate of about fifty-five thousand acres annually." At the time of the exposition in 1907, Black Virginians paid taxes on real estate and personal property worth $17,442,227.[39]

Jackson and Davis hoped that *The Industrial History*'s narrative and the many photographs could serve three goals. "We propose," as they explained the first, "to place this book, if possible, in the hands of every Negro school boy and girl in the land, that he may know his own people, and, by virtue of that knowledge, be inspired to do his part to build up to greater heights, the race with which he is identified. We feel that this book, teeming with information, is an absolute necessity if we are to be in the future what the present progress would indicate." In pursuit of their second goal, Jackson and Davis also wanted white men and women to read the book. "When our white friends shall read this book," they continued, in a direct appeal for continued white support from sympathetic Northern people who had helped finance Black participation in the Jamestown Exposition, "they will feel encouraged to know that their labors have not been in vain." By thus hinting to white readers that they, too, could take pride in their own (modest) contributions and were in (some small) part responsible for the industrial progress that the book celebrated, Jackson and Davis tried to draw in their white readers, feed their vanities, and stimulate them to continue their support. They stated their third purpose plainly, that "When our enemies and villifiers read it they must at least have a greater respect for our people or prove themselves too prejudiced to accept of indisputable evidence of the powers of a people."[40]

The figures on landownership and taxes were impressive, but with Black Virginians constituting about one-third of the whole population, ownership of "one-twenty-eighth of all the land in Virginia" was a much less-impressive figure than it appeared out of context. Ownership of one-sixteenth of all the land east of the Blue Ridge, where the vast majority of Black men and women lived, was not so impressive per capita, either. Even in Charles City County, where Black men and women owned one-third of all the private property, that was still well below the standard of white property ownership statewide because Black people constituted a majority in Charles City County. Jackson and Davis did not include information about the many obstacles that Black Virginians had not been able to overcome.

Community Organizations

Similar to the segregated economy, Black women and men were also compelled to establish their own social clubs or other organizations to work on civic betterment projects, to improve public schools, and for other purposes. Robert Gilbert Griffin, who served one term in the House of Delegates, was a founder of the Yorktown lodge of the Grand United Order of Odd Fellows and rose to become president of the international organization.[41] At about the same time that white women began forming women's clubs in Virginia cities, Black women began doing the same thing. In 1895, Rosa Dixon Bowser, a Richmond teacher who was active in state and national educational organizations, was founding president of the Richmond Woman's League. With Maggie Walker and others, Bowser formed the Woman's Department of the Negro Reformatory Association of Virginia and helped raise money to establish the Virginia Manual Labor School for Colored Boys and the Industrial Home School for Colored Girls, both in Hanover County.[42] The founding superintendent of the girls' school, Janie Porter Barrett, was a graduate of Hampton and sponsor of the Locust Street Social Settlement to assist poor women and children in Hampton, and in 1908 was the first president of the Virginia State Federation of Colored Women's Clubs.[43]

As in the cities, residents of small towns and the countryside also created institutions to serve their needs, including county agricultural fairs

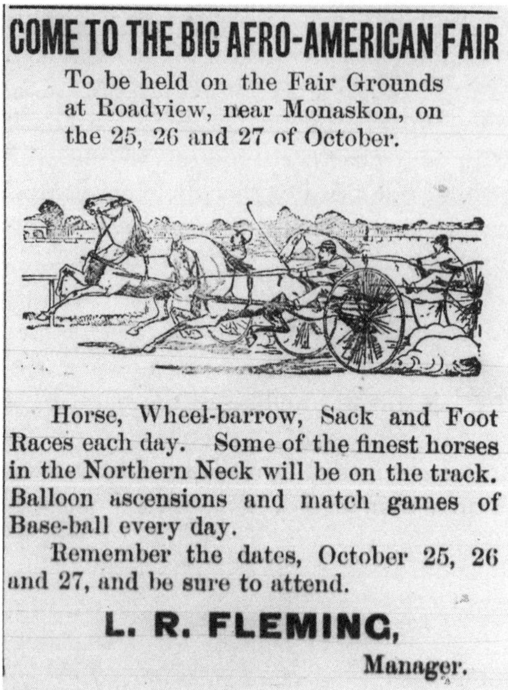

"Come to the Big Afro-American Fair" headlines an advertisement in the Irvington *Virginia Citizen*, October 12, 1900, for a fair in Lancaster County, one of a number of county or regional fairs that Black Virginians sponsored in parallel with county and state fairs that white people staged. (Library of Virginia)

and an occasional state fair separate from the long-running state fair that white planters had created before the Civil War. At the end of the nineteenth century Leonard R. Flemings, a freeborn storekeeper in Lancaster County, managed the county's "Afro-American Fair" that was often held on his property for more than a decade. County residents revived the event in 1927 after whites banned them from attending the local Chesapeake Fair.[44]

Early in the twentieth century, Wiley Horace Crocker, who had taught agriculture at Hampton Institute, purchased land in Suffolk, where in 1914 the newly incorporated Tidewater Fair Association held the first of many decades of annual fairs. The association became one of the largest and most successful incorporated Black business enterprises in the state.[45]

Denied access to established white medical institutions, which created dire consequences, Black men and women were compelled to develop similar institutions for their own communities. Hampton Institute opened Dixie Hospital early in the 1890s and created the first school in the state for Black women to learn nursing.[46] About the same time, Isaac David Burrell began practicing medicine in Roanoke and also opened a drugstore. He was an elder of Fifth Avenue Presbyterian Church and a member of the Masons, the Knights of Pythias, and the Odd Fellows. He was also president of the Magic City Medical Society, the professional association of Black physicians in the Roanoke area. Its members hoped to establish a hospital for Black people but had not yet achieved their objective when in 1914 Burrell had to travel to Washington, DC, for gallstone surgery because Roanoke hospitals refused to treat him. He died shortly after the operation, but his widow, Margaret H. Barnette Burrell, carried on as best she could and ran the drugstore. The year after his death, Black physicians opened Burrell Memorial Hospital, which served the Roanoke area until 1978.[47]

Not long after Burrell began his practice in Roanoke, William Tecumseh Foreman and three other Black physicians rented rooms to open a hospital in Newport News, which evolved into Whittaker Memorial Hospital, named for Robert L. Whittaker, one of the early doctors. The hospital was very much a creation of the community. Carrie J. Clarke Bolden, following the death of her clergyman husband, studied nursing at Dixie Hospital and used her connections with local women's clubs to raise money for the hospital;[48] and John Christopher Allen, a longshoreman who was also on the board of directors of the Crown Savings Bank,

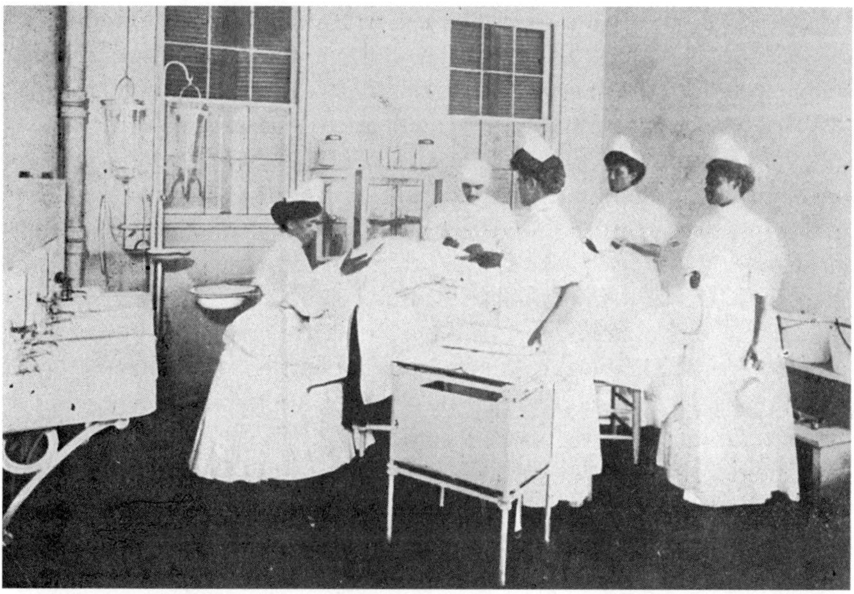

"An Emergency Case" shows nurses assisting a doctor in the operating room at Richmond Hospital. (*Souvenir Views: Negro Enterprises & Residences, Richmond, Va.* Richmond: D. A. Ferguson, 1907, Library of Congress)

served on the board of the hospital for thirty-five years.[49] Physician Sarah Garland Boyd Jones helped organize in 1902 the Richmond Hospital Association, which opened a hospital for Black patients in February 1903, and a school to train nurses scheduled to begin a month later. The hospital had rooms for twenty-five patients and a charity ward with sixteen beds. In March 1905, it became the Richmond Hospital Association and Medical College, and Training School for Nurses, Incorporated, and was later named for Jones after her untimely death at the age of thirty-nine.[50]

Success in Many Forms

Success for Black men and women who lived in Virginia during the decades before and after the turn of the twentieth century took many forms—ownership of a farm or business; holding a professional job that paid a steady income; educational achievement; membership in fraternal, social, or church organizations; family or personal connections with other successful people. The most important predictors of their success, in whatever field, appear to have remained as before: because they possessed valuable skills; because they lived in a town or city; and/or because they were fortunate enough to obtain a good education. With those advantages, they were able to launch the next generation into potentially successful lives, too. A few examples indicate the many fields in which some of them succeeded.

Probably the most famous Virginian at the end of the century was a clergyman, John Jasper, long-time minister at Sixth Mount Zion Baptist Church in Richmond. By all accounts a riveting speaker, Jasper delivered his most famous sermon, "The Sun Do Move," more than 250 times throughout the United States. The title referred to the passage in Joshua chapter 10, verses 12 and 13, that recorded that at Joshua's request, God bid the sun to stop its course through the sky long enough for the Israelites to prevail against the Amorites on the battlefield at Gibeon. From that miracle, Jasper deduced that the sun revolved around the earth, not the earth around the sun, as astronomers had believed for centuries. For Jasper and for many of his followers, the Bible was to be read as literally true in every particular; and if Scripture recorded that God commanded the sun to stand still, it stood still, which proved that it normally moved.

Although some critics faulted Jasper's theology and rejection of modern science, his sermon was immensely popular both because of his powerful delivery and his message that the Bible was the literal truth. Some of the many thousands of white men and women who sought opportunities

The Burke family of Fairfax County and Alexandria: Florence Burke (left), Willie Burke (right), and their children (left to right) William Tilman Burke, Bessie Payne Burke, and Viola Burke, circa 1890. Portraits like this of members of professional, middle-class families were prized possessions and documented economic and social success in the era of freedom. (Burke Family Papers, 1847–1924, Accession 29879, Personal Papers Collection, Library of Virginia)

to hear Jasper preach his sermon may have quietly looked down on him as unsophisticated and failed to appreciate his natural genius. Contemporary publications of the sermon text were all in a demeaning dialect that could indicate to readers that Jasper could not even speak English properly and that therefore the poorly educated preacher need not be taken seriously and was merely an entertaining performer. But in his strict, literal interpretation of Scripture, Jasper in fact shared a religious outlook with millions of other Americans, both white and Black.[51]

A Virginian who succeeded in his chosen calling through a subtle use of diplomacy was Thomas Calhoun Walker (no relation to Maggie Walker). He was much more influential and successful than most of his contemporary Black Virginians, but his method for succeeding was rooted in subtle exploitation of some common understandings about race relations that nearly all white Virginians shared. After the end of slavery, men, women, and children, Black and white, learned an etiquette of race relations that reinforced white supremacy. For instance, white people expected that Black people address them respectfully as Mr. or Mrs., but white people almost never addressed Black people with those polite courtesy titles. They might address a Black clergyman as Reverend, a Black teacher as Professor, or a Black physician as Doctor, which acknowledged their educational qualifications and the dignity of their professional callings, but in virtually all other cases white people addressed Black people familiarly or condescendingly by their given names, only, as was done during slavery. Conversely, Black adults and children addressed white boys and girls as Mr. James or Miss Eleanor, always including the courtesy title. In those and many other ways, language and behavior conformed to the expectations of white, not Black, society.[52]

T. C. Walker, or Lawyer Walker, as he was known, understood and exploited those white beliefs. He was born into slavery during the Civil War, attended Hampton Institute, and studied law to become the first Black attorney in Gloucester County, practicing law well into the 1930s. No stranger to working with whites—he studied law under two former Confederate officers—Walker worked effectively behind the scenes with business, judicial, and political leaders to help Black men and women in core areas of education, health, home ownership, foster care, and citizenship. He succeeded in achieving his goals in part because he chose not to challenge white supremacy directly. Unlike *Richmond Planet* editor John Mitchell Jr., who boldly spoke out in public, when faced with Jim Crow segregation Walker advised Blacks to behave courteously and not spark white antagonism. As a result, like Booker T. Washington, he was vulnerable to charges of being labeled an Uncle Tom who acted the part of a subservient supplicant in corridors of white power. Yet, Walker's conduct enabled his remarkable success in his decades-long career working on behalf of Black men, women, and children. Believing that Black prosperity was the most effective challenge to white supremacy, he maneuvered within the strict confines that Jim Crow racism imposed. Within those confines, however, Walker managed to undermine a measure of white supremacy's power to enable some Black people to obtain that prosperity.[53]

James Apostle Fields, whom we met in the introduction, escaped from slavery, as did the other members of his family, attended Hampton Institute and the law school at Howard University, and became a prosperous and successful lawyer in Hampton. His brother, George Washington Fields, also became a locally influential lawyer, and in turn his daughter, Inez Catherine Fields, became one of the first Black women attorneys in Virginia.[54] They were unusually successful and illustrated through their lives that Black Virginians could take maximum advantage of their opportunities and could achieve a large part of the American dream.

John Dabney is a prime example of a man with fewer advantages but who also succeeded with the abilities that he possessed. Born into slavery about 1824, he worked as a bartender and earned enough money to purchase his wife out of slavery and may have purchased and freed his mother, too. Dabney expanded his business after the Civil War to include catering and earned a wide reputation for his mint juleps as well as for his memorable personality. He was hospitable to white customers who paid their bills and outwardly conformed to their expectations, but he was also cautious about trusting them too far and kept a revolver handy under his bar. Dabney had a realistic view of the challenges that he and people like him faced. He told a son that "White folks are awfully wicked" and that "If you do everything white folks want you to do, you will go either to the penitentiary or the gallows."[55] Dabney was not well educated, but he raised his sons to respect education. John Milton Dabney (originally Milton Williamson Dabney) grew up to play professional baseball, and Wendell Phillips Dabney had a long and successful career as a music educator and newspaper editor in Ohio.[56]

John Wesley Cromwell was born into slavery in Portsmouth but was freed as a boy and educated in Philadelphia. He returned to Portsmouth in 1865 to teach school. He participated in Republican Party politics in the 1860s and while working as a clerk in the Department of the Treasury in Washington, DC, attended the law school of Howard University, from which he graduated in 1874. He published and edited the *People's Advocate*, headquartered in Alexandria and later in Washington, DC, from 1874 until at least 1884. For almost half a century, Cromwell worked both in and out of Virginia to promote education, mostly industrial education, and the welfare of Black Americans.[57]

Newspapers throughout Virginia and the nation took notice of Bettie Thomas Lewis, of Richmond, who in June 1892 became what one of them called "the richest colored woman in Virginia."[58] She was the daughter of a wealthy white businessman and former planter, William A. Thomas, and one of his formerly enslaved women whom surviving records do not clearly identify. Thomas told his lawyer that he wanted Lewis to inherit his estate and asked the lawyer to come to the house to write a will to that effect. That very night, though, Thomas died after handing his daughter a quantity of gold and bonds, the keys to his bank box, and his savings account passbook. He told her, in a companion's presence, that she was to be his sole heir. Following his death later that night, the whole of his estate was valued at about $225,000, including the house and real estate which alone were worth about $20,000.

Thomas's white relatives, to whom he left nothing at all, sued to invalidate the bequest on the grounds that he had not followed all of the legal steps necessary to make a proper gift *causa mortis*, that is, a valid gift, equivalent to a bequest, made in anticipation of imminent death. When the Supreme Court of Appeals ruled on *Thomas's Administrator v. Bettie Thomas Lewis*, in 1892, two and a half years after Thomas's death, the white judges by a four to one vote affirmed his bequest, which made Lewis rich and famous. With her new wealth, Lewis and her husband were able to escape from the constraints of Virginia's culture. In the mid-1890s she and her husband moved to Philadelphia, where he died in 1898. She did not return to Virginia.[59]

Andrew William Ernest Bassette, who was born in 1857 (whether free or enslaved is not certainly known) and lived until 1940, attended Hampton Institute and taught school in Greensville, Sussex, and Surry Counties before he returned to his native Elizabeth City County, where he taught, farmed, and studied law. Lawyer Bassette, as he became known, was a founder of the People's Building and Loan Association of Hampton, purchased several lots in the city, and joined local lodges of the Freemasons and Odd Fellows. He presided several times at the annual celebrations of Emancipation Day and was superintendent for many years of the Sunday School of First Baptist Church in Hampton. Three of his sons attended Howard University; one became a lawyer, one a doctor, and one a dentist. Bassette's grandsons also successfully pursued careers in law and medicine.[60]

The children of William Roscoe Davis and Nancy Moore Davis also had successful professional careers for which their parents' belief in the value of education certainly helped pave the way. Among the first refugees from slavery who entered the army encampment in Hampton in the spring of 1861, they and their children were able to take advantage of their freedom and education. Their descendants, both those who knew them and those who were born too late to remember them personally, grew up inspired by their example and achieved careers as distinguished educators, scholars, artists, and other professionals. Davis was a man of great dignity who in old age sported a long beard that made him resemble a Biblical patriarch, fitting as he served as minister at Hampton's First Baptist Church for decades. By force of personality he even required white people to address him formally and properly as Mr. Davis.[61]

By the end of the 1800s, Black Virginians like Davis and his descendants indeed took their places in the business world and helped create a thriving—though separate—economy and society with its own educators, business and professional class, religious leaders, and community organizations. The divide between the races would increase into the new century as white supremacists sought to end permanently the political gains Black people had made in the decades immediately after the end of the Civil War.

Epilogue

"To Set Up Lofty Landmarks"

"We are now surely and firmly placed upon the path of progress," Willis A. Hodges had optimistically told his twenty-three fellow Black delegates during the Constitutional Convention of 1867–68, "and it becomes us, and the people whom we represent, to set up lofty landmarks at every point in our onward road to the position of freemen."[1] Despite temporary political gains in the decades after freedom—peaking with the Readjusters—Hodges's optimistic forecast would be dashed completely early in the new century. The Constitutional Convention of 1901–2 destroyed any hopes that Black Virginians could reach any of their lofty landmarks through political action and left them few options other than to try to exploit such educational opportunities as they had and to work together to thrive in the segregated economy—or to leave the state.

Disfranchisement

That convention concluded almost two decades of a campaign that white supremacists conducted to disfranchise Black voters and drive Black men out of public life. They began in 1884, immediately after Readjusters lost their majorities in the General Assembly in the November 1883 election. The assembly passed over Readjuster governor William E. Cameron's veto a law known for its sponsors as the Anderson-McCormick Act. It created new electoral boards in the cities and counties and authorized the General Assembly to name all members of the boards.[2] For years thereafter, Democratic majorities in the assembly appointed all of the state's election officers. That gave white Democrats almost a complete monopoly on who conducted elections, which made it very difficult for Black and white

Republican voters to cast their ballots and to have those ballots accurately counted and for Republicans to win elections.[3]

In 1894, the Democratic majority in the assembly enacted what was called the Walton Act. It appeared to be a progressive reform of the sort popular elsewhere in the United States. The law required the state to print ballots with the names of all candidates on them and allowed voters to mark their ballots in secret. Poll watchers could no longer see how voters intended to vote, which made intimidation more difficult. The printed secret ballot, though, operated as a literacy test because voters had to be able to read the names on the ballot. The law required voters to draw a line through at least three-quarters of the name of every candidate they wished to vote against.[4] Black voters were at a disadvantage because literacy rates remained lower for Black Virginians than for white Virginians. Democratic election officials had wide leeway to decide that a line through part of a Democratic candidate's name was not long enough, which disqualified the ballot; or to decide that a line through part of a Republican candidate's name was legally long enough, so the ballot could be counted and counted for the Democrat. The law effectively deprived thousands of men of both races of the ability to cast votes for candidates of their choice or have their votes accurately tabulated. The two laws together contributed to a notable drop in voter totals in Virginia at the time.[5]

George H. Stephens, a Hampton graduate who lived in Roanoke in 1896, published an essay entitled "The Southern Negro." In it he concluded, "The right of suffrage in the South, as is well-known, has become in general a meaningless privilege to the Negro. The intelligent colored voter, side by side with the illiterate one, has been silenced as a political factor."[6] The number of Black men who won election to the General Assembly declined to zero early in the 1890s, and the number who won election to local offices declined almost to zero by the end of the decade.

By the 1890s, as Peter Randolph wrote in his 1893 autobiography, Black men in the Southern states had few allies left. Nearly twenty-five years after he left the pulpit of Ebenezer Baptist Church in Richmond and moved to Boston, he charged that "The white South seems to think the colored Americans have but few rights that they are bound to respect, and they have the colored people in their hands, as clay in the hands of the potter, to mould into shape, or dash into pieces. The North—judging from its indifference and non-interference—are gradually turning the whole 'Negro question' over to the South to take care of."[7]

Randolph stated that white people explained and excused their harsh treatment of Black people because of their many alleged vices; but,

Randolph bluntly responded, "Slavery taught them to steal food, by depriving them of sufficient food. It taught them to lie, by punishing them severely when detected, and taught them to be immoral by compelling men and women to marry again and again, after their husbands and wives had been sold, that they may raise a new set of children for the slave market. Also, by the forced relation of some of the masters and slave-drivers, who begot children by slave women, and sold the females at a high price to become mistresses for white men."[8]

Without allies, without the vote, and as a shrinking minority, Black men had few means to protect their liberties and the interests of their families. White men betrayed or sabotaged their chances for better lives in freedom. The Supreme Court of the United States ruled in *Williams v. Mississippi* in 1898 that state constitutions and laws that placed restrictions on the suffrage that applied to all potential voters irrespective of race, such as payment of poll taxes or literacy tests, did not violate the Fifteenth Amendment or the equal protection clause of the Fourteenth Amendment.[9] The way was wide open for almost complete disfranchisement of Black men so long as race was not the stated purpose.

It was therefore surprisingly easy in 1900 for a few Democrats in the General Assembly to order a referendum on holding the constitutional convention. There were no longer any Black members in the assembly to protest, white Republicans offered no effective opposition, and most white Democrats agreed with George H. Stephens that the Black vote was then practically "meaningless." The law required that voters deposit in the ballot box a ballot with the printed words "for constitutional convention" if they wished to vote for the convention. If they wished to vote against the convention, the law required them to erase or strike out the words before they placed the ballot in the box.[10] If a voter cast a ballot in the referendum but did not indicate on it in the correct manner that he opposed holding a convention, the ballot was counted in favor; or if a voter did not know what to do when handed an affirmative ballot and did not know that there was no negative ballot, then he lost an opportunity to register a negative vote.

The law scheduled the referendum for the fourth Thursday in May 1900. That was the day for electing county officers, traditionally the election with the lowest voter participation. The referendum passed by a margin of 77,362 to 60,375.[11] Of the 447,815 adult men eligible to vote in Virginia then, only 30.1 percent of them voted,[12] about half the number who voted in that autumn's presidential election.[13] A small minority of adult men in Virginia, 17.2 percent of them, actually voted the convention into being.[14]

John Mitchell Jr. repeatedly advised readers of his *Richmond Planet* that the convention was an "unconstitutional 'Constitutional' Convention." Its stated purpose, to disfranchise as many Black voters as possible, was in his opinion a plain violation of the Fifteenth Amendment and also of the January 1870 act of Congress (which he quoted) that approved the Constitution of 1869 and readmitted Virginia senators and representatives to their seats in Congress and thus ended military oversight of the state government.[15] That law had prohibited changes to the state's constitution "to deprive any citizen or class of citizens of the United States of the right to vote who are entitled to vote by the Constitution"; to deny any person the right to hold office "on account of his race, color, or previous condition of servitude"; or "to deprive any citizen or class of citizens of the United States of the school rights and privileges secured by the constitution of said State."[16]

A group of men that included lawyer Thomas C. Walker, former legislator Alfred W. Harris, and former *Staunton Tribune* editor Willis McGlascoe Carter circulated a public letter in the summer of 1900 calling for a public meeting to "let our neighbors know how we feel the injustice of the act proposed, after all the years of toil and labor we have spent in helping to build up the waste places of the old Commonwealth." At meetings held in 1900 and 1901, men and women hoped to devise a strategy to save public schools and "other matters of grave importance." The recently organized Negro Industrial and Educational Association explained in an open letter to the constitutional convention shortly after it opened in June 1901 that "We know when the principles laid down in the Declaration of Independence are being violated; we know when the national Constitution is being abrogated in letter, as well as spirit." The authors protested "disfranchisement of any class of citizens of the State, which does not apply equally to all," perhaps not ready to believe that the convention intended to do exactly that.[17]

The one hundred white members whom voters elected to the convention followed the lead of the zealous advocates of white supremacy who had brought the convention into being. Twenty years after the Readjusters' highly successful legislative reforms of 1882, which included abolition of the poll tax, the Virginia Constitution of 1902 reinstated the poll tax as a prerequisite to register and vote. The constitution and the enabling legislation that the General Assembly passed created such a complex and protracted process for paying the tax and registering that it effectively disfranchised about 90 percent of the Black voters in the state, not because of "race, color, or previous condition of servitude," but because most of

....THE....
Constitutional
Convention.
Help Save Our Public Schools.
A public meeting under the auspices of the Negro Educational and Industrial Association of Virginia, will be held at the
MT. ZION BAPTIST CHURCH,
To-Night,
FRIDAY, MAY 3RD, 1901,
To consider plans looking to the the saving of our public schools and other matters of grave importance to be brought before the Constitutional Convention.
JAS. H. HAYES, Esq., of the Richmond Bar, Willis M. Carter, of the City Schools, and Rev. W. H. Moses, pastor of the church, Revs. C. I. Withrow, of M. E. Church and H. W. Williams will speak.
All are invited male and female. Rev. A. A. Galvin and all Ministers of the city will be present and participate.
COMMITTEE.

Advertisement for a meeting organized by Staunton Black leaders in May 1901, shortly before the election of delegates to the Constitutional Convention of 1901–2 that was expected to disfranchise a large proportion of Black voters. The organizers had hopes of being able to prevent the convention from taking any action that might endanger or reduce support for the public schools. (Special Collections, Library of Virginia)

them were poor, could not read, or could not as the law required write out an application to register in their own handwriting without assistance.[18]

The author of the disfranchisement provision was Carter Glass, a former member of the Senate of Virginia, future member of Congress and secretary of the treasury, and long-time owner of a Lynchburg newspaper. Using what was at the time a common—and derogatory—term for Blacks, he explained that the provisions of the constitution would completely "eliminate the darkey as a political factor in this State." Glass boasted, "we have accomplished our purpose strictly within the limitations of the Federal Constitution by legislating against the characteristics of the black race, and not against the 'race, color or previous condition' of the people themselves. It is a fine discrimination, indeed, that we have practiced in the fabrication of this plan."[19] By the phrase "the characteristics of the black race," Glass evidently meant the characteristics that members of the convention had repeatedly described, including illiteracy, ignorance, incompetence, untrustworthiness, and dishonesty—the lesson that the song "Jump Jim Crow" taught—not to mention a thirty-five-year history of voting for Readjusters and Republicans.[20]

Rather than submit the new constitution to almost certain defeat in a ratification referendum, the members of the convention voted by a narrow margin to proclaim it in effect without a referendum. What Virginia did was not unique. The apparently irresistible force of widespread belief in white supremacy enabled white men in most of the states of the former Confederacy to rewrite state constitutions and laws to disfranchise Black men. State conventions wrote new constitutions and proclaimed them in effect without ratification referenda in Mississippi in 1890, in South Carolina in 1895, in Louisiana in 1898, and in Alabama in 1901.

The Virginia convention appended to the constitution a Schedule so that "no inconvenience may arise from the adoption of this Constitution, and in order to provide for carrying it into complete operation." Section 22 of the Schedule required that all public officials in the state swear allegiance to the new constitution. It also dropped an axe: "upon the failure of any such officer, executive or judicial, to take such oath by the day named, his office shall thereby become vacant."[21]

The coercive requirement in Section 22 was part of the implementation of the constitution—it forced public officials to acknowledge its legitimacy or lose their jobs—and worked to secure it against legal challenges. Eleven months after the constitution went into effect, the Supreme Court of Appeals decided a criminal case, *Taylor v. Commonwealth,* that was appealed to the court on the grounds, among other things, that the constitution was not properly ratified and therefore prosecution under its authority was not legal. The judges unanimously cited the taking of the oath required in the Schedule as acceptance of the legitimacy of the new constitution by all the state's legislative, executive, and judicial officials, including themselves. The constitution "having been thus acknowledged and accepted by the officers administering the government and by the people of the State, and being, as a matter of fact, in force throughout the State" it was therefore "the only rightful, valid, and existing Constitution of this State, and that to it all the citizens of Virginia owe their obedience and loyal allegiance."[22]

In 1904 the Supreme Court of the United States ruled on two pleas that officers of election not conduct elections under authority of the new constitution, but by then the elections in question had already been held. The court stated in *Jones v. Montague* and then cited that case in *Selden v. Montague* that "the thing sought to be prohibited has been done and cannot be undone by any order of court."[23] Fait accompli. Those three court opinions settled the legal question about the proclamation and legal legitimacy of the Constitution of 1902. Few or no other white men challenged the proclamation of the new constitution. Many of them lost the right to vote as a consequence of the constitution that was intended to disfranchise Black men. Thousands of white men involuntarily paid the price to disfranchise Black men.

When voter registration began under the new constitution in the summer of 1902, former convention delegate Walter Watson recorded in his diary that he "came across an old slave darkey"—that is, a man who had been born into slavery—"who believed great harm of the new Constitution and told me the negroes held me accountable for what they considered a serious attempt upon their liberty."[24] One of the most outspoken racists in the convention, a former judge, and a future congressman, Watson reacted with surprise that a Black man could have had the presumption to believe that he was entitled to any rights at all.

The new constitution granted registrars almost unlimited power to reject applicants who failed to give satisfactory answers to any questions that the registrar posed. When a registrar in Warren County asked Charles Wilson Butler in 1902 to give an acceptable interpretation of a portion of the new constitution, he indignantly responded, "you men have no right to refuse to register me";[25] but they had the power, and they used it for decades. Still, leaders like John Mitchell Jr. (who did register in September 1902) and Maggie Walker continued to encourage Black men to register as well as Black women after ratification in 1920 of the Nineteenth Amendment granting women the right to vote.[26] At that time investigators for the National Association for the Advancement of Colored People documented the obstruction that white registrars in Hampton Roads imposed on Black women attempting to register.[27]

By the time of the 1901–2 constitutional convention, Black officeholding was almost unknown in Virginia. A very small number of men held on as justices of the peace, largely unnoticed even in their own counties as the job had relatively minor responsibilities. Daniel Norton, who had been a member of the Convention of 1867–68 and of the Senate of Virginia for several terms, served as a justice of the peace in York County until 1917.[28] Most remarkably, Leonard R. Flemings, of Essex County, was reelected more or less continuously from 1887 until he died in office in 1937.[29] At the end of May 1901 on the same day that voters elected members of the constitutional convention, a Black Republican, J. D. Pearman, won election as a justice of the peace in Henrico County. The Democratic candidate and incumbent failed to file his reelection papers in time, and therefore his name was not on the ballot. He was probably the voter who wrote in his name on election day, but two Black voters wrote in Pearman's name, and he literally won the election by a two to one majority.[30] Norton, Flemings, and Pearman were the exceptions that proved the rule.

Until the 1960s, Black voters were too few in number to worry white politicians of either party. That allowed the campaign of white supremacists against Black Virginians to continue unabated for decades after the constitutional convention. In 1924, the General Assembly passed An Act to Preserve Racial Integrity that defined all people with any known (or even suspected) African ancestry as "colored" and therefore subjected them to all of the state's racially discriminatory laws; and in 1925 the assembly passed one of the strongest state laws in the country to enforce racial segregation in public meetings.[31] The disfranchisement convention of 1901–2 destroyed all hopes of creating an egalitarian, democratic society in Virginia of the sort that radical Republicans had tried to create in the 1860s and that Black men and some white Readjusters tried to create in the 1880s. White supremacists imposed Jim Crow, the American apartheid, on Virginia.

Into the Twentieth Century

Some individual Virginians achieved impressive success in spite of Jim Crow restrictions, but by such measures as literacy rates, average annual income, infant mortality, and quality of housing, Black men and women remained far behind most white Virginians. The same could be said for comparisons of Black Americans to white Americans. In those and other important matters Black Virginians had not been able to reach any of their lofty landmarks or fully realize the dreams of American citizenship that had inspired men and women after the abolition of slavery.

Racism, embodied in the disfranchisement of 1902 and the legal constraints of Jim Crow, was responsible. White domination of political life after the destruction of the Readjuster Party in the 1880s virtually guaranteed that state and local governments appropriated tax money collected from all residents disproportionately to the benefit of white people. That was almost universally the case with appropriations for public education. The severely restricted electorate resulting from the Constitution of 1902 enabled a small minority of elite white male politicians to control politics and government at all levels and manage everything as they wanted. The Democratic Party founded in the 1880s controlled the state until the 1960s and was firmly committed to maintaining white supremacy and racial segregation. It was the most undemocratic and long-lasting political machine in the history of the United States. This is abundantly documented in a very large scholarly literature with no dissent and very little disagreement even on matters of detail.[32]

Black men and women in Virginia, without enough voters to exercise any meaningful political leverage, even in Black majority areas, were generally unable to make many significant improvements in their lives except within the limited and limiting confines of the segregated economy. The exodus of Black Virginians continued at a high rate until the middle of the twentieth century. They composed more than a third of the state's population in 1900, but by the 1950s, those who remained were less than a quarter of the state's population.[33] On the whole, the prospects for men, women, and children in the three-quarters of a century after the demise of the Readjuster Party in the 1880s were deeply dispiriting.

However, some men and women who grew up early in the twentieth century in that grim social climate and with those limited options boldly undertook as adults to fight back, to resume the work that Black Virginians had begun with the abolition of slavery. The state's most able and successful civil rights lawyers all grew up then, including Samuel W. Tucker, Spottswood Robinson Jr., Oliver W. Hill, Ruth Harvey Charity, and Victor Ashe. They all had the same motivation, understood the root cause of the problem in the same way, and knew that they had few white allies they could rely on. They had to take care of themselves and, as Willis Hodges had put it, "the people whom we represent." Like T. C. Walker, they attacked the injustices and practices that white people's prejudices created by skillfully wielding white people's law. Unlike Walker, though, this generation of Black leaders directly attacked Jim Crow itself rather than take small steps within the limits that Jim Crow imposed. Racism was the enemy to be vanquished. As Samuel W. Tucker recalled late in life, "I got involved in the civil rights movement on June 18, 1913, in Alexandria" because on that date and in that place, "I was born black."[34]

Afterword

AJENA CASON ROGERS

THE VIDEO clip is long gone, but I can still replay it in my mind. My sixteen-year-old son Joseph is running, as if running for his life, through brambles and briars, over hills and down berms, darting here and there between trees. He's dressed in clothing borrowed from a Civil War–era history site where I used to work and where he once, as a mere three-year-old, portrayed Baby Booker T. Washington. Here, too, he is portraying an enslaved person, but this time it is for a media production for his high school TV studio trying to capture on film the desperation, terror, and determination of someone who would risk all to run, run, run for the chance to own his own body. Running to secure freedom for himself.

Even as I replay that scene in my mind today, I recall the deep ache I felt, putting myself in the place of that boy's long-ago mother who could only wonder what had happened to her child, perhaps never knowing whether he lived or died free. Good thing, I said to myself, that this is only a production, a reenactment. I know Joseph will be coming home, eating me out of house-and-home as teen boys do. Years later, though, we all found out that reenactment was closer to the truth than we could ever have dreamed.

In 2012 *Come On Children*, the memoirs of my third great uncle George Washington Fields, were rediscovered in the archives of the Hampton History Museum. This copy typed on onion skin paper had been tucked away, unseen since Sandidge "Sis" Evans's papers had been merged into the museum's collections a few decades before. I got a copy from my friend and fellow researcher Drusilla Pair and began to read his account. *Come On Children* was written by a man whom my maternal grandmother once knew in her youth as Uncle George. Suddenly I was reading and learning the parts of my family's history that had over the course of the decades dropped out of our oral tradition: I devoured details such as the name of his mother (Martha Ann), the day-to-day experiences he had when he was enslaved from birth to age nine, and then . . . his detailed account of how his brother James—my grandmother's grandfather—escaped from slavery at age seventeen. As I read, I could see my son Joseph's face on James's face, and I could feel Martha Ann's tears in my tears. I had always been proud of the accomplishments of my great-great grandfather—lawyer, educator, property owner—but truth be told, knowing the details of what he went through just so we could be here made me stand even taller.

Therein lies the power of story. As a Virginian, I was born and raised steeped in the lore of our great Commonwealth. I was proud to be born in the state of the "Mother of Presidents," the land of George Washington and Thomas Jefferson and Woodrow Wilson, a land of abundant resources and pay-as-you-go fiscal responsibility. Yet deep down I felt something was missing. I sensed that the stories I was hearing and learning were not complete. Where did James Fields fit in? Where did my grandmother Margaret Fields Johnson fit in? Where did I fit in? Weren't we Virginians too?

History partially and incompletely told leads to stereotyping and misunderstanding. As the novelist Chimamanda Ngozi Adichie says in her TED Talk titled "The Danger of a Single Story," the consequence of a single story prevailing to the exclusion of all others is that it robs people of dignity, makes recognition of our equal humanity difficult, and emphasizes how we are different rather than how we are similar. Stories matter. Details matter. Telling inclusive human stories matters. When we know the struggles and triumphs of a wide range of people, we get a fuller sense and a fuller appreciation of why things are the way they have become, and how we might be able to steer things in the future.

That is what this book has done. It uses the stories of individuals to create a more nuanced understanding or portrait of the whole. It looks in overlooked places and challenges stereotypes. These stories were there all along, being told but not widely heard, recorded in archives but not widely seen, often undervalued and given less weight than other narratives. This book will help public historians like me access more of the vast number of under-told stories and gain the courage to become better facilitators and stewards of the history we share. Books like this one encourage us in the journey to discover and to raise the voices of those who were not able to tell their stories themselves.

This kind of story stewardship is a balancing act, however. As Brené Brown, researcher and author of *Atlas of the Heart,* so wonderfully puts it, "Story stewardship means honoring the sacred nature of the story—the ones we share and the ones we hear—and knowing that we've been entrusted with something valuable or that we have something valuable that we should treat with respect and love." She continues with a caution: "Narrative takeover is a huge problem in our world. It impacts one-on-one conversations and cultural conversations. Rather than be good stewards of a story, we hijack the story and center ourselves." We must stay ever mindful of the responsibility that comes with telling stories that might not be our own, and sensitive to the need to enable others to tell their own stories.

The stories in *Justice for Ourselves* are hard history to tell and will cause discomfort and perhaps some anxiety and stress. These stories at times can be hard to hear. It is hard to hear how people can be so cruel to other people. At the same time, it is also hard to hear stories that challenge some long-held beliefs and undermine stereotypes and tropes.

In my experience, making audiences feel causes action and can prompt readers and listeners to do something—if nothing other than to go back to the primary documents to see for themselves. This book is a beginning, an encyclopedia, a primer, a guide map to encourage deeper exploration.

When there are gaps, we can't help but try to fill in those gaps with what we know—or think we know—if we have only been taught a single story. Or worse, we dismiss as implausible or unacceptable historical stories that do not fit our paradigm. What does reading these stories provoke you to do? What are you now inspired to discover? What are you waiting for?

Appendix

VIRGINIA'S BLACK LEADERS, 1850–1900

All of these Black leaders have online biographies in the *Dictionary of Virginia Biography* (www.lva.virginia.gov/public/dvb), an ongoing biographical reference work published by the Library of Virginia, or in Virginia Humanities' *Encyclopedia Virginia* (encyclopediavirginia.org), a reliable resource on the history and culture of Virginia.

Members of the Virginia Constitutional Convention, 1867–1868

William H. Andrews (b. ca. 1839), Isle of Wight and Surry Counties, teacher

James D. Barrett (1833–1903), Fluvanna County, carpenter and minister

Thomas Bayne (ca. 1824–1888), Norfolk City, dentist and minister

James William D. Bland (1844–1870), Appomattox and Prince Edward Counties, carpenter and teacher

William Breedlove (ca. 1820–1871), Essex and Middlesex Counties, blacksmith and ferry operator

John Brown (ca. 1830–after 1900), Southampton County, carpenter and farmer

David Canada (fl. 1867–1869), Halifax County, stonemason

James B. Carter (ca. 1816–1870), Chesterfield and Powhatan Counties, shoemaker and grocer

Joseph Cox (ca. 1835–1880), Richmond City, laborer and custodian

Willis Augustus Hodges (1815–1890), Princess Anne County, minister and newspaper editor

Joseph R. Holmes (ca. 1838–1869), Charlotte and Halifax Counties, shoemaker

Peter K. Jones (ca. 1834–1895), Greensville and Sussex Counties, carpenter and watchman

Samuel F. Kelso (ca. 1825–1880), Campbell County, teacher and post office worker
Lewis Lindsey (1843–1908), Richmond City, musician and custodian
Peter George Morgan (1817–1890), Petersburg, shoemaker and saloon keeper
William P. Moseley (ca. 1819 or 1820–1890), Goochland County, boatman
Francis "Frank" Moss (d. by Aug. 6, 1884), Buckingham County, farmer and liquor merchant
Edward Nelson (fl. 1867–1869), Charlotte County, laborer
Daniel M. Norton (d. 1918), James City and York Counties, physician and barber
John Robinson (1825 or 1826–1908), Cumberland County, saloon keeper and wagon driver
James Thomas Sammons Taylor (1840–1918), Albemarle County, shoemaker
George Teamoh (1818–after 1887), Norfolk County and Portsmouth, shipyard worker and tailor
Burwell Toler (ca. 1822–1880), Hanover and Henrico Counties, minister and carpenter
John Watson (d. 1869), Mecklenburg County, shoemaker

Members of the House of Delegates, 1869–1890

William H. Andrews (b. ca. 1839), Surry County, 1869–1871, teacher
William Horace Ash (1859–1908), Amelia and Nottoway Counties, 1887–1888, teacher and attorney
Britton Baskervill (1863–1892), Mecklenburg County, 1887–1888, teacher and farmer
Edward David Bland (1848–1927), Prince George and Surry Counties, 1879–1884, shoemaker
Phillip S. Bolling (ca. 1849–1892), Buckingham and Cumberland Counties, 1883, farmer and brickmason
Samuel P. Bolling (1819–1900), Buckingham and Cumberland Counties, 1885–1887, entrepreneur
Tazewell Branch (1828–1925), Prince Edward County, 1874–1877, shoemaker and grocer
William Henry Brisby (1836–1916), New Kent County, 1869–1871, blacksmith and sawmill operator
Goodman Brown (1840–1929), Prince George and Surry Counties, 1887–1888, farmer

Peter Jacob Carter (1845–1886), Northampton County, 1871–1878, farmer and merchant

Matt Clark (ca. 1844–after 1892), Halifax County, 1874–1875, farmer

George William Cole (d. after June 10, 1880), Essex County, 1879–1880, teacher and farmer

Asa Coleman (d. after Feb. 24, 1893), Halifax County, 1871–1873, carpenter

Johnson Collins (1847–1906), Brunswick County, 1879–1880, watchman and laborer

Aaron Commodore (1819 or 1820–1892), Essex County, 1875–1877, shoemaker

Miles Connor (d. 1893), Norfolk County, 1875–1877, laborer

Henry Cox (1832–after 1910), Chesterfield and Powhatan Counties, 1869–1877, shoemaker and farmer

Isaac Dabbs (ca. 1848–after 1910), Charlotte County, 1875–1877, laborer

McDowell Delaney (1844–1926), Amelia County, 1871–1873, teacher and minister

Amos Andre Dodson (1856–1888), Mecklenburg County, 1883–1884, teacher and carpenter

Shed Dungee (1831–1900), Buckingham and Cumberland Counties, 1879–1882, shoemaker, farmer, and minister

Jesse Dungey (ca. 1820–1884), King William County, 1871–1873, shoemaker, census taker, and minister

Isaac Edmundson (ca. 1840–1927), Halifax County, 1869–1871, barber and laborer

Ballard Trent Edwards (ca. 1828–1881), Chesterfield and Powhatan Counties, 1869–1871, brickmason and carpenter

Joseph P. Evans (1835–1889), Petersburg, 1871–1873, minister

William Dennis Evans (ca. 1831–1900), Prince Edward County, 1877–1880, grocer and house painter

William W. Evans (d. 1892), Petersburg, 1887–1888, newspaper editor and attorney

William Faulcon (1841–by 1904), Prince George and Surry Counties, 1885–1887, blacksmith and farmer

George Fayerman (d. 1890), Petersburg, 1869–1871, grocer and butcher

James Apostle Fields (1844–1903), Elizabeth City, James City, Warwick, and York Counties, Williamsburg, 1889–1890, attorney and teacher

Alexander Quincy Franklin (1852–1924), Charles City and New Kent Counties, 1889–1890, teacher

John Freeman (d. 1876), Halifax County, 1871–1873, farmer and plasterer

William Gilliam (d. 1893), Prince George County, 1871–1875, farmer

James P. Goodwyn (d. after April 1910), Petersburg, 1874–1875, lighthouse keeper and whitewasher

Armistead Green (d. 1892), Petersburg, 1881–1884, grocer and mortician

Robert Gilbert Griffin (1847–1927), Elizabeth City, James City, Warwick, and York Counties, Williamsburg, 1883–1884, miller and farmer

Nathaniel Matthew Griggs (d. 1919), Prince Edward County, 1883–1884, tobacco factory worker and department store employee

Ross Hamilton (1843–1901), Mecklenburg County, 1870–1882, 1889–1890, carpenter and shopkeeper

Alfred William Harris (1853–1920), Dinwiddie County, 1881–1888, attorney

Henry Clay Harris (d. after Oct. 5, 1905), Halifax County, 1874–1875, watchman and census taker

Henry C. Hill (ca. 1815–1905), Amelia County, 1874–1875, farmer

Charles E. Hodges (1819–after Apr. 15, 1910), Norfolk County and Portsmouth, 1869–1871, minister and farmer

John Quincy Hodges (1841–after June 1, 1900), Princess Anne County, 1869–1871, claims agent and clerk

Henry Johnson (1842–1922), Amelia and Nottoway Counties, 1889–1890, farmer and teacher

Benjamin F. Jones (d. after 1911), King William County, 1869–1871, farmer

James Richard Jones (d. after August 20, 1902), Mecklenburg County, 1885–1887, farmer and postmaster

Peter K. Jones (ca. 1834–1895), Greensville County, 1869–1877, carpenter and watchman

Robert G. W. Jones (1826–1900), Charles City County, 1869–1871, farmer

Rufus Sibb Jones (ca. 1834–1897), Elizabeth City and Warwick Counties, 1871–1875, barber and teacher

William H. Jordan (1860 or 1861–d. after 1889), Petersburg, 1885–1887, merchant and clerk

Alexander G. Lee (d. by Oct. 10, 1901), Elizabeth City and Warwick Counties, 1877–1879, oysterman and boatman

Neverson Lewis (ca. 1839–1918), Chesterfield and Powhatan Counties, Manchester, 1879–1882, farmer and census taker

James F. Lipscomb (1830–1893), Cumberland County, 1869–1877, farmer and grocer

William P. Lucas (ca. 1843–1887), Louisa County, 1874–1875, teacher and postal clerk

John Walter Boyd Mathews (1840–1879), Petersburg, 1871–1873, barber

John B. Miller Jr. (fl. 1859–1875), Goochland County, 1869–1871, barber and teacher

Peter George Morgan (1817–1890), Petersburg, 1869–1871, shoemaker and saloon keeper

Francis "Frank" Moss (d. by Aug. 6, 1884), Buckingham County, 1874–1875, farmer and liquor merchant

Armistead S. Nickens (1836–1906), Lancaster County, 1871–1875, farmer and sawyer

Frederick Smith Norton (d. 1893), James City County, Williamsburg, 1869–1871, shoemaker

Robert Norton (d. by Oct. 17, 1898), Elizabeth City, James City, Warwick, and York Counties, Williamsburg, 1869–1875, 1877–1882, barber and shopkeeper

Alexander Owen (ca. 1830–ca. 1898), Halifax County, 1869–1871, ditcher and farmer

Littleton Owens (ca. 1842–1894), Princess Anne County, 1879–1882, farmer and lighthouse keeper

Richard Gault Leslie Paige (1846–1904), Norfolk County, 1871–1875, 1879–1882, attorney and metalworker

William Harvey Patterson (1810–1895), Charles City County, 1871–1873, farmer and minister

Caesar Perkins (1839–1910), Buckingham and Cumberland Counties, 1869–1871, 1887–1888, grocer and minister

Fountain Perkins (1816 or 1817–1896), Louisa County, 1869–1871, minister and farmer

John William Poindexter (ca. 1848–1889), Louisa County, 1875–1877, teacher

Guy Powell (d. 1900), Brunswick County, 1881–1882, minister and farmer

William H. Ragsdale (d. 1871), Charlotte County, 1869–1871, teacher

John H. Robinson (1857–1932), Elizabeth City, James City, Warwick, and York Counties, Williamsburg, 1887–1888, teacher and attorney

Robert Davis Ruffin (1842–1916), Dinwiddie County, 1875–1876, attorney and grocer

Archer Scott (1836–1909), Amelia and Nottoway Counties, 1875–1877, 1879–1884, farmer

George Lewis Seaton (ca. 1822–1881), Alexandria City, 1869–1871, carpenter

Dabney N. Smith (1846–1920), Charlotte County, 1881–1882, farmer and shopkeeper

Henry D. Smith (d. 1901), Greensville and Sussex Counties, 1879–1880, carpenter, farmer, and distiller

Robert M. Smith (d. 1923), Elizabeth City and Warwick Counties, 1875–1877, wheelwright and grocer

William Nash Stevens (1847–1891), Sussex County, 1869–1871, attorney and clerk

John Bryce Syphax (d. 1916), Alexandria County, 1874–1875, laborer and political leader

Henry Turpin (1836–1908), Goochland County, 1871–1873, painter and porter

John Watson (d. 1869), Mecklenburg County, 1869, shoemaker

Maclin C. Wheeler (1854 or 1855–1916), Brunswick County, 1883–1884, farmer

Robert H. Whittaker (d. 1905), Brunswick County, 1873–1877, farmer

Ellis Wilson (1818–1904), Dinwiddie County, 1869–1871, farmer and minister

Members of the Senate of Virginia, 1869–1890

James William D. Bland (1844–1870), Charlotte and Prince Edward Counties, 1869–1870, carpenter and teacher

Cephas L. Davis (ca. 1839–1907), Charlotte and Mecklenburg Counties, 1879–1880, minister and teacher

John Montgomery Dawson (1829–1913), Charles City, Elizabeth City, James City, Warwick, and York Counties, 1874–1877, barber and minister

Joseph P. Evans (1835–1889), Prince George and Surry Counties, Petersburg, 1873–1875, minister

Nathaniel Matthew Griggs (d. 1919), Amelia, Cumberland, and Prince Edward Counties, 1887–1890, tobacco factory worker and department store employee

James Richard Jones (d. after Aug. 20, 1902), Charlotte and Mecklenburg Counties, 1876–1877, 1881–1883, farmer and postmaster

Isaiah Leonard Lyons (1843–1871), Elizabeth City, Surry, Warwick, and York Counties, 1869–1871, clerk and drugstore proprietor

William P. Moseley (ca. 1819 or 1820–1890), Fluvanna, Goochland, and Powhatan Counties, 1869–1871, boatman

Francis "Frank" Moss (d. by Aug. 6, 1884), Appomattox and Buckingham Counties, 1869–1871, farmer and liquor merchant

Daniel M. Norton (d. 1918), Charles City, Elizabeth City, James City, Warwick, and York Counties, Williamsburg, 1871–1873, 1877–1887, physician and barber

Guy Powell (d. 1900), Brunswick, Lunenburg, and Nottoway Counties, 1875–1879, minister and farmer

John Robinson (1825 or 1826–1908), Amelia, Cumberland, Nottoway, and Prince Edward Counties, 1869–1873, saloon keeper and wagon driver

William Nash Stevens (1847–1891), Dinwiddie, Greensville, and Sussex Counties, 1871–1879, 1881–1883, attorney and clerk

George Teamoh (1818–after 1887), Norfolk County, Portsmouth, 1869–1871, shipyard worker and tailor

House of Representatives

John Mercer Langston (1829–1897), Fourth District (Petersburg, counties of Amelia, Brunswick, Dinwiddie, Greensville, Lunenburg, Mecklenburg, Nottoway, Powhatan, Prince Edward, Prince George, and Sussex), 1890–1891, attorney, law professor, and college president

Civic/Community Leaders

Joseph Abrams (1791–1854), Richmond City, minister

John Henry Adams (ca. 1848–1934), Richmond City, councilman and alderman

Beverly Allen (1859–1918), King William County, educator

John Christopher Allen (1876–1953), Newport News, labor leader and hospital director

Dana Olden Baldwin (1881–1972), Martinsville, physician and real estate developer

Janie Aurora Porter Barrett (1865–1948), Hanover County, social worker, educator, and school superintendent

Andrew William Ernest Bassette (1857–1942), Hampton, attorney and entrepreneur

Carrie J. Clarke Bolden (ca. 1869–1973), Newport News, nurse

Rosa L. Dixon Bowser (1855–1931), Richmond City, educator

Lucy Goode Brooks (1818–1900), Richmond City, founder of Friends' Asylum for Colored Orphans

Edward C. Brown (1877–1928), Newport News, entrepreneur

William Washington Browne (1849–1897), Richmond City, fraternal organization leader

Isaac David Burrell (1865–1914), Roanoke City, physician and pharmacist

Willis McGlascoe Carter (1852–1902), Staunton, educator and newspaper editor

Amanda Virginia Thomas Clark (1869–1952), Newport News, educator

Reuben Turner Coleman (1844–1909), Cumberland County, entrepreneur
Edna Meade Colson (1888–1985), Petersburg, educator
James Major Colson (1855–1909), Petersburg, educator
Fields Cook (ca. 1817–1897), Richmond City, minister and Republican Party leader
Wiley Horace Crocker (1873–1943), Suffolk, real estate developer and manager of Tidewater Fair Association of Suffolk
John Wesley Cromwell (1846–1927), Alexandria City, educator, attorney, and journalist
John Dabney (ca. 1824–1900), Richmond City, restaurateur
Noah Davis (1804–1867), Fredericksburg, minister and author
William Roscoe Davis (d. 1904), Hampton, minister and orator
Jennie Serepta Dean (1848–1913), Prince William County, educator
Mark Renie (or Réné) DeMortie (1829–1914), Nottoway County, anti-slavery activist and entrepreneur
John E. Ferguson (1810–1859), Richmond City, entrepreneur
Leonard R. Flemings (d. 1937), Lancaster County, grocer and local official
Joseph Dennis Harris (ca. 1833–1884), Hampton, physician
William Johnson Hodges (d. 1872), Norfolk County, anti-slavery activist and political leader
John Jasper (1812–1901), Richmond City, minister
Sarah Garland Boyd Jones (1866–1905), Richmond City, physician
John Mitchell Jr., (1863–1929), Richmond City, newspaper editor, civil rights activist, councilman, and banker
Josephine B. Mathews Norcom (1873–1927), Portsmouth, teacher and organization leader
John Oliver (d. 1899), Richmond City, educator and local official
Mary Smith Kelsey Peake (1823–1862), Hampton, educator
James Solomon Russell (1857–1935), Brunswick County, educator
Maggie Lena Draper Mitchell Walker (1864–1934), Richmond City, bank president, social reformer, and civil rights advocate
Thomas Calhoun Walker (1862–1953), Gloucester County, attorney and entrepreneur
Joseph Thomas Wilson (1837–1890), Norfolk City, historian

NOTES ON SOURCES

Modern scholarship on emancipation and its consequences in Virginia have largely focused on a locality or a region. Each has its own virtue. Robert Francis Engs's 1979 *Freedom's First Generation: Black Hampton, Virginia, 1861–1890* and John Thomas O'Brien's doctoral dissertation published in 1990 as *From Bondage to Citizenship: The Richmond Black Community, 1865–1867* were the first studies on freed people in cities. Engs's has the special virtue of the long view that exhibits how the consequences of the end of slavery played out across three decades; O'Brien's has the special virtue of a deep analysis during the critical short period of the capital city's freed people. Steven Elliott Tripp's 1996 *Yankee Town, Southern City: Race and Class Relations in Civil War Lynchburg* treats that city between 1850 and the 1870s to illuminate how freedom changed Lynchburg and its people. Peter J. Rachleff's *Black Labor in the South: Richmond, Virginia, 1865–1890* carefully chronicles the city's working men through a quarter of a century and treats some interracial cooperation during that time. Crandall A. Shifflett's 1982 *Patronage and Poverty in the Tobacco South: Louisa County, Virginia, 1860–1890,* like Engs's *Freedom's First Generation,* is a long-term study, but like O'Brien's it is focused on one community, the rural, central Piedmont county and within that context on the economics of freedom and also compares and contrasts the simultaneous experiences of Black and white people.

Lynda J. Morgan's 1992 *Emancipation in Virginia's Tobacco Belt, 1850–1870* is a regional study that, unlike most of the other scholarship, looks backward into the decade before the Civil War to assess emancipation in the context of long-term continuities and changes. Jonathan Noyales's 2021 *Slavery and Freedom in the Shenandoah Valley during the Civil War Era* treats in detail how enslaved people in that region became free. Jeffrey R. Kerr-Ritchie's 1999 *Freedpeople in the Tobacco South: Virginia, 1860–1900* concentrates on roughly the same region as Morgan but carries its analysis all the way up to the end of the nineteenth century. Daniel B. Thorp's 2017 *Facing Freedom: An African American Community in Virginia from Reconstruction to Jim Crow* on Montgomery County combines the many virtues of a local study with a long view that reaches through the remainder of the century. Nicole Myers Turner's 2020 *Soul*

Liberty: The Evolution of Black Religious Politics in Postemancipation Virginia, closely examines the essential role that Black churches played not only in the spiritual life of their congregations but also in political organization and mobilization, especially during the brief Readjuster period. Mary Farmer-Kaiser's 2010 *Freedwomen and the Freedmen's Bureau: Race, Gender, and Public Policy in the Age of Emancipation* is not confined to Virginia but examines the important subject of gender relationships immediately after the Civil War.

THE WORK OF the Library of Virginia's award-winning *Dictionary of Virginia Biography* (*DVB*) is the foundation for *Justice for Ourselves: Black Virginians Claim Their Freedom after Slavery.* Beginning with print volumes in 1998, 2001, and 2006, the ongoing authoritative reference work is currently published digitally, comprising at present more than 1,800 encyclopedia-length biographies (including a thousand online entries) of Virginians from all walks of life and every region of the colony and state, spanning more than four hundred years. The *DVB* has moved beyond the traditional focus of reference works on white male political and military subjects to broaden the definition of who, and what, is important to Virginia history. This is especially true in telling the stories of Black Virginians whose lives have been too-little studied.

Challenging this endeavor is the underrepresentation of Black people in such traditional research materials as letters, diaries, and journals. Public records, therefore, are the essential means to delve into the lives of Black Virginians. Fortunately, the *DVB* has been aided by the emergence of essential primary source materials that have been made more accessible in recent decades through diligent archival work and digitization. This is especially true with respect to the Library of Virginia's projects, Virginia Untold: The African American Narrative, which provides greater accessibility to pre-1865 records, and Virginia Chronicle, which presents full text searchable and digitized images of more than 3.5 million newspaper pages.

The authors, situated at the Library of Virginia, benefited from ready access to manuscript and digitized public sources, including vital records, contemporary newspapers, deeds of emancipation, freedom suits, registers of "free negroes," election records, legislative petitions, cohabitation registers, chancery causes, convention and legislative journals, and local, state, and federal records of various kinds. *DVB* research uncovered heretofore largely unknown Black delegates and revealed some who were thought to be Black delegates but were, in fact, found to be white.

Research folders that often began with only a short paragraph from Luther Porter Jackson's seminal *Negro Office-Holders in Virginia, 1865–1895* (1945), were developed into research folders several inches thick with dozens of primary source materials. Perhaps most importantly, with contributions from scholars across the country, these entries are the first reliable biographies ever written about these men and women.

NOTES

Abbreviations and Short Titles

Acts of Assembly	*Acts of the General Assembly of Virginia, Passed at the Session of . . .* (1730–). Title varies over time.
BRFAL	Records of the Bureau of Refugees, Freedmen, and Abandoned Lands, RG 105, NARA.
Census	Records of the Bureau of the Census, Record Group 29, National Archives and Records Administration, Washington, DC.
Debates and Proceedings of 1867–1868 Convention	*Debates and Proceedings of the Constitutional Convention of the State of Virginia* (1868)
DVB Files	*Dictionary of Virginia Biography* Editorial Files, LVA
DVB Online	*Dictionary of Virginia Biography* (Library of Virginia, 1998–), accessible at the Library of Virginia website (www.lva.virginia.gov/public/dvb/)
DVB on *EV*	Entries from the *Dictionary of Virginia Biography,* Library of Virginia (1998–), published on *Encyclopedia Virginia,* accessible at www.encyclopediavirginia.org/
JHD	Virginia General Assembly, House of Delegates, *Journal of the House of Delegates of the Commonwealth of Virginia* (1776–)
Journal of 1867–1868 Convention	*Journal of the Constitutional Convention of the State of Virginia* [1868]
JSV	Virginia General Assembly, Senate, *Journal of the Senate of Virginia* (1776–)
LC	Library of Congress, Washington, DC
LVA	The Library of Virginia, Richmond
NARA	National Archives and Records Administration, Washington, DC
RG	Record Group
US	*Cases Argued and Decided in the Supreme Court of the United States*

Va.	*Cases Decided in the Supreme Court of Appeals of Virginia*
VMHB	*Virginia Magazine of History and Biography*
VMHC	Virginia Museum of History and Culture

Notes on Language

1. *Scott v. Raub* 88 Va. 721 (1892), quotations on 728–29.

Introduction

1. *Equal Suffrage: Address from the Colored Citizens of Norfolk, Va., to the People of the United States. Also an Account of the Agitation among the Colored People of Virginia for Equal Rights. With an Appendix Concerning the Rights of Colored Witnesses before the State Courts* (New Bedford, Massachusetts, 1865), 4.
2. Tommy Bogger, "Thomas Bayne (ca. 1824–1888)," *DVB* on *EV* (https://encyclopediavirginia.org/entries/bayne-thomas-ca-1824-1888, accessed Dec. 29, 2021).
3. Ira Berlin et al. eds., *Freedom: A Documentary History of Emancipation, 1861–1867* (Cambridge, UK, 1985–), ser. 1, 2:128–30, quotation on 128; Amy Murrell Taylor, *Embattled Freedom: Journeys through the Civil War's Slave Refugee Camps* (Chapel Hill: University of North Carolina Press, 2018).
4. *Richmond Planet*, Oct. 11, 1890; J. H. Chataigne, comp., *Chataigne's Directory of Richmond, Virginia, To Which is Added a Street and Number Directory, Giving Names and Occupations After the Numbers* (Richmond, 1889).
5. E.g. among the books, Robert Francis Engs, *Freedom's First Generation: Black Hampton, Virginia, 1861–1890* (Philadelphia: University of Pennsylvania Press, 1979); Crandall A. Shifflett, *Patronage and Poverty in the Tobacco South: Louisa County, Virginia, 1860–1890* (Knoxville: University of Tennessee Press, 1982); Peter J. Rachleff, *Black Labor in the South: Richmond, Virginia, 1865–1890* (Philadelphia: Temple University Press, 1984); John Thomas O'Brien, *From Bondage to Citizenship: The Richmond Black Community, 1865–1867* (New York: Garland, 1990); Lynda J. Morgan, *Emancipation in Virginia's Tobacco Belt, 1850–1870* (Athens: University of Georgia Press, 1992); Steven Elliott Tripp, *Yankee Town, Southern City: Race and Class Relations in Civil War Lynchburg* (New York: New York University Press, 1996); Jeffrey R. Kerr-Ritchie, *Freedpeople in the Tobacco South: Virginia, 1860–1900* (Chapel Hill: University of North Carolina Press, 1999); Mary Farmer-Kaiser, *Freedwomen and the Freedmen's Bureau: Race, Gender, and Public Policy in the Age of Emancipation* (New York: Fordham University Press, 2010); Edward L. Ayres and Scott Nesbit, "Seeing

Emancipation: Scale and Freedom in the American South," *Journal of the Civil War Era* 1 (2011): 3–24; Glenn David Brasher, *The Peninsula Campaign and the Necessity of Emancipation: African Americans and the Fight for Freedom* (Chapel Hill: University of North Carolina Press, 2012); Jaime Amanda Martinez, *Confederate Slave Impressment in the Upper South* (Chapel Hill: University of North Carolina Press, 2014); Daniel B. Thorp, *Facing Freedom: An African American Community in Virginia from Reconstruction to Jim Crow* (Charlottesville: University of Virginia Press, 2017); Jonathan A. Noyalas, *Slavery and Freedom in the Shenandoah Valley during the Civil War Era* (Gainesville: University Press of Florida, 2021).

6. https://www.lva.virginia.gov/public/dvb/.
7. https://encyclopediavirginia.org/.
8. Donald W. Gunter, "James Apostle Fields (1844–1903)," *DVB* on *EV* (https://encyclopediavirginia.org/entries/fields-james-a-1844-1903, accessed Dec. 29, 2021).
9. *Acts of Assembly*, 1830–1831 sess., 107.

1. "I Ain't No Slave"

1. Charles Perdue et al., eds., *Weevils in the Wheat: Interviews with Virginia Ex-Slaves* (Charlottesville: University Press of Virginia, 1976), 163.
2. Ira Berlin, *Slaves without Masters: The Free Negro in the Antebellum South* (New York: Pantheon Books, 1974); Tommy L. Bogger, *Free Blacks in Norfolk, Virginia, 1790–1860: The Darker Side of Freedom* (Charlottesville: University Press of Virginia, 1997); Warren Eugene Milteer Jr., *Beyond Slavery's Shadow: Free People of Color in the South* (Chapel Hill: University of North Carolina Press, 2021).
3. Berlin had access to only three book-length studies and some article-length studies or chapters that treated free people in the decades before the Civil War: John H. Russell, *The Free Negro in Virginia, 1619–1865* (Baltimore: Johns Hopkins Press, 1913); Luther Porter Jackson, "Free Negroes of Petersburg," *Journal of Negro History* 12 (1927): 372–73; Luther Porter Jackson, "The Virginia Free Negro Farmer and Property Owner, 1830–1860," *Journal of Negro History* 24 (1939): 390–439; Virginia Writers' Project, *The Negro in Virginia* (New York: Arno Press, 1940); Luther Porter Jackson, *Free Negro Labor and Property Holding in Virginia, 1830–1860* (New York: Russell and Russell, 1942); James Hugo Johnston, "Race Relations in Virginia and Miscegenation in the South" (PhD diss., University of Chicago, 1937, which was published in 1970).
4. Melvin Patrick Ely, *Israel on the Appomattox: A Southern Experiment in Black Freedom from the 1790s through the Civil War* (New York: A. Knopf, 2004).
5. The leading works on free people in mid-nineteenth-century Virginia are Ellen D. Katz, "African-American Freedom in Antebellum Cumberland

County, Virginia—Freedom: Personal and Liberty and Private Law," *Chicago-Kent Law Review* 70 (1995): 927–92; Brenda E. Stevenson, *Life in Black and White: Family and Community in the Slave South* (New York: Oxford University Press, 1996); Bogger, *Free Blacks in Norfolk;* Kirt van Daacke, *Freedom Has a Face: Race, Identity, and Community in Jefferson's Virginia* (Charlottesville: University of Virginia Press, 2012); Eva Sheppard Wolf, *Almost Free: A Story about Family and Race in Antebellum Virginia* (Athens: University of Georgia Press, 2012); Ellen Eslinger, "Free Black Residency in Two Antebellum Virginia Counties: How the Laws Functioned," *Journal of Southern History* 79 (2013): 261–98; Kirk Mariner, *Slave and Free on Virginia's Eastern Shore: From the Revolution to the Civil War* (Onancock, Va.,: Miona Publications, 2014); Ted Maris-Wolfe, *Family Bonds: Free Blacks and Re-enslavement Law in Antebellum Virginia* (Chapel Hill: University of North Carolina Press, 2015); Carey H. Latimore, *The Role of Southern Free Blacks during the Civil War Era: The Life of Free African Americans in Richmond, Virginia, 1850 to 1876* (Lewiston, N.Y.: Edwin Mellen Press, 2015); Marcus P. Nevius, *City of Refuge: Slavery and Petit Marronage in the Great Dismal Swamp, 1763–1856* (Athens: University of Georgia Press, 2020).

6. Milteer, *Beyond Slavery's Shadow.*
7. John T. O'Brien, "Joseph Abrams (1791–1854)," *DVB* on *EV* (https://encyclopediavirginia.org/entries/abrams-joseph-1791-1854, accessed Jan. 5, 2022); Robert Ryland, "Reminiscences of First African Church, Richmond, Virginia," *American Baptist Memorial* 14 (1855): 354 (quotation); *Richmond Dispatch*, June 7, 1854.
8. Plea of James Z. Matthews, n.d., copies of deed of trust, will of Rebecca Matthews, and will of Walter Boyd Gilliam, with valuation of her estate and list of enslaved people, all in *Mathews v. Mathews' Exec. et al*, Petersburg Chancery Cause 1854–038, LVA; Brent Tarter, "John Walter Boyd Matthews (1840–1879)," *DVB* on *EV* (https://encyclopediavirginia.org/entries/john-walter-boyd-matthews-1840-july-11-1879, accessed Jan. 5, 2022). She is mentioned briefly in Jackson, *Free Negro Labor and Property Holding*, 223–24, but unaccountably not in Suzanne Lebsock, *The Free Women of Petersburg: Status and Culture in a Southern Town, 1784–1860* (New York: Norton, 1984).
9. Ervin L. Jordan Jr., "James William D. Bland (1844–1870)," *DVB* on *EV* (https://encyclopediavirginia.org/entries/bland-j-w-d-1844-1870, accessed Jan. 7, 2022).
10. Philip W. Stanley, "Peter George Morgan (1817–1890)" *DVB* on *EV* (https://encyclopediavirginia.org/entries/morgan-peter-g-1817-1890, accessed Jan. 10, 2022).
11. Alexander H. Lorch III, "Reuben Turner Coleman (d. Feb. 14, 1909)," *DVB* Online, published 2006, rev. 2021 (https://www.lva.virginia.gov/public/dvb/bio.php?b=Coleman_Reuben_Turner, accessed Jan. 15, 2022).

12. Tarter, "Henry Turpin (1836–1908)," *DVB* on *EV* (https://encyclopedia virginia.org/entries/turpin-henry-1836-1908, accessed Dec. 28, 2021).
13. Carolyn Durham and Diana Durham, "A. Q. Franklin (1852–1924)," *DVB* on *EV* (https://encyclopediavirginia.org/entries/franklin-a-q-1852-1924, accessed Dec. 28, 2021).
14. Tarter, "William Gilliam (d. 1893)," *DVB* on *EV* (https://encyclopedia virginia.org/entries/gilliam-william-d-1893, accessed Dec. 29, 2021).
15. Jennifer R. Loux, "William D. Evans (1831–1900)," *DVB* on *EV* (https://encyclopediavirginia.org/entries/evans-william-d-ca-1831-1900, accessed Dec. 30, 2021).
16. Matthew S. Gottlieb, "Armistead S. Nickens (1836–1906)," *DVB* on *EV* (https://encyclopediavirginia.org/entries/nickens-armistead-s-1836-1906, accessed Jan. 8, 2022).
17. Michael Plunkett, "Goodman Brown (1840–1929)," *DVB* on *EV* (https://encyclopediavirginia.org/entries/brown-goodman-1840-1929, accessed Jan. 9, 2022).
18. Sally Phillips, "John Robinson (1825 or 1826–1908)," *DVB* on *EV* (https://encyclopediavirginia.org/entries/robinson-john-1825-or-1826-1908, accessed Jan. 11, 2022).
19. Tarter, "James F. Lipscomb (1830–1893)," *DVB* on *EV* (https://encyclo pediavirginia.org/entries/lipscomb-james-f-1830-1893, accessed Jan. 11, 2022).
20. Milteer, *Beyond Slavery's Shadow*, 134, 135.
21. *The Charters and Ordinances of the City of Richmond . . .* (Richmond, 1859), 193–200, second quotation on 196, first quotation on 198.
22. *The Revised Ordinances of the Borough of Norfolk . . .* (Norfolk, 1852), 135.
23. *Acts of Assembly*, 1831–1832 sess., 22.
24. Philip J. Schwarz, *Twice Condemned: Slaves and the Criminal Laws of Virginia, 1705–1865* (Baton Rouge: Louisiana State University Press, 1988).
25. *Cropper v. Commonwealth* 42 Va (2 Robinson) 842 (1843) quotation on 844. Note: Accomac County was the spelling until 1940 when the General Assembly adopted the current spelling, Accomack.
26. *Acts of Assembly*, 1848 sess., 117–21.
27. Tarter, *The Grandees of Government: The Origins and Persistence of Undemocratic Politics in Virginia* (Charlottesville: University of Virginia Press, 2013), 150–59; Marie Tyler-McGraw, *An African Republic: Black and White Virginians in the Making of Liberia* (Chapel Hill: University of North Carolina Press, 2007); Maris-Wolf, *Family Bonds*.
28. *Dred Scott v. Sandford* 60 US 393 (1857).
29. Reginald D. Butler, "Evolution of a Rural Free Black Community: Goochland County, Virginia, 1728–1832" (PhD diss., Johns Hopkins University, 1989); Ely, *Israel on the Appomattox*; Eslinger, "Free Black Residency in Two Antebellum Virginia Counties"; Katz, "African-American Freedom."

30. Arlington County (Alexandria County) Free Negro Register, 1749–1841 (entry no. 749), LVA.
31. Marianne E. Julienne, "George Lewis Seaton (ca. 1822–1881)." *DVB* on *EV* (https://encyclopediavirginia.org/entries/seaton-george-lewis-ca-1822-1881, accessed Jan. 13, 2022).
32. Tarter, "William P. Moseley (ca. 1819 or 1820–1890)," *DVB* on *EV* (https://encyclopediavirginia.org/entries/moseley-william-p-ca-1819-or-1820-1890, accessed Jan. 15, 2022).
33. *Daily Richmond Enquirer,* Apr. 18, 1860.
34. Petersburg *Daily Express,* Dec. 2, 1859.
35. *Norfolk and Portsmouth Herald,* Mar. 16 (quotations), 18, 1829.
36. William Bland Whitley, "Joseph Cox (ca. 1835–1880)," *DVB* on *EV* (https://encyclopediavirginia.org/entries/cox-joseph-ca-1835-1880, accessed Feb. 12, 2022).
37. Whitley, "Joseph P. Evans (1835–1889)," *DVB* on *EV* (https://encyclopediavirginia.org/entries/evans-joseph-p-1835-1889, accessed Feb. 20, 2022).
38. Stanley, "Lewis Lindsey (1843–1898)," *DVB* on *EV* (https://encyclopediavirginia.org/entries/lindsey-lewis-1843-1908, accessed Feb. 15, 2022).
39. Gottlieb, "George Teamoh (1818–after 1887)," *DVB* on *EV* (https://encyclopediavirginia.org/entries/teamoh-george-1818-after-1887, accessed Feb. 12, 2022).
40. Suzanne Gehring Schnittman, "Slavery in Virginia's Urban Tobacco Industry, 1840–1860" (PhD diss., University of Rochester, 1987), 287–300.
41. Bogger, *Free Blacks in Norfolk,* 153–54.
42. Lebsock, *Free Women of Petersburg,* 96.
43. Bogger, *Free Blacks in Norfolk,* 120–38.
44. Ibid., 103–19, 138–45.
45. *Acts of Assembly,* 1831–1832 sess., 20.
46. Ryland, "Reminiscences of First African Church," 354.
47. O'Brien, "Joseph Abrams (1791–1854)," *DVB* on *EV.*
48. Deborah Lee, "Noah Davis (1804–1867)," *DVB* on *EV* (https://encyclopediavirginia.org/entries/davis-noah-1804-1867, accessed Feb. 16, 2022).
49. John J. Zaborney, *Slaves for Hire: Renting Enslaved Laborers in Antebellum Virginia* (Baton Rouge: Louisiana State University Press, 2012).
50. Perdue, *Weevils in the Wheat,* 150.
51. Ibid., 68.
52. Especially Bogger, *Free Blacks in Norfolk,* 103–19.
53. Eva Sheppard Wolf, *Race and Liberty in the New Nation: Emancipation in Virginia from the Revolution to Nat Turner's Rebellion* (Baton Rouge: Louisiana State University Press, 2006), and Wolf, *Almost Free.*
54. Maris-Wolf, *Family Bonds.*
55. Philip J. Schwarz, *Migrants Against Slavery: Virginians and the Nation* (Charlottesville: University Press of Virginia, 2001).

56. Tarter, "William Johnson Hodges (d. 1872)," *DVB* on *EV* (https://encyclopediavirginia.org/entries/hodges-william-johnson-d-1872, accessed Mar. 1, 2022).
57. Tarter, "Willis A. Hodges (1815–1890)," *DVB* on *EV* (https://encyclopediavirginia.org/entries/hodges-willis-a-1815-1890, accessed Mar. 18, 2022); Willard B. Gatewood, ed., *Free Man of Color: The Autobiography of Willis Augustus Hodges* (Knoxville: University of Tennessee Press, 1982).
58. Tarter, "Charles E. Hodges (1819–after Apr. 15, 1910)," *DVB* on *EV* (https://encyclopediavirginia.org/entries/hodges-charles-e-1819-after-april-15-1910, accessed on Mar. 14, 2022).
59. James Hugo Johnston, *Race Relations in Virginia and Miscegenation in the South, 1776–1860* (Amherst: University of Massachusetts Press, 1970), 166–71, 175–79, 217–27, 251–68.
60. Petition of Basil Brawner, n.d. [received Feb. 20, 1835], Records of the General Assembly, Legislative Petitions, Prince William Co., RG 78, LVA.
61. *Hudgins v. Wright* 11 Va (1 Hening and Munford) 133 (1806), quotation on 134.
62. Ibid., 141.
63. *Hook v. Nanny Pagee and Her Children* 16 Va. (2 Munford) 379 (1814).
64. James M. Campbell, *Slavery on Trial; Race, Class, and Criminal Justice in Antebellum Richmond, Virginia* (Gainesville: University Press of Florida, 2007), 167–73.
65. Christopher Tucker, "John E. Ferguson (1810–1859)," *DVB* on *EV* (https://encyclopediavirginia.org/entries/ferguson-john-e-1810-1859, accessed Mar. 10, 2022); Richmond City Hustings Court Minute Book, 20:401 (quotation); trial covered in Richmond *Daily Dispatch*, Aug. 21 (misidentified as "Wm. Purkinson"), 25, Sept. 1, Nov. 9, Dec. 16, 1858.
66. George Wythe Munford, comp., *The Code of Virginia, Second Edition, Including Legislation to the Year 1860* (Richmond, 1860) (also known as the *Code of 1860*), chap. 103, sect. 9 (page 510).
67. Tucker, "John E. Ferguson," *DVB* on *EV.*
68. Depositions and letters with family history, in *Maria Griffin et al. v. Executors of Helen M. Anderson et al.*, James City Co. Chancery Cause 1873–005, LVA; Brent Tarter, "Robert Gilbert Griffin (ca. 1847–1927)," *DVB* on *EV* (https://encyclopediavirginia.org/entries/robert-gilbert-griffin-march-1847-february-9-1927, accessed Jan. 18, 2022).

2. "We Will All Be Free"

1. *Richmond Enquirer*, Jan. 4, 1861.
2. Transcription of trial record, *Commonwealth v. Sam (a slave)*, Mecklenburg Co., May 21, 1861, Executive Papers of Governor John Letcher, Pardons, May 1861, RG 3, LVA.

3. George Wythe Munford, comp., *The Code of Virginia, Second Edition, Including Legislation to the Year 1860* (Richmond, 1860) (also known as the *Code of 1860*), 816 (Title 54, Chap. 200, Sec. 7).
4. Transcription of trial record, *Commonwealth v. Reuben*, Greenbrier Co., May 27, 1861, Executive Papers of Governor John Letcher, Pardons, May 1861, RG 3, LVA (quotations); Secretary of the Commonwealth Executive Journal (1861), RG 13, LVA.
5. Jonathan A. Noyalas, *Slavery and Freedom in the Shenandoah Valley during the Civil War Era* (Gainesville: University Press of Florida, 2021), 45.
6. Virginia Writers' Project, *The Negro in Virginia* (New York: Arno Press, 1940), 188–214; Ervin L. Jordan Jr., *Black Confederates and Afro-Yankees in Civil War Virginia* (Charlottesville: University Press of Virginia, 1995), 69–90.
7. Isabella Neeson Woods to Samuel Woods, Sept. 16, Oct. 8, 1861, in Ruth Woods Dayton, ed., *Samuel Woods and His Family* (Charleston, W.Va.: Hood-Hiserman-Brodhag Company, 1939), 37, 47.
8. Susan Miranda Holt Berlin to George W. Berlin, Jan. 3, 1862, Berlin-Martz Family Papers, LVA; see also Brent Tarter, *Daydreams and Nightmares: A Virginia Family Faces Secession and War* (Charlottesville: University of Virginia Press, 2015), 25–26, 62, 68, 96, 99, 100, 102.
9. Noyalas, *Slavery and Freedom*, 45, 46, 66.
10. Undated clipping, ca. Sept. 8, 1910, *Brooklyn Eagle*, and obituary in *Long Islander*, May 2, 1917, both Greenlawn-Centerpoint Historical Association, Greenland, New York; John Blassingame, ed., *Slave Testimony: Two Centuries of Letters, Speeches, Interviews and Autobiographies* (Baton Rouge: Louisiana State University Press, 1977), 543–47.
11. Pay Roll of Slaves employed by the Commonwealth of Virginia, for Coast, Harbor and River defenses, on the defensive works at Gloucester Point in the Month of April 1861, Slave Rolls, May–Oct. 1861, Records of the Engineer Department, 1861–1865, RG 46, LVA.
12. James H. Brewer, *The Confederate Negro: Virginia's Craftsmen and Military Laborers, 1861–1865* (Durham, N.C.: Duke University Press, 1969); Jaime Amanda Martinez, *Confederate Slave Impressment in the Upper South* (Chapel Hill: University of North Carolina Press, 2014).
13. James W. Hunnicutt, *The Conspiracy Unveiled: The South Sacrificed; Or, The Horrors of Secession* (Philadelphia: J. B. Lippincott & Co, 1863), 355 (first quotation), 368 (third quotation), 376 (second quotation), 379 (fourth quotation), 380–83; Matthew S. Gottlieb, "James W. Hunnicutt (1814–1880)," *DVB* on *EV* (https://encyclopediavirginia.org/entries/hunnicutt-james-w-1814-1880/, accessed Feb. 12, 2021).
14. Katherine E. Harbury and Brent Tarter, "William Roscoe Davis (d. 1904)," *DVB* on *EV* (https://encyclopediavirginia.org/entries/davis-william-roscoe

-d-1904, accessed Feb. 12, 2021); *American Missionary* 5 (1861): 246–49, quotations on 248 and 249.

15. *My Poor Dear Syl . . . The Upshur County Civil War Diary and Letters of Marcia Louise Sumner Phillips* (Buckhannon, W.Va.: Ralston Press, 2013), 71.
16. Wilder Dwight, *Life and Letters of Wilder Dwight, Lieut.-Col. Second Mass. Inf. Vols.* (Boston: Ticknor and Fields, 1868), 205.
17. *New York Times,* June 22, 1862.
18. *Southern Workman* 21 (1892), 46–47, 62.
19. J. Z. Hearst to Alice Hearst, Aug. 1, 1862, Accession 53157, LVA.
20. E.g., Noyalas, *Slavery and Freedom,* 106–11.
21. David Hunter Strother, "Personal Recollections of the War," *Harper's New Monthly Magazine* 34 (1867): 446 (quotation).
22. Amy Murrell Taylor, *Embattled Freedom: Journeys through the Civil War's Slave Refugee Camps* (Chapel Hill: University of North Carolina Press, 2018), 58–59.
23. Robert Francis Engs, *Freedom's First Generation: Black Hampton, Virginia, 1861–1890* (Philadelphia: University of Pennsylvania Press, 1979), 17–31, 34; Taylor, *Embattled Freedom,* 58–59; Glenn David Brasher, *The Peninsula Campaign and the Necessity of Emancipation: African Americans and the Fight for Freedom* (Chapel Hill: University of North Carolina Press, 2012), 50, 79.
24. Engs, *Freedom's First Generation,* 14–15.
25. Taylor, *Embattled Freedom,* 19–56; Herbert G. Gutman, *The Black Family in Slavery and Freedom, 1750–1925* (New York: Pantheon Books, 1976), 412–13.
26. Engs, *Freedom's First Generation,* 17–61.
27. Brasher, *Peninsular Campaign.*
28. Roberta Schildt, "Freedman's Village: Arlington, Virginia, 1863–1900," *Arlington Historical Magazine* (Oct. 1984): 11–21; Joseph P. Reily, "'Coming from the Shadow of the Past': The Transition from Slavery to Freedom at Freedmen's Village, 1863–1900," *VMHB* 95 (1987): 403–28; Lindsey Bestebreurtje, "Beyond the Plantation: Freemen, Social Experimentation, and African American community in Freedman's Village," *VMHB* 126 (2018): 334–65.
29. Dorothea E. Abbott, "The Land of Maria Syphax and the Abbey Mausoleum," *Arlington Historical Magazine* 7 (1984): 64–80; *Washington Bee,* Feb. 6, 1886; Tarter, "John Bryce Syphax (d. by Sept. 8, 1916)," *DVB* on *EV* (https://encyclopediavirginia.org/entries/john-bryce-syphax-d-september-8-1916, accessed July 28, 2021); Sara B. Bearss, "George Washington Parke Custis (1781–1857)," *DVB* on *EV* (https://encyclopediavirginia.org/entries/custis-george-washington-parke-1781-1857, accessed July 6, 2021).
30. John E. Stealey III, *West Virginia's Civil War–Era Constitution: Loyal Revolution, Confederate Counter-Revolution, and the Convention of 1872* (Kent, Ohio: Kent State University Press, 2013), 103–5.

31. Charles Henry Ambler, *Francis H. Pierpont, Union War Governor and Father of West Virginia* (Chapel Hill: University of North Carolina Press, 1937), 30, 34–42, 160, 201, 219.
32. *JHD*, 1863–1864 Alexandria sess., 15–16.
33. *Journal of the Constitutional Convention Which Convened at Alexandria on the 13th Day of February, 1864* (1864), 3–4.
34. *New York Times*, Mar. 11, 1864; *Journal of 1864 Convention*, 18; *Constitution of the State of Virginia, and the Ordinances Adopted by the Convention which Assembled at Alexandria, on the 13th Day of February, 1864* (Alexandria, 1864), 14.
35. Bearss, "'Restored and Vindicated': The Virginia Constitutional Convention of 1864," *VMHB* 122 (2014): 156–81; Tarter, *Constitutional History of Virginia* (Athens: University of Georgia Press, 2023), 137–38; see also Richard G. Lowe, *Republicans and Reconstruction in Virginia, 1856–70* (Charlottesville: University Press of Virginia, 1991), 21–23.
36. *Acts of the Legislature of West Virginia at Its Third Session Commencing January 17, 1865* (Wheeling, 1865), 6, 14; Stealey, "Free at Last: W.Va.'s Tortuous Road to Emancipation," *Sunday Gazette-Mail* (Charleston, W.Va.), Mar. 8, 2015.
37. *JSV*, 1864–1865 Alexandria sess., 127–29; *JHD*, 1864–1865 Alexandria sess., 54–56; Tarter, "Thirteenth Amendment to the U.S. Constitution," *Encyclopedia Virginia* (https://encyclopediavirginia.org/entries/thirteenth-amendment-to-the-u-s-constitution-the/, accessed Dec. 7, 2020).
38. Jordan, *Black Confederates and Afro-Yankees*, 201–15.
39. Warren Eugene Milteer Jr., *Beyond Slavery's Shadow: Free People of Color in the South* (Chapel Hill: University of North Carolina Press, 2021), 224–27; List of enslaved persons ordered to be sent to work on fortifications, made on Sept. 22, 1863, in Cumberland County, in compliance with requisitions of the Governor for 80 slaves from said County, Cumberland Co. Free Negro and Slave Records, LVA; Sally Phillips "John Robinson (1825 or 1826–1908)," *DVB* on *EV* (https://encyclopediavirginia.org/entries/robinson-john-1825-or-1826-1908, accessed Apr. 2, 2021).
40. *Commonwealth v. Breedlove and Chandler* and accompanying documents, Pardon Papers, Dec. 1863, Executive Papers of Governor John Letcher, RG 3, LVA.
41. John T. Kneebone, "William Breedlove (ca. 1820–1871)," *DVB* on *EV* (https://encyclopediavirginia.org/entries/breedlove-william-ca-1820-1871, accessed Feb. 12, 2021).
42. Kneebone, "William Henry Brisby (1836–1916)," *DVB* on *EV* (https://encyclopediavirginia.org/entries/brisby-william-h-1836-1916, accessed Feb. 12, 2021).
43. Jordan, *Black Confederates and Afro-Yankees*, 264–90.
44. Joseph T. Wilson, *The Black Phalanx: A History of the Negro Soldier of the United States in the Wars of 1775–1812, 1861–'65* (Hartford, Conn.: American

Publishing Company, 1888), 377–462, estimates of number on 123, 142; Andre Fleche, "United States Colored Troops," *Encyclopedia Virginia* (https://encyclopediavirginia.org/entries/united-states-colored-troops-the/, accessed June 22, 2021).

45. Tarter, "'Gallantry in Action': Medal of Honor Winners from Virginia, 1862–1865," *Virginia Cavalcade* 37 (1987): 28–37.
46. Ibid.
47. Ibid.; quotation in A. G. Draper to Surgeon in Charge US Gen. Hosp. Fort Monroe Va., Feb. 4, 1865, Miles James, Compiled Service Military Records of Volunteer Union Soldiers Who Served With the US Colored Troops: Infantry Organizations, 36th through 40th, Records of the Adjutant General's Office, RG 94, NARA.
48. Wilson, *Black Phalanx*, 424–28.
49. Tarter, "'Gallantry in Action,'" 33.
50. Donald W. Gunter, "Peter Jacob Carter (1845–1886)," *DVB* on *EV* (https://encyclopediavirginia.org/entries/carter-peter-jacob-1845-1886, accessed Feb. 12, 2021); Compiled Service Military Records of Volunteer Union Soldiers Who Served With the US Colored Troops: Infantry Organizations, 8th through 13th, Records of the Adjutant General's Office, RG 94, NARA. Family history information and documents, including discharge papers (copies in *DVB* Files), provided by grandson, Arthur Treherne Carter (2004).
51. Mar. 28 [1865] enlistment date in Compiled Service Military Records of Volunteer Union Soldiers Who Served With the US Colored Troops: Infantry Organizations, 20th through 25th, Records of the Adjutant General's Office, RG 94, NARA; United States Census, Veteran Schedule, 1890, Records of the Bureau of the Census, RG 29, NARA; Samuel P. Bates, *History of Pennsylvania Volunteers, 1861–5*, 10 vols. [Harrisburg: B. Singerly, State Printer, 1869–1871], 10:1024–25.
52. Jennifer Loux, "John M. Dawson (1829–1913)," *DVB* on *EV* (https://encyclopediavirginia.org/entries/dawson-john-m-1829-1913, accessed Feb. 12, 2021).
53. Christopher T. Brooks, "James T. S. Taylor (1840–1918)," *DVB* on *EV* (https://encyclopediavirginia.org/entries/taylor-james-t-s-1840-1918/, accessed Jan. 13, 2022); Compiled Service Military Records of Volunteer Union Soldiers Who Served with the US Colored Troops, 2d through 7th Colored Infantry, 1861–1865, Records of the Adjutant General's Office, RG 94, NARA.
54. Interview with Mrs. Eliza Ann Taylor by Susie R. C. Byrd, 5 Mar. 1937, LH01410, Virginia Writers' Project, Accession 36002, Federal Records Collection, LVA, rendered in Black dialect.
55. *Richmond Times-Dispatch*, June 4, 1999.
56. Jordan, *Black Confederates and Afro-Yankees*, 83–286; Lois Leeven, "Mary Richards Bowser (fl. 1846–1867)," *Encyclopedia Virginia* (https://

encyclopediavirginia.org/entries/bowser-mary-richards-fl-1846-1867/, accessed Jan. 12, 2022); Elizabeth R. Varon, "Elizabeth L. Van Lew (1818–1900)," *DVB* Online, published 2018 (http://www.lva.virginia.gov/public/dvb/bio.asp?b=Van_Lew_Elizabeth, accessed Jan. 13, 2022).

57. *Acts of the Assembly,* 1924 sess., 297; Jordan, *Black Confederates and Afro-Yankees,* 185–200; Bill Archer, "'I was sent to the service of the Confederacy'; Samuel Walker: Slave, Freedman, and Pensioner, 1842–1933," *Virginia Cavalcade* 50 (2001): 40–47.
58. Virginia Confederate Pension Application, Act of 1902 (Servants), Department of Accounts, RG 6, LVA; Tarter, "Isaac Edmundson (ca. 1840–1927)," *DVB* on *EV* (https://encyclopediavirginia.org/entries/edmundson-isaac-ca-1840-1927, accessed Jan. 13, 2022).
59. Bruce C. Levine, *Confederate Emancipation: Southern Plans to Free and Arm Slaves during the Civil War* (New York: Oxford University Press, 2006); Kevin M. Levin, *Searching for Black Confederates: The Civil War's Most Persistent Myth* (Chapel Hill: University of North Carolina Press, 2019).
60. Tarter, *The Grandees of Government: The Origins and Persistence of Undemocratic Politics in Virginia* (Charlottesville: University of Virginia Press, 2013), 353–54.
61. Telegram, James R. Branch to Thomas Branch, Apr. 22, 1862, Executive Papers of Governor John Letcher, RG 3, LVA.
62. Kneebone, "James Read Branch (1828–1869)," *DVB* on *EV* (https://encyclopediavirginia.org/entries/branch-james-read-1828-1869, accessed Jan. 15, 2022).
63. Levine, *Confederate Emancipation;* Levin, *Searching for Black Confederates.*
64. Pardon Requests, 1865 March Pardons, Executive Papers of Governor William Smith, RG 3, LVA; Richmond *Daily Dispatch,* Mar. 18, 1865.
65. Richmond *Daily Dispatch,* Mar. 22, 1865 (quotation); Thomas M. Preisser, "The Virginia Decision to Use Negro Soldiers in the Civil War, 1864–1865," *VMHB* 83 (1975): 98–113.
66. Jordan, *Black Confederates and Afro-Yankees,* 114; Cumberland Baptist Church Record Book, entries for July 10, 13, 1862, Oct. 10, 1863, Accession 41989, LVA.
67. Sally E. Hadden, *Slave Patrols: Law and Violence in Virginia and the Carolinas* (Cambridge, Mass.: Harvard University Press, 2001).
68. Kristen Green, *The Devil's Half Acre: The Untold Story of How One Woman Liberated the South's Most Notorious Slave Jail* (New York: Seal Press, 2022), 173–74, 188.
69. Virginia Writers' Project, *Negro in Virginia,* 201, 212 (quotation).
70. Nelson D. Lankford, *Richmond Burning: The Last Days of the Confederate Capital* (New York: Viking, 2002); Michael D. Gorman, "A Conqueror or a Peacemaker? Abraham Lincoln in Richmond," *VMHB* 123 (2015): 2–88.

71. Chris M. Calkins, *The Battles of Appomattox Station and Appomattox Court House, April 8–9, 1865,* 2d ed. (Lynchburg, Va.: H. E. Howard, 1987), 138–39; Levin, *Searching for Black Confederates,* 174.
72. Jordan, *Black Confederates and Afro-Yankees,* 299–301.
73. Virginia Writers' Project, *Negro in Virginia,* 201–14; Charles Perdue et al., eds., *Weevils in the Wheat: Interviews with Ex-Slaves* (Charlottesville: University Press of Virginia, 1976), 367–76.
74. *Richmond Planet,* Oct. 11, 1890; Registers of Signatures of Depositors in Branches of the Freedman's Savings and Trust Company, 1865–1874, RG 101, NARA; J. H. Chataigne, comp., *Chataigne's Directory of Richmond, Va.* (Richmond, 1889), 110, 134, 320, 462; Census, Richmond, Virginia, 1880, 1900.
75. Matthew Gottlieb, "R. D. Ruffin (1842–1916)," *DVB* on *EV* (https://encyclopediavirginia.org/entries/ruffin-r-d-1842-1916, accessed Jan. 17, 2022); deposition of Robert D. Ruffin, May 16, 1873, Records of the Southern Claims Commission, Disallowed and Barred Claims, RG 233, NARA, quotation.
76. *New-York Tribune,* June 23, 1864.
77. United States War Department, *The War of the Rebellion: A Compilation of the Official Records of the Union and Confederate Armies* (Washington, DC, 1880–1901), ser. 1, vol. 46, part 1:1,237–38 (quotation).
78. Perdue, *Weevils in the Wheat,* 242.

3. "To Own Oneself Is to Own One's Future"

1. Thomas Calhoun Walker, "Lawyer Walker of Gloucester—As Told to Two Northern Friends," ca. 1950, Special Collections Research Center, Earl Gregg Swem Library, College of William and Mary, Williamsburg, 45.
2. *Southwestern Christian Advocate,* July 6, 1882.
3. Compiled in *Last Seen: Finding Family after Slavery* at https://informationwanted.org (accessed Dec. 12, 2020).
4. Jennie Brown to the Sheriff of Mecklenburg Co., June 18, 1882, Mecklenburg Co. Free Negro and Slave Records, 1781–1882, LVA.
5. *Staunton Daily Leader,* Jan. 9, 1905.
6. Daniel W. Crofts, "John Brown (ca. 1830–after 1900)," *DVB* on *EV* (https://encyclopediavirginia.org/entries/brown-john-ca-1830-after-1900, accessed Mar. 4, 2021).
7. Stephen Flemming to Governor Francis H. Pierpont, May 21, 1865, Executive Papers of Governor Francis H. Pierpont, RG 3, LVA.
8. George Teamoh, *God Made Man, Man Made the Slave: The Autobiography of George Teamoh,* eds. F. N. Boney, Richard L. Hume, and Rafia Zafar (Macon, Ga.: Mercer University Press, 1990), 115; Matthew S. Gottlieb, "George

Teamoh (1818–after 1887)," *DVB* on *EV* (https://encyclopediavirginia.org/entries/teamoh-george-1818-after-1887, accessed Feb. 12, 2021).

9. Walker, "Lawyer Walker of Gloucester," 8–13, later published in revised form as *The Honey-Pod Tree: The Life Story of Thomas Calhoun Walker* (New York: John Day Company, 1958); John G. Deal, "Thomas Calhoun Walker, (1862–1953)," *DVB* Online, published 2022 (https://www.lva.virginia.gov/public/dvb/bio.php?b=Walker_Thomas_Calhoun, accessed May 1, 2022).
10. Hawkins Wilson to Chief of Freedman's Bureau, Richmond, Virginia, May 11, 1867, enclosing letter to Sister Jane, Records of the Field Officers for the State of Virginia, 1865–1872, BRFAL.
11. Catherine A. Jones, *Intimate Reconstructions: Children in Postemancipation Virginia* (Charlottesville: University of Virginia Press, 2015), 103–32; John T. Kneebone, "Lucy Goode Brooks (1818–1900)," *DVB* on *EV* (https://encyclopediavirginia.org/entries/brooks-lucy-goode-1818-1900, accessed Jan. 10, 2022).
12. *Acts of Assembly*, 1865–1866 sess., 84–85.
13. Ibid., 85–86; J. Tivis Wicker, "Virginia's Legitimization Act of 1866," *VMHB* 86 (1978): 339–44; Brent Tarter, "Cohabitation Act of 1866," *Encyclopedia Virginia* (https://encyclopediavirginia.org/entries/cohabitation-act-of-1866/, accessed Jan. 15, 2022); Catherine A. Jones, "More than a Contract, Less than a Right: Regulating Marriage in Postwar Virginia, 1865–1885" (unpublished essay, 2018).
14. Tarter, "Robert G. W. Jones (1826–1900)," *DVB* on *EV* (https://encyclopediavirginia.org/entries/robert-g-w-jones-july-10-1826-by-march-15-1900, accessed Jan. 18, 2022).
15. Virginia Writers' Project, *The Negro in Virginia* (New York: Arno Press, 1940), 86.
16. The Library of Virginia has digitized many Cohabitation Registers. To see images of those records, go to bit.ly/VaUntold, select Search by Record Type tab, then select Cohabitation Registers Sub-Collection; some marriage records also in Marriage records of the Office of the Commissioner, Washington Headquarters, 1861–1869, M1875; and Records of the Field Offices for the State of Virginia, 1865–1872, both BRFAL.
17. Edward L. Ayers and Scott Nesbit, "Seeing Emancipation: Scale and Freedom in the American South," *Journal of the Civil War Era* 1 (2011): 3–24, on 12–17.
18. Scott Nesbit, "Scales Intimate and Sprawling: Slavery, Emancipation, and the Geography of Marriage in Virginia," *Southern Spaces*, July 19, 2011, https://southernspaces.org/2011/scales-intimate-and-sprawling-slavery-emancipation-and-geography-marriage-virginia/.
19. Jones, *Intimate Reconstructions*, 47–54.
20. *Acts of Assembly*, 1865–1866 sess., 91–93.

21. Tarter, "Vagrancy Act of 1866," *Encyclopedia Virginia*, https://encyclopedia virginia.org/entries/vagrancy-act-of-1866/, accessed Apr. 20, 2022.
22. *Daily Richmond Whig*, Jan. 26, 1866; Tarter, "Vagrancy Act of 1866."
23. *Code of 1860*, 492–96; Drew Addison Swanson, "Fighting over Fencing: Agricultural Reform and Efforts to Close the Virginia Open Range," *VMHB* 117 (2009): 104–39.
24. *Acts of Assembly*, 1865–1866 sess., 203–4; Shawn Everett Kantor and J. Morgan Kouser, "Common Sense or Commonwealth? The Fence Law and Institutional Change in the Postbellum South," *Journal of Southern History* 59 (1993): 201–42; Steven Hahn, "A Response: Common Cents or Historical Sense?," Ibid., 243–58.
25. John O. Peters, "New Law for a Shocking New Reality" (unpublished essay, 2018).
26. Crandall A. Shifflett, *Patronage and Poverty in the Tobacco South: Louisa County, Virginia, 1860–1900* (Knoxville: University of Tennessee Press, 1982).
27. Daniel B. Thorp, *Facing Freedom: An African American Community in Virginia from Reconstruction to Jim Crow* (Charlottesville: University of Virginia Press, 2017), 75.
28. Slaughter B. Bullock Papers, 1760–1910, Accession 23932, Personal Papers Collection, LVA.
29. Amy Murrell Taylor, *Embattled Freedom: Journeys through the Civil War's Slave Refugee Camps* (Chapel Hill: University of North Carolina Press, 2018), 223.
30. Gregg L. Michel, "From Slavery to Freedom: Hickory Hill, 1850–80," in Edward L. Ayers and John C. Willis, eds., *The Edge of the South: Life in Nineteenth-Century Virginia* (Charlottesville: University Press of Virginia, 1991), 109–33; Mary Farmer-Kaiser, *Freedwomen and the Freedmen's Bureau: Race, Gender, and Public Policy in the Age of Emancipation* (New York: Fordham University Press, 2010), 59–60, 64–70.
31. Amy Feely Morsman, *The Big House after Slavery: Virginia Plantation Families and Their Postbellum Domestic Experiment* (Charlottesville: University of Virginia Press, 2010).
32. *Freedmen's Record* 3 (June 1867): 104–5.
33. Labor Agreement between William H. Eubank and his Laborers, Jan. 1, 1866, Lunenburg County Freedmen's Contracts, 1865–1866, Lunenburg County Court Records, Local Government Records Collection, LVA.
34. *Acts of Assembly*, 1865–1866 sess., 83.
35. Ibid., 89–90.
36. William J. McGehee to Maj. Jordan, June 6, 1866, Freedmen's Bureau Field Office Records, BRFAL; Lynda Morgan, *Emancipation in Virginia's Tobacco Belt, 1850–1870* (Athens: University of Georgia Press, 1992), 193.
37. Jeffery R. Kerr-Ritchie, *Freedpeople in the Tobacco South, 1860–1900* (Chapel Hill: University of North Carolina Press 1999), 171–73.

38. Ibid., 157–80.
39. *Parrish v. Commonwealth* 81 Va. 1 (1884).
40. C. P. Goodyear to Paul R. Hambrick, Oct. 31, 1867, Records of the Assistant Commissioner for the State of Virginia, 1865–1869, M1048, BRFAL; Ervin L. Jordan Jr., "Jesse Dungey (ca. 1820–1884)," *DVB* on *EV* (https://encyclopediavirginia.org/entries/dungey-jesse-ca-1820-1884, accessed Dec. 22, 2021).
41. *National Anti-Slavery Standard,* Nov. 13, 1869; Tarter, "William P. Moseley (ca. 1819 or 1820–1890)," *DVB* on *EV* (https://encyclopediavirginia.org/entries/moseley-william-p-ca-1819-or-1820-1890, accessed Dec. 22, 2021).
42. Gottlieb, "Daniel M. Norton, later Daniel McNorton (d. 1918)," *DVB* on *EV* (https://encyclopediavirginia.org/entries/norton-daniel-m-later-daniel-mcnorton-d-1918, accessed Dec. 22, 2021); Gottlieb, "Robert Norton (d. by Oct. 17, 1898)," *DVB* on *EV* (https://encyclopediavirginia.org/entries/norton-robert-d-by-october-17-1898, accessed Dec. 22, 2021); Zachary Newkirk, "A Brief Moment in the Sun: The Reconstruction-Era Courts of the Freedman's Bureau," *Judicature* 101 (2017): 9–55 (https://judicature.duke.edu/articles/a-brief-moment-in-the-sun-the-reconstruction-era-courts-of-the-freedmans-bureau/, accessed 22 Dec. 2021).
43. Richmond *Daily Dispatch,* Oct. 4, 1866.
44. William Thomas Alderson, "The Influence of Military Rule and the Freedmen's Bureau on Reconstruction in Virginia, 1865–1870" (PhD diss., Vanderbilt University, 1952).
45. C. P. Goodyear to Paul R. Hambrick, Aug. 13, 1868, King William Courthouse, 1867–1868, Records of the Field Offices for the State of Virginia, 1865–1872, M1913, BRFAL; Leila Christenbury, "Benjamin Jones (d. after 1911)," *DVB* on *EV* (https://encyclopediavirginia.org/entries/benjamin-f-jones-d-after-1911/, accessed Jan. 21, 2022).
46. Alexander D. Bailie to Major J. R. Stone, May 31, 1867, Records of the Assistant Commissioner for the State of Virginia, 1865–1869, M1048, BRFAL.
47. William F. Mugleston, ed., "The Freedmen's Bureau and Reconstruction in Virginia: The Diary of Marcus Sterling Hopkins, a Union Officer," *VMHB* 86 (1978): 55.
48. Jones, *Intimate Reconstructions,* 64–73.
49. *Acts of Assembly,* 1865–1866 sess., 86.
50. Jones, *Intimate Reconstructions,* 118–32.
51. Diana Kristine Durham, "Mary Smith Kelsey Peake (1823–1862)," *DVB* Online, published 2023 (https://www.lva.virginia.gov/public/dvb/bio.asp?b=Peake_Mary, accessed June 15, 2023).
52. "Sarah A. Gray," Virginia Changemakers, LVA (https://edu.lva.virginia.gov/changemakers/items/show/216, accessed Feb. 28, 2022).
53. Thomas P. Jackson to A. S. Flagg, Sept. 21, 1865 (first quotation), Princess Anne County Letters and Orders Received, July–Dec. 1865 and Jackson to

Flagg, Oct. 9, 1865 (second quotation), Endorsement Book of Applications for Restoration of Property, Norfolk, both Records of the Field Offices for the State of Virginia, 1865–1872, M1913, BRFAL.

54. Marianne E. Julienne, "George Lewis Seaton (ca. 1822–1881)," *DVB* on *EV* (https://encyclopediavirginia.org/entries/seaton-george-lewis-ca-1822-1881, accessed Jan. 13, 2022).
55. Ronald Butchart, "Freedmen's Education in Virginia, 1861–1870," *Encyclopedia Virginia* (https://encyclopediavirginia.org/entries/freedmens-education-in-virginia-1861-1870/, accessed Jan. 15, 2022); J. W. Alvord, *Tenth Semi-Annual Report on Schools for Freedmen, July 1, 1870* (Washington, DC, 1870), 15.
56. Jones, *Intimate Reconstructions*, 158–88; *Semi-Annual Report on Schools for Freedmen* (1867–1870).
57. Butchart, "Freedmen's Education in Virginia."
58. Samuel L. Horst, ed., *The Fire of Liberty in Their Hearts: The Diary of Jacob E. Yoder of the Freedmen's Bureau School, Lynchburg, Virginia, 1866–1870* (Richmond: Library of Virginia, 1996), 32.
59. Ibid., 39.
60. Steven Tripp, *Yankee Town, Southern City: Race and Class Relations in Civil War Lynchburg* (New York: New York University Press, 1996), 186.
61. Jody Lynn Allen, "Roses in December: Black Life in Hanover County, Virginia during the Era of Disfranchisement" (PhD diss., College of William and Mary, 2007), 56.
62. Tarter, "William P. Lucas (ca. 1843–1887)," *DVB* on *EV* (https://encyclopediavirginia.org/entries/william-p-lucas-ca-1843-may-30-1887, accessed Dec. 22, 2021).
63. Tarter, "Samuel F. Kelso (ca. 1825–1880)," *DVB* on *EV* (https://encyclopediavirginia.org/entries/kelso-samuel-f-ca-1825-1880, accessed Dec. 22, 2021); *Journal of 1867–1868 Convention*, 28, 29.
64. Kristen Green, *The Devil's Half Acre: The Untold Story of How One Woman Liberated the South's Most Notorious Slave Jail* (New York: Seal Press, 2022), 207–14, 220–26, 247.
65. Robert Francis Engs, *Freedom's First Generation: Black Hampton, Virginia, 1861–1890* (Philadelphia: University of Pennsylvania Press, 1979), 87–90, 111–27.
66. Watkins James to Hon. Jacob M. Howard, Feb. 12, 1866, *Report of the Joint Committee on Reconstruction*, 39th Congress, 1st session, Report No. 30 (Washington, DC, 1866), Part II, *Virginia, North Carolina, South Carolina*, p. 43–44.
67. *Freedmen's Record* 2 (Jan. 1866): 25–26.
68. *American Missionary* 11 (May 1867): 111.
69. Alvord, *Tenth Semi-Annual Report on Schools for Freedmen*, 11–15.
70. Michael B. Chesson, *Richmond after the War, 1865–1890* (Richmond: Virginia State Library, 1981), 88–96; John Thomas O'Brien, "Reconstruction

in Richmond: White Restoration and Black Protest, April–June 1865," *VMHB* 89 (1981): 259–81; O'Brien, *From Bondage to Citizenship: The Richmond Black Community, 1865–1867* (New York: Garland, 1990), 116–33, 148–54, 160–85.

71. *New-York Tribune*, June 17, 1865.
72. LeRoy P. Graf et al., eds., *The Papers of Andrew Johnson*. 16 vols. (Knoxville, University of Tennessee Press, 1967–2000), 8:210–13.
73. Tripp, *Yankee Town, Southern City*, 224–49.
74. Jones, *Intimate Reconstructions*, 112–15.
75. Peter Randolph, *From Slave Cabin to the Pulpit, The Autobiography of Rev. Peter Randolph: The Southern Question Illustrated and Sketches of Slave Life* (Boston: J. H. Earle, 1893), 70–71.
76. *Report of the Joint Committee on Reconstruction at the First Session of the Thirty-Ninth Congress*, 3 vols. (Washington, DC, 1866), House Report No. 30, 39th Cong., 1st sess., 2:52; Richard Lowe, "Testimony from the Old Dominion before the Joint Committee on Reconstruction," *VMHB* 104 (1996): 373–98.
77. *Report of the Joint Committee on Reconstruction*, 2:59.
78. Ibid., 54–55.
79. Ibid., 56.
80. Records of the Assistant Commissioner for the State of Virginia, Records Relating to Murders and Outrages, Descriptive List of Reports of Outrages, Mar.–June 1866, p. 1 (first quotation), 2–3 (second quotation), 4 (third quotation), 15 (fourth quotation), and Register of Outrages Committed on Freedmen, Jan.–Dec. 1868, both M1048, BRFAL.
81. Christenbury, "Benjamin F. Jones"; quotation in Jones to Col. Ira Ayer Jr., July 30, 1867, and documentation in other letters, Records of the Field Offices for the State of Virginia, 1865–1872, M1913, BRFAL .
82. Richmond *Daily Dispatch*, May 2, 3, 1866; *Harper's Weekly*, May 19, 1866, 317.
83. William A. Blair, *The Record of Murders and Outrages: Racial Violence and the Fight over Truth at the Dawn of Reconstruction* (Chapel Hill: University of North Carolina Press, 2021), 37–39, 86–87.
84. *Papers of Andrew Johnson*, 8:210–14, quotations on 211; Tarter, "Conference with President Andrew Johnson (June 16, 1865)," *Encyclopedia Virginia*, https://encyclopediavirginia.org/entries/conference-with-president-andrew-johnson-june-16-1865/, accessed Dec.12, 2021.
85. Cumberland Baptist Church Minute Book, 1856–1896, Accession 41989, LVA, entry for May 12, 1866.
86. Thorp, *Facing Freedom*, 171.
87. Tripp, *Yankee Town, Southern City*, 208–9.
88. Randolph, *From Slave Cabin to the Pulpit*, 76–126 (quotation on 89).
89. Nancy A. Hillman, "Drawn Together, Drawn Apart: Black and White Baptists in Tidewater Virginia, 1800–1875" (PhD diss., College of William and Mary, 2013), 295–396.

90. Thorp, *Facing Freedom*, 172, 176.
91. *Acts of Assembly*, 1866–1867 sess., 649–50.
92. Tarter, "Charles E. Hodges (1819–after April 15, 1910)," *DVB* on *EV* (https://encyclopediavirginia.org/entries/hodges-charles-e-1819-after-april-15-1910, accessed Dec. 22, 2021); Jennifer Loux, "John M. Dawson (1829–1913)," *DVB* on *EV* (https://encyclopediavirginia.org/entries/dawson-john-m-1829-1913, accessed Dec. 22, 2021).
93. O'Brien, "Fields Cook (ca. 1817–1897)," *DVB* on *EV* (https://encyclopediavirginia.org/entries/cook-fields-ca-1817-1897, accessed Dec. 15, 2021); Mary J. Bratton, ed., "Fields's Observations: The Slave Narrative of a Nineteenth-Century Virginian," *VMHB* 88 (1980): 75–83.
94. Randolph, *From Slave Cabin to the Pulpit*, 58–59.
95. Elna C. Green, *This Business of Relief: Confronting Poverty in a Southern City, 1740–1940* (Athens: University of Georgia Press, 2003), 85–102.
96. Washington, DC, *Evening Star*, May 17, 1867 (quotation); Richmond *Daily Dispatch*, Sept. 11, 1867; *Alexandria Gazette*, Sept. 13, 1867.
97. *Alexandria Gazette*, Feb. 23, 1867.
98. Gottlieb, "George Teamoh," *DVB* on *EV*.
99. Joshua Shaffer, "Armistead Green (d. 1892)," *DVB* on *EV* (https://encyclopediavirginia.org/entries/green-armistead-d-1892, accessed Dec. 22, 2021).
100. Morgan, "Samuel P. Bolling (1819–1900)," *DVB* on *EV* (https://encyclopediavirginia.org/entries/bolling-samuel-p-1819-1900, accessed Dec. 22, 2021).
101. Julienne, "James B. Carter (ca. 1816–1870)," *DVB* on *EV* (https://encyclopediavirginia.org/entries/carter-james-b-ca-1816-1870/, accessed Dec. 22, 2021).
102. Tripp, *Yankee Town, Southern City*, 181, 251.
103. Mehrsa Baradaran, *The Color of Money: Black Banks and the Racial Wealth Gap* (Cambridge: Harvard University Press, 2017), 22–30; Carl R. Osthaus, *Freedmen, Philanthropy, and Fraud: A History of the Freedman's Savings Bank* (Urbana: University of Illinois Press, 1976), 5–6, 64–70, 153.
104. O'Brien, *From Bondage to Citizenship*, 328–34.
105. Richmond *Daily Dispatch*, Jan. 1, 1874.
106. Clarksville *Tobacco Plant*, Apr. 12, 1867.
107. Gottlieb, "Daniel M. Norton, later Daniel McNorton," *DVB* on *EV*; Gottlieb, "Robert Norton," *DVB* on *EV*; Richmond *Daily State Journal*, July 10, 1871.

4. "We Claim the Right of Suffrage"

1. *Proceedings of the Black State Conventions, 1840–1865*, ed. Philip S. Foner and George E. Walker, 2 vols. (Philadelphia: Temple University Press, 1979–1980), 258–76.
2. *Equal Suffrage: Address from the Colored Citizens of Norfolk, Va., to the People of the United States* (New Bedford, Mass., 1865), 10–11.

3. *Equal Suffrage*, 13–14; Michael Hucles, "Many Voices, Similar Concerns: Traditional Methods of African-American Political Activity in Norfolk, Virginia, 1865–1875," *VMHB* 100 (1992): 545–50.
4. *Equal Suffrage*, 1.
5. *Equal Suffrage*, 4.
6. *Equal Suffrage*, unnumbered pp. 27–28.
7. C. Peter Ripley et al., eds., *The Black Abolitionist Papers* 5 vols. (Chapel Hill: University of North Carolina Press, 1992), 5:324–29, from New York *Weekly Anglo-African*, June 24, 1865.
8. *Equal Suffrage*, unnumbered p. 27.
9. Paul D. Escott, *Black Suffrage: Lincoln's Last Goal* (Charlottesville: University of Virginia Press, 2022).
10. Richard Lowe, "The Freedmen's Bureau and Local Black Leadership," *Journal of American History* 80 (1993): 989–98.
11. Harold S. Forsythe, "'But My Friends are Poor': Ross Hamilton and Freedpeople's Politics in Mecklenburg County, Virginia, 1869–1901," *VMHB* 105 (1997): 412–13.
12. Elsa Barkley Brown, "To Catch the Vision of Freedom: Reconstructing Southern Black Women's Political History, 1865–1880," in *African American Women and the Vote, 1837–1965*, ed. Ann D. Gordon et al. (Amherst: University of Massachusetts Press, 1977), 73–74.
13. Richard G. Lowe, *Republicans and Reconstruction in Virginia, 1856–70* (Charlottesville: University Press of Virginia, 1991), 22–24; *Daily Richmond Whig*, July 6, 1865 (quotation).
14. Brent Tarter, "John C. Underwood (1809–1873)," *DVB* on *EV* (https://encyclopediavirginia.org/entries/underwood-john-c-1809-1873/, accessed Mar. 5, 2022).
15. 39th Cong., 1st sess., chap. 31.
16. Tarter, "Fourteenth Amendment," *Encyclopedia Virginia* (https://encyclopediavirginia.org/entries/fourteenth-amendment-to-the-u-s-constitution/, accessed Mar. 10, 2022).
17. John Hammond Moore, "The Norfolk Riot, 16 April 1866," *VMHB* 90 (1982): 155–64 (banner quotations on 157); Hucles, "Many Voices, Similar Concerns," 551–552; House Executive Document No. 72, 39th Cong., 2d sess.
18. Dan T. Carter, *When the War was Over: The Failure of Self-Reconstruction in the South, 1865–1867* (Baton Rouge: Louisiana State University Press, 1985).
19. 39th Cong., 2d sess., chap. 63.
20. *Alexandria Gazette*, Mar. 4, 5, 7, 1867; Alrutheus A. Taylor, *The Negro in the Reconstruction of Virginia* (Washington, DC: Association for the Study of Negro Life and History, 1926), 208.
21. *Consolidated List of Persons Registered as Voters in the State of Virginia, December 12, 1867*, printed as Doc. 5 in *Documents of the Constitutional Convention of the State of Virginia* (Richmond, 1868), 51–52.

22. Election poll books in Secretary of the Commonwealth Military Rule Election Records, 1867, 1869, Accession 50706, RG 13, LVA (online at bit.ly/VaUntold, select Search by Record Type tab, then select Election Records Sub-Collection); election accounts in Taylor, *Negro in Reconstruction*, 208–26; Jeffrey R. Kerr-Ritchie, *Freedpeople in the Tobacco South: Virginia, 1860–1900* (Chapel Hill: University of North Carolina Press, 1999), 71–91; Hucles, "Many Voices, Similar Concerns," 552–54; Daniel W. Crofts, *Old Southampton: Politics and Society in a Virginia County, 1834–1869* (Charlottesville: University Press of Virginia, 1992), 243–57, 355–56; Daniel B. Thorp, *Facing Freedom: An African American Community in Virginia from Reconstruction to Jim Crow* (Charlottesville: University of Virginia Press, 2007), 193–99; *Consolidated Vote of the State of Virginia at the Election Held October 22, 1867*, printed as Doc. 5 in *Documents of the Constitutional Convention of the State of Virginia*, 53–56.
23. Tarter, *Constitutional History of Virginia*, 148.
24. *Consolidated Vote.*
25. Secretary of the Commonwealth, Election Records, 1776–1941, No. 427, State Government Records Collection, RG 13, LVA.
26. Jack P. Maddex Jr. *The Virginia Conservatives, 1867–1879: A Study in Reconstruction Politics* (Chapel Hill: University of North Carolina Press, 1970), 51–56; Tarter, "The Conservative Party of Virginia," *Encyclopedia Virginia* (https://encyclopediavirginia.org/entries/conservative-party-of-virginia/, accessed Mar. 15, 2022).
27. Taylor, *Negro in Reconstruction*, 208–26; *Debates and Proceedings of 1867–1868 Convention*, 43–45, 60–82, 112–13, 135, 462–63.
28. *Daily Richmond Whig*, June 27, 1867; Richmond *Daily Dispatch*, Oct. 24, 1867.
29. Richmond *Daily Enquirer and Examiner*, Oct. 29, 1867; Woodstock *Shenandoah Herald*, Oct. 31, 1867 (quotation); Taylor, *Negro in Reconstruction*, 227; Luther Porter Jackson, *Negro Office-Holders in Virginia, 1865–1895* (Norfolk: Guide Quality Press, 1945), 35; Richard G. Lowe, "Virginia's Reconstruction Convention: General Schofield Rates the Delegates," *VMHB* 80 (1972): 353; W. W. Scott, *A History of Orange County, Virginia, from its Formation in 1734 to the End of Reconstruction in 1870* (Richmond: E. Waddey Co., 1907), 163, 164, 278; obituary in *Washington Post*, Feb. 1, 1892.
30. Lowe, "Virginia's Reconstruction Convention."
31. Tarter, *Constitutional History*, 164.
32. Tarter, *The Grandees of Government: The Origins and Persistence of Undemocratic Politics in Virginia* (Charlottesville: University of Virginia Press, 2013), 213–28.
33. Tarter, *Constitutional History*, 193–94.
34. Fiske Kimball, *The Capitol of Virginia, A Landmark of American Architecture*, Jon Kukla, Martha C. Vick, and Sarah Shields Driggs, eds. (Richmond: Virginia State Library and Archives, 1989), 66–67, 83.

35. Richard L. Hume, "The Membership of the Constitutional Convention of 1867–1868: A Study of the Beginnings of Congressional Reconstruction in the Upper South," *VMHB* 86 (1978): 461–84; Hume and Jerry B. Gouch, *Blacks, Carpetbaggers, and Scalawags: The Constitutional Conventions of Radical Reconstruction* (Baton Rouge: Louisiana State University Press, 2008).
36. Richmond *Daily Whig*, Dec. 6, 1867; *Frank Leslie's Illustrated Newspaper* 25 (Feb. 15, 1868): 345–46; *Journal of 1867–1868 Convention*, 147.
37. Matthew S. Gottlieb, "James W. Hunnicutt (1814–1880)," *DVB* on *EV* (https://encyclopediavirginia.org/entries/hunnicutt-james-w-1814-1880/, accessed Mar. 17, 2022); Steven E. Nash "'The Devil Let Loose Generally': James W. Hunnicutt's Conceptualization of the Union in Fredericksburg," *VMHB* 126 (2018): 334–65.
38. E.g., Richmond *Southern Opinion*, Dec. 7, 21, 1867, Feb. 15, Mar. 28, 1868.
39. Richmond *Southern Opinion*, Dec. 21, 1867; John T. Kneebone, "David Canada (fl. 1867–1869)," *DVB* on *EV* (https://encyclopediavirginia.org/entries/canada-david-fl-1867-1869/, accessed Dec. 22, 2021).
40. *Journal of 1867–1868 Convention*, 173.
41. Maddex, *Virginia Conservatives*, 51–56; Raleigh Travers Daniel, "Conservative Party State Committee Circular No. 4," Feb. 12, 1868, broadside, LVA (quotation).
42. Richmond *Daily Enquirer and Examiner*, Dec. 11, 12, 1867.
43. *Debates and Proceedings of 1867–1868 Convention*, 60–64, quotations on 60, 61.
44. Ibid., 68.
45. Ibid., 62–64 (quotation on 64).
46. Ibid., 81–82 (quotation on 81); Ervin Jordan, "James William D. Bland (1844–1870)," *DVB* on *EV* (https://encyclopediavirginia.org/entries/bland-j-w-d-1844-1870/, accessed Mar. 15, 2022).
47. *Journal of 1867–1868 Convention*, 197–98, quotation on 198.
48. *Debates and Proceedings of 1867–1868 Convention*, 522–26.
49. Ibid., 165–69, 175–76.
50. Ibid., 205.
51. Ibid., 162–65.
52. *Journal of 1867–1868 Convention*, 118.
53. *Debates and Proceedings of 1867–1868 Convention*, 211–12.
54. Ibid., 546.
55. Ibid., 164.
56. *Journal of 1867–1868 Convention*, 88.
57. Ibid., 104.
58. Ibid., 94.
59. *Journal of 1867–1868 Convention*, 101, nature of resolution not reported in journal but in *Debates and Proceedings of 1867–1868 Convention*, 520–21 (quotation).

60. *Journal of 1867–1868 Convention,* 45.
61. Ibid.
62. Ibid., 92–93, 95.
63. Ibid., 326.
64. Ibid., 55.
65. Ibid., 196–97.
66. Ibid., 382.
67. Ibid., 247, 249.
68. Ibid., 100–1.
69. Ibid., 82–83, 93.
70. Ibid., 116–17.
71. Ibid., 62.
72. Ibid., 35.
73. *Debates and Proceedings of 1867–1868 Convention,* 96.
74. *Journal of 1867–1868 Convention,* 333–34.
75. Ibid., 301.
76. E.g., Tarter, *Grandees of Government,* 224, 244.
77. *Journal of 1867–1868 Convention,* 338.
78. Ibid., 138.
79. Ibid., 100.
80. Ibid., 111.
81. Ibid., 174.
82. Ibid., 95–96.
83. Ibid., 37, 39–40.
84. Ibid., 111.
85. Ibid., 110 (quotation), 111.
86. Ibid., 87–89.
87. Ibid., 101.
88. Ibid., 122.
89. *Debates and Proceedings of 1867–1868 Convention,* 575.
90. *Journal of 1867–1868 Convention,* 93.
91. Ibid., 88.
92. *Debates and Proceedings of 1867–1868 Convention,* 199.
93. Ibid., 713–14.
94. Richmond *Daily Enquirer and Examiner,* June 24, 1868.
95. *Alexandria Gazette,* Mar. 4, 1867.
96. Tarter, "John Hawxhurst (1817–1881)," *DVB* on *EV* (https://encyclopediavirginia.org/entries/hawxhurst-john-1817-1881/, accessed Feb. 17, 2022).
97. Ted Tunnell, "Edgar Allan (1842–1904)," *DVB* on *EV* (https://encyclopediavirginia.org/entries/allan-edgar-1842-1904/, accessed Feb. 21, 2022).
98. *Journal of the 1867–1868 Convention,* 90, 114.
99. *Debates and Proceedings of 1867–1868 Convention,* 104.
100. Ibid., 458–68, quotation on 467.

101. Ibid., 557–58 quotation on 557.
102. Richmond *Daily Enquirer and Examiner,* Jan. 22, 1868.
103. The official, enrolled Constitution is in Records of the Virginia Constitutional Convention of 1867–1868, RG 96, LVA; *The Constitution of Virginia Framed by the Convention Which Met in Richmond, Virginia, on Tuesday, December 3, 1867* (Richmond, 1868); verified texts, including notes about discrepancies between the original manuscript and printed versions, on LVA's Constitutions of Virginia webpage at https://www.lva.virginia.gov/constitutions/discover/.
104. Laura E. Free, *Suffrage Reconstructed: Gender, Race, and Voting Rights in the Civil War Era* (Ithaca, N.Y.: Cornell University Press, 2015).
105. *Journal of 1867–1868 Convention,* 27.
106. Ibid., 286–87.
107. Catherine A. Jones, "More than a Contract, Less than a Right: Regulating Marriage in Postwar Virginia, 1865–1885" (unpublished essay, 2018).
108. *Acts of Assembly,* 1876–1877 sess.,333–34; Tarter, "When 'Kind and Thrifty Husbands' Are Not Enough: Some Thoughts on the Legal Status of Women in Virginia," *Magazine of Virginia Genealogy* 33 (1995): 86–91.
109. Unratified provision at https://www.lva.virginia.gov/constitutions/discover/#constitution-1868.
110. Paul Goodman, "The Emergence of Homestead Exemption in the United States: Accommodation and Resistance to the Market Revolution, 1840–1880," *Journal of American History* 80 (1993): 470–98; James W. Ely, Jr., "Homestead Exemption and Southern Legal Culture," in *Signposts: New Directions in Southern Legal History,* ed. Sally E. Hadden and Patricia Hagler Minder (Athens: University of Georgia Press, 2013): 289, 291–92, 294, 298–99.
111. B. A. Glasrud, "African American Militia Units in Virginia (1870–1899)," *Encyclopedia Virginia* (https://encyclopediavirginia.org/entries/african-american-militia-units-in-virginia-1870-1899/, accessed Mar. 3, 2022).
112. Albert Ogden Porter, *County Government in Virginia: A Legislative History, 1607–1904* (New York: Columbia University Press, 1947), 241–303.
113. Joseph P. Harahan, "Politics, Political Parties, and Voter Participation in Tidewater Virginia during Reconstruction, 1865–1900" (PhD, diss., University of Michigan, 1973).
114. *Journal of 1867–1868 Convention,* 389.
115. Ibid., 390; John C. Underwood to editor, *Washington Chronicle,* Jan. 7, 1868 [*sic*], reprinted in *New York Times,* 10 Jan. 1869.
116. Tarter, "John C. Underwood"; *Annual Report of the Joint Committee on the State Library* printed as Doc. No. 13 with *JSV,* 1872–1873, sess.; *New York Times,* Feb. 22, 1873; see also, Marianne E. Julienne and Brent Tarter, "The Virginia Ordinance of Secession: A Research Note on Contemporary Copies," *VMHB* 119 (2011): 155–59.

117. James L. McDonough, "John Schofield as Military Director of Reconstruction in Virginia," *Civil War History* 15 (1969): 237–56; Tarter, "First Military District," *Encyclopedia Virginia* (https://encyclopediavirginia.org/entries/first-military-district/, accessed Mar. 3, 2022).
118. Richmond *Daily Dispatch*, Apr. 18, 1868; Lowe, *Republicans and Reconstruction*, 144–48.
119. Alexander F. Robertson, *Alexander Hugh Holmes Stuart* (Richmond: William Byrd Press, 1925), 272–77, 278–85, and including the important documents, on 430–45, 448–56; Maddex, *Conservative Party*, 67–73; Lowe, *Republicans and Reconstruction*, 159–63.
120. *General Orders and Circulars, Headquarters First Military District, 1869* (Richmond, 1870), 3–7.
121. *JSV*, 1869 special sess., 27–28; *JHD*, 1869 special sess., 36.
122. *JSV*, 1869 special sess., 27–28; *Richmond Whig and Advertiser*, Oct. 12, 1869; Emily Jones Salmon, "Isaiah L. Lyons (1843–1871)," *DVB* on *EV* (https://encyclopediavirginia.org/entries/lyons-isaiah-l-1843-1871/, accessed Apr. 4, 2022).
123. 41st Cong., 2d sess., chap. 10.
124. Tarter, *Gerrymanders: How Redistricting Has Protected Slavery, White Supremacy, and Partisan Minorities in Virginia* (Charlottesville: University of Virginia Press, 2019), 10–39.
125. Tarter, *Constitutional History of Virginia*, 191–94.
126. *Debates and Proceedings of 1867–1868 Convention*, 164.

5. "Send a Colored Man"

1. Petersburg *Lancet*, May 31, 1884.
2. *Acts of Assembly*, 1883–1884 sess., 183.
3. Brent Tarter, "Mark Renie (or Réné) DeMortie (1829–1914)," *DVB* on *EV* (https://encyclopediavirginia.org/entries/demortie-mark-1829-1914/, accessed Dec. 22, 2021).
4. Tarter, "The Republican Party of Virginia in the Nineteenth Century," *Encyclopedia Virginia* (https://encyclopediavirginia.org/entries/the-republican-party-of-virginia-in-the-nineteenth-century/, accessed Jan. 5, 2022).
5. Emily Jones Salmon, "J. D. Harris (ca. 1833–1884)," *DVB* on *EV* (https://encyclopediavirginia.org/entries/harris-j-d-ca-1833-1884/, accessed Jan. 17, 2022).
6. Richard Lowe, *Republicans and Reconstruction in Virginia, 1856–1870* (Charlottesville: University Press of Virginia, 1991), 191–95.
7. Michael Chesson, "John H. Adams (ca. 1848–1934)," *DVB* on *EV* (https://encyclopediavirginia.org/entries/adams-john-h-ca-1848-1934, accessed June 4, 2022).
8. Chesson, "John Oliver (d. 1899)," *DVB* Online, published 2021 (https://www.lva.virginia.gov/public/dvb/bio.php?b=Oliver_John, accessed June 3, 2022);

Washington, DC, *New Era*, Apr. 21, 1870 (quotation); Peter J. Rachleff, *Black Labor in the South: Richmond, Virginia, 1865–1890* (Philadelphia: Temple University Press, 1984), 13–39, 55–69.

9. Brent Tarter, "The Remarkable Hodges Family of Princess Anne County and Norfolk," *Uncommonwealth*, LVA (https://uncommonwealth.virginiamemory.com/blog/2019/03/06/the-hodges-family, accessed June 15, 2022).
10. The Black delegates were elected in July 1869, although John Watson died before taking his seat and Ross Hamilton was later elected, meaning a total of twenty-five men ultimately won election to this term in the House.
11. Robert Somers, *The Southern States Since the War, 1870–1* (New York: Macmillan, 1871), 17.
12. *JSV*, 1869–1870 sess., 32, 206; Washington, DC, *New Era*, June 2, 1870 (quotation).
13. Ervin L. Jordan Jr., "James William D. Bland (1844–1870)," *DVB* on *EV* (https://encyclopediavirginia.org/entries/bland-j-w-d-1844-1870/, accessed June 4, 2022).
14. Census, Richmond City, 1870; Richmond *Daily Dispatch*, Oct. 4, 1869; Richmond *Daily State Journal*, Oct. 23, 1873.
15. John G. Deal, "Guy Powell (d. by November 19, 1900)," *DVB* on *EV* (https://encyclopediavirginia.org/entries/powell-guy-d-by-november-19-1900/, accessed June 4, 2022).
16. United States Census Office, *Compendium of the Tenth Census: 1870* (44 percent not literate), *Compendium of the Eleventh Census: 1880* (34 percent not literate), Government Printing Office, Washington, DC.
17. Matthew S. Gottlieb and Brent Tarter, "Frank Moss (d. by Aug. 6, 1884)," *DVB* on *EV* (https://encyclopediavirginia.org/entries/moss-frank-d-by-august-6-1884/, accessed May 1, 2022); Joshua Shaffer, "Armistead Green (d. 1892)," *DVB* on *EV* (https://encyclopediavirginia.org/entries/green-armistead-d-1892/, accessed May 1, 2022); Marianne E. Julienne, "William Faulcon (1841–by 1904)," *DVB* on *EV* (https://encyclopediavirginia.org/entries/faulcon-william-1841-by-1904/, accessed May 1, 2022).
18. Julienne, "Henry D. Smith (d. by December 2, 1901)," *DVB* on *EV* (https://encyclopediavirginia.org/entries/henry-d-smith-d-by-december-2-1901, accessed May 2, 2022); Tarter, "Robert M. Smith (d. Feb. 13, 1923)," *DVB* on *EV* (https://encyclopediavirginia.org/entries/robert-m-smith-d-february-13-1923, accessed May 2, 2022); Tarter, "Robert Gilbert Griffin (1847–1927)," *DVB* on *EV* (https://encyclopediavirginia.org/entries/robert-gilbert-griffin-march-1847-february-9-1927/, accessed May 5, 2022).
19. Tarter, "Alexander G. Lee (d. by Oct. 10, 1901)," *DVB* on *EV* (https://encyclopediavirginia.org/entries/alexander-g-lee-d-by-october-10-1901/, accessed May 5, 2022); Tarter, "James Richard Jones (d. after Aug. 20, 1902)," *DVB* on *EV* (https://encyclopediavirginia.org/entries/james-richard-jones-d-after-august-20-1902/, accessed May 5, 2022).

20. Sally Phillips, "John Robinson (1825 or 1826–1908)," *DVB* on *EV* (https://encyclopediavirginia.org/entries/robinson-john-1825-or-1826-1908/, accessed May 6, 2022); John T. Kneebone, "William H. Brisby (1836–1916)," *DVB* on *EV* (https://encyclopediavirginia.org/entries/brisby-william-h-1836-1916/, accessed May 6, 2022).
21. Diane Kiesel, "R. G. L. Paige (1846–1904)," *DVB* on *EV* (https://encyclopediavirginia.org/entries/paige-r-g-l-1846-1904/, accessed May 6, 2022).
22. Tarter, "Ellis Wilson (1818–1904)," *DVB* on *EV* (https://encyclopediavirginia.org/entries/ellis-wilson-1818-1904/, accessed May 7, 2022).
23. Tarter, "Robert G. W. Jones (1826–1900)," *DVB* on *EV* (https://encyclopediavirginia.org/entries/robert-g-w-jones-july-10-1826-by-march-15-1900/, accessed May 7, 2022).
24. Kiesel, "R. G. L. Paige," *DVB* on *EV*; Julienne, "George Lewis Seaton (ca. 1822–1881)," *DVB* on *EV* (https://encyclopediavirginia.org/entries/seaton-george-lewis-ca-1822-1881/, accessed May 7, 2022); Lynda J. Morgan, "Tazewell Branch (1828–1925)," *DVB* on *EV* (https://encyclopediavirginia.org/entries/branch-tazewell-1828-1925/, accessed May 8, 2022).
25. Michael Woods, "Alfred W. Harris (1853–1920)," *DVB* on *EV* (https://encyclopediavirginia.org/entries/harris-alfred-w-1853-1920/, accessed May 8, 2022); Tarter, "William H. Jordan (1860 or 1861–after 1889)," *DVB* on *EV* (https://encyclopediavirginia.org/entries/william-h-jordan-1860-or-1861-d-after-1889/, accessed May 8, 2022); *JHD*, 1885–1886 sess., 129; *Acts of Assembly*, 1885–1886 sess., 34–36.
26. Julienne, "Shed Dungee (1831–1900)," *DVB* on *EV* (https://encyclopediavirginia.org/entries/dungee-shed-1831-1900/, accessed May 10, 2022); Tarter, "Charles E. Hodges (1819–after Apr. 15, 1910)," *DVB* on *EV* (https://encyclopediavirginia.org/entries/hodges-charles-e-1819-after-april-15-1910/, accessed May 10, 2022); Lisa Clemmer, "Fountain M. Perkins (1816 or 1817–1896)," *DVB* on *EV* (https://encyclopediavirginia.org/entries/perkins-fountain-m-1816-or-1817-1896/, accessed May 10, 2022); Dustin Landon Robinette, "Caesar Perkins (1839–1910)," *DVB* on *EV* (https://encyclopediavirginia.org/entries/perkins-caesar-1839-1910/, accessed May 10, 2022); Jennifer R. Loux, "John M. Dawson (1829–1913)," *DVB* on *EV* (https://encyclopediavirginia.org/entries/dawson-john-m-1829-1913/, accessed May 10, 2022).
27. Philip W. Stanley, "Peter G. Morgan (1817–1890)," *DVB* on *EV* (https://encyclopediavirginia.org/entries/morgan-peter-g-1817-1890/, accessed May 10, 2022).
28. *JHD*, 1874–1875 sess., 102; *Acts of Assembly*, 1874–1875 sess., 110–11 (quotation on 110).
29. *Acts of Assembly*, 1876–1877 sess., 357–58.
30. Ibid., 1883–1884 sess., 408–9.

31. *JHD*, 1887–1888 sess., 48; *Acts of Assembly*, 1887–1888 sess., 163–64.
32. *JHD*, 1887–1888 sess., 213; *Acts of Assembly*, 1887–1888 sess., 465–66.
33. *JHD*, 1887–1888 sess., 156, 257, 287.
34. Ibid., 1869–1870 sess., 249.
35. Ibid., 1874 sess., 316, 1874–1875 sess., 28.
36. Ibid., 1869–1870 sess., 270.
37. Ibid., 235.
38. Ibid., 1874 sess., 160, 250, 1874–1875 sess., 39.
39. Ibid., 1877–1878 sess., 204, 1878–1879 sess., 118.
40. Ibid., 1872–1873 sess., 234; *Acts of Assembly*, 1872–1873 sess., 167 (quotation).
41. *JHD*, 1872–1873 sess., 25, 1874 sess., 236.
42. Ibid., 1869–1870 sess., 146.
43. Ibid., 1884 sess., 554.
44. *Norfolk Virginian*, Mar. 15, 1870 (first and third quotations); *Acts of Assembly*, 1869–1870 sess., 189 (second quotation); *Alexandria Gazette*, Apr. 8, 1870.
45. *JHD*, 1872–1873 sess., 79 (quotation), 124–25; Leila Christenbury, "Rufus Sibb Jones (ca. 1834–1897)," *DVB* on *EV* (https://encyclopediavirginia.org/entries/rufus-sibb-jones-ca-1834-july-17-1897/, accessed May 8, 2022).
46. *JHD*, 1872–1873 sess., 320.
47. Ibid., 1877–1878 sess., 369 (quotation), 487.
48. Ibid., 1872–1873 sess., 78, 124; 1875–1876 sess., 193.
49. Kiesel, "R. G. L. Paige (1846–1904)," *DVB* on *EV*; *New York Herald*, Jan. 22, 1880.
50. *JHD*, 1869–1870 sess., 101.
51. *JHD*, 1879–1880 sess., 212; *Acts of Assembly*, 1874–1875 sess., 269–71, 1877–1878 sess., 138–39.
52. *JHD*, 1874 sess., 93.
53. Ibid., 1874–1875 sess., 344, 1875–1876 sess., 366.
54. Ibid., 1874 sess., 78; George Wythe Munford, comp., *Third Edition of the Code of Virginia: Including Legislation to January 1, 1874* (Richmond, 1873), 1196.
55. *JHD*, 1874–1875 sess., 47.
56. Ibid., 1879–1880 sess., 32, 252, 256.
57. Ibid., 1872–1873 sess., 498, 1875–1876 sess., 245, 250, 252.
58. Ibid., 1874 sess., 207, 442.
59. Ibid., 1872–1873 sess., 77.
60. Ibid., 1871–1872 sess., 63–64, 170.
61. Ibid., 40, 90, 195, 410–11; Edward L. Ayers, *Vengeance and Justice: Crime and Punishment in the 19th-Century American South* (New York: Oxford University Press, 1984), 176–80, 225–27.
62. *JHD*, 1869–1870 sess., 666.
63. Ibid., 1871–1872 sess., 97; Richmond *Daily State Journal*, Dec. 21, 1871.
64. *JHD*, 1881–1882 sess., 293.

65. *JHD,* 1869–1870 sess., 74, 106–7, 112 (quotation), 208, 269, 308, 348, 393, 1870–1871 sess., 126.
66. Richmond *Daily State Journal,* Feb. 28, 1872, although *JHD,* 1871–1872 sess., 367, does not indicate who offered the amendment or what it was; but the language in the newspaper report is almost identical to the language in *Acts of Assembly,* 1871–1872 sess., 441 (quotation).
67. Donald W. Gunter, "Peter Jacob Carter, (1845–1886)" *DVB* on *EV* (https://encyclopediavirginia.org/entries/carter-peter-jacob-1845-1886/, accessed June 7, 2022).
68. Harold S. Forsythe, "'But All My Friends Are Poor': Ross Hamilton and Freedpeople's Politics in Mecklenburg County, Virginia, 1869–1901," *VMHB* 105 (1997): 409–38.
69. Silver Persinger, "Miles Connor (d. 1893)," *DVB* on *EV* (https://encyclopediavirginia.org/entries/connor-miles-d-1893/, accessed June 7, 2022).
70. Tarter, "Johnson Collins (1847–1906)," *DVB* on *EV* (https://encyclopediavirginia.org/entries/collins-johnson-1847-1906/, accessed June 7, 2022).
71. Tarter, "Nathaniel M. Griggs (d. 1919)," *DVB* on *EV* (https://encyclopediavirginia.org/entries/griggs-nathaniel-m-d-1919/, accessed June 7, 2022).
72. William Bland Whitley, "George William Cole (d. after June 10, 1880)," *DVB* on *EV* (https://encyclopediavirginia.org/entries/cole-george-william-d-after-june-10-1880/, accessed June 8, 2022).
73. Kneebone, "William H. Andrews (b. ca. 1839)," *DVB* on *EV* (https://encyclopediavirginia.org/entries/andrews-william-h-b-ca-1839/, accessed June 9, 2022).
74. *Acts of Assembly,* 1870–1871 sess., 378–81; *JSV,* 1870–1871 sess., 294–95; *JHD,* 1870–1871 sess., 387; Tarter, *A Saga of the New South: Race, Law, and Public Debt in Virginia* (Charlottesville: University of Virginia Press, 2016), 22–26.
75. Tarter, *Saga of the New South,* 26–28.
76. Ibid., 15.
77. Allen W. Moger, "Railroad Practices and Politics in Virginia after the Civil War," *VMHB* 59 (1951): 423–457; Maddex, *Virginia Conservatives,* 92–99, 113–20, 143–65; George Harrison Gilliam, "Building a Modern South: Political Economy in Nineteenth-Century Virginia" (PhD diss., University of Virginia, 2013), 200–45, 276–85, 295–96.
78. George Teamoh, *God Made Man, Man Made the Slave: The Autobiography of George Teamoh,* eds. F. N. Boney, Richard L. Hume, and Rafia Zafar (Macon, Ga.: Mercer University Press, 1990), 129–35, quotations on 131 and 132.
79. *Staunton Spectator,* 14 June 1870.
80. Richmond *Daily Dispatch,* Feb. 18, 1871 (square brackets in original).
81. Christenbury, "Alexander Owen (ca. 1830–ca. 1899)," *DVB* on *EV* (https://encyclopediavirginia.org/entries/alexander-owen-ca-1830ca-1898, accessed June 1, 2022).

82. *Acts of Assembly*, 1869–1870 sess., 402–17.
83. *Journal of 1867–1868 Convention*, 333–34.
84. *JSV*, 1869–1870 sess., 485, 489, 507; Tarter, "William P. Moseley (ca. 1819 or 1820–1890)," *DVB* on *EV* (https://encyclopediavirginia.org/entries/moseley-william-p-ca-1819-or-1820-1890/, accessed June 15, 2022).
85. *JHD*, 1869–1870 sess., 606–7, 610 (quotation), 615; Tarter, "John B. Miller Jr. (fl. 1859–1875)," *DVB* on *EV* (https://encyclopediavirginia.org/entries/john-b-miller-jr-fl-1859-1875/, accessed June 8, 2022); Tarter, "William Nash Stevens (1847–1891)," *DVB* on *EV* (https://encyclopediavirginia.org/entries/william-nash-stevens-1847-april-18-1891/, accessed June 8, 2022); Julienne and Tarter, "Establishment of the Public School System in Virginia," *Encyclopedia Virginia* (https://encyclopediavirginia.org/entries/public-school-system-in-virginia-establishment-of-the/, accessed June 9, 2022).
86. Tarter, "James P. Goodwyn (d. after Apr. 1910)," *DVB* on *EV* (https://encyclopediavirginia.org/entries/james-p-goodwyn-d-after-april-1910/, accessed June 15, 2022); Richmond *Daily State Journal*, Sept. 23, Oct. 9, 1873; Richmond *Daily Dispatch*, Nov. 5, 1873; William D. Henderson, *The Unredeemed City: Reconstruction in Petersburg, Virginia: 1865–1874* (Washington: University Press of America, 1977), 249–51.
87. *Richmond Daily Whig*, Aug. 17, 1876; Richmond *Daily Dispatch*, Aug. 17, 18, 1876; *Petersburg Index and Appeal*, Aug. 17, 18, 28, 29, Sept. 9, 11, 19, 30, Oct. 18, 20, Nov. 3, 6, 7, 10, 1876.
88. Tarter, *The Grandees of Government: The Origins and Persistence of Undemocratic Government in Virginia* (Charlottesville: University of Virginia Press, 2013), 262–64 and sources cited on 426 n. 21–23.
89. Tarter, "African Americans and Politics, 1865–1902," *Encyclopedia Virginia* (https://encyclopediavirginia.org/entries/african-americans-and-politics-in-virginia-1865-1902/, accessed June 15, 2022); Tarter, *Constitutional History*, 188.
90. Pippa Holloway, "'A Chicken-Stealer Shall Lose His Vote': Disfranchisement for Larceny in the South, 1874–1890," *Journal of Southern History* 75 (2009): 931–62; see also Holloway, *Living in Infamy: Felon Disfranchisement and the History of American Citizenship* (New York: Oxford University Press, 2014); Tarter, *Constitutional History*, 188, 189.
91. Tarter, "African Americans and Politics."
92. Luther Porter Jackson, *Negro Office-Holders in Virginia, 1865–1895* (Norfolk, Va.: Guide Quality Press, 1945), 57–67.
93. Joseph P. Harahan, "Politics, Political Parties, and Voter Participation in Tidewater Virginia during Reconstruction, 1865–1900" (PhD diss., University of Michigan, 1973).
94. Chesson, "Richmond's Black Councilmen, 1871–96," in *Southern Black Leaders of the Reconstruction Era*, ed. Howard N. Rabinowitz (Urbana: University of Illinois Press, 1992), 193.

95. Chesson, "Richmond's Black Councilmen," 194; Richmond *Daily State Journal*, Apr. 24, 1871.
96. Chesson, "Richmond's Black Councilmen," 191–222.
97. Richmond *Daily Dispatch*, Jan. 18, 1871.
98. *JHD*, 1874–1875 sess., 439–40; Meghan Townes, "Statue Stories: Thomas J. Jackson and Civil War Remembrance," *Uncommonwealth*, LVA (https://uncommonwealth.virginiamemory.com/blog/2017/10/26/statue-stories-thomas-j-jackson-and-civil-war-remembrance/, accessed June 15, 2022).
99. *Richmond Enquirer*, Aug. 22, 1875.
100. Fair but differing accounts in Richmond *Daily Dispatch*, Aug. 20, 21, 23, 1875, and *Richmond Enquirer*, Aug. 20, 21, 22 (quotation), 1875.

6. "Without Distinction of Color"

1. *Richmond Daily Whig*, Feb. 26, 27 (quotation), 1879.
2. Marianne E. Julienne and Brent Tarter, "Establishment of the Public School System in Virginia," *Encyclopedia Virginia* (https//encyclopediavirginia.org/entries/public-school-system-in-virginia-establishment-of-the/, accessed July 6, 2022).
3. Senate Doc. 6, printed with *JSV*, 1869–1870 sess. (quotation on 1), and also printed as House Doc. 13, with *JHD*, 1869–1870 sess.; *Virginia School Report, 1871. First Annual Report of the Superintendent of Public Instruction for the Year Ending August 31, 1871* (Richmond, 1871), 4–5, 9, 12–13.
4. *Virginia School Report, 1871*, 15 (quotation), 23, 173.
5. J. L. Blair Buck, *The Development of Public Schools in Virginia, 1607–1952* (Richmond: Commonwealth of Virginia State Board of Education, 1952), 65–93; Walter J. Fraser Jr. "William Henry Ruffner and the Establishment of Virginia's Public School System, 1870–1874," *VMHB* 79 (1971): 259–79; Julienne, "William Henry Ruffner (1824–1908)," *DVB* on *EV* (https://encyclopediavirginia.org/entries/ruffner-william-henry-1824-1908/, accessed June 19, 2022); *Virginia School Report, 1871*, 106–31.
6. Walter C. Daniel, *Black Journals of the United States* (Westport, Conn.: Greenwood Press, 1982), 350–58; Sidonia Serafini, "Black, White, and Native: The Multiracial Writing Community of Hampton Institute's *Southern Workman*," *Southern Quarterly* 56 (winter 2019): 63–81.
7. William A. Link, *A Hard Country and a Lonely Place: Schooling, Society, and Reform in Rural Virginia, 1870–1920* (Chapel Hill: University of North Carolina Press, 1986).
8. *Southern Workman* 2 (Feb. 1873): 2.
9. Ibid., 3 (1874): 39.
10. Ibid., 4 (1875): 47.
11. Ibid., 7 (1878): 20.
12. Ibid., 7 (1878): 60.

13. Ibid., 10 (1881): 122.
14. Ibid., 8 (1879): 100.
15. Ibid., 12 (1883): 80.
16. Jane Dailey, *Before Jim Crow: The Politics of Race in Postemancipation Virginia* (Chapel Hill: University of North Carolina Press, 2000), 70–76.
17. *Richmond Daily Whig*, July 9, 1880.
18. Petersburg *Lancet*, Jan. 19, 1884.
19. Brent Tarter, "Samuel F. Kelso (ca. 1825–1880)," *DVB* on *EV* (https://encyclopediavirginia.org/entries/kelso-samuel-f-ca-1825-1880/, accessed Mar. 4, 2022).
20. Alonzo Thomas Dill, "Beverly Allen (1859–1918)," *DVB* Online, published 1998, revised 2022 (https://www.lva.virginia.gov/public/dvb/bio.php?b=Allen_Beverly, accessed Mar. 4, 2022).
21. *Annual Report of the Superintendent of Public Instruction* (1870), 219, (1880), 95, (1890), 10.
22. Cassandra L. Newby-Alexander, "Amanda Virginia Thomas Clark (1869–1952)," *DVB* Online, published 2006, (https://www.lva.virginia.gov/public/dvb/bio.php?b=Clark_Amanda, accessed Mar. 4, 2022).
23. Julienne, "Josephine B. Mathews Norcom (1873–1927)," *DVB* Online, published 2019 (https://www.lva.virginia.gov/public/dvb/bio.php?b=Norcom_Josephine_Mathews, accessed Mar. 5, 2022).
24. Lauranett L. Lee, "Maggie Lena Draper Mitchell Walker (1864–1934)," *DVB* Online, published 2020 (https://www.lva.virginia.gov/public/dvb/bio.php?b=Walker_Maggie_Lena, accessed Mar. 5, 2022).
25. Veronica Davis, "Rosa L. Dixon Bowser (1855–1931)," *DVB* on *EV* (https://encyclopediavirginia.org/entries/bowser-rosa-l-dixon-1855-1931/, accessed Mar. 6, 2022).
26. Tarter, "John William Poindexter (ca. 1848–1889)," *DVB* on *EV* (https://encyclopediavirginia.org/entries/john-william-poindexter-ca-1848-february-16-1889/, accessed Mar. 7, 2022).
27. John T. Kneebone, "William H. Ash (1859–1908)," *DVB* on *EV* (https://encyclopediavirginia.org/entries/ash-william-h-1859-1908/, accessed Mar. 7, 2022).
28. Philip Stanley, "James Solomon Russell (1857–1935)," *DVB* on *EV* (https://encyclopediavirginia.org/entries/russell-james-solomon-1857-1935/, accessed Mar. 7, 2022).
29. "Autobiography of Wendell Phillips Dabney," undated typescript, 27–28, Wendell Phillips Dabney Collection, Cincinnati Historical Society Library, Cincinnati Museum Center.
30. Tarter, *A Saga of the New South: Race, Law, and Public Debt in Virginia* (Charlottesville: University of Virginia Press, 2016), 28.
31. Julienne and Tarter, "Establishment of the Public School System."

32. Nelson Morehouse Blake, *William Mahone of Virginia: Soldier and Political Insurgent* (Richmond: Garret and Massie, 1935); Jack P. Maddex Jr., *The Virginia Conservatives, 1867–1879: A Study in Reconstruction Politics* (Chapel Hill: University of North Carolina Press, 1970), 248–54; Tarter, *Saga of the New South*, 46.
33. *Richmond Daily Whig*, Jan. 30, 1878 (quotation); John W. Daniel to W. T. Taliaferro, Sept. 19, 1879, in Richmond *Daily Dispatch*, Sept. 24, 1879; William Bland Whitley, "John Warwick Daniel (1842–1910)," *DVB* on *EV* (https://encyclopediavirginia.org/entries/daniel-john-warwick-1842-1910/, accessed May 18, 2022); Tarter, *Saga of the New South*, 49–50.
34. *JHD*, 1877–1878 sess., 425–30 (quotation on 428).
35. Tarter, *Saga of the New South*, 8–9.
36. Dailey, *Before Jim Crow*; Tarter, *Saga of the New South*, 57–58.
37. Richmond *Virginia Star*, 27 Sept. 1879.
38. *Southern Workman* 8 (1879): 122 (quotations); 9 (1880): 6, 42.
39. Tarter, *Saga of the New South*, 59–61.
40. *JHD*, 1879–1880 sess., 142, 172, 179, 381–86; *JSV*, 1879–1880 sess., 156–57, 204, 267–68.
41. Staunton *Valley Virginian*, Apr. 8, 1880, copied from a lost issue of the *Richmond Star*.
42. Richmond *Daily Dispatch*, July 8, 1880.
43. Full accounts of the meeting in *Richmond Daily Whig*, Mar. 16 (quotations), 18, 1881; Tarter, "Petersburg Convention of March 14, 1881," *Encyclopedia Virginia*, (https://encyclopediavirginia.org/entries/petersburg-convention-of-march-14-1881/, accessed on May 18, 2022).
44. Richmond *Daily Dispatch*, June 3 (quotations), 4, 1881. Files of the more sympathetic *Richmond Daily Whig* are lost for the month.
45. *JHD*, 1881–1882 sess., 33.
46. Ibid., 30–31.
47. Ibid., 26, 36, 79, 84, 85, 109, 138, 158–59, 173, 188, 196, 202, 255, 263, 286, 294.
48. Ibid., 216.
49. Ibid., 1881–1882 sess., 88, 279, 1882 special sess., 16.
50. Ibid., 1881–1882 sess., 310.
51. Ibid., 168, 1882, special sess., 110.
52. Ibid., 1881–1882 sess., 293, 1882 special sess., 15.
53. Ibid., 1881–1882 sess., 302.
54. Ibid., 1882 special sess., 20.
55. Ibid., 1881–1882 sess., 333.
56. Ibid., 67 (first quotation), 137 (second quotation).
57. Tarter, *The Grandees of Government: The Origins and Persistence of Undemocratic Politics in Virginia* (Charlottesville: University of Virginia Press, 2013), 245–48.

58. Secretary of the Commonwealth, 1776–1941, MS Election Record No. 104, State Government Records Collection, RG 13, LVA.
59. *Acts of Assembly*, 1881–1882 sess., 88–98.
60. *JHD*, 1881–1882 sess., 244, 1882 special sess., 63; *Acts of Assembly*, 1881–1882 sess., 283–87; *Richmond Daily Whig*, Feb. 15, 1882 (quotation).
61. *JHD*, 1882 extra sess., 257.
62. *Acts of Assembly*, 1901–1902 sess., 397
63. *JHD*, 1881–1882 sess., 84; *Acts of Assembly*, 1881–1882 sess., 246–48 (quotation on 246). The hospital had been in existence since 1870 (see *Acts of Assembly*, 1869–1870 sess., 189) and was still known as Central Lunatic Asylum until the 1890s. The 1882 act directed the asylum directors to construct new buildings at a new site near Petersburg.
64. *JHD*, 1881–1882 sess., 37; *Acts of Assembly*, 1881–1882 sess., 401–4.
65. Tarter, *Saga of the New South*, 69–72.
66. *JHD*, 1883–1884 sess., 17–23, quotation on 20.
67. William Mahone to John D. Long, Feb. 11, 1882, printed in *Richmond Daily Whig*, Mar. 15, 1882.
68. *Richmond Daily Whig*, Oct. 24, 1883.
69. "Public Free Schools!" Broadside (n.d. [ca. 1883]), LVA.
70. Isaac Dabbs to William Mahone, Nov. 25, 1882, William Mahone Papers, David M. Rubenstein Rare Book & Manuscript Library, Duke University, Durham, N.C.
71. Willis William Robinson to William Mahone, May 27, 1882, Mahone Papers.
72. George Washington to William Mahone, Dec. 19, 1882, Mahone Papers.
73. Richmond *Daily Dispatch*, July 26, 1883.
74. Address of Oct. 23, 1883, reported in Richmond *Daily Dispatch*, Oct. 26, 1883.
75. *Richmond Daily Whig*, July 31, 1884.
76. Dailey, *Before Jim Crow*, 79; Marion *Conservative Democrat*, Nov. 1, 1883, quotation.
77. Tarter, *Saga of the New South*, 76–80.
78. Ibid., 179–80.
79. Tarter, "Francis Simpson Blair (1839–1899)," *DVB on EV* (https://encyclopediavirginia.org/entries/blair-francis-s-1839-1899/, accessed May 12, 2022); Tarter, "Robert William Blair (1873–1924)," *DVB on EV* (https://encyclopediavirginia.org/entries/blair-robert-w-1873-1924/, accessed May 12, 2022).
80. Luis-Alejandro Dinnella-Borrego, "John Mercer Langston (1829–1897)," *DVB on EV* (https://encyclopediavirginia.org/entries/langston-john-mercer-1829-1897/, accessed May 12, 2022); *John M. Langston v. E. C. Venable*, 51st Cong, 1st sess., House Report no. 2462.
81. Matthew Gottlieb, "Daniel M. Norton later McNorton (d. 1918)" (https://encyclopediavirginia.org/entries/norton-daniel-m-later-daniel

-mcnorton-d-1918/), "F. S. Norton (d. 1893)" (https://encyclopediavirginia.org/entries/norton-f-s-d-1893/), and "Robert Norton (d. 1898)" (https://encyclopediavirginia.org/entries/norton-robert-d-by-october-17-1898/), *DVB on EV* (accessed May 12, 2022).

82. *Daily Richmond Whig*, Oct. 24, 1883; Tarter, "John Bryce Syphax (d. 1916)," *DVB on EV* (https://encyclopediavirginia.org/entries/john-bryce-syphax-d-september-8-1916/, accessed May 13, 2022).

7. "I Am Constantly Busy"

1. Lucy in *Southern Workman* 22 (1893): 153, identified in *Twenty-Two Years' Work of the Hampton Normal and Agricultural Institute at Hampton, Virginia* (1893), 125.
2. H. in *Southern Workman* 17 (1888): 41.
3. H. in *Southern Workman* 19 (1890) 125.
4. *Southern Workman* 7 (1878): 4.
5. Brent Tarter, *Virginians and Their Histories* (Charlottesville: University of Virginia Press, 2020), 315.
6. W. T. Fuller, "The Farmers' Alliance, Its Aims and the Means by Which it Wishes to Accomplish Them," *Southern Workman* 20 (1891): 228.
7. Theodore Saloutos, *Farmer Movements in the South, 1865–1933* (Berkeley: University of California Press, 1960), 119–22; William Edward Spriggs, "The Virginia Colored Farmers' Alliance: A Case Study of Race and Class Identity," *Journal of Negro History* 64 (1979): 191–204; Omar H. Ali, *In the Lion's Mouth: Black Populism in the New South, 1886–1900* (Jackson: University Press of Mississippi, 2010), 48–77; Tarter, "Colored Farmers' Alliance and Cooperative Union of Virginia," *Encyclopedia Virginia* (https://encyclopediavirginia.org/entries/colored-farmers-alliance-and-cooperative-union-of-virginia-the/, accessed June 10, 2022); Richmond *Virginia Sun*, June 1, 1892.
8. Spriggs, "Virginia Colored Farmers' Alliance," 193–94.
9. July 1862 birth date in Census, Warren Co., N.C.; signed public letters from Boydton in *Richmond Planet*, Oct. 10, 1890; Richmond *Virginia Sun*, June 1, 1892.
10. Richmond *Times*, Aug. 22, 1890 (quotation).
11. Ibid.; *Southern Workman* 19 (1890): 103.
12. Richmond *Times*, Aug. 22, 23, 1890; *Richmond Planet*, Aug. 30, 1890.
13. Samuel Proctor, "The National Farmers' Alliance Convention of 1890 and its 'Ocala Demands,'" *Florida Historical Quarterly* 28 (1950): 161–81.
14. William DuBose Sheldon, *Populism in the Old Dominion; Virginia Farm Politics, 1885–1900* (Princeton: Princeton University Press, 1935), 22–75.
15. Proctor, "National Farmers' Alliance Convention of 1890," 175–81; Spriggs, "Virginia Colored Farmers' Alliance," 200.

16. Spriggs, "Virginia Colored Farmers' Alliance," 199.
17. *Richmond Dispatch,* Aug. 11, 1891; full report in *Richmond Planet,* Aug. 15, 1891.
18. *Richmond Dispatch,* Aug. 11, 1891; not included in otherwise full report of the convention in *Richmond Planet,* Aug. 15, 1891.
19. Richmond *Virginia Sun,* June 1, 1892.
20. Ibid., July 13, 1892.
21. Spriggs, "Virginia Colored Farmers' Alliance," 200–1.
22. Holmes, "Demise of the Colored Farmers' Alliance," 187–200.
23. Helen G. Edmonds, *The Negro and Fusion Politics in North Carolina* (Chapel Hill: University of North Carolina Press, 1951), 109; obituary in Norfolk *Journal and Guide,* North Carolina edition, Feb. 7, 1940.
24. W. E. Burghardt Du Bois, "The Negroes of Farmville, Virginia: A Social Study," *Bulletin of the Department of Labor,* No. 14 (Jan. 1898): 1–38, quotations on 5, 6, 8, and 9.
25. Ibid., 15, 16 (second and third quotations), 17 (first quotation).
26. Ibid., 20 (first quotation), 21 (second quotation).
27. Ibid., 25–26.
28. Ibid., 34 (first quotation), 35 (second quotation).
29. Ibid., 36.
30. Peter J. Rachleff, *Black Labor in the South: Richmond, Virginia, 1865–1890* (Philadelphia: Temple University Press, 1984).
31. Jane Dailey, *Before Jim Crow: The Politics of Race in Postemancipation Virginia* (Chapel Hill: University of North Carolina Press, 2000), 159.
32. Rachleff, *Black Labor in the South,* 141–42; Michael B. Chesson, *Richmond after the War, 1865–1890* (Richmond: Virginia State Library, 1981), 187–89.
33. Charles E. Wynes, *Race Relations in Virginia, 1870–1902* (Charlottesville: University of Virginia Press, 1960), 68–83.
34. *Virginia v. Rives,* 100 US 313 (1880): 313; *Ex Parte Virginia,* 100 US 339 (1880); *The Civil Rights Cases,* 109 US 3 (1883); Brent Tarter, "*Ex Parte Virginia* (1880)," *Encyclopedia Virginia,* https://encyclopediavirginia.org/entries/ex-parte-virginia-1880/, accessed June 16, 2022.
35. Alan B. Bromberg, "John Strode Barbour (1820–1892)," *DVB* on *EV* (https://encyclopediavirginia.org/entries/barbour-john-s-1820-1892/, accessed June 17, 2022).
36. Wynes, *Race Relations in Virginia,* 68–83, esp. 70–73.
37. *Plessy v. Ferguson* 163 US 537 (1896).
38. Tarter, *Virginians and Their Histories,* 319–20.
39. William Waller Hening ed., *The Statutes at Large: Being a Collection of All the Laws of Virginia, from the First Session of the Legislature, in the Year 1619 . . .* (Richmond, etc., 1809–23) 3:87; George Webb, *The Office and Authority of a Justice of the Peace* (Williamsburg, 1736), 220.
40. Wynes, *Race Relations in Virginia,* 92–95.

41. George W. Munford, comp., *Third Edition of the Code of Virginia: Including Legislation to January 1, 1874* (Richmond, 1873), 850.
42. *Kinney v. Commonwealth* 71 Va. 858 (1878).
43. *Acts of Assembly*, 1877–1878 sess., 302.
44. *Jones v. Commonwealth* 79 Va. 213 (1885), quotation on 216.
45. *Jones v. Commonwealth*, 80 Va. 538 (1885), quotation on 542.
46. *Loving v. Virginia* 388 US 1 (1967); Walter Wadlington, "The *Loving* Case: Virginia's Anti-Miscegenation Statute in Historical Perspective," *Virginia Law Review* 52 (1966): 1189–223; Peter Wallenstein, *Tell the Court I Love My Wife: Race, Marriage, and Law—An American History* (New York: Palgrave Macmillan, 2002).
47. Joshua D. Rothman, *Notorious in the Neighborhood: Sex and Families across the Color Line in Virginia, 1787–1861* (Chapel Hill: University of North Carolina Press, 2003).
48. Alexander H. Lorch III, "Reuben Turner Coleman (1844–1909)," *DVB* Online, published 2006, rev. 2021 (http://www.lva.virginia.gov/public/dvb/bio.asp?b=Coleman_Reuben_Turner, accessed June 15, 2022); Richmond *Daily Dispatch*, July 2, 1879.
49. Marilyn Mildred White, "'We Lived on an Island': An Afro-American Family and Community in Rural Virginia, 1865–1940" (PhD diss., University of Texas at Austin, 1983), 61–68.
50. Thomas Calhoun Walker, "Lawyer Walker of Gloucester—As Told to Two Northern Friends," ca. 1950, Special Collections Research Center, Earl Gregg Swem Library, College of William and Mary, Williamsburg, 76 (second quotation), 77, 187 (first quotation).
51. Brent Tarter, "Lynch, Charles," *American National Biography*, ed. John A. Garraty and Mark C. Carnes, 24 vols. (New York, 1999), 14:104–5.
52. John G. Deal, "Thomas Calhoun Walker (1862–1953)," *DVB* Online, published 2022 (https://www.lva.virginia.gov/public/dvb/bio.php?b=Walker_Thomas_Calhoun, accessed July 14, 2022); Walker, "Lawyer Walker of Gloucester," 231 (quotation).
53. Gianluca De Fazio, "Improving Lynching Inventories with Local Newspapers: Racial Terror in Virginia, 1877–1927," *Current Research in Digital History* 2 (Aug. 25, 2019), https://crdh.rrchnm.org/essays/v02-04-improving-lynching-inventories/ (quotation), accessed June 9, 2022.
54. Gianluca De Fazio et al., "Racial Terror: Lynching in Virginia," https://sites.lib.jmu.edu/valynchings/, accessed June 9, 2022; De Fazio, "Improving Lynching Inventories."
55. *Richmond Dispatch*, Nov. 9, 1889.
56. Ann Field Alexander, "'Like an Evil Wind': The Roanoke Riot of 1893 and the Lynching of Thomas Smith," *VMHB* 100 (1992): 173–206.
57. Dolores Flamiano, "'Virginia's Shame': The 1891 Lynching of Three Black Miners in Clifton Forge" ("Racial Terror: Lynching in Virginia," n.d.).

58. "Racial Terror: Lynching in Virginia," n.d.
59. Ibid.; *Clinch Valley News,* Feb. 17, 1893 (quotation).
60. Alexander, *Race Man: The Rise and Fall of the "Fighting Editor," John Mitchell Jr.* (Charlottesville: University of Virginia Press, 2002).
61. *Richmond Planet,* Dec. 13, 1890.
62. See, for example, *Richmond Planet,* Jan. 30, 1897.
63. Suzanne Lebsock, *A Murder in Virginia: Southern Justice on Trial* (New York: W.W. Norton, 2003).
64. Diane Miller Sommerville, *Rape and Race in the Nineteenth-Century South* (Chapel Hill: University of North Carolina Press, 2004).
65. Leila Christenbury, "Edmonia Carter Powers Barksdale (1847–1918)," *DVB* Online, published 2019 (https://www.lva.virginia.gov/public/dvb/bio.php?b=Barksdale_Edmonia_Carter_Powers, accessed June 15, 2022); quotation in Richmond *Times-Dispatch* and Richmond *Evening Journal,* both Feb. 13, 1914.
66. John Stewart Bryan, *Joseph Bryan: His Times, His Family, His Friends* (Richmond, 1935), 160–61.
67. *Southern Workman* 17 (1888): 17.
68. Ibid., 20 (1891): 149.
69. Tarter, "Willis A. Hodges (1815–1890)," *DVB* on *EV* (https://encyclopediavirginia.org/entries/hodges-willis-a-1815-1890, accessed June 14, 2022); Tarter, "John Q. Hodges (1841–after June 1, 1900)," *DVB* on *EV* (https://encyclopediavirginia.org/entries/hodges-john-q-1841-after-june-1-1900/, accessed June 14, 2022).
70. Walker, "Lawyer Walker of Gloucester," 187.
71. Charles Perdue et al., eds., *Weevils in the Wheat: Interviews with Virginia Ex-Slaves* (Charlottesville: University Press of Virginia, 1976), 128.

8. "To Take Our Place in the Business World"

1. *Fiftieth Anniversary—Historical Report of the R. W. G. Council, I. O. Saint Luke, 1867–1917* (Richmond, 1917), 58–59 (quotation on 58).
2. J. L. Blair Buck, *The Development of Public Schools in Virginia, 1607–1952* (Richmond: Commonwealth of Virginia State Board of Education, 1952), 85–86, 156–62; school funding addressed in published annual and biennial reports of the Virginia Superintendent of Public Instruction.
3. John T. Kneebone, "Britton Baskervill (1863–1892)," *DVB* on *EV* (https://encyclopediavirginia.org/entries/baskervill-britton-1863-1892/, accessed June 15, 2022).
4. Daniel B. Thorp, *Facing Freedom: An African American Community in Virginia from Reconstruction to Jim Crow* (Charlottesville: University of Virginia Press, 2017), 148–55; Marianne E. Julienne, "Graham Cox Campbell

(1847–1915)," *DVB* Online, published 2001, rev. 2022 (https://www.lva.virginia.gov/public/dvb/bio.php?b=Campbell_Graham_Cox, accessed Aug. 19, 2022); Antoinette van Zelm, "Jennie Serepta Dean (1848–1913)," *DVB* on *EV* (https://encyclopediavirginia.org/entries/dean-jennie-serepta-1848-1913, accessed Aug. 19, 2022).

5. Jennifer Loux, "Carrie Victoria Dyer (1839–1921)," *DVB* on *EV* (https://encyclopediavirginia.org/entries/dyer-carrie-victoria-1839-1921/, accessed Aug. 19, 2022); *Annual Catalogue of Hartshorn Memorial College, Richmond, Virginia 1899–1900* (Richmond: Whittet and Shepperson, 1900), 9 (quotation).
6. Douglas Thompson, "Virginia Baptist State Convention" *Encyclopedia Virginia* (https://encyclopediavirginia.org/entries/virginia-baptist-state-convention/, accessed June 9, 2022); Tommy Bogger, "John M. Armistead (1852–1929)" *DVB* on *EV* (https://encyclopediavirginia.org/entries/armistead-john-m-1852-1929/, accessed Sept. 29, 2023); Ralph Reavis, *Virginia Seminary: A Journey of Black Independence* (Bedford, Va.: The Print Shop, 1990).
7. Eve Gregory, *Claremont Manor* (Petersburg, Va.: Plummer Printing Company, Inc., 1990), 99–102; *Temperance, Industrial and Collegiate Institute, 1906–1907 Catalogue* (Richmond: St. Luke Herald Press, 1906); W. N. Hartshorn and George W. Penniman, eds., *An Era of Progress and Promise, 1863–1910* (Boston: Priscilla Publishing Co., 1910), 363 (first quotation); Claremont *Monthly Advocate*, June 13, 1896 (second quotation).
8. Donald W. Gunter, "James Major Colson (1855–1909)," *DVB* Online, published 2006 (https://www.lva.virginia.gov/public/dvb/bio.php?b=Colson_James_Major, accessed July 24, 2022).
9. Lauranett L. Lee, "Edna Meade Colson (1888–1985)," *DVB* Online, published 2006 (http://www.lva.virginia.gov/public/dvb/bio.asp?b=Colson_Edna_Meade, accessed July 25, 2022).
10. Robert Francis Engs, *Freedom's First Generation: Black Hampton, Virginia, 1861–1890* (Philadelphia: University of Pennsylvania Press, 1979), 111–27.
11. Jeremy Wells, "Booker T. Washington (1856–1915)," *Encyclopedia Virginia* (https://encyclopediavirginia.org/entries/washington-booker-t-1856-1915/, accessed June 23, 2022); Louis Harlan, *Booker T. Washington: The Making of a Black Leader, 1856–1901* (New York: Oxford University Press, 1972).
12. James D. Watkinson, "William Washington Browne and the True Reformers of Richmond, Virginia," *VMHB* 97 (1989): 375–98; Watkinson, "William Washington Browne (1849–1897)," *DVB* on *EV* (https://encyclopediavirginia.org/entries/browne-william-washington-1849-1897/, accessed Feb. 12, 2021).
13. Shennette Garrett-Scott, *Banking on Freedom: Black Women in U.S. Finance Before the New Deal* (New York: Columbia University Press, 2019).

14. Garrett-Scott, *Banking on Freedom*, 99, quoting Maggie L. Walker, "Benaiah's Honor—For Men Only" (1906), 19–20. Folder 24, box 3, Maggie Lena Walker Papers, Maggie Lena Walker National Historic Site, Richmond, Va.
15. Gertrude Woodruff Marlowe, *A Right Worthy Grand Mission: Maggie Lena Walker and the Quest for Black Economic Empowerment* (Washington, DC: Howard University Press, 2003); Garrett-Scott, *Banking on Freedom*; Lauranett L. Lee, "Maggie Lena Draper Mitchell Walker (1864–1934)," *DVB* Online, published 2020 (https://www.lva.virginia.gov/public/dvb/bio.php?b=Walker_Maggie_Lena, accessed Aug. 8, 2022).
16. Marlowe, *Right Worthy Grand Mission*, 171–72.
17. "O." in *Southern Workman* 19 (1890): 6; identified by name in *Twenty-Two Years' Work of the Hampton Normal and Agricultural Institute at Hampton, Virginia* (Hampton, 1893), 93.
18. Henry Lewis Suggs, "Virginia," in *The Black Press in the South, 1865–1979*, ed. Henry Lewis Suggs (Westport, Conn.: Greenwood Press, 1983), 379–95; "Virginia Newspaper Project Seeks Copies of African-American Newspapers," *Library of Virginia Newsletter* (Jan-Feb. 1995), 4–5; some Black newspapers in LVA's collection are online at Virginia Chronicle: https://virginiachronicle.com/.
19. Nicole Myers Turner, *Soul Liberty: The Evolution of Black Religious Politics in Postemancipation Virginia* (Chapel Hill: University of North Carolina Press, 2020), 6–7.
20. Ibid., 57–80, 97–100.
21. W. E. Burghardt Du Bois, "The Negroes of Farmville, Virginia: A Social Study," *Bulletin of the Department of Labor*, No. 14 (Jan. 1898): 18.
22. Lynda J. Morgan, "Samuel P. Bolling (1819–1900)," *DVB* on *EV* (https://encyclopediavirginia.org/entries/bolling-samuel-p-1819-1900/, accessed Aug. 1, 2022).
23. *Southern Workman* 26 (1897): 67 (quotations), 29 (1900): 134, 30 (1901): 698–99.
24. F. D. Banks, "The Negro in Business," *Southern Workman* 30 (1901): 783 (quotation), 784; first name in *Twenty-Two Years Work*, 64–65.
25. Garrett-Scott, *Banking on Freedom*, 103–4.
26. John T. Kneebone, "Edward C. Brown (ca. 1877–1928)," *DVB* Online, published 2001 (https://www.lva.virginia.gov/public/dvb/bio.php?b=Brown_Edward_C., accessed Aug. 8, 2022).
27. Judith P. Justus and John P. Bing, "Dana Olden Baldwin (1881–1972)," *DVB* Online, published 1998 (https://www.lva.virginia.gov/public/dvb/bio.php?b=Baldwin_Dana_Olden, accessed Aug. 8, 2022).
28. Alexander H. Lorch III, "Reuben Turner Coleman (1844–1909)," *DVB* Online, published 2006, rev. 2021 (http://www.lva.virginia.gov/public/dvb/bio.asp?b=Coleman_Reuben_Turner, accessed July 25, 2022).

29. Department of the Interior, Current Reports, vol. 5, *Twelfth Census of the United States, Taken in the Year 1900, Agriculture: Pt. 1: Farms, Live Stock, and Animal Products* (Washington, DC: Government Printing Office, 1902), 14.
30. Department of Commerce, Bureau of the Census, *Negro Population, 1790–1915* (Washington, DC: Government Printing Office, 1918), 557, 588–89.
31. Crandall A. Shifflett, *Patronage and Poverty in the Tobacco South: Louisa County, Virginia, 1860–1900* (Knoxville: University of Tennessee Press, 1982), 19, 52–53.
32. Giles B. Jackson and D. Webster Davis, *The Industrial History of the Negro Race of the United States* (Richmond: The Virginia Press, 1908), 104–5.
33. Ibid., 107–108.
34. Ibid.
35. Ibid., 109, 119.
36. *The Official Blue Book of the Jamestown Ter-Centennial Exposition, A.D. 1907* (Norfolk: Colonial Publishing Co., 1909); Brent Tarter, *Virginians and Their Histories* (Charlottesville: University of Virginia Press, 2020), 316–17.
37. W. Fitzhugh Brundage, "Meta Warrick's 1907 'Negro Tableaux' and (Re) Presenting African American Historical Memory," *Journal of American History* 89 (2003): 1,368–1,400.
38. Jackson and Davis, *Industrial History of the Negro Race*, 6.
39. Ibid., 102 (quotation), 156.
40. Ibid., 7.
41. Tarter, "Robert Gilbert Griffin (1847–1927)," *DVB* on *EV*, (https://encyclopediavirginia.org/entries/robert-gilbert-griffin-march-1847-february-9-1927/, accessed June 25, 2022).
42. Veronica Alease Davis, "Rosa L. Dixon Bowser (1855–1931)" *DVB* on *EV* (https://encyclopediavirginia.org/entries/bowser-rosa-l-dixon-1855-1931//, accessed July 15, 2022).
43. Anne Firor Scott, "Janie Aurora Porter Barrett (1865–1948)," *DVB* Online, published 1998, rev. 2021 (http://www.lva.virginia.gov/public/dvb/bio.php?b=Barrett_Janie_Porter, accessed July 25, 2022).
44. Irvington *Virginia Citizen*, Oct. 12, 1900; Tarter, "L. R. Flemings (d. 1937)," *DVB* on *EV* (https://encyclopediavirginia.org/entries/flemings-l-r-d-1937/, accessed July 25, 2022).
45. Gunter, "Wiley Horace Crocker (1873–1943)," *DVB* Online, published 2006 (https://www.lva.virginia.gov/public/dvb/bio.php?b=Crocker_Wiley_Horace, accessed July 25, 2022); Sarah S. Hughes, "The Suffolk Fair," in Jane H. Kobelski, ed., *Readings in Black and White: Lower Tidewater Virginia* (Portsmouth, Va.: Portsmouth Public Library, 1982), 34–38.
46. Alice M. Bacon, "The Dixie Hospital," Supplement to *Southern Workman* 21 (Feb. 1892), and Bacon, "The Dixie, its Progress and its Needs," *Southern Workman* 23 (1894): 30–32.

47. Ann Field Alexander, "Isaac David Burrell (1865–1914)," *DVB* Online, published 2001, rev. 2018 (http://www.lva.virginia.gov/public/dvb/bio.asp?b=Burrell_Isaac_David, accessed July 25, 2022).
48. Patricia E. Sloan, "Carrie J. Clarke Bolden (ca. 1869–1973)," *DVB* Online, published 2001 (http://www.lva.virginia.gov/public/dvb/bio.php?b=Bolden_Carrie_Clarke, accessed July 25, 2022).
49. Earl Lewis, "John Christopher Allen (1876–1953)," *DVB* Online, published 1998 (http://www.lva.virginia.gov/public/dvb/bio.asp?b=Allen_John_Christopher, accessed July 25, 2022).
50. Marianne E. Julienne, "Sarah Garland Boyd Jones (1866–1905)," *DVB* on *EV*, (https://encyclopediavirginia.org/entries/jones-sarah-garland-boyd-1866-1905, accessed July 25, 2022).
51. Mary J. Bratton, "John Jasper of Richmond: From Slave Preacher to Community Leader," *Virginia Cavalcade* 29 (summer 1979): 32–39; Brent Tarter, "John Jasper (1812–1901)," *DVB* Online, published 2023, (https://www.lva.virginia.gov/public/dvb/bio.asp?b=Jasper_John, accessed June 15, 2023).
52. Jennifer Lynn Ritterhouse, *Growing up Jim Crow: Black and White Southern Children Learn About Race* (Chapel Hill: University of North Carolina Press, 2006).
53. John G. Deal, "Thomas Calhoun Walker (1862–1953)," *DVB* Online, published 2022 (https://www.lva.virginia.gov/public/dvb/bio.php?b=Walker_Thomas_Calhoun, accessed July 14, 2022); Thomas Calhoun Walker, "Lawyer Walker of Gloucester—As Told to Two Northern Friends," ca. 1950, Special Collections Research Center, Earl Gregg Swem Library, College of William and Mary, Williamsburg.
54. Brittany N. Heyward, "Inez Catherine Fields (1895–1978)," *DVB* Online, published 2015 (http://www.lva.virginia.gov/public/dvb/bio.asp?b=Fields_Inez_Catherine, accessed July 25, 2022).
55. "Autobiography of Wendell Phillips Dabney," undated typescript, Wendell Phillips Dabney Collection, Cincinnati Historical Society Library, Cincinnati Museum Center, 46 (first quotation), 50 (second quotation), 67.
56. Philip J. Schwarz, "John Dabney (ca. 1824–1900)," *DVB* on *EV* (https://encyclopediavirginia.org/entries/dabney-john-ca-1824-1900/, accessed Aug. 11, 2022).
57. Gunter, "John Wesley Cromwell (1846–1927)," *DVB* on *EV* (https://encyclopediavirginia.org/entries/cromwell-john-wesley-1846-1927/, accessed Aug. 11, 2022).
58. Richmond *Times*, June 19, 1892.
59. *Thomas's Administrator v. Bettie Thomas Lewis*, 89 Va. 36 (1892); Tarter, "*Thomas's Administrator v. Bettie Thomas Lewis* (1892)," *Encyclopedia Virginia* (https://encyclopediavirginia.org/entries/thomass-administrator-v-bettie-thomas-lewis-1892/, accessed July 20, 2022).

60. Michael E. Hucles, "Andrew W. E. Bassette (1857–1942)," *DVB* on *EV* (https://encyclopediavirginia.org/entries/bassette-andrew-w-e-1857-1942/, accessed July 22, 2022).
61. Katherine Harbury and Brent Tarter, "William Roscoe Davis (d. 1904)," *DVB* on *EV* (https://encyclopediavirginia.org/entries/davis-william-roscoe-d-1904/, accessed July 22, 2022).

Epilogue

1. *Debates and Proceedings of 1867–1868 Convention*, 364.
2. *Acts of Assembly*, 1884 special sess., 146–51.
3. Brent Tarter, *The Grandees of Government: The Origins and Persistence of Undemocratic Politics in Virginia* (Charlottesville: University of Virginia Press, 2013), 262–64.
4. *Acts of Assembly*, 1893–1894 sess., 862–67.
5. Tarter, *Grandees of Government*, 264–65; Beth Barton Schweiger, "Putting Politics Aside: Virginia Democrats and Voter Apathy in the Era of Disfranchisement," in *The Edge of the South: Life in Nineteenth-Century Virginia*, ed. Edward L. Ayers and John C. Willis (Charlottesville: University Press of Virginia, 1991), 194–218.
6. George H. Stephens, "The Southern Negro," *Southern Workman* 25 (1896): 58–59, quotation on 58.
7. Peter Randolph, *From Slave Cabin to the Pulpit: The Autobiography of Rev. Peter Randolph: The Southern Question Illustrated and Sketches of Slave Life* (Boston: J. H. Earle, 1893), 133–34.
8. Ibid., 138.
9. *Williams v. Mississippi* 170 US 213 (1898).
10. Tarter, *Constitutional History of Virginia* (Athens: University of Georgia Press, 2023), 201; *Acts of Assembly*, 1899–1900 sess., 835.
11. Tarter, *Constitutional History*, 201–2; Secretary of the Commonwealth, 1776–1941, MS Election Records No. 104, State Government Records Collection, RG 13, LVA.
12. Computed from *Twelfth Census*, 10 vols. (Washington, DC, 1902), 2:100–101.
13. Edgar Eugene Robinson, *The Presidential Vote, 1896–1932* (Stanford, Ca.: Stanford University Press, 1934), 354.
14. Tarter, *Constitutional History*, 201.
15. *Richmond Planet*, Oct. 5, Nov. 9, 1901, June 7, 28, July 5, 1902.
16. 42d Cong., 2d sess., chap. 10.
17. Richmond *Times*, July 24, 1900 (first quotation); Charlottesville *Daily Progress*, Aug. 23, 1900; "The constitutional convention: help save our public schools: a public meeting under the auspices of the Negro Educational and Industrial Association of Virginia . . . ," May 3, 1901, Broadside collection,

LVA (second quotation); Richmond *Dispatch*, June 20, 1901 (third quotation); Deborah Harding, "Willis McGlascoe Carter (1852–1902)," *DVB* Online, published 2016 (http://www.lva.virginia.gov/public/dvb/bio.asp?b=Carter_Willis_McGlascoe, accessed Nov. 30, 2022).

18. Herman L. Horn, "The Growth and Development of the Democratic Party in Virginia since 1890" (PhD diss., Duke University, 1949), 102–13.
19. *Report of the Proceedings and Debates of the Constitutional Convention State of Virginia Held in the City of Richmond June 12, 1901, to June 26, 1902*, 2 vols. (Richmond, 1906), 2:3,076 (first quotation)–3,077 (second quotation).
20. Tarter, *Constitutional History*, 217–19.
21. *The Constitution of the State of Virginia. Adopted by the Convention of 1901–2* (Richmond, 1902), Schedule, 66, sec. 22: 72–73.
22. *Taylor v. Commonwealth* 101 Va. 829 (1903), quotation on 831.
23. *Jones v. Montague* 194 US 147 (1904) quotation on 153, and *Selden v. Montague* 194 US 153 (1904).
24. Mrs. Walter A. Watson [Constance Tinsley Watson], ed., *Notes on Southside Virginia* (Richmond: Virginia State Library, 1925), 220.
25. Warren Co. List of Colored Applicants Refused Registration, 1901–1902, Accession 37579, Local Records Collection, LVA.
26. *Richmond Planet*, June 7, 28, July 5, 1902; Richmond City Election Records, Rolls of Registered Colored Voters, Madison Ward, 1st Precinct, 1902–1920, LVA; *New York Times*, Aug. 10, 1903; Lauranett L. Lee, "Maggie Lena Draper Mitchell Walker (1864–1934)," *DVB* Online, published 2020 (https://www.lva.virginia.gov/public/dvb/bio.php?b=Walker_Maggie_Lena, accessed Mar. 5, 2022).
27. Brent Tarter, Marianne E. Julienne, and Barbara C. Batson, *The Campaign for Woman Suffrage in Virginia* (Charleston, S.C.: History Press, 2020), 149–51.
28. Matthew Gottlieb, "Daniel M. Norton later Daniel McNorton (d. 1918)," *DVB* on *EV* (https://encyclopediavirginia.org/entries/norton-daniel-m-later-daniel-mcnorton-d-1918/, accessed July 1, 2022).
29. Tarter, "L. R. Flemings (d. 1937)," *DVB* on *EV* (https://encyclopediavirginia.org/entries/flemings-l-r-d-1937/, accessed July 7, 2022).
30. *Richmond Planet*, June 1, 1901.
31. *Acts of Assembly*, 1924 sess., 534–35 (quotation), 1925 sess., 945–46; Richard B. Sherman, "The 'Teachings at Hampton Institute': Social Equality, Racial Integrity, and the Virginia Public Assemblage Act of 1926," *VMHB* 95 (1987): 275–300; Sherman, "'The Last Stand': The Fight for Racial Integrity in Virginia in the 1920s," *Journal of Southern History* 54 (1988): 69–92.
32. V. O. Key, *Southern Politics in State and Nation* (New York, A. A. Knopf, 1949); Herman L. Horn, "The Growth and Development of the Democratic Party in Virginia since 1890" (PhD diss., Duke University, 1949); Charles E. Wynes, *Race Relations in Virginia, 1870–1902* (Charlottesville: University of Virginia Press, 1961); Andrew Buni, *The Negro in Virginia Politics, 1902–1965*

(Charlottesville: University Press of Virginia, 1967); Allen W. Moger, *Virginia: Bourbonism to Byrd, 1870–1925* (Charlottesville: University Press of Virginia, 1968); Raymond H. Pulley, *Old Virginia Restored: An Interpretation of the Progressive Impulse, 1870–1930* (Charlottesville: University Press of Virginia, 1968); J. Harvie Wilkinson III, *Harry Byrd and the Changing Face of Virginia Politics, 1945–1966* (Charlottesville: University Press of Virginia, 1968); Larry J. Sabato, *The Democratic Party Primary in Virginia: Tantamount to Election No Longer* (Charlottesville: University Press of Virginia, 1977); Ronald L. Heinemann, *Depression and New Deal in Virginia: The Enduring Dominion* (Charlottesville: University Press of Virginia, 1983); Paul T. Murray, "Who Is an Indian; Who Is a Negro: Virginia Indians in the World War II Draft," *VMHB* 95 (1987): 215–31; Sherman, "'Teachings at Hampton Institute'"; Sherman, "'The Last Stand': The Fight for Racial Integrity in Virginia"; Holt, *Virginia's Constitutional Convention of 1901–1902;* Ronald L. Heinemann, *Harry Byrd of Virginia* (Charlottesville: University Press of Virginia, 1996); Winnett W. Hagens, "The Politics of Race: The Virginia Redistricting Experience, 1991–1997," in *Race and Redistricting in the 1990s*, ed. Bernard Grofman (New York: Agathon Press, 1998), 315–19; J. Douglas Smith, *Managing White Supremacy: Race, Politics, and Citizenship in Jim Crow Virginia* (Chapel Hill: University of North Carolina Press, 2002); Pippa Holloway, *Sexuality, Politics, and Social Control in Virginia, 1920–1945* (Chapel Hill: University of North Carolina Press, 2006); Paul A. Lombardo, *Three Generations, No Imbeciles: Eugenics, the Supreme Court, and Buck v. Bell* (Baltimore: Johns Hopkins University Press, 2008); Arica L. Coleman, *That the Blood Stay Pure: African Americans, Native Americans, and the Predicament of Race and Identity in Virginia* (Bloomington: Indiana University Press, 2013); Tarter, *Grandees of Government, 281–304;* William P. Hustwit, *James J. Kilpatrick: Salesman for Segregation* (Chapel Hill: University of North Carolina Press, 2013); Julian Maxwell Hayter, *The Dream Is Lost: Voting Rights and the Politics of Race in Richmond, Virginia* (Lexington: University Press of Kentucky, 2017); Tarter, *Gerrymanders: How Redistricting has Protected Slavery, White Supremacy, and Partisan Minorities in Virginia* (Charlottesville: University of Virginia Press, 2019), 50–57.

33. Bureau of the Census, *Census of Population: 1950, A Report of the Seventeenth Decennial Census of the United States.* Volume II: "Characteristics of the Population Number of Inhabitants, General and Detailed Characteristics of the Population." Part 46: Virginia (Washington, DC, 1952), 31.
34. *Richmond Times-Dispatch,* Feb. 10, 1986.

INDEX

Italicized page numbers refer to illustrations.

Abernathy, Mary, 190
Abrams, Joseph, 13, 24, 25, 241
Accomack County, 19, 45
Acres, Jackson, 58
Adams, John, 86, 123
Adams, John Henry, 123, 241
Albemarle County, 38, 98
Alexandria, 40, 45, 75, 89, 95, 112, 132; Beulah Normal and Theological School, 75–76; Ebenezer Baptist Church, 86; Excelsior School, 75; First Free School Society of Alexandria, 76; *People's Advocate*, 217; Third Baptist Church, 86
Alexandria County (later Arlington County), 20–21, 148
Allan, Edgar, 112
Alleghany County, 187–88
Allen, Beverly, 156, 241
Allen, John Christopher, 213–14, 241
Amelia County, 129, 136, 146, 183, 196
American Baptist Home Missionary Society, 196
American Baptist Missionary Convention, 26
American Beneficial Insurance Company, 206
American Missionary Association, 6, 14, 38–39, 41–42, 75, 78
Amherst County, 135
Anderson, Owen (or Orion), 186
Anderson, Robert (of Hagerstown, Md.), 61
Anderson, Robert (of Williamsburg), 31–32
Anderson-McCormick Act, 221–22
Andrews, William H., 98, 140, 141, 235, 236
Anna T. Jeanes Fund, 195
Appomattox Court House, 56–57
apprenticeship, 16, 74
Arlington (estate), 42–43
Armstrong, Samuel Chapman, 59, 78
artisans and skilled workers, 12, 31; after slavery, 71–72, 98, 123, 129–30, 179, *199*, 206–8
Ash, William Horace, 157, 236
Ashe, Victor, 229
attorneys, 7, 129, 131, 185, 206, 218, 229
Augusta County, 20, 183

Baker, Frank, 41
Baldwin, Dana Olden, 204–5, 241
Ballton, Samuel, 37
banking. *See under individual cities*
Banks, Frank D., 204
Baptist Foreign Mission Convention of the United States of America, 164–65
Barber, Kate, 201
Barbour, John Strode, 181
Barbour County, 36
Barksdale, Edmonia, 190
Barnes, Mary, 190
Barnes, Pokey, 190
Barrett, James D., 96, 235
Barrett, Janie Aurora Porter, 211, 241
Baskervill, Britton, 195–96, 236
Bassette, Andrew William Ernest, 218, 241
Bayne, Thomas, 1, 2, 81–82, 90; convention delegate, 98, 104, 105, 106, 109, 112–13, 235
Beaty, Powhatan, 52
Bedford County, 153
Bell, William, 2, 58
Blair, Francis Simpson, 163
Blake, Robert, 49–50

Bland, Edward David, 164, 236
Bland, Hercules, 14
Bland, James William D., 14, 105–6, 108, 112, 125–26, 235, 240
Bland, Mary, 14
Blow, Sam, 188
Bolden, Carrie J. Clarke, 213, 241
Bolling, Eliza W., 204
Bolling, Phillip S., 129, 236
Bolling, Samuel P., 87, 129, 203–4, 236
Bowden, Henry Moseley, 113
Bowden, Thomas R., 122
Bowser, Mary Richards (or Mary Elizabeth), 52
Bowser, Rosa L. Dixon, 157, 211, 241
Boyd, William C., 153–54
Boydton: Boydton Academic and Bible Institute, 195; *Midland Express*, 177
Branch, James Read, 53
Branch, Spencer, 188
Branch, Tazewell, 132, 236
Breedlove, William, 47, 110, 235
Brewers, Ann, 60
Brisby, William Henry, 47, 130, 140, 236
Brooks, Albert R., 62, 79
Brooks, Lucy Goode, 62–63, 241
Brown, Amy Johnson, 16
Brown, Benjamin, 16
Brown, Edward C., 204, 241
Brown, Goodman, 16, 237
Brown, Herbert, 16
Brown, Jennie, 61
Brown, Jerry, 188
Brown, John, 61, 96, 97, 235
Brown, Parthenia Bell, 16
Brown, Scipio, 16
Browne, William Washington, 200, 242
Brunswick County, 129, 136, 139, 146
Bryan, Joseph, 191
Buckhannon County, 39
Buckingham County, 111, 127, 129, 183; Baptist Aid Society, 132
Bullock, Slaughter B., 68
Bureau of Refugees, Freedmen, and Abandoned Lands, 61–62, 66–68, *67*, 70, 72–74, 92; criticized, 72–73, 106
Burke family, *215*
Burrell, Isaac David, 212–13, 242
Burrell, Margaret H. Barnette, 213
Burton, Robert, 187
Butler, Benjamin F., 41
Butler, Charles Wilson, 227

Cameron William E., 162, 163, 166
Campbell County, 78, 112
Canada, David, 103, 107, 235
Caroline County, 40, 62
Carter, James B., 87, 106, 109, 235
Carter, Matilda, 27
Carter, Peter Jacob, 50, 137–38, 148, 237
Carter, Willis McGlascoe, 224, 225, 242
Central Lunatic Asylum, 134–35, 166
chain gangs, 136, 147
Chandler, William, 47
Charity, Ruth Harvey, 229
Charles City County, 45, 63, 131, 134, 183, 211; Union Baptist Church, 131
Charles Town, 39
Charlotte County, 96–97, 107, 125, 134, 136, 169, 188–89
Charlottesville, 51, 69
Chesterfield County, 80–81, 86, 87, 106, 166, 173
children, 9, 22, 26–27, 73–74, 76–77, *77*, 80, 179. *See also* schools
Christiansburg Institute, 196, 199
churches and ministers, 25–26, *84*, 84–87, 132, 134, 179, 180, 203, 214. *See also under individual cities and counties*
cities. *See* local officeholders; urban (city and town) life; *and individual cities*
civic and service (including fraternal) organizations, 9, 72, 88, 131–33, 157, 180, 200–204, *201*, 211–14. *See also under individual cities and counties*
Civil War, 16, 34, 43, 46–48; women, 52–57. *See also* Confederate Army; United States Army
Clark, Amanda Virginia Thomas, 156–57, 242
Clark, Matt, 134, 237
Clarksville, 153
Clifton Forge, 187
Cohabitation Act of 1866, 63–64

Cole, George William, 139, 237
Coleman, Asa, 136, 237
Coleman, Reuben Turner, 15, 184, 205, 242
Colemanville Hotel, 205
Colemanville Mineral Springs Company, 205
Collins, Johnson, 139, 237
Colored Agricultural and Industrial Association of Virginia, 132
Colored Farmers' Alliance and Cooperative Union of Virginia, 175–78
Colored National Labor Union, 123
Colored Shiloh Baptist Association, 132
Colored State Convention (1865), 89
Colored Valley Baptist Association, 85
Colson, Edna Meade, 197, 242
Colson, James Major, 197, 242
Commodore, Aaron, 169–70, 237
Confederate Army, 52–54
Confederate States of America, 37–38
Connor, Miles, 138–39, 237
Conservative Party, 104, 116, 121–23, 125, 144–45, 161, 169, 170–71
Constitution of 1869, 113–19, 145
Constitution of 1902, 224–27
contraband, 41
Convention of 1867–68, *105*; delegates, 96–104, *119*, 235–36; election of delegates, 94–97, *95*, *97*
Convention of 1901–2, 223–26, 228
Cook, Fields, 79, 86, 89, 242
corruption, 141–42, 143–44
Cox, Eliza, 23
Cox, Henry, 126, 237
Cox, Joseph, 23, 108, 235
criminal law, 136–37, *137*, 145
Crocker, Wiley Horace, 212, 242
Cromwell, John Wesley, 217, 242
Cropper, Elkaney, 19
Culpeper County, 38
Cumberland County, 15, 16, *17*, 47, 60, 110, 205; Cumberland Baptist Church, 55, 85; legislators, 127, 129, 130, 132, 183, 184–85; New Constitution Baptist Church, 85
Cummings, Kate, 181
Custis, George Washington Parke, 43

Dabbs, Isaac, 169, 237
Dabney, John, 158, 217, 242
Dabney, John Milton (Milton Williamson), 217
Dabney, Wendell Phillips, 158, 217
Daniel, John Warwick, 159, 163, 169
Danville, 24; riot, 170
Davis, Cephas L., 136, 240
Davis, Daniel Webster, 209–11
Davis, Jefferson, 23, 52, 56, 93
Davis, Nancy Moore, 38, 41, 46, 218
Davis, Noah, 26, 242
Davis, William Roscoe, 38–39, 41, 46, 218, 242
Dawson, John Montgomery, 50–51, 86, 132, 148, 240
Dean, Jennie Serepta, 196, 242
Delancy, Eliza Ann, 52
Delaney, McDowell, 136, 237
Democratic Party, 121, 144–45, 169–72, 181, 228–29
DeMortie, Mark Renie (or Réné), 120, 121, 143, 242
DeRosario, John Wallace, 18
Dillard, Mary E., *209*
Dinwiddie County, 23, 129, 131, 132, 148, 165
disfranchisement, 145, 221–28. *See also* suffrage
Dodson, Amos Andre, 132, 138, 237
Dred Scott v. Sanford, 20
Dungee, Shed, 132, 237
Dungey, Jesse, 71, 237

Edmundson, Isaac, 53, 237
education. *See* schools
Edwards, Ballard Trent, 137, 237
elections, *121*, *144*; 1867, 94–96; 1869, 116–17, 122, 124–25, 143; 1871, 143; 1873, 143; 1875, 143; 1876, 143; 1877, 145; 1879, 160–61; 1881, 163–64; 1883, 167–70, *168*, 171; 1885, 170; 1888, 171; 1889, 145; 1892, 178; 1900, 223–24; 1901, 227
Elizabeth City County, 6, 7, 45, 117, 130, 133, 135, 218
Ellerson (or McDonald), Sam, 188
Emancipation Proclamation, 42, 43–44, 56, 58, 89

emigration, 178–79, 191–93, 205, 218, 229
entrepreneurs, 15, 31; after slavery, 87–88, 120, 127, 130, 179, 194, 200–207, 218
equal rights, 89, 91, 106–7, 109–10, 111, 113, 136, 148, 161–62
Essex County, 47, 110, 139, 169–70, 227
Evans, Josephine, 23
Evans, Joseph P., 23, 129, 135, 237, 240
Evans, Margaret, 16
Evans, William Dennis, 15–16, 134, 237
Evans, William W., 23, 129, 237
Ex Parte Virginia, 181

Fairfax County, 45, 171
fairs, 211–12, *212*
families, 9, 16–17, 26–29, *27*, *39*, 39–40, 54–55, 60–64, 74, *215*, 218–19
Farmville, 87, 105, 139, 178–80, 203–4; Beulah African Methodist Episcopal Church, 132; First Baptist Church, 180; Freemasons, 180; Good Samaritans, 180; Loving Sisters of Worship, 180; Odd Fellows, 180; True Reformers, 180; "The Negroes of Farmville, Virginia" (Du Bois), 178–80. *See also* Prince Edward County
Farr, Richard Ratcliffe, 165
Faulcon, William, 129–30, 132, 237
Fauntleroy, Thomas Turner, 184
Fauquier County, 135
Fayerman, George, 126, 128, 136, 237
Fence Law of 1866, 65–66, 136, 137, 164
Ferguson, Harriet F., 31
Ferguson, John E., 31, 242
Ferguson, William, 31
Fields, George Washington, *7*, 216
Fields, Inez Catherine, *7*, 216
Fields, James Apostle, 5–8, *6*, 40, 216, 237
Fields, Martha Ann, 5, 40
Fields, Washington, 5
Fifteenth Amendment, 113, 117, 118, 223
firearms, 18, 36, 45, 50, 72, 143, 188, 190
Flemings, Leonard R., 212, 227, 242
Flemmings family, 61–62
Floyd County, 64
Fluvanna County, 96
Foreman, William Tecumseh, 213
Fort Monroe, 38–39, 40, 41–43, 75. *See also* Hampton
Fourteenth Amendment, 93, 117, 118, 143, 181, 223
Fowlkes, Thaddeus, 188
Franklin, Alexander Quincy, 15, 237
Franklin County, 153–54
fraternal organizations. *See* civic and service (including fraternal) organizations
Fredericksburg, 26, 38; Shiloh Baptist Church, 169
free Blacks, 11–33, *17*, 46–48
Freedman's Savings and Trust Company (Freedman's Bank), 88, 148
Freedman's Village, 43
Freedmen's Bureau. *See* Bureau of Refugees, Freedmen, and Abandoned Lands
freedom, 36–40, *39*, 56–59
free labor economy, 65–68, 69–71, 179; labor contract, *68*, 69–71; women in, 68
Freeman, John, 134, 238
Fugitive Slave Act of 1850, 24, 37
Funders, 159, 169
Funding Act of 1871, 140–41, 151, 159

Gardiner, James, 48–49
General Assembly, 63, 65, *119*, 120–21, 124, 133–40, 143, 161, 172; House of Delegates, 125–40, *126*, 160, 170, 236–40; Senate, 125, 141, 142, 160, 170, 240–41; session of 1882, 164–66
Gibbons, Isabella, 69
Gibson, Eustace, 109
Gilliam, William, 15, 134, 136, 238
Glass, Carter, 225–26
Gloucester County, 60, 62, *155*, 185
Goochland County, 15, 20, 21, 72, 133, 134, 142
Goodwyn, James P., 133, 134, 143, 238
Gordonsville, 73
Grand Fountain United Order of True Reformers, 9, 200, *201*, 206
Grand Lodge of Good Templars, 200
Grand United Order of Odd Fellows, 133
Grant, Ulysses S., 112, 116, 117, 121, 143
Gray, Martha A., 184
Gray, Sarah A., 75

Green, Armistead, 87, 129, 134, 165, 166, 238
Greenbrier County, 36
Green family, 60
Greensville County, 130
Griffin, Maria, 31–32, 40, 46, 50
Griffin, Robert Gilbert, 32, 50, 130, 133, 211, 238
Griggs, Nathaniel Matthew, 139, 238, 240

Halifax County, 53, 97, 103, 107, 129, 134, 141–42, 154
Hamilton, Ross, 127, 138, 164, 238
Hampton, 42, 82, 91, 130, 133, 204, 216; Dixie Hospital, 212, 213; First Baptist Church, 218; Locust Street Social Settlement, 211; People's Building and Loan Association, 218; Third Baptist Church, 7. *See also* Fort Monroe; refugee camps
Hampton Normal and Agricultural Institute (Hampton University), 75, 78, 125, 136, 151–52, 196, *198*, 198–99, *199*, 216; Hampton Singers, 198. See also *Southern Workman*
Hanover County, 5, 27, 40, 59, 67–68, 77, 98, 211
Harris, Alfred William, 132, 164–65, 165–66, 224, 238
Harris, Anna, 192–93
Harris, Frances (or Francis) J. A., 63
Harris, Henry Clay, 136, 163, 238
Harris, Joseph Dennis, 122, 242
Harrisonburg, 39
Hartshorn Memorial College, 196, 207
Hawxhurst, John, 112
Hayden, William, 29–30
Henrico County, 183, 227–28
Hill, Henry C., 136, 238
Hill, Oliver W., 99, 229
Hill, Richard R., 82
Historically Black Colleges and Universities, 9, 78. *See also under individual schools*
Hodges, Charles A., 28
Hodges, Charles E., 28–29, 86, 124, 129, 132, 238
Hodges, John Quincy, 28, 29, 75, 124, 129, 191, 238
Hodges, Julia Nelson Willis, 28, 29
Hodges, William Johnson, 28, 75, 90, 242
Hodges, Willis Augustus, 28–29, 75, 191; convention delegate, 98, 104–5, *105*, 106–7, 124, 221, 229, 235
Holliday, Frederick William Mackey, 159–60
Holmes, Joseph R., 96–97, 107, 111, 235
homestead exemption, 111, 114
Hopkins, Marcus Sterling, 73–74
Hunnicutt, James W., 38, 102–3, 112
Hunter, Caroline, 26–27

Independent Order of the Sons and Daughters of Saint Luke, 9, 194, 200–202, 206–7
Ingleside Seminary, 157, *195*, 196
Industrial History of the Negro Race of the United States (Giles B. Jackson and Daniel Webster Davis), 210–11
Industrial Home School for Colored Girls, 211
interracial sex and marriage, 82, 135, 183–84
Isle of Wight County, 78, 82, 156
Israel Hill (Prince Edward County), 12, 14

Jackson, Giles B., 209–11
Jackson, Luther Porter, 2–3, 98, 146, 245
Jackson, Thomas J. "Stonewall" (statue), 147
Jackson Ward. *See* Richmond
James, Mary, 15, 21
James, Miles, 49
James City County, 7, 18, 45
Jamestown Exposition of 1907, 207–10, *208*, *209*
Jasper, John, 214–15, 242
Jefferson, William T., 150, 160
Jefferson County, 39
Jim Crow, 9, 175, 183–84. *See also* racism; segregation
Johnson, Henry, 146, 238
Johnson, John, 188
Johnson, Sarah Woodson, 11

Jones, Benjamin F., 73, 83, 126, 238
Jones, James Richard, 130, 138, 238, 240
Jones, Peter K., 107, 236, 238
Jones, Robert E., 58
Jones, Robert G. W., 63, 131, 238
Jones, Rufus Sibb, 135, 238
Jones, Sarah Garland Boyd, 214, 242
Jones v. Montague, 226–27
Jordan, William H., 132, 238
Jorgensen, Joseph, 143
juries, 23, 93, 114, 135, 148, 162, 181

Kelso, Samuel F., 77–78, 108, 109–10, 112–13, 115, 156, 236
King and Queen County, 58, 154–55
King William County, 71, 73, 83
Kinney v. Commonwealth, 183
Knights of Labor, 180
Ku Klux Klan, 84, *144*

labor contract. *See* free labor economy
Laboring Men's Mechanics' Union Association, 148
labor organizations, 88, 123–24, 148, 180
Lacy, Benjamin Watkins, 184
Lancaster County, 16, 212; Afro-American Fair, *212*
Langston, John Mercer, 6, 171, 197, 241
Lee, Alexander G., 130, 135, 238
Lee, Fitzhugh, 170
Lee, Hugh, 112
Lee, Mary Custis, 43
Lee, Robert E., 43, 93; portrait, 147
Lewis, Bettie Thomas, 217–18
Lewis, John Francis, 163
Lewis, Neverson, 135–36, 238
Lincoln, Abraham, 26, 34, 35, 43, 56–57, *57*
Lindsey, Lewis, 23, 107, 109, 110, 111, 236; caricatured, *103*
Lipscomb, Catharine, 16
Lipscomb, James F., 17, 238
Lipscomb, John. *See* Robinson, John
Lipscomb, Martha, 16–17
Lipscomb, William, 17
literacy, 5, 15, 24, 66, 98, 222; in Convention of 1867–68, 128; literacy tests, 222, 223
local officeholders, 138–39, 145, 146–47, 172, 227–28. *See also under individual cities and counties*
Logan, Minnie, 63
Loudoun County, 45, 186
Louisa County, 132, 136, 157, 205
Loving v. Virginia, 184
Lucas, William P., 77–78, 136, 238
Lumpkin, Mary, 78
Lumpkin, Robert, 56, 62, 78
Lunenburg County, 69, 190
Lynchburg, 16–17, *17*, 24, 80, 87, 108–9, 112, 157; bus boycott, 182; schools in, 76–77, *77*, 156
Lynchburg Baptist Seminary (Virginia Theological Seminary and College, Virginia University of Lynchburg), 196
lynching, 185–91, *187*. *See also* violence
Lyons, Isaiah Leonard, 117, 240

Madison County, 38
Mahone, William, 159, 161, 166–67, 169, 170, 171
Mallory, Shepard, 41
Manassas Industrial School for Colored Youth, 196
Manchester, 26, 34, 137
Marable, William Henry (or Solomon), 190
Martinsville, 204–5
Mason, James M., 37
Matthews, James Z., 13
Matthews, John Walter Boyd, 13, 136, 239
Matthews, Rebecca A. Gilliam, 13–14, 24, 25
May, Godfrey, 143
Mayo, Joseph, 80
McKenzie, Lucy Smith, 173
Mecklenburg County, 34–35, 61, 73, 88, 111, 129, 195; legislators from, 127, 129, 130, 132, 136, 138, 164
medicine, 99, 203, 205, 206, *213*; women in healthcare, 212–14, *213*. *See also under individual cities*
militia, 114

Miller, Charles, 187
Miller, John B., Jr., 133–34, 135, 142, 239
Miller, L. Clarence, 194, 200, 202
Minor, Jane, 25
Mitchell, A. J., 71
Mitchell, John, Jr., 182, 187, 188–89, *189*, 190, 216, 224, 227, 242
Montague, Robert Latané, 47
Montgomery County, 67, 85, 184
Morgan, Peter George, 14–15, 96, 132–33, 146, 236, 239
Moseley, Martha Catherine Turpin, 15, 21
Moseley, William P., 15, 21, 71–72; convention delegate, 107, 236; senator, 142, 240
Moss, Francis "Frank": convention delegate, 111, 236; delegate, 127, 129–30, 147, 239; senator, 127, 147, 240

Nansemond County, 82
Negro Industrial and Educational Association, 224
Negro in the Reconstruction of Virginia (Alrutheus Taylor), 2,
Negro Office-Holders in Virginia, 1865–1890 (Luther Porter Jackson), 2–3, 98, 146, 245
Nelson, Edward, 96–97, 236
Newby, Madison, 82
New England Freedmen's Aid Society, 69, 157
New Kent County, 45, 47, 130, 134, 150
Newport News, 1, 7, 156; bus boycott, 182; Crown Savings Bank, 204, 213; Newport News Cemetery Company (Greenlawn Memorial Park), 133; Whittaker Memorial Hospital, 213
newspapers, 9, 58, 60, 152, 157, 183, 203, 207, *207*. *See also under individual cities and towns*
Nickens, Armistead, 16
Nickens, Armistead S., 16, 239
Nickens, Polly Weaver, 16
Nixon, Samuel. *See* Bayne, Thomas
Norcom, I. C., 157
Norcom, Josephine B. Mathews, 156–57, 242
Norfolk, 1, 26, 40, 41, 44, 45, 78, 90; Brown Savings Bank, 204; bus boycott, 182; Colored Monitor Union Club, 86, 90–91; free Blacks in, 18, 24, 25; members of Convention of 1867–68, 104, 113; Mount Olive Cemetery, 131; Norfolk Virginia Union Baptist Association, 132; riot in, 93–94; Virginia Building and Savings Association, 132
Norfolk County, 45, 75, 124, 129, 131, 138, 164; Churchland Grove Baptist Church, 139; Little Zion Baptist Church, 164
Northampton County, 45, 50, 137–38
Norton, Daniel M., 72, 81, 88, 130, 146, 163, 171, 227; convention delegate, 98, 236; senator, 127, 129, 162, 170, 241
Norton, Frederick Smith, 129, 171, 239
Norton, Robert, 72, 88, 129, 130, 163, 171, 239
Nottoway County, 14, 112, 120, 129, 135, 195, 196

Oliver, John, 123–24, 242
Oliver, Patrick W., 203
Orange and Alexandria Railroad, 181
Orange County, 38, 97
Owen, Alexander, 134, 141–42, 239
Owen, William L., 141–42
Owens, Littleton, 165, 239

Page County, 78
Paige, Lillie, 131
Paige, Richard Gault Leslie, 131, 132, 135, 164, 239
Pamunkey, 127, 130
Parrish v. Commonwealth, 71
passes, 47, 55; after slavery, 79–80
patrols, 55–56
Patterson, William Harvey, 134, 239
Peabody Education Fund, 195
Peake, Mary Smith Kelsey, 75, 242
Pearman, J. D., 227–28
Pennsylvania Freedmen's Relief Association, 76

People's (Populist) Party, 178
Perkins, Caesar, 127, 132, 163, 239
Perkins, Fountain, 132, 239
Petersburg, 22, 25, 26, 53, 59, 83–84, 87; bus boycott, 182; Colored Baptist Church of Harrison Street, 83–84, *84*; Colored High School (Peabody High School), 195; election of 1867, 96; election of 1873, 143; First Baptist Church, 203; free Blacks in, 13–14, 23, 24, 53; Freedmen's Bureau in, *67*; Impartial Relief Association, 133; *Lancet*, 23, 120, 156; legislators, 128–29, 132, 133, 134, 135, 136, 142, 165; local officeholders, 146; Masonic Temple Association of the City of Petersburg, 133; members of Convention of 1867–68, 107; Petersburg Relief Association, 133; Republican Convention (1879), 162–63
Pierpont, Francis H., 45, 80–81
Pittsylvania County, 181
Poindexter, John William, 157, 239
political organizing, 89–92. *See also* Readjuster Party; Republican Party
Pollard, Lucy Jane, 190
poll tax. *See* suffrage
Poor, Frederick W., 97–98
poor relief, 110–12, 132–33
Portsmouth, 45, 62, 87, 98, 124, 157; bus boycott, 182; Colored Woman's Club, 157
Powell, Guy, 127, 239, 241
Powhatan County, 16, 135
Prince Edward County, 55, 70, 125, 132, 134, 183; free Blacks in, 12, 14–16, 20. *See also* Farmville
Prince George County, 15, 129, 134, 164
Princess Anne County, 28–29, 45, 75, 86, 98, 104, 191; legislators, 124, 129, 165
Prince William County, 29–30
property ownership, 7, 114, 130–31, 153, 210, 211; rural, 14, 15, 16, 111, 205; urban (town and city), 13–14, 31, 203–5, 207
Pryor, Ida, 61
public debt, 115, 140–41, 150–51, 158–60, 165
Pulaski County, 157
racism, 21–22, 29–33, 80, 103–4, 169, 215–16, 222–29
Ragsdale, William H., 134, 239
Randolph, Peter, 80–81, 85, 86–87, 222–23
Ratcliff, Edward, 48
Readjuster Party, 9, 150, 159, 160–72
Reconstruction, xiii, 94; Act to Admit the State of Virginia to Representation in Congress, 117; Civil Rights Act of 1866, 93; Civil Rights Act of 1875, 181; First Military District, 94, 98; Joint Committee on Reconstruction, 81–82. *See also* Bureau of Refugees, Freedmen, and Abandoned Lands
refugee camps, 41–43
Reid, William Ferguson, 99
Republican Party, 92, 138, 143, 148–49, 162–71; radicals in, 96, 102, 116, 122–23
Reynolds, Hannah, 56–57
Rich, Peggy, 83
Richmond, 56–57, *57*, 58, 62–63, 82–83, *83*, 87, 88, 108, 126–27; banks in, 88, 200, 201–2; burned, 56, 99–100, *100*; bus boycott, 182; churches in, 26, 84–85, 134, 156, 214; Colored Men's Equal Rights League, 91; First African Baptist Church, 13, 25, 26, 79, 92; free Blacks in, 13, 18, 21–22, 23, 24, 31; Friends' Asylum for Colored Orphans, 63; hotels, 126–27; Jackson Ward, 9, 194, 146, 147, 206–7; local officeholders, 146–47; Mayor's Court, 21, 31, 80; *Reformer*, 200; Richmond Beneficial Insurance Company, 206; Richmond Hospital, *213*; Richmond Hospital Association and Medical College, 214; *Richmond Planet*, 58, 182, 187, 188–89, *207*, 224; Richmond Theological School for Freedmen (Richmond Theological Institute), 196, 207; Richmond Woman's League, 211; *Saint Luke Herald*, 194; Saint Luke Penny Savings Bank, 201–2; Southern Aid Insurance Company, 206; teachers, 156, 157; Training School for Nurses, Incorporated, 214; United Aid Insurance Company, 206
Richmond and Danville Railroad, 181–82

Riddleberger, Harrison Holt, 165
Roanoke, 186–87, 212–13; Burrell Memorial Hospital, 213; Fifth Avenue Presbyterian Church, 212; Magic City Medical Society, 213
Roanoke County, 183; Elon Colored Baptist Church, 85
Roanoke Missionary Baptist Association, 132
Robertson, William H., 112
Robinson, Clement, 75–76
Robinson, Jeter, 16
Robinson, John, 16, *17*, 47, 110, 130, 236, 241
Robinson, John H., 133, 239
Robinson, Mary C., 153
Robinson, Nathaniel, 16
Robinson, Spottswood, Jr., 229
Robinson, Willis William, 169
Rockbridge County, 20
Rose, Louise Bowes, 59
Ruffin, Robert Davis, 58–59, 148, 239
Ruffner, William Henry, 151, 158, 165
rural life, 11, 28–29; after slavery, 65–69, 77, 106, 164, 173–78. *See also* sharecropping; Vagrancy Act of 1866
Russell, James Solomon, 157, 242

Saint Paul Normal and Industrial School, 157
Schofield, John McAllister, 98, 116
schools, 9, 148, 151–57, *152*, *155*, 170, 194–99; burned, 78; Freedmen's Bureau, 74–78; higher education, 78, 136, 196–99, 207; industrial, 199, 217; normal schools, 109, 136, 151, 166; private schools, *195*, 195–96; public, *77*, 109–10, 115, 140–41, 142–43, 151, 194–95, 224, *225*, 228; public school funding, 150–51, 158–60, 165, 166, *168*; in refugee camps, 42, 43; segregated, 109, 142, 181; teachers, 76, *77*, 153–57, *197*, *198*. *See also* Hampton Normal and Agricultural Institute; Virginia Normal and Collegiate Institute; Virginia Union University; *and under individual cities and counties*
Scott, Archer, 135, 239
Scott, John, 187
Seaton, George, 21
Seaton, George Lewis, 20–21, 76, 126, 132, 239
Seaton, Lucinda, 21
secession, 35, *35*
segregation, 87, 107, 114, 126–27, 134, 137, 180–82, 228; in public schools, 109, 142–43, 151–52
Selden, William S., 2, 58
Selden v. Montague, 226–27
sharecropping, 71, 205
Sheler, Martha, 64
Shiloh Baptist Association, 85
Slate River Colored Baptist Association, 132
slavery, 11, 34–40, 54–56, *126*; abolition, 43–46; self-emancipation, 36–43
slave trade, 55, 56, 60–63
Smallwood, John J., 196
Smith, Dabney N., 137, 239
Smith, Henry D., 130, 240
Smith, James B., 83
Smith, Robert M., 130, 133, 136, 240
Smith, Thomas, 187
Smyth County, 183
Southampton County, 96, 97
South Boston, 134
Southern Claims Commission, 58–59
Southern Workman, 152, 154, 160, 173, 204
Spotsylvania County, 38
Staunton, 59, 225; *Staunton Tribune*, 224
Stephens, George H., 222, 223
Stevens, William Nash, 142, 163, 240, 241
Suffolk, 41, 82, 212
suffrage, 89–92, 107–8, 114, 116–17, 137, 227; poll tax, 110, 145, 148, 160, 161, 165, 167, 223, 224; white opposition to, 92, 104; white support for, 93, 112, 161. *See also* disfranchisement; voting
Surry County, 82, 98, 117, 129, 132, 140, 164; Temperance, Industrial, and Collegiate Institute, 196
Sussex County, 130, 156
Syphax, John Bryce, 43, 171, 240
Syphax, Maria Carter, 43
Syphax, William, 43

taxes, 110, 111. *See also* suffrage
Taylor, Ellen Sammons, 51
Taylor, Fairfax, 51
Taylor, James Thomas Sammons, 51–52, 98, 107, 110, 163, 236
Taylor v. Commonwealth, 226
teachers, 153, 154, 155–56, *197*. *See also* Richmond; schools
Teamoh, George, 24, 62, 87; convention delegate, 98, 103, 110, 236; senator, 141, 241
Teamoh, Sallie, 24
Thirteenth Amendment, 43, 46, 89, 118
Thomas's Administrator v. Bettie Thomas Lewis, 218
Tidewater Fair Association, 212
Toler, Burwell, 98, 111, 236
towns. *See* urban (city and town) life
Townsend, James, 41
Tucker, Samuel W., 229
Turpin, Edwin, 15, 21
Turpin, Henry, 15, 137, 240

Underwood, John C., 93, 112, 115–16
United States Army, 37, 38, 40–44, 46, 58, 65; United States Colored Troops (USCT), 48–52, *51*, 59, 137; veterans in Convention of 1867–68, 98, 117; veterans in General Assembly, 32, 50, 128, 135, 138. *See also* refugee camps
United States House of Representatives, 28, 117, 120, 171, 224, 241
United States Navy, 16, 49–50
Upshur County, 36, 39
urban (city and town) life, 22–26, 76–77, 87–88, 178–80, 203–5. *See also* Vagrancy Act of 1866

Vagrancy Act of 1866, 64–65, 137
Van Lew, Elizabeth, 52
Veal, Charles, 49
violence, 12, 79–84, *84*, 135, 143, *144*. *See also* lynching
Virginia, Restored Government, 44–46, 57–58, 113
Virginia Industrial, Mercantile, and Building Association, 177
Virginia Manual Labor School for Colored Boys, 211
Virginia Normal and Collegiate Institute (Virginia State University), 9, 138, 156–57, 165–66, 197, *197*
Virginia State Federation of Colored Women's Clubs, 157, 211
Virginia Teachers' Reading Circle, 157
Virginia Union Association, 93
Virginia Union Baptist Association, 132
Virginia Union University, 78, 196
Virginia v. Rives, 181
voting, *95*, 95–97, *97*, 107, 143–45, 162, 163, 222, 223. *See also* suffrage; elections

Walker, Armstead, 157
Walker, Gilbert Carlton, 122
Walker, Grace Herbert, 62
Walker, Maggie Lena Draper Mitchell, 157, 200–202, 211, 227, 242
Walker, Thomas Calhoun, 60, 62, 155, 185, 192, 215–16, 224, 229, 242
Wallace, Nancy Ellison, 153
Warren County, 227
Warrick, Meta, 208–9, 210
Warwick, William H., 176–78
Warwick County, 7, 45, 117, 133, 135
Washington, Booker T., 78, 198–99, 200
Washington, George, 169
Washington, Martha Dandridge Custis, 43, 171
Watson, John, 73, 88, 111, 138, 236, 240
Watson, Walter, 227
Wells, Brock, 64
Wells, Henry Horatio, 122
Westmoreland County, 37
West Point, 156
West Virginia, 44, 45, 46, 57
Wheeler, Maclin C., 146, 240
whipping (stripes), 18, 19, 34, 136, 166, 167
Whitehurst, Edward, 1–2, 35, 41–42
Whitehurst, Emma, 1–2
Whittaker, Robert H., 136, 213, 240
Williamsburg, 7, 26, 45, 86; Colored Union League, 91; First Baptist Church, 51, 148
Wilson, Ellis, 131, 240

Wilson, Joseph Thomas, 48, 242
Wilson family, 62
Winchester, 36, 37, 44
Woman's Department of the Negro Reformatory Association of Virginia, 211
women, 92, 102, 112, 167–68, 192, *201*, 201–2, *202*, 204, *209*; health care, 212–14, *213*; property ownership, 13, 113–14; rural life, 173, 176; teachers, 153, 154, 155–56, *197*; urban life, 12, 179. *See also* children; families
Wright, Jonathan Jasper, 181–82
Wythe County, 183

Yoder, Jacob, 76–77, *77*
York County, 7, 18, 117, 146, 227; Freedmen's Bureau in, 72; Lone Star, 72, 88
Yorktown, 32, 40, 59, 88, 130, 211

RECENT BOOKS IN

The American South Series

After Emancipation: Racism and Resistance at the University of Virginia
Kirt von Daacke and Andrea Douglas, editors

Driven to the Field: Sharecropping and Southern Literature
David A. Davis

The Princess of Albemarle: Amélie Rives, Author and Celebrity at the Fin de Siècle
Jane Turner Censer

In the True Blue's *Wake: Slavery and Freedom among the Families of Smithfield Plantation*
Daniel B. Thorp

Against the Hounds of Hell: A Life of Howard Thurman
Peter Eisenstadt

Facing Freedom: An African American Community in Virginia from Reconstruction to Jim Crow
Daniel B. Thorp

Capital and Convict: Race, Region, and Punishment in Post–Civil War America
Henry Kamerling

The Uplift Generation: Cooperation across the Color Line in Early Twentieth-Century Virginia
Clayton McClure Brooks

The Risen Phoenix: Black Politics in the Post–Civil War South
Luis-Alejandro Dinnella-Borrego

Designing Dixie: Tourism, Memory, and Urban Space in the New South
Reiko Hillyer

A Deed So Accursed: Lynching in Mississippi and South Carolina, 1881–1940
Terence Finnegan

Radical Reform: Interracial Politics in Post-Emancipation North Carolina
Deborah Beckel

Religion and the Making of Nat Turner's Virginia: Baptist Community and Conflict, 1740–1840
Randolph Ferguson Scully

From Yeoman to Redneck in the South Carolina Upcountry, 1850–1915
Stephen A. West

What Reconstruction Meant: Historical Memory in the American South
Bruce E. Baker

Black, White, and Olive Drab: Racial Integration at Fort Jackson, South Carolina, and the Civil Rights Movement
Andrew H. Myers

Murder, Honor, and Law: Four Virginia Homicides from Reconstruction to the Great Depression
Richard F. Hamm

South by Southwest: Planter Emigration and Identity in the Slave South
James David Miller

A Way out of No Way: Claiming Family and Freedom in the New South
Dianne Swann-Wright

The Lynching of Emmett Till: A Documentary Narrative
Christopher Metress, editor

Ladies and Gentlemen on Display: Planter Society at the Virginia Springs, 1790–1860
Charlene M. Boyer Lewis

Forgotten Time: The Yazoo-Mississippi Delta after the Civil War
John C. Willis

Bloody Promenade: Reflections on a Civil War Battle
Stephen Cushman

Slave in a Box: The Strange Career of Aunt Jemima
M. M. Manring

Haunted Bodies: Gender and Southern Texts
Anne Goodwyn Jones and Susan V. Donaldson, editors